Power and Pleasure

Louis Barthou and the Third French Republic

ROBERT J. YOUNG

McGill-Queen's University Press
Montreal & Kingston • London • Buffalo

© McGill-Queen's University Press 1991
ISBN 0-7735-0863-5

Legal deposit fourth quarter 1991
Bibliothèque nationale du Québec

Printed in Canada on acid-free paper

This book has been published with the help of a
grant from the Social Science Federation of Canada,
using funds provided by the Social Sciences and
Humanities Research Council of Canada.
Publication has also been supported by the Canada
Council through its block grant program.

Photographs 1–4, 7–10, and 12, collection of Mâi-
tre Marcel Gilbert, Paris; photographs 5 and 6, collection of Mme. Pierre Bouchet, Paris; photograph 11,
Musées Royaux des Beaux-Arts de Belgique, Brussels.

Canadian Cataloguing in Publication Data

Young, Robert J., 1942–
 Power and pleasure: Louis Barthou and the Third
 French Republic

 Includes bibliographical references and an index.
 ISBN 0-7735-0863-5

 1. Barthou, Louis, 1862–1934. 2. France – Politics
 and government – 1870–1940. 3. France – History –
 Third Republic, 1870–1940. 4. Politicians – France –
 Biography. I. Title.

 DC342.8.B37Y69 1991   944.081'092   C91-090374-3

This book was typeset by Typo Litho composition inc.
in 10/12 Baskerville.

For
Kendal, Kevin, and Christopher

In Memory of
Agnes, Clarence, and John

Contents

Introduction

History demands impartiality, not indifference. It is a
type of resurrection. It needs emotion to make it live.
... It is as much art as science.[1]

We agree on this, Monsieur Barthou and I, however conscious one must be of a contrary view. Not that such agreement between author and subject need imply universal accord. Who could subscribe to another of his judgments? "One never dies completely, particularly if one dies well."[2] He did die "well," in 1934, gunshot victim in a public assassination, yet he is on the point of passing into total obscurity, remembered only by a rapidly declining number of loyal friends and unrepentant enemies. Will he be just one name among many, fading and merging with those of how many other statesmen and servants of the Third French Republic? History and historians, one senses, are subject to the ups and downs of professional fashion, some reference to which doubtless could be used to explain the collective act of forgetfulness which has removed Barthou and so many others from the public consciousness. But there are signs of a recent change, and it may well be that Barthou's prediction could prove valid after all. For the fact is that, recently, there has been a perceptible renaissance of interest in the Third Republic and in its class of political *dirigeants*. This work is part of that revival, however inadvertently it may have slipped into a current not of its own making.

For it is less in trends than in Barthou himself that my interest lies. He was seventy-two years of age at the time of his death, and the Republic's foreign minister; by then, he had surveyed the affairs of France for well over forty years, as lawyer, journalist, deputy, senator, and cabinet minister. He had fought a duel with Jean Jaurès and flown with Wilbur Wright. He had been implicated in a murder and publicly accused of sexual impropriety. Prime minister in 1913, entrusted by fate with parliamentary passage of the three-year military service law, he was celebrated by some as a national hero in 1914 when the French armies managed to contain the German offensive into northern France. For that service, as well as in recognition of his work as an author, Barthou was elected to the Académie Française just at the end of the war, in some respects the crowning achievement of his career.

Or so he frequently maintained, for he was one in whom politics had many rivals. Louis Barthou, like others better known, also had a certain idea of France, the more vibrant for not being unique to him. Cultural life, in the broadest sense, was an imperative for Barthou. For him, it had the distinction of being at one and the same time an expression of France's greatness and – remarkably – greater even than France herself. Music he so considered, and theatre, and prose, and poetry, and all manner of plastic art. All this he enjoyed out of a dual conviction: that a people confirmed its inherent goodness by the pursuit of whatever was beautiful, and that true creative genius transcended the petty squabbles of nations and stood as eloquent testament to the concept of humanity.[3]

As vulnerable to the seduction of Art as to that of Politics, Barthou was just as constant to many other personal *divertissements*: historical research, journalism, aviation, travel, bibliophilia, and physical exercise. With little exaggeration, Claude Farrère once described him as "knowledgeable about everything, interested in everything, excited by everything."[4] That included, to be sure, an interest in his parental family in Béarn, and his family in Paris – Alice, his wife of thirty-five years, and Max, the only child, symbol first of hope and then of tragedy. These, too, singly and in combination, are all part of the flame which has drawn me to Louis Barthou. Next to these, were I to be believed, the other facets had less allure: his role in the murder of Gaston Calmette, his alleged propensity for theft, erotica, whips, and *séances à trois*. Vile but baseless, authentic but irrelevant? At this point we need venture nothing but an undertaking to explore the dark as well as the light, conscious again of Barthou's counsel: "One never diminishes a great man by showing that he was in fact a man."[5]

Accordingly, the task at hand is to fashion a full-length portrait of Louis Barthou, a biography, to put it more conventionally. But it is to literature as well as to historical science that I have turned for advice, confident that these two apparent solitudes have much in common. Maupassant, for instance, encouraged novelists to illuminate what he called "the essential events." Do so, he said, by treating all the other events with the emphasis they warrant, and thus isolate the "special truth it is desired to reveal."[6] Though offered to the artist, this fare seems just as wholesome for the historian. In any event, the objective of this volume is to weave together a complete life, using the skein of what is "essential." And that means discarding the strict and confining measurements of politics.

I believe that my subject would have approved the attempt. Indeed, he doubted that politics were much of a mirror of a man's inner substance. What is said in the corridors, in the committee rooms, on the floor of the House is certainly some measure of intellect; but words, Barthou observed, do not necessarily reveal "character."[7] What is needed, to supplement rather than replace politics, is evidence of another order – that which calls up private behaviour and modes of recreation, that which reflects opinion on myriad subjects, from education to health care, religion to feminism, judicial reform to trade unions. At the same time, such opinions need to be examined within the context in which they were first articulated. Again, it was he who remarked, "There is a private world inside every man"; and in keeping with this nostrum it is essential to place him *chez lui*, a personal expression of his own times and his own social milieu.[8] Unique, undeniably, though no more so than any other, Barthou was in many respects reflective of a "type," the eminent bourgeois in that middle-aged Third Republic: from the cut of his clothes and his beard to his dextrous balancing of journalism, politics, and cultural activism, and from his tranquil and stable domestic foyer to the animated Assembly meetings where moderate men tried to contain both revolution and reaction. Although hardly smothered by the folds of bourgeois convention, Louis Barthou was unmistakably a man of his times. This portrait thus requires a tableau large enough to accommodate background as well as the human form.

It is just as well that I adopt this particular conceptual approach by preference, for the nature of the source materials would have made it imperative. There are no Barthou papers, in the sense of a single, substantial collection deriving from his estate and housed under one roof. Instead, what one has in the way of unpublished documentation are several hundred letters, scattered from Paris to Pau, deposited in small and, in some cases, private collections. For the rest – apart from the surfeit of materials from press, parliamentary, and diplomatic publications – one is left to contemplate a massive corpus of books, articles, speeches and prefaces, published by Barthou himself over the space of some fifty years and addressed to a taxing range of topics. In short, and only partly by design, Louis Barthou told us a great deal about himself. But what he was saying, measured in part by his tone and form of expression, has to be filtered through the familiar interpretive screen. To the historian, there is nothing new about this, but summits are no easier to climb because they have been mastered by others. The task of illuminating the "essential," to invoke Maupassant again, is as formidable as ever, particularly when one agrees with Barthou that there are "in every one of us hidden corners where no one else ever enters."9

There is more to be said about the connection between the nature of the source materials and the way in which any work is conceived. The fact that Barthou wrote extensively on a multitude of subjects encourages one to focus on the "whole" man over his entire life, as opposed to confining attention to his role and behaviour as a politician. In my estimation, the former has greater potential than the latter. To take the more obvious first, a high percentage of what Barthou wrote had nothing to do with politics, at least ostensibly. Therefore, one might simply ignore such materials, make sporadic use of them to illustrate aspects political, or accept the invitation offered by Barthou's eclectic interests and opt for a wide conceptual sweep.

Second, and for reasons yet unfathomed, the archives are exceptionally sparse when it comes to correspondence relating to his political career. This goes far beyond the destruction of his private papers, only two decades ago. That was tragic, but at least explicable. What is remarkable is the near-absence of Barthou in the otherwise voluminous archival *fonds* of long-time collaborators like Raymond Poincaré, or of his sometime political allies like Millerand, Sarraut, Jonnart, Leygues, Deschanel, and Hanotaux. Here, in the papers of political friends, Barthou comes close to vanishing without a trace, a condition confirmed by an altogether surprisingly large number of memoir accounts of this period. Often, his name will not even figure in an index. What, then, are we to make of this? Does it support the view that, because friends relied on personal contact rather than written correspondence, the absence of a paper record is evidence of intimacy? Is it, in fact, precisely the reverse? Or are we reduced to some archivally sinister phenomenon to explain how Barthou's correspondence was plucked from otherwise intact collections? Since none of this seems to fit within the range of the probable, the mystery remains, and with it the difficulty of over-estimating the political side of Barthou's career. He may well have been right when he observed that a man's character was reflected in the choice of his friends; but if such is the case, the papers and recollections of most of his political friends certainly inspire some despair.10

A third observation may be offered on this matter of sources and conception. Just as there are considerable lacunae to impede a book-length study too tightly focused on politics, so there are also pockets of documentation which, if anything, are too rich. Barthou's role at the Genoa Conference in 1922, his subsequent work at the Reparations Commission, his tour of duty as foreign minister in 1934, each of these has behind it a formidable mass of documentation which could well overshadow – and misleadingly – longer and comparably important stages of his political career. The problem of documentary unevenness, therefore, is one that I have had to confront from the outset. And once again, I have addressed it by adopting the vehicle of a "whole-life" perspective, insurance of a sort against allowing the quantity of documentation to define what is "essential."

There is a final point about sources and the road taken in this study. It is one which invokes the earlier admission that, in this case, necessity was the offspring of preference. That point is this. If we do not appreciate the inspiration he drew from the French cultural tradition, Louis Barthou will defy interpretation for an eternity. He was animated by the Idea of France, rhetorically at times to be sure, but never disingenuously. He defined himself by this Idea, and saw himself as as intellectual descendant of all who had gone before him. A republican, he could still admire Napoleon; a moderate, he could still respect Robespierre. Corneille, Racine, and Diderot belonged to him, as part of his day-to-day patrimony, as did Lamartine, de Vigny, and Hugo, as did the contemporary giants of his own day – Rostand, Loti, and Anatole France. For Barthou there was nothing here that was trivial, peripheral, or pretentious. His duty as a public servant of France was to serve her interests and promote her glory; and she, quite simply, was the accumulated genius of centuries. This is the key to Louis Barthou; and this is why circumstance and temperament alike have combined to suggest to me a way of unlocking the personality of this statesman and of placing it within its generational and social milieu.

Enough said for the moment about objectives and material resources. But there are other kinds of resources of which the reader has a right to be aware; for instance, the historian himself. Too often, indeed customarily, we prefer not to mention this; but by this false and sometimes uncharacteristic modesty, do we not imply that we are something we are not – the detached observer, who enters events in a copybook or on a silicon screen, without personal response, ruthlessly impartial? In this case, such an impression would be misleading. Anxious to be fair, I doubt very much that I am impartial. Like Nigel Nicolson I am both persuaded and reassured by the dictum that it is more important for a biographer to be "compassionate than clever."[11]

Indeed, years of cohabitation have made me sympathetic to Barthou, and I am likely to give him the benefit of a doubt. Having read almost everything he wrote over some fifty years, and much of what he said privately and in public, I would not readily grant that I have been badly deceived, that somewhere beneath a consummate disguise of candour and principle there lurked a man who was at heart an unscrupulous opportunist and a hypocrite.[12] Bias, too, might be admitted on the grounds of temperament. Bound to no party, and like Professor Higgins a creature of no eccentric whim, I have a native sympathy for a moderate of Barthou's stamp and some respect for his detachment from party apparatus. These, no doubt, constitute a mixture of assets and liabilities. What matters is that the reader is under no illusion about the author's continued presence. For the fact is, or so I believe, that the historian and the novelist are both after Maupassant's "special truth," a truth we "desire" to reveal. In neither case is the author's interpretive hand incidental or gratuitous, a fact of which Barthou was fully aware when he recalled de Vigny's remarks on the subject of one's antecedents: "No matter that the blood has flown from them to me. When I write their history, they are my descendants."[13] And so, for better or worse, is Barthou from me.

The interpretation has then but one provenance. The effort, however, has been more evenly distributed; and accordingly I have many people to thank for their assistance. Indeed, and once again because of the dispersed character of the documentation on Barthou, I have drawn widely from the advice and aid of many benefactors. Apart from a few, whose services were of a particularly scholarly order and whom I identify below, the names of the others will be found in an extended note on sources toward the end of this volume.

Those to whom an expression of thanks can wait no longer include my excellent research assistant, Elizabeth Beazley, and her predecessor, Cynthia Adam; my friend and industrious aide in Pau, Jean-François Saget; and a host of scholarly friends and acquaintances who have helped with their expertise and their encouragement: Michel Papy, Patrick Fridenson, Maurice Vaïsse, Pierre Albert, Claude Lévy, Alain Quella-Villeger, Martin Alexander, John Kieger, and Brian R. Sullivan. A special vote of thanks is owing to Gerald Friesen, whose care as a reader matched his support as a friend.

I also record my gratitude to the Social Sciences and Humanities Research Council of Canada, and the University of Winnipeg, both of which have been generous in their financial support for this project.

Finally, I turn to the greatest of my creditors, my wife, Kathryn, to whom I remain hopelessly, happily, indebted.

None of those named above is responsible for what I have written, but all should know that they have made it possible. I hope it will not disappoint. Less at risk in this sense are those dearest to me, for they will welcome having "Barthou" finished. They have lived with him for long enough, and in their own way have said what Barthou once said in his: "Libraries lead everywhere, as long as one knows when to leave."[14]

1   Isidore Barthou's Hardware Store, Oloron-Sainte-Marie

2 Barthou arrives with his mother for his wedding at the Madeleine,
January 1895

3 Barthou and Alice leave the Madeleine

4　Minister of the Interior 1896

5 Barthou's familiar ex libris, designed by Jean-Louis Forain

6 The rare ex libris, designed by Pierre Bouchet and
donated to the author by Mme Bouchet

7 Max shortly before his death in 1914

8 Alice and Max

9   Alice circa 1920

10   Barthou the
Academician, 1922

11   Louis Barthou
   by Cornelius Van Dongen

12   Barthou some months
      before his death

Power and Pleasure

First Impressions, 1862–1889

The nest is not always a measure of the flight to
come, but the child is the forecast of the man.[1]

September 1887. He had the look of someone impatient and displeased. The luggage suggested a vacationer, not a man on business;
yet he looked anything but relaxed. Neither labourer nor patrician,
judging by the hands and the clothes, he had rather to be a bourgeois
of modest station, if possibly immodest ambition. Short of stature –
perhaps 5'4 or 5'5 – but of wiry physique, he was quick of gesture,
alert, restless, not a man accustomed to having time on his hands.
A university man by the look of him; and if one were to divine a
lawyer, one would not have been mistaken. About twenty-five years
of age, and going places, he looked for all the world like a man stuck
in some station at Aachen. Which is where he was, waiting for the
next train to Cologne. Caught, for once, without a thing to read, he
sat, fidgeting with the lorgnon on the bridge of his nose, gazing out
beyond the tracks into the past.

Louis Barthou was annoyed. Liège had had its moments for the
sightseer, but Namur had been as disappointing as his idol, Hugo,
had predicted it would be.[2] Aachen itself had been better, the cathedral certainly, but he had become uncomfortable in the presence
of so many Germans. Indeed, he felt like a foreigner for the first
time, largely because his self-acquired German was much weaker
than the Spanish he had learned in school and had been able to
practise during previous visits to Spain.[3] This linguistic isolation,
which had brought on a new wave of resentment about the quality
of language instruction he had received in France, had been doubly
unnerving. Faced with a long wait for his train to Cologne, he had
repaired to the municipal library, a natural recourse for a recent
recipient of a doctorate of law from the University of Paris. But the

cupboard had been bare: there was nothing in French but a few of Zola's tasteless novels and, as if for contrast, some predictably dull fare from the unremarkable Georges Ohnet. It was a disgrace, he thought, that French literature should be so poorly represented, and evidence enough that the conservative press had been right to complain about the trend in popular culture toward pornography and lascivious lifestyles.[4] There had been nothing left to do but return to the railway terminal and, in his confessed loneliness, think about his loved ones.

Having been called to the bar that very spring, at the Appeals Court in Pau, he had been able to celebrate his twenty-fifth birthday at home, before embarking on a brief vacation. The entire family had been there: Isidore and Marie, his parents, now resident in Pau; his sister Clémence, who, though two years his junior, was already married; his brother Joseph, twenty-two years of age, and still a bit adrift and aimless; finally Léon, the *benjamin*, a strong student and already on the track of a law degree and a prosperous career. Two lawyers in any family was something to be proud of, but given the modest home of Isidore and Marie, achievement like this was on a scale much closer to hope than realistic expectation.[5]

"They raised me above their own social station," he thought, as his mind wandered to his parents.[6] Limited himself to a primary school education, Isidore Barthou had had to work hard all of his life. Wounded at Sebastopol, in the name of a France he loved but of an emperor he detested, he had re-entered civilian life in the accounting branch of the Compagnie des Chemins de Fer du Midi. Four years later, in 1859, he had left the railroad in order to open a small business – a hardware shop in Oloron-Sainte-Marie. Of Béarnais stock himself, in 1861 Isidore had married a relative newcomer. His bride, Marie Octavie Noé, although recently educated in the convent at Oloron, was the daughter of an illiterate blacksmith from Champagne, a man who had settled in Béarn following a long period of military service in the region. It was to Isidore and Marie that a first child had been born in 1862, a son, at one in the morning of 25 August, the traditional feast day of Saint Louis. Accordingly, he had been named Jean-Louis-Firmin Barthou.[7]

Put out briefly to a wet nurse in the neighbouring village of Ledeuix, the infant was soon returned to the family hearth above the hardware store in the Rue Sablière. It was here that his education had begun, formally and informally. Isidore's ambition quickly enveloped his son, and directed his gaze upwards, to the bourgeoisie – men who had no dirt on their hands, and wore no peasant's blouse, and who were addressed as "Monsieur." To that end, the boy's ed-

ucation began, first at Oloron's local *école laïque*, and then in the
town's seminary. By the age of thirteen the young Barthou had
proven himself to be an exceptional student, thanks to the disciplined
direction formally provided by his local teachers, thanks as well to
the late evenings he had put into his homework, under the dim light
cast by flickering candles.[8] But it had been worth it. His performance
had been strong enough to secure entrance as a *pensionnaire* in the
lycée at Pau. There he was destined to complete the final four years
of his progress toward the coveted *baccalauréat*.

Long before then, however, Barthou had learned lessons of an
altogether different character. No friend of Emperor Napoleon III,
Isidore Barthou had followed intently the daily developments in the
Franco-Prussian War of 1870. Confined during business hours to
his store, he had been in the habit of sending his eight-year-old son
to the sub-prefecture in Oloron with instructions to copy down the
latest news posted outside the government office. On the very day
of the Prussian victory at Sedan, in early September 1870, the young
messenger returned with two lessons learned. It had been a day of
tears. A bully had run off with his pencil before he had been able
to complete his father's mission. Louis had been crushed and indignant. A stupid, cruel, unfair act, which had given him his first, lasting
taste of malice. Neither could he forget the tears of his father, whom
he had found with their neighbour, the draper Touan, a Bona-
partist! Both men had been dumbfounded, imperialist and republican both, and quietly shared their sorrow over the defeat of
France.[9]

Five years later, the thirteen-year-old Barthou was to find himself
in a student residence in Pau, the provincial capital some twenty
miles to the north of Oloron but still within sight of the snow-capped
Pyrenees. He could no longer remember whether it had been on
the very first day of school that he had been led into the large
assembly hall, but the message inscribed on its walls was unforget-
table: "Enfants, n'oubliez jamais 1870–1871."[10] This immediately
had become another important step in his political education. Not
that the lycée had forgotten for a moment its primary mandate,
which was to produce informed, disciplined scholars. It prided itself
in providing a strong classical education, precisely the sort of emphasis and subject matter which appealed to the new arrival from
Oloron.

Science was not where he shone, at least by his own reckoning.
He later joked about having been no favourite of his physics teacher,
although in 1879–80 he delivered nearly prize-winning performances in both physics and chemistry. Physical education, too, he

considered at the time to be an unnecessary intrusion. Compulsory
morning exercises soon became a target for clandestine rebellion, as
clever lads like Barthou tried to excuse themselves at every opportunity. And it was here as well that he had the distinction of being
assured by a classmate, named Jean Moréas, that poetry too he
should leave to others more talented. But Latin, Greek, and French
were consistently strong subjects, ones in which he delivered award-
winning performances, as indeed he was to do at various times in
history, geography, music, and Spanish. The latter, taken on his
father's urging, he had come close to mastering; Béarnais too, although the latter was acquired from home and countryside rather
than from the French state's textbooks.[11] But neither, he now reflected, was of much use in Aachen, a fact which reminded him of
how unpopular German had been as a language at school.[12] Still,
he had every reason to be proud of his academic training, for which
his darting intelligence and exceptional memory had served him
well. Indeed, it was that alert and restless mind which had earned
for him the nickname "quicksilver," although he sometimes privately
wondered if the real reason was not his inability to sit still for long.[13]

There was in fact a perceptible inner tension, an ambition, which
could not be curbed, an edge which was never completely covered
behind the lorgnon or beneath his customary basque béret. Part of
it was the mark of a generation, teenagers who were not allowed to
forget their past or the responsibility which military defeat had thrust
upon them all. Some of their teachers could not speak of 1870
without their eyes filling with tears, and others clearly regarded
instruction in republicanism as a sacred cause. Such a one had been
the popular Georges Edet, teacher of rhetoric, a man who had used
the closing exercises in August 1879 to make the boys' eyes sparkle
with his passionate speech on the glorious victory of Valmy and on
the obligations of republican sacrifice. Sparkle too with lessons on
Michelet and Victor Hugo, republican patriots whose works still
remained proscribed in the schools of Béarn – curricular remnants
of the imperial regime which had been swept away in 1870. What
better way to inspire young scholars than to offer them *en cachette*
the forbidden fruit of illicit literature? Before long, the diminutive
seventeen-year-old from Oloron had been overwhelmed by Hugo
in particular, "possessed" by Hugo, "intoxicated by Hugo," and by
the sheer beauty of the republican ideal.[14]

Not even he could explain the strength of his response. Part of
it, probably, lay in the collision between a spirited youth and the
discipline imposed by school authorities and their unrelenting routine: compulsory exercise, the study hour before breakfast in the

refectory, a breakfast observed in silence, lunch always at twelve, dinner always at eight, newspapers forbidden within the school. Barthou had fought back, resisting these petty tyrannies by making no secret of his admiration for Léon Gambetta, a radical republican who seemed forever to be upsetting political assemblies at Versailles or Paris. Indeed, had he not found a cause in which he and the great patriot might share – the heavy-handedness of religious authority? With memories still fresh of the bully in Oloron, Barthou had been enraged by the scolding and threats delivered by the school chaplain to boys who skipped confession. Not as yet associating this with a breach of his freedom of conscience, the young scholar nonetheless was quick to see such official intimidation as an act of injustice.[15]

It was then that the train for Cologne drew up to the platform, whisking him away from Aachen and, for a time, interrupting his reflections. Cologne proved more to his liking, especially its breath-taking cathedral which, he conceded, defied even Hugo's descriptive powers. Indeed, and to their credit, its builders had been better planners than had Barthou for his trip. It was 1 September 1887. The next day would mark the seventeenth anniversary of the German victory at Sedan. Suddenly, it became unthinkable that he should spend it surrounded by Germans, subject to their celebrations.[16] And so, on impulse, he took the next train for Holland, and promptly returned to the past.

His studies at the lycée had been so distinguished that he had been accepted into the Bordeaux law faculty in November 1880. And as usual, he had proven no disappointment. Installed in a residence at 31 rue des Remparts, he had blossomed quickly as a promising newcomer, an all-rounder. Literature continued to attract him, none more powerfully than that of Hugo, whose autographs he already had started to collect; and his infatuation with Beethoven and Wagner, especially Richard Wagner, had also begun.[17] Less smitten was he by the young women of Bordeaux, although he confided to his friend, Robert Lacoste, that his unattached status allowed him to enjoy the romantic side of his life. Sport, too, was a regular feature of his days on the Garonne. Pelote especially, a game which was well suited to his speed and reflexes, as well as his sense of timing and anticipation – qualities which of course could be put to other uses. He had in fact become involved in student politics, an activity which not only called upon his speaking and writing skills but also led to his role in the founding of the Association Générale des Étudiants de Bordeaux.[18]

None of these activities had adversely affected his scholarly performance in law school. In 1881 and 1882 he had secured first prize in both civil law and Roman law, although the latter induced "acute indigestion" on the eve of examinations. At the same time, he earned a diploma in political economy for courses taken under the auspices of the Bordeaux Chamber of Commerce, even though he admitted privately that he was more taken by Jules Claretie's *Les Amours d'un interne*.[19] By then, the end of his third year of studies at Bordeaux, the way was clear for a swift passage to the Paris Faculty of Law and to the doctoral degree, particularly as his severe myopia had excused him from the rigours and career-interruption of military service.[20] The call to Paris had been strong and inviting, and he had gone. But he had heard yet another siren by then, that of journalism. As the blurred images of the landscape along the northern Rhine flashed past the carriage windows, it was becoming even more obvious than ever before how his involvement with the press was leading him deeper and deeper into the world of politics.

He no longer recalled precisely how this passion for politics had started, but it had been during the Bordeaux years that he had made his first, occasional contributions to *La Petite Gironde*. By 1883 he had attracted the attention of Emile Garet, the founder and editor-in-chief of the Pau-based *L'Indépendant des Basses Pyrénées*. It was Garet who had enlisted him as a journalist to accompany the public works minister, Raynal, during the latter's trip to the south-west to open the new rail-line between Pau and Oloron. Garet, a passionate republican, had been using his newspaper for almost twenty years to refute and discredit the secular ambitions of the Church and the clerical resources of imperialists and monarchists alike. Sympathetic, therefore, to the current government of Jules Ferry, and disposed to promote its accomplishments, Garet had drawn upon the resourceful law student in Bordeaux. What more fitting than to have an Oloron product report, with enthusiasm, the achievements of a republican government, and in the pages of *L'Indépendant*?[21] Now, in 1887, having returned to Pau with a law degree in hand, Barthou was certain that this collaboration with Garet was likely to intensify.

Returned to Pau. He still had no reservations about the move back, about having left Paris for a distant, provincial city, having accepted a call to the bar from the Appeals Court there rather than one of several offers of employment in Paris.[22] For all that, he had enjoyed the last three years in Paris. His dissertation had been defended just over a year ago, in June 1886, in front of a jury of four eminent professors from the Paris Faculty; and it had been published by Arthur Rousseau before the year was out. The subject, it would be fair to say, had already ceased to excite him, but the conclusions he had drawn were likely to stay with him for a lifetime. Very briefly, he had discovered that the current tax structures, designed by the

1804 civil code to discriminate in favour of propertied wealth and against mobile wealth, were simply out of touch with the nature of the economy and attendant financial realities in the 1880s. The courts, he knew, had tried to adjust their judgments accordingly, but what really was needed was an overhauling of the law by parliament. He could still recall, word for word, his concluding statement: "Best expressed: revise without rupturing and repair without renouncing, that should be the motto of the lawmaker bent on reform." It still seemed sensible, adjusting to new realities, but prudently and pragmatically.[23]

Paris, to be sure, had been rich in many other attractions. Beyond everything else, there had been that irrepressible urge to be informed, to know more. He had made a point of reading *Le Temps* through the week, a paper animated by the insight and wit of Françisque Sarcey; and on the weekends he had exchanged his subscriptions for those of a medical student who took the *Journal des Débats* of Jules Lemaître.[24] Beyond the press, and surely above it, there remained the deity Hugo, whose mortal presence disappeared in 1885, Barthou's second year in Paris. And thus there had just been time to do the nearly unthinkable, to actually meet the man whose writings he and so many other students had come to adore. It had taken a little audacity. Having spotted a press notice about a reception to honour the elderly writer, Barthou had rented whatever formal attire he could afford and guessed would be appropriate, and duly arrived at Hugo's home – a delegate, he mumbled, of some students' association; and he had been admitted. Admitted to meet the author of *Hernani* and *Ruy Blas*, and of how many other stories and verses already savoured and consumed since the days of Georges Edet and the classrooms in Pau![25]

Unabashedly "hugolâtre" from an artistic point of view, Barthou also applauded the writer's enduring crusade for continuing political reform in France. He and his idol, as the young man saw it, were deeply committed to the notion that the Third Republic would be reformist in character. And that in turn strengthened even further his ties with Garet in Pau, and drew Barthou to the fellowship of another law student in Paris, a man of Lorraine and his senior by a year, Raymond Poincaré. Through him, Barthou had entered the parapolitical world of the Union de la Jeunesse Républicaine, under whose auspices he had embarked on a speech-making circuit in sundry Paris meeting halls. Not always to large audiences: he now remembered with a smile the night last year that he had run into Octave Aubert, an old school friend from Pau. It had been the 22nd of June, the day after he had defended his dissertation. On a wave of enthusiasm he had swept Aubert off to that horrible, tiny, and

unseasonably cold room in the rue Bolivar, where he had spoken of
Cavour and Garibaldi, with more passion than might have been
called for by an audience of seven huddled around a crude stove.
That explained everything, or so he had insisted to Aubert. Nothing
but inclement weather could possibly explain why so few had turned
out to hear him speak on such an exciting topic![26]

The train had crossed the Dutch border. Before long, he found
himself in Amsterdam, amid a people whom he found phlegmatic
and over-large. It was a relief to have escaped from the Germans,
but the Dutch had such prodigious appetites and loved such rich
food. He was sure that he could see a connection between their diet,
their physique, and their stolid temperament. The galleries of Amsterdam, however, were a pure delight. The Rembrandts, in such
abundance, left him in awe. Later, on the train to Haarlem and La
Haye, he could not get the images out of his mind, especially those
of the *Ronde de Nuit* and the *Syndic des Drapiers*. They were with him
for life, he knew, indelible, always ready to revive "the inexpressible
joy ... of someone possessed." The other cities had proven memorable
too, for the same reasons, and for one other. Never before had he
seen such a plenitude of Dutch masters, so numerous that their
names ran together in his mind, at random: Rembrandt still, Van
Dyck, Rubens, Holbein, Steen and Téniers, Jordaens and Wouwer-
man.[27]

La Haye had brought another experience, less agreeable but
equally indelible. A music-lover, he found himself at a café-concert,
one which started badly with several pedestrian pieces for piano and
several tiringly repetitive marches. He began to lose a battle with his
patience, the more so in the presence of a dull and unresponsive
bourgeois audience whose interests seemed confined to their beer.
And so they remained, indifferent to the departure of "l'horrible
petit pianiste," and to the arrival on stage of some ten garishly
dressed women who were pretending to be singers. One by one they
came forward to howl some banal little number in Dutch, English,
or, more often, German. Until the arrival of the star herself. He had
strained to make out what she was singing, "over the wheeze of an
indescribable voice," only to be stunned, appalled, to conclude that
it was a type of military ballad, in French! This was too much for
someone with a common love of music and language. Incensed, he
fled the place, before the unseeing eyes of the Dutch burghers and
their ladies, intent as always on their "bière détestable."[28] It was time
to catch a train for Belgium.

En route to Anvers, he found another opportunity to reflect on
where he had been, and where he still wished to go. He was not yet

fully convinced that he wanted to make the jump from law to politics.[29] Returning to Pau would give him some time to decide. His work for the Appeals Court would not be so taxing as to preclude the exploration of political possibilities, perhaps on the municipal level, or that of the department; perhaps even nationally. What was already clear was the need to learn from Emile Garet, the need to have the assured support of this man who personified republican politics in a region where the Republic was still regarded with much suspicion.

He knew as well that something out of the ordinary existed between himself and Garet. There was an exceptional temperamental affinity, something natural and intrinsic in part. Acquired too, in part, for Garet had been an established republican leader even before 1870, and therefore his name had been spoken with respect in the home of Isidore Barthou. Active on the Pau municipal council for a time, the city's parliamentary representative in Paris between 1882 and 1885, and still a member of the departmental *conseil général*, Garet was a superb local illustration of how politics and press could be fused. All that, Barthou had known for some time. But he had recognized more recently other qualities in Garet which he either knew to be part of himself or intended to emulate. Garet, for instance, was a man of great erudition, a man who had a profound appreciation of history and who therefore knew that the affairs of nation states could not possibly be understood if they were measured only by the hour just passed. Indeed, he was himself an expert of sorts on the French Revolution, on the subject of which he was to write two books, one dedicated to his protégé Louis Barthou. There was also in him an especially fine blend of political consistency, intellectual independence, and shrewd pragmatism. An inflexible republican, Garet was no creature of party apparatus; and he was realistic enough to know that "By wanting to do everything one risks succeeding in nothing." Admirably put, thought Barthou, but guaranteed to provoke criticism from hardliners on every front, even one's own. Garet certainly had borne his share, and had endured it all in disciplined silence. No one knew better than he how easily moderation could be portrayed as weakness. And his friend, the young lawyer, had learned from it all.[30]

The days which followed in Belgium were days of continued personal exploration for Louis Barthou, though in the immediate rather than in the recollected sense. In Anvers he pursued an already developed interest by visiting the Plantin Museum, that treasure-house of early printed books, manuscripts, and rare engravings. There too he had been overwhelmed by yet more Ruebens. Especially moving, in his estimation, was the *Descente de la Croix*, a work which he characterized as "a sublime demonstration of genius." Although it was not the religious motif which touched him, he was once more impressed by how frequently religious inspiration had contributed to the aesthetic delights of nominal Catholics like himself. Some of Memling's work in Bruges he found similarly affective, although he told himself that his "enchantment" was of purely intellectual origin. In quite a different mood, and pursuing another interest, he visited the municipal prison in Gand, a visit which reminded him that Belgium had led on the road to civilization by abolishing the death penalty. Finally, something thrilling had happened to him in Brussels. Although he was generally disappointed by the International Exhibition of that year, he had viewed the entire site from four hundred meters in a tethered observation balloon. It was his introduction to recreational aviation, one which delighted him and to which he knew at once that he would return.[31]

The journey home by train was less novel, but it was the journey home. And that to Louis Barthou had an excitement of its own, for he cherished his regional roots and his complex cultural ancestry. He had enjoyed his first major trip abroad, by and large, and he had soaked up the artistic and architectural delights of many foreign places. But he had seen nothing to compare with the majesty of his corner of the world, with its snow-covered peaks, "its forests, meadows and vineyards ... the murmuring, growling mountain stream, and where on the cloudless horizons, under a luminous sky, celebrated vineyards and gentle rolling slopes take on a distant, bluish cast."[32] Absence only strengthened the association, underscored the pride he felt in knowing old men who still remembered de Vigny's stay in Oloron and Pau, knowing too that other men of genius – Hugo, Sainte-Beuve, Lamartine – had known his valleys and mountains and written about them.[33] This was not, for a particle of a second, to disclaim France in favour of Béarn. It was rather a wedding of the two, and in a way that most Frenchmen would find quite unexceptional. On the one hand, there was his "pays"; on the other, there was France, unidentical but complementary, two indispensable points of reference. Family and the memories of youth were part of it, and the classrooms, and a landscape fleshed out with a cultural history of the region, some of which had been taught, some simply learned. Basque bérets and the tongue of the Béarnais, pelote and garbure, Henry IV and the legends of Navarre, the springs of Eaux Bonnes, the racing *gaves* of Oloron and of Pau, the river Adour, the peaks of Anie and of the Midi de Bigorre, Sainte Bernadette of Lourdes and the miraculous Grotto of Massabielle.

Such had been his cradle, and from it had grown a young man of great promise and, for all of his twenty-five years, of considerable accomplishment. Prize-winning student, public speaker of acknowledged talent, a writer solicited by the republican press, a man with an expanding knowledge of art, history, music, language, and literature. No mean achievement this, for the grandson of an illiterate smith, and the son of a man who had never entered secondary school. But like Isidore, the young Barthou was energetic, industrious and ambitious. His father's words were never to leave him; indeed they became a kind of emblem for this lower-middle-class family from Oloron-Sainte-Marie: "Go on, my son, you don't win battles you don't fight."[34] Already, Barthou had the reputation for being a scrapper, agile, witty, ingratiating – all of these – but as well, a tenacious little man who would not let go. Indeed, his future wife would later describe him as a fox terrier, a breed known for its tenacity and lightning reflexes.[35] With one exception, he even looked the part – in everything but the ever-present pince nez, without which he could see almost nothing. Otherwise, he was trim and finely boned, inquisitive and alert, short-haired – thanks to a barber's tight clip and to an already receding hairline – wearing a trimmed Edwardian beard, with full moustache, and a rounded goatee. Terrier or not, this was the image he never abandoned, barely altered, over the span of his entire life.

In fact, much of the personality was already set by the time he returned from his vacation in the autumn of 1887. He had fully assimilated the family and class aversion to wasting time, just as he had long since accepted the notion that a gentleman – if such he were to be – ought to be a genuine "renaissance" man, capable of speaking intelligently on everything from prison reform to poetry, or from art to aviation. There was too, deep within him, a wide vein of romanticism which, when tapped, often delivered rapturous responses to canvases, cathedrals, and country – the latter especially, for he had been well moulded in that generation of humiliated patriots. Although a sense of humour was also already in evidence – one that would become increasingly manifest over the years – there was in the twenty-five-year-old Barthou a tone of surprising sobriety. The rather prudish comments about Emile Zola, the over-stern assessment of the Brussels fair, the disapproving characterization of the Dutch, each of these may suggest the presence of a man still young enough to confound wisdom with gravity.

It is more probable than certain that his brief escape to the Low Countries had given him time to ruminate on the future as well as on the past. Clearly, he was approaching an important intersection in his life. For seven months he had been wearing two hats, that of a lawyer and that of a journalist. On the one hand, he had been registered at the bar since February 1887; but his few cases had made future prospects seem limited.[36] On the other hand, he had also begun writing regularly for Emile Garet in February 1887; that is to say, that it was then that Barthou began to sign or initial the columns he had been writing on a range of subjects, including politics at the local, national, and international levels. As important as the topics themselves, however, was the fact that his name was appearing almost daily in the most important republican paper in Béarn. He was becoming a celebrity, drawing both applause and criticism for his unconcealed admiration of "Opportunist" republicans like Jules Ferry, cautious reformers whose agendas were mainly political in character. Not surprisingly, Barthou's was the vision of Emile Garet, and of men resolved to rekindle the freedom impulse of the French Revolution: political freedom based on popular sovereignty, civil freedom based on the equality of all citizens, and religious freedom based on the liberty of conscience.[37]

By early 1888 Barthou had resolved to try his hand at municipal politics. He would be a candidate in the elections scheduled in Pau for the month of May. It would mean curtailing his legal activities, but not those of his partisan journalistic career. Indeed, there was very little slackening in his output for the sympathetic Garet, especially when it came to addressing the threat they perceived to the Republic in the form of General Boulanger. By the spring of 1888 Barthou was writing lead editorials in L'Indépendant, urging parliament to constrain this maverick soldier who betrayed all the signs of a nascent dictator. Boulanger's recent decision to defy the government by running for election in the department of the Nord was – so an irate Barthou proclaimed – "shamelessly illegal," the action of "an insubordinate soldier."[38] Next to the nationally contentious Boulanger, and the opportunities the general was inadvertently opening up to ambitious young opponents, the municipal scene must have seemed like a quiet and undemanding backwater. An excellent spot, however, to be inducted into formal politics.

Running on a slate of republican candidates headed by Henri Faisans, Barthou cleared his first electoral hurdle on 13 May. Before many weeks had passed he had proven himself a conscientious attender of council meetings, and had been elected to serve on various council committees – including education, public works, tramways, and finance. It was in the latter capacity that he was able to further his reputation for financial prudence and republican fidelity. With an eye to both, he recommended modest cutbacks in the administrative costs of the municipal police and reductions in the salaries of two parish priests, but increases in the salaries paid to the city's lay teachers.[39]

Diligent as he was, and impressively active, Barthou was not destined to remain for long on the municipal stage. In all, he served for just over a year; but it would not have been long after his election that shrewd observers noticed that his eye was already elsewhere. Some public figures, he later remarked, were really not "politicians" at all, in the sense of being interested in "policy." Rather, what interested them, including many city councillors, was only the administration of policy. Whether he could have articulated this at twenty-six years of age, he certainly knew by then that he was driven by something else, by an ambition more powerful. He never referred to it as some profound impulse to do good works, to serve others. It was more like a microbe, some "démon" in his bloodstream that drove him to achieve at an even higher level.[40] In this case, it had to be in the form of either departmental or national politics, or both. In any event, instinct told him what recollection was to do later, namely that an apprenticeship had to be served somewhere, and that municipal politics was as promising a place to start as anywhere else. Speaking later of the experience gained among city councillors, Barthou observed:

When one is clever, attentive, approachable, open, eager, obliging, dedicated, you quickly earn both popularity and a clientele. You are the instrument, the intermediary, the voter's commissioner to the administration. You make yourself known to the sub-prefect, the prefect, the city engineer, the comptroller, the school inspector. You make things happen, while making news. Little by little you secure control of the situation, and make yourself indispensable.[41]

Barthou may be forgiven for attributing to this shrewd public servant the quality of indispensability. One thing is certain, however. He was by no means so regarded, even by republicans, when he was chosen by their local congress in July 1889 to stand for national election. The fact was that they believed the opposition candidate unbeatable, too strong to throw a really serious challenger against. Hence they chose the novice Barthou, ambitious and presumptuous enough to insert his head into the jaws of defeat, attractive and local enough to earn some sympathy while doing so.[42] Indeed, the ease with which he secured the nomination for Oloron only confirmed how depressed were the local republican notables of Béarn.*

The *arrondissement* into which Barthou had been cast by his republican elders was familiar enough ground. One of the seven national ridings within the department of the Basses-Pyrénées, Oloron comprised eight cantons and a total of some seventy communes, half of which were villages of fewer than five hundred inhabitants. The centre of activity was Oloron-Sainte-Marie itself, a town with a population of nearly ten thousand residents, in fact the third most populous centre in the department. Thus accredited by demography, the town accordingly enjoyed the distinction of having a sub-prefecture, a court of first instance, a publicly financed elementary school, a Catholic-run secondary school, and a Spanish consulate.[43]

Here was the terrain on which Barthou would make his first run at national politics. Home ground. But so was it too for Jacques LaCaze, the scion of an affluent, politically prominent family of the region, and the apparently unstoppable conservative candidate. Indeed, LaCaze's chances seemed only to have improved with the Floquet government's recent decision to abandon the voting system of *scrutin de liste* – which had returned an entire block of conservative representatives from the Basses-Pyrénées in 1885 – in favour of voting by single-member constituencies, the *scrutin d'arrondissement*. This meant a direct, head-on clash between Barthou and LaCaze, one which was expected by most to confirm again the riding's essentially conservative temperament. After all, behind the one high-profile local candidate there existed a tenuous alliance of regional conservative forces: monarchists of varying stripes who simply detested the Republic; monarchists, imperialists, and republicans who for disparate reasons were drawn to General Boulanger; clerics and militant lay members of the Church whose condemnation of the Republic on religious grounds usually preceded their condemnation on the grounds of politics. Little wonder that the Catholic-monarchist papers like *Mémorial* and *L'Écho d'Oloron* showered their support on the like-minded LaCaze, and their opprobrium on the candidate of the godless Republic. And easy was it for them to counter the opposition's use of the endearing Béarnais diminuitive "Louiset," with the demeaning, pejorative "Barthouet."[44]

Nevertheless, Barthou did have his supporters. Here, one can identify in the front ranks of the local republican electoral machine some one hundred prominent figures from banking and accounting, law, industry, and commerce.[45] These were the men who had taken advantage of a very recent upturn in republican fortunes in the summer of 1889, and thus in the July elections had secured control of local government administration at both the department and *arrondissement* levels. This development in itself had improved the odds against Barthou. A second and more surreptitious source of support lay within the forces of the central administration, the prefect and his various deputies. Nominally neutral in electoral affairs, these men nevertheless had a commission to advance the interests of the central government in the department to which they had been assigned. If that meant, as it often did, aiding and abetting the electoral campaigns of candidates sympathetic to the government, then so be it. Thus, with the benign approval of Ernest Constans, the interior minister in Paris, the prefect in Pau did what he could for the campaign of the tyro Barthou. As it happened, this included the summary dismissal of two mayors – one in Lanne, the other in Arudy – nominally for spreading false political rumours, in fact because of of their active association with the electoral campaign of Jacques LaCaze.[46] And behind them all, behind the entire republican presence in Béarn, were heard the voices of Garet's *L'Indépendant* and *Le Glaneur* of Oloron, spreading the word of the Republic and – despite Béarn's minimal interest in Boulangism – using the General as proof of a republic *toujours en danger*.

Included among the resources marshalled by the republicans of Béarn was, of course, Louis Barthou himself: his cause, his energies, his native instinct for campaigns. The former, to be sure, was only his in part. The republicans of Oloron, confronted by a popular conservative, had not plumped for any radical visionary. Barthou, we are told on excellent authority, was not about to dispute traditional values or promote a major rethinking of established political and social structures. In a riding where Boulangism was not much of a threat, and where neither labour unions nor a socialist press had made significant inroads, his task was to hold the traditional monarchist-clerical forces at bay while promoting the redressment of local grievances and the realization of local aspirations. As for the first, his electoral *profession de foi* of July 1889 opened with a reaffirmed commitment to republican principles, to the current government in Paris of Paul Tirard, and to the fight against Boulangism. In principle a proponent of constitutional revisionism – where such could be seen to advance progressive change – for the moment he opposed any tinkering with the constitution for fear of doing anything that might play into the hands of demagogues like Boulanger. He adopted an equally elastic position on the delicate question of the Church. He was in favour of the separation of Church and State, but not for the present. In fact, and if elected, he would vote in parliament for the maintenance of the religious budget under the provision of the Concordat. For the truth was, he said, that any attempt to separate now would only lend credence to the Church's cry of persecution and thus would further inflame opposition to the Republic itself. Less equivocal altogether, albeit on a less sensitive subject, Barthou endorsed the colonial policy of the Republic as part of the country's legitimate pursuit of prestige and strategic advantage.[47]

Addressing matters of more immediate local concern, Barthou presented himself as an enthusiastic supporter of a railway line between Pau and Canfranc in Spain, via Oloron and Somport. A Franco-Spanish convention to that effect had been concluded in 1885, but now, he said, construction had to proceed at once on the section of the new line between Pau and Oloron – an enterprise calculated to turn heads in his birthplace. Land taxes, he continued, needed revision downward in view of the ongoing slump in agricultural prices, and a four year tax moratorium ought to be declared on vineyards devastated by the phylloxera. Patent and tariff policy also needed rethinking in ways more compatible with the concerns of both agricultural and industrial producers, and the system by which land was still being surveyed and registered needed to be made more efficient. The young candidate also went on record as supporting the government's recent reduction of military service to three years, a view which accorded with that of farmers anxious to regain the labour of their sons as soon as possible. Finally, in language which has stood the test of time, he pledged himself to the more sensible, prudent, and efficient use of public funds, and to what he called a fairer distribution of the tax burden – pledges which are guaranteed to play wherever there are citizens upset by government profligacy and high-handedness.[48]

There was nothing exceptional in any of this. Candidates, whatever their allegiance, must play to the local stage, making promises that prove them innovative but disclaim extravagance. Similarly on national issues, especially those which might have delicate local roots, the art is to place one's feet decisively in both camps. Nothing was more natural to Barthou. Partly, to be sure, this derived from the instincts of a fighter who knew the importance of presenting a fleeting target. Partly too it stemmed from something equally instinctive, an inherent temperamental centrism. If, like Garet, he was always going to have to face charges of being too flexible and too moderate, it was better that he should sometimes be able to capitalize on those same qualities. The fact was that he did feel strongly about the national danger presented by Boulanger, and about persistent clerical intrusions into secular affairs of state. But he was not yet ready to go as far as Separation, any more than he was ready to insist on the sacrosanct untouchability of the Republic's constitution. Lack of real principles, his opponents would charge; an instinctive dislike of simplistic formulae, his supporters would retort. It was an exchange that would ring in Barthou's ears for forty years, becoming more shrill with every new election, with every new issue, with every time he was considered for a cabinet portfolio.

What was exceptional in 1889, or at least remarkable, was the tireless, dogged campaign waged by the twenty-seven-year-old republican underdog. His rival, LaCaze, was well known, reasonably well liked, and a moderate himself, if within the camp of traditional antirepublicans. Not being a Boulangist worked as much to LaCaze's advantage in Béarn as it did to Barthou's. But LaCaze had the disadvantage of being seen as a sure thing, and this expectation qualified the ardour of his own supporters and at the same time suggested the wisdom of a low-key campaign that would not antagonize potential backers or lend any kind of credence to the Barthou camp. Conversely, Barthou had little to lose, beyond his already considerable pride. Rising to the challenge, he stumped the constituency of Oloron with characteristic vigour, discreetly avoiding reference to his educational qualifications while exploiting the role of local boy and blacksmith's grandson.[49] No commune was left to wonder about the identity of the young republican, for he made a point of visiting each one – sometimes enjoying, sometimes merely enduring, the unpredictable lurches of his campaign fortunes. Unlike Jacques LaCaze, Louis Barthou was to this manner born.

Two qualities in particular he reckoned indispensable to electoral success. First, one had to exude confidence and, in that demeanour, to avoid being provoked by the indifferent or hostile. Years later he could still recall one old mayor, of suspect political loyalty in 1889, who had tested the candidate's patience with a wine long since turned to vinegar. Declining an uncertain provocation, Barthou had declared the wine excellent and toasted his host's good health.[50] Peasants, too, could be equally taciturn. Octave Aubert recalled one meeting in a mountain meadow between the candidate and a béret-topped peasant struggling down the slopes with a load of cheese. Having tried a friendly introduction, Barthou was visibly surprised to hear the man grunt, without stopping for a second, "I'm Cazassus." Recovering in an instant, Barthou forecast with a chuckle: "When I'm elected, this same Cazassus will say that he has known me for ages."[51]

To be what he called *serviable* was the second criterion. It was something that he had learned on the municipal council and that he was to spend a lifetime perfecting. Even in that first campaign of 1889 he had learned the importance of being useful and of being accommodating – even when it came to having to consume endless quantities of home-cooked meals at the kitchen tables of constituents from Laruns to Lasseube and Arudy to Aramits. Good republican tables, he recalled years later, laden with huge bowls of *garbure*, that thick soup of the south-west made with cabbage, beans, potatoes, preserved goose, and bacon. One ate from hunger, briefly, and then from tact, even of fare which looked as if it had seen better days: the lobster, for example, which had been served one day as a mark of particular respect for the visiting candidate. He had been doubtful from the moment it had arrived on the table – its aroma unusual – but had finished the plate in reciprocal deference to the cook and voter's wife. It was not long before lobster and stomach both had rebelled; but the candidate later noted with satisfaction that the voter had not.[52]

In fact, most voters did not. Of nearly fourteen thousand votes cast in September 1889, a very slim majority had gone to Barthou. Indeed, he owed his victory to a margin of barely three hundred votes.[53] Narrow as it was, however, this was an unexpected victory for the republicans of Oloron, one that had been won less on issues than on the relentless campaign waged by the candidate himself. Backed by loyal republican activists in press and local government, and relying on a platform that accorded exceptionally well with his centrist temperament, the candidate had taken charge of his own campaign and waged it with a charming ferocity. His reward was to be able to bear the republican colours to Paris and into the fifth legislature of the Third Republic. His lesson was of another order. Despite his victory, Barthou stored away another telling campaign incident. Accustomed though he had been to campaigning in nothing more grand than a modest two-horse carriage, on one occasion he had been obliged to hire a four-horse livery. Instantly, the style had changed, appearances, and so confounded one old peasant into cheering the arrival of the affluent LaCaze. Once corrected, however, the same voter had begun an equally enthusiastic cheer for Barthou. Then and there, the young candidate recognized a certain "fragilité" in the ideal of universal suffrage.[54] Though not his first, it was yet another collision with human nature, one which helped nurture an unmistakable if disciplined cynicism about the behaviour and motives of men and women. Nevertheless, he was not about to taint the cup of victory. As he put it, with his familiar eagerness: "Imagine that! A member of parliament!"[55] His articles for Garet would continue for several years to come, if on a declining scale, but his career in municipal politics was at an end. He was about to return to Paris, the arch-achiever still driven in search of a new challenge, the precious young collaborator who Emile Garet could only hope would not lose his way in the intellectual congestion of the nation's capital.[56]

CHAPTER TWO

Points of Departure:
Paris circa 1890

Elites, as long as all those who are worthy have had
access to such a station, are not an affront to the
principle of equality; on the contrary, they are
evidence of that sovereign idea.[1]

The national stage upon which Louis Barthou had arrived in the
autumn of 1889 extended in all directions and, for someone of
twenty-seven years of age, without measure. His own sense of its
dimensions, therefore, was necessarily incomplete; and yet it could
hardly have been less so than that with which a foreign reader would
try to follow his career a century later. It is with such a person in
mind that we make some attempt to raise slowly the curtain on this
deputy's first performance in Paris.

The optimism which he brought to the nation's capital in 1889
was symptomatic of the national mood, at least that which prevailed
among those electors who had just returned a firm republican majority to the National Assembly. Boulangism had been outman-
oeuvred and with it, if less explicitly, monarchism and bonapartism.
More than coincidentally, the economy too was beginning to emerge
from the doldrums of the past decade, a revival that could be measured by the familiar yardsticks of modern economic performance
– intensified industrialization and urbanization. In these respects, of
course, France was part of a broad pattern of development which
applied to European competitors like Britain, Germany, and Italy.
The 1890s were going to record the arrival of more industrial workers, more urban residents, simply more citizens than ever before.

But the pace of these developments in France was characteristically
more restrained. If, for example, 29 per cent of the active French
work force had been employed in industry in the 1860s, that figure
had risen to a bare 31 per cent by the first decade of the twentieth
century. Growth, to be sure, but contained growth, the sort of pace
which spelled change clearly enough but which did not dictate emer-

gency responses. The same judgment applied to the nation's overall demographic growth, which did not increase by even as much as 1 per cent in the forty years after 1870. The growth of the urban population, it is true, was much healthier, at 10 per cent for the corresponding forty-year period; but this had little to do with any fundamental shift in the nature of the economy. Rather, the urbanization figures reflect the proportionate growth of the lower middle class, particularly among the ranks of shopkeepers, such as Isidore Barthou, and of functionaries within the steadily expanding public service.[2]

If, therefore, too rapid change can leave its own explosive residue – as Barbara Tuchman has argued – the Third Republic was able to confront the controlled growth of the 1890s with confidence. Or rather did its *dirigeants*, for these were men unafraid of change as long as it could be forecast and directed. As Barthou had remarked in his dissertation of 1886, the nation's wealth was no longer being generated along traditional lines and according to traditional proportions. Much of that wealth no longer had anything to do with agricultural land, despite the fact that well over 40 per cent of the work force derived its income from agriculture. Instead, even by 1880, less money was being invested in agriculture than in the shares of transportation, public utility, and construction companies. The latter, especially, proved attractive to middle-class investors in the 1890s, as the quickened pace of urbanization swept away the stodgy housing market of the 1880s and sharply revived real estate values in the urban suburbs.[3] The attendant land speculation, together with investments in apartment block construction, thus proved to be important stimuli for the generation and preservation of bourgeois wealth. Examples like that of Ivry, on the periphery of Paris, where land prices multiplied sixfold in just over two decades, are eloquent expressions of the opportunities which presented themselves to the wealthy of the nation's capital.[4]

Paris, predictably, was one of the hottest points on the nation's economic element; and so this centre of nearly 2.5 million people continued to attract even more residents and investors alike – some drawn by employment prospects, some by the vaunted profit margins of the new omnibus and railroad companies, or those of gas, chemicals, and electricity. With them came significant alterations of the city's demographic profile. The uncomfortably high population density in the city centre – around Châtelet, Maubert, Louvre, and Cité – encouraged the exodus of those more fortunate to the suburban developments. Those of more modest means tended to gravitate toward the north, settling between Clichy and Aubervilliers, where new jobs in the food industry and metallurgy were opening up, or from which they could still commute to their old situations by means of the urban railroad. Those more fortunate still often migrated from the city centre or from the provinces to a new suburban belt which stretched from the southern quarter of Montrouge toward Vincennes in the east, whereas the wealthy took themselves out to the garden suburbs which extended leisurely from Neuilly west to Saint Germain-en-Laye. In fact, it was here in this prime quarter – at Châtou-Vézinet – that Barthou's future father-in-law was already acquiring very substantial real estate holdings.

There was nothing novel in the way income determined the disposition of urban residence. The city had never been, and was not now becoming, that great equalizer where those of high and low station could mix in republican fraternity. Instead, there were discernible internal frontiers, crossable of course, but on one side of which one felt more comfortable than on the other. Barthou was no exception. He had lived in the Latin Quarter during his days as a law student, neither rich nor impoverished; and in 1889 he was to take up residence on familiar ground, at the corner of the boulevards Saint-Germain and Saint Michel, just opposite the gardens of the Cluny museum. Apart from what he may have read, life had taught him nothing of the city's undernourished and inadequately housed, the men, women, and children of the 18th, 19th, and 20th districts, most of whom lived in one or two small rooms, who suffered from a rate of indigency twice that of the city average, and who were about to prove so ripe for the cholera epidemic that descended in 1892.[5] Like most bourgeois, especially those of professional background, he saw little of them. It is true that he might have found his inspiration in their suffering, as many socialist deputies were to do. But he did not. His inspiration came from that class of men whose accomplishments had been twofold. They had ensured the financial security of themselves and their families – and with it the accoutrements of social influence and respectability – and they had done so while rendering conscientious public service to France.

This was the elite to which Louis Barthou aspired. He was not yet of them, a resident of the Chaussée d'Antin or the Faubourg Saint-Honoré with a country home at Châtou or Asnières. But he was among them – at the National Assembly, but also as a member of a social class which emulated an aristocratic lifestyle while vaunting its own success in banking, industry, and commerce. Accordingly, young men like Barthou, ambitious and able but with personal fortunes still unsecured, were drawn into the social maelstrom of their more affluent elders – banquets and balls, races at Auteuil and

Longchamp, flower festivals in the Bois de Boulogne, and dazzling fund-raisers for charities.[6] At the same time, his future as a successful public servant lay in part in the hands of the *grande bourgeoisie* who had gradually assumed the positions of aristocratic notables in the first two decades of the Third Republic. Here were men who insisted on the complementarity of republican politics and modern business and who, in that belief, were prepared to enlist the talents of younger men of better education but smaller fortunes than themselves. Here were industrialists like the iron-steel magnate Schneider, the chemical industrialist Poulenc, Motte of the northern textile factories, Cail and Cavillier of the giant engineering enterprises: men who had been prepared to offer support for the Republic once it had become clear that the Republic intended to be no threat to them.[7] Their collective experience, to say nothing of their vested interests, was much more extensive than those of young deputies from small towns like Oloron-Sainte-Marie; however, such young men often shared with them the vision of a fiscally responsible regime which had not to pitch itself recklessly into all manner of social reform. The insurance of the individual's full political and legal equality was paramount, as it had been for the radicals of the 1870s and 1880s. That of economic equality, they admitted, was more problematical. That injustice existed was clear enough, as was the need to eliminate it. But precisely how, and with what despatch, and with what implications, were all questions which needed to be explored in the long light of unhurried inquiry and public discussion.

Unmistakably, this was a bourgeois Republic, at long last secure in the hardiness of its constitution and the steadiness of its leadership. With no trace of embarrassment, the regime stood for private property, individual initiative, and hard work, for education as a vehicle for personal success and family responsibility as the motive to succeed. It took pride in orderly change, partly because Comte's positivism inspired confidence in a scientifically addressed future, and partly because order itself ranked so highly in the pantheon of bourgeois virtues. True, much of this was derided by some as the mark of small minds and crabbed spirits – Gustave Flaubert, for one. But Barthou was unimpressed by the profundity of such literary critics, a sentiment expressed in his recollection of Henry Roujon's retort to Flaubert: "To work, hope and aspire, to love, marry and have a family, how is that more silly than spending one's time putting black on white, and wrestling all night with an adjective?"[8] Like Roujon, whose chair he would one day occupy in the Académie Française, Barthou was not forsaking literature or writers. Rather, he was reaffirming something which he had been taught in a hardware store in Oloron-Saint-Marie. One earned one's place in the world by dint of hard work, personal drive, and honourable conduct. And that is what the Republic meant to him, a regime where men of modest ancestry but exceptional talent could fulfil their potential to serve and to receive.[9]

In the meantime, Paris was more than a workplace, even to the serious-minded. It was a theatre of countless recreations, particularly for a class which applied itself to leisure with the same intensity it used for work. The city was opening itself to them, extending its new boulevards and its new bridges so as to carry them into the aristocratic enclaves of both Left and Right Bank, shifting some of its luxury trade south from the Boulevard des Italiens toward the Place Vendôme and west toward the newly fashionable quarter of the Champs Elysées where the residences of aristocrats were giving way to the new six story apartment blocks of the affluent bourgeoisie.[10] Indeed, it was precisely in this quarter that Barthou, once married, would settle and remain for the whole of his wedded life. How much evidence of progress could one ask from an elite which saw its own good fortune as proof of the democratic ideal? And of what genre? Perhaps the medical discoveries of the 1880s which had finally made treatable typhoid, pneumonia, tuberculosis, diphtheria, and cholera. Perhaps the presence of forty thousand automobiles which, by 1890, were already transforming the sounds and odours of Paris. Perhaps the advent of the telephone and the telephonic link established between Paris and London in 1891. Or the decision by the prefect of the Seine, M. Poubelle, to ensure that all residences would be equipped with garbage cans the contents of which would be collected daily from the pavement kerbs. Perhaps, but could there be any possible doubt? It was that urban extravaganza known as the 1889 Exhibition.[11]

The Republic had resolved to mark with all possible éclat the one hundredth anniversary of the French Revolution, a series of events which would associate past, present, and anticipated glories. It was in that year, therefore, that the Gare Saint-Lazare was opened, and the new Sorbonne, and the statue to Camille Desmoulins in the gardens of the Palais Royal. More dramatic by far was the celebration of March 1889, marking the completion of the Eiffel Tower, and then in May the official opening of the Exhibition by President Carnot before an estimated audience of five hundred thousand visitors. There had been some sour notes, of course, notably over Gustave Eiffel's "useless and monstrous" creation, a judgment publicly delivered by men of letters – and presumed good taste – like Alexandre Dumas, François Coppée, Sully Prudhomme and de Maupassant.[12]

But for all that, there were few who could resist the exotic cosmopolitan village that was laid out at the foot of the Tower, along the Champs de Mars, and which featured food, curios, and entertainment from all corners of the French empire, from Tahiti to Madagascar and from Annam to Senegal. And fewer still who wished to deny the exceptional benefits that were to be derived from modern science and engineering – whether they took the form of technically exquisite structures like Eiffel's Tower, gas-lit at night in the colours of the Republic, or of the displays of dynamos, transformers, electric motors, and even electrically illuminated water fountains.[13] Not even the severe strain of influenza which swept the city so effortlessly at the end of the year was enough to tarnish the memories of this, man's tribute to his own genius.

Even without the Exhibition, however, Paris seemed overrun by novelty, though not always of a sort to evoke universal acclaim. Popular literature was intensifying its fascination with sexual motifs, starting from the naturalist fortress manned by Zola, running through the more explicit and contrived pages of *Gil Blas*, down to the smuttier ranks of *Boudoir* and *Grivoiserie Parisienne*, and still further down to the pornography and "the infatuation with filth" of *Bavarde*.[14] This trend toward the sexually explicit had accelerated during the 1880s and betrayed no sign of faltering at the onset of the 1890s. Equally enduring in 1889 was the bicycle craze which had captured so many bourgeois around the mid-point of that decade. Although he remained free from the contagion, and was still some years away from his conversion to regular daily exercise, Louis Barthou observed with interest the number of public figures who paraded themselves and their cycles at Saint Cloud or in the Bois de Boulogne between Maillot and the Porte Dauphine.[15] Tennis, too, was making steady inroads in France of the 1880s, as were golf and football. And just as one might experiment with one of these for a little fun and exercise, so one might also try out the new "skating" on the rue Pergolèse or watch the authentic Buffalo Bill perform before thousands of equally transfixed Parisiens.[16]

There was one current which Barthou did find irresistible. That was the music of Richard Wagner. It may have started, like his Hugophilia, with the knowledge that Wagner's music had been disdained by musical circles of the Second Empire. But as with Hugo, what may have started as an *amour de circonstance* quickly developed into a passionate, lifelong affair. In this respect, and unusually, Barthou was in the vanguard of artistic taste, for even in the 1880s Wagner's music was still the subject of some derision in France. Only very gradually in the 1890s, with the successful staging of works like

Die Walküre by directors like Calonne at the Châtelet, did the genius of Wagner command rapt and attentive audiences in France.[17] For a time they continued to boo and hiss, just as they were to do at the 1891 début of Victorien Sardou's *Thermidor* at the Comédie Française, a play which incensed radical republicans with its unflattering characterization of Robespierre and which was in fact shut down after only two performances in the interests of public order.[18] Whether Barthou attended either performance we do not know. But we do know that he had in common with playwright and critics a consuming interest in the personalities and issues of the French Revolution and would, in the fullness of time, write at length on Robespierre as well as on Mirabeau and Danton.

Such were some of the other avenues in Paris with which Louis Barthou had become familiar by the early 1890s. Unlike Saint-Germain or Saint-Michel, these defined a cultural *quartier* within which this educated, energetic achiever operated during the early years of his return to Paris. But adjacent to that quarter there stretched another, at the heart of which was a major intersection of two other *grands boulevards*, that of the deputy and that of the minister. Without some sense of the milieu which each of these invokes, one would be hard pressed to understand a man of Barthou's time, role, and character.

Autumn 1889, the twenty-seven-year-old deputy arrives at the National Assembly, situated on the Quai d'Orsay just across the Seine from the Place de la Concorde. He is beside himself with excitement. "He who has not lived through ... these impressions, these sensations, these sentiments, cannot grasp the intensity and emotional truth contained in those simple words: 'Member of Parliament,' especially for those who come to public life in the very flower of their youth."[19] Looming above him is the spendid façade of the Palais Bourbon, executed by Payet on Napoleon's orders. Moving to the main gate, he is asked for proof of identity by a cautious doorman, a minor embarrassment which Barthou laughs off with a joke about the man's appalling ignorance.[20] On to the *questure*, the reception office where they hand out a supply of envelopes and stationery, everything bearing the insignia of the National Assembly. Then a brisk tour of the corridors, undertaken with the energy of a schoolboy: past the Salle des Pas-Perdus, the statue of Laocoön, the long tables manned by the national and international press, to the Salle des Quatre Colonnes with its periphery of bust-filled niches – Solon, Cato, Lycurgus. ... From here, which way? Straight ahead to the Assembly's stenographic offices, telephones, committee rooms, and the members' smoking room. Back to the Salon Delacroix, toward the cloakrooms, post office, and barber. Here too is the *buvette* which overlooks the Seine, and the *tabac* run by "La Tante," the best-informed person in the House, where everyone collects gossip and newcomers go with relish to buy "les cigars de député."[21]

Or one could proceed directly to the Salle des Séances, the famous hemicycle with its great sloping bank of deputies' desks, row on row, ascending from the floor toward the two spectators' galleries high above. Redesigned fifty years earlier by Jules de Joly, and intended for some three hundred deputies, the Salle is now seriously over-crowded with roughly twice that number trying to attend, with vary-ing degrees of earnestness and success. More comfort is to be found among the spectators, who, in the gods, can look down upon the proceedings of the House. Indeed, from here they can even monitor the votes taken below, as they watch the urns passed by ushers along the benches – with the white ballots (For) competing with the blues (Against) – or the deputies presenting themselves for an even more openly recorded *scrutin public* at the tribune. The tribune, the focal point of the Salle, eight steps above the Assembly room floor, and the coveted spot from which all speeches are delivered. Behind it the desk of the secretary-general, and seated another tier above, the elevated chair of the Président de la Chambre.[22] But it is the tribune to which Barthou's gaze returns, the place where so many of his heroes have stood. "A man is not worthy to climb these steps," he thinks, "and to strike this marble with his hand, unless he recalls – with a pious, almost religious respect – the grave, even tragic, events which have occurred here."[23]

It did not take long, however, before the dreams of oratorical triumphs were interrupted by the address of the Assembly's Presi-dent, opening this, the Fifth Legislature (1889–1893) of the Third Republic. Thereafter, the Chamber was immediately divided by lot into eleven bureaus, each sharing in the task of validating the recent election results in every national riding. Given the house member-ship of over six hundred deputies, each bureau was to have a com-plement of some sixty members. Barthou's own experience proved not entirely typical. By whatever means – perhaps the influence of the eminent Jules Ferry, with whom Barthou had established cordial relations – he was selected as one of the six *secrétaires d'âge*.[24] This meant that he would be on call to serve any of the bureaus during his first term as deputy, a service function which had the advantage of bringing him into direct contact with many more deputies than otherwise would have been the case. In common with others, how-ever, he was nominated through the bureau system to serve on one of the House standing committees – in his case, that of labour regulation, a subject in which he had little previous experience. Characteristically, therefore, he started to remedy his deficiencies by absorbing much of the available literature, especially that already accumulated in the records of the committee. It was tiring work, frustrating and unrewarding. Proposed legislation that was poorly prepared by ministerial staff, he discovered, became a nightmare to the relevant parliamentary committee. It took ages to clean things up, and only by dint of dull slogging. Although forever a potential star at the tribune, the deputy of the committees was just a workhorse, or so the young Barthou quickly learned: "he asks questions, he investigates, he counts, he weeds out, he revises, he edits."[25]

Seasoned parliamentary hands, one suspects, welcomed the process by which novitiates like Barthou were soon set to work and perhaps brought down a peg with reminders that there was still much to learn. At the same time there was a certain internal dynamic that was at work among the newly arrived deputies, especially the younger ones. On the one hand, their arrival at the Palais Bourbon was confirmation of something in which they had already come to believe. They were indeed members of a meritocratic elite, men of proven industry and intellectual capacity; it was but doubly reassuring to find oneself among others of the same cast. On the other hand, one's self-esteem had to adjust to the fact that, in these corridors, there were many others of similar talent and ambition. This is not at all that impulse to equality with which democracy – French in particular – is customarily associated. But it is, in its ironic if familiar way, an expression of the bond between democracy and elitism, a bond on which Barthou looked with approval.

The trajectory traced by Barthou's early career, from Oloron to Paris, was unique by definition. But the fact remains that when he found himself at the Palais Bourbon in 1889, he was only one of many similarly unique individuals. In a society where less than 1 per cent of all French males went on to higher education, 70 per cent of the corps of deputies had been university educated.[26] Some had become teachers and doctors, others journalists, engineers, and architects, but the concentration, unmistakably, was in the field of law. Indeed, as many as 174 deputies elected in 1889 had first approached politics as lawyers or notaries. That in itself may carry a particular significance. Barthou himself believed that lawyers were well suited to politics because of their professional training to serve the interests of their clients. Scholars of our own day, however, have added to that observation the comment that this service function also renders them polyvalent, men elastic enough to sustain multiple pressures. However, this apparent absence of firm ideological fibre, or principle, sometimes means that beneath the smokescreen laid down by rhetoric and sophistry, there is nothing more grand than personal rivalries and competing ambition.[27] Whether it is the law that makes such men, or such men the law, the association of law and politics has become commonplace. Barthou as lawyer, though younger and even more educated than most deputies, thus continued to show further traces of conformity to patterns inscribed by broader social and generational forces.

This impression strengthens with the inclusion of other social data. Like him, most candidates in legislative elections were men of some local political experience, men who had served some apprenticeship in municipal, *arrondissement*, or departmental government and, often, who continued to hold some kind of local office even after their election as deputy.[28] Many, again like the deputy from Oloron, had used journalism as part of their springboard into politics and, again like him, would continue to contribute to that profession as writers or members of editorial boards. For the most part this had little to do with strict economic necessity, for something in the order of 40 per cent of the deputies in the Fifth Legislature enjoyed the affluence of the upper middle class or aristocracy.[29] However, since the number of deputies of working class origin was still very small, the fact remained that more than half of the members of parliament were of lower middle class background – again, men of wholly exceptional education but of quite unexceptional personal fortune. Thus, although they may not have been desperate for the income supplement that would come their way from journalism or local government service, neither could many of them afford to be indifferent to the prospect of some additional income.

The fact is that deputies were not handsomely paid in 1889. Indeed, their base salary of nine thousand francs per annum had not changed in fifty years[30] – proof, some might say, that money was not a motive to enter politics; proof, others might retort, that only the already affluent were intended to apply. There were other perquisites, to be sure, including very cheap rail fare, reductions in private telephone rates, and subsidized bar and restaurant prices at the Palais Bourbon. However, in 1898, the year before parliament voted *not* to increase deputies' indemnities to fifteen thousand francs, one member calculated that many colleagues were actually losing money every year. By his reckoning, a married deputy with two children and a maid would spend far more on accommodation, food and clothing, office expenses and taxes than he earned from his parliamentary salary. It is not surprising, therefore, that many deputies continued in some measure to practise law, journalism, medicine, and engineering, especially in the early years of their political career. Later, with the improved indemnities of 1906, and with more assets acquired through investment, marriage, or both, many deputies like Barthou certainly came to enjoy a much higher degree of economic security than they had known before.[31]

That they worked for it, at least the conscientious, seems quite beyond doubt. On the surface, admittedly, this may not have been obvious. The Chamber did not meet in the mornings or – in response to deputies' concerns about having time to spend in their constituencies – on Saturdays or Mondays. But this apparently abbreviated working week was illusory. The competent, conscientious, and ambitious in fact led a demanding existence. Their mornings customarily were given over to a variety of tasks: studying the morning press, both first hand and through the services of the press-clipping agency *Argus*; undertaking more work for yet another parliamentary committee or putting the final touches on a speech intended for delivery that afternoon. But more important – in so far as time is concerned – was the correspondence, an incessant current of written exchanges which swirled back and forth between the deputy, his local constituents, and the central administration. Here, in this triangular flow, were suspended so many traces of what constituted a deputy's strength and weaknesses, so much in fact of what is both good and questionable in modern representative politics.

Very simply, the deputy was bombarded, daily, by requests and demands from constituents in search of jobs for their children, exemptions from military service for their sons, scholarships for the studious, subventions for the schools, contracts for road construction; or requests for interventions within the local administration to prevent or rectify some alleged act of injustice, or for personal attendance at this gala opening, or that unveiling, or such and such a banquet. Often as not, a definitive, singular reply was impossible. It might require a letter to the Finance ministry, or to that of the Interior, advancing the constituent's case; then a letter to the latter assuring him that something was being done; eventually a letter reporting the outcome, and then a letter acknowledging the elector's gratitude, or his resolve to vote for the opposition for the rest of his life.[32]

Rendering "service" of this order involved a host of psychological complexities. For instance, the reply which promised future action was actually declaring that the deputy himself had to ask someone else, that he too was a pleader, as dependent on the system in his own way as the hopeful elector. Should the deputy's intervention fail, one had further proof of impotence and thus further reason to doubt the wisdom of his re-election. In short, an important key to continued electoral success was a deputy's capacity to be a "fixer," someone who was more than a skilful solicitor, someone who actually wielded some power. There had to be a subtle balancing of servant and master roles. On the one hand, and in Barthou's eyes, the public man "belongs to everyone. They demand from him what they cannot expect from anyone else ... He is constantly subjected to the tyranny of severe criticism." [33] On the other hand, in order to avoid total subordination, the deputy must have something to compensate for his chronic electoral vulnerability. In a word, power. And this is why, in the decades before the First World War, French deputies continued to poach on the powers that were intended to be wielded by the state's representatives in the provinces, namely the prefects and sub-prefects.[34] A deputy with powerful friends in the Interior ministry, or a deputy still active in departmental press and political circles, could so impede a prefect's effectiveness, and, thereafter, his career prospects, that cooperation between these two local notables seemed a mutually advantageous course. Accordingly, in exchange for support he was to deliver in Paris and department, the deputy secured some access to the powers of patronage which were wielded by the state's senior agents in the provinces. By so doing, the elected official was able to strengthen his own ability to deliver favours of all descriptions and, as a direct consequence, enhance his chances of being re-elected.[35]

This happy balancing of service and power is not easily or quickly achieved. It is earned, laboriously, in the country and capital both; and success in the former is very closely associated with career progress in the latter. Success in Paris is mandatory, although, as with Rome, there is more than one way to get there. Outside parliament, in the 1890s, there was a political culture of private salons in which prominent people of like minds discussed the ways, means, and sometimes personnel which could be relied upon to get or keep the French state on course. Barthou does not appear to have profited much from such associations, any more than he owed his political rise to Catholic or Masonic networks.[36] Conversely, it was not long before he became active in the leading press association in Paris, a professional and, no doubt, political interest which he was to retain for the whole of his life. Perhaps for that reason, and despite the fact that he never assumed owner or editorial board responsibilities, he seemed assured of sympathetic support from the journalists of the nation's centrist press. Inside parliament, there were two devices upon which aspiring deputies relied, apart from the work they undertook in the bureaus and committees, and from the opportunities which arose from within one's own political party or group. One was the way in which one could "work the corridors," those subtle, psychological negotiations by which one impressed colleagues and reminded them of one's much tapped but inexhaustible utility.[37] Another was the way one performed at the tribune, whether or not one's remarks were measured and dignified, informed and informative, apparently spontaneous but in fact premeditated. Such at least were Barthou's criteria, together with the strictures that a speaker should never allow himself to be interrupted – unless he had something to gain from it – should never try to outshout opponents, and above all should never say that he really did not want to be a cabinet minister![38] Finally, inside oneself one had to construct a certain self-containment, a self-defence mechanism with the aid of which one tried to struggle toward the top. Defence, in part, against the disappointments brought on by one's own ambition, for, as Barthou said, "the politician never loses hope." Defence, in part, against the isolation which came with the incomprehension of others, all those who cannot understand the compulsion to soldier on despite the press of one's constituents or of one's colleagues. They tell you to resign, he said, without realizing that "there is no retirement from politics," that politics is the mistress one can never bring oneself to abandon.[39]

The transformation from deputy to minister is dependent on the full range of such techniques, whether publicly evident or tended only in private. Sometimes, too, although one might prefer to believe rarely, it may owe something to the clumsy solicitations which occur in the anterooms of incoming premiers. Accustomed as they have been to pleading in countless ministerial offices, ostensibly in the interests of others, it is just as natural for deputies to put themselves forward for a cabinet portfolio. Whether or not this practice paid dividends, there is little doubt that emerging prime ministers found themselves inundated by ambitious hopefuls, reminding Barthou of the benches packed with immigrants at the Gare Saint Lazare.[40] To be sure, there were other, less obvious, ways of pursuing cabinet portfolios, some not much more laudatory than the brassy, direct approach. Patronage, invoked by powerful friends, wives, and mistresses – the so-called *ministresses* – often played a part. So too, however, did regional loyalties, religious or Masonic associations, and party affiliation. Talent even played a role, as intellectual capacity, acquired expertise, and skilful parliamentary tactics were included on the long list of variables which prospective heads of government had to weigh in the balance.

For their part, the ministers themselves were quickly transformed from supplicants to patrons. By Barthou's reckoning, three mornings per week were regularly given over to audiences with a succession of favour-seekers. There were, for instance, the press directors, ably seconded by a cloud of editors, writers, and office personnel; and there were hordes of "former" ministers, more numerous still; and finally, numberless, there were those who were seeking to pave the way to their first cabinet appointment, and deluging anyone capable of offering assistance with a flood of telegrams, letters, and telephone calls.[41]

Whatever the credentials responsible for securing a given portfolio, elevation to the rank of minister was an achievement of very considerable proportion. It brought one into a new and still more particular elite; and having so risen once, one long remained among the ranks of *ministrables*, future as well as past cabinet material. Louis Barthou, of course, was not a minister in 1889; however, he was able to secure that distinction by the spring of 1894, at thirty-two years of age the youngest cabinet minister in the Republic's history. For this reason, there is something to be said for anticipating that success and sketching at this point a rough profile of the ministerial elite. It may thus be possible to illustrate more fully still how Louis Barthou, for all of his inherent qualities, assumed the contours typical of a certain class, *métier*, and time. Thanks to the exceptional work of Jean Estèbe, it is possible to identify, if briefly, some of the more salient features of this group profile.[42]

Returning to a familiar theme, one finds that the educational background of most ministers in the period before 1914 is highly illuminating. Like Barthou, they had been raised in homes where the religious influence was not very marked. Thus anticlericalism came more easily to those who had fewer inhibitions to surmount, even when the influence of typically more pious mothers may explain the politician's reluctance to break formally with the Church. Some, including Barthou, had had experience with local seminary schools, but the majority, again like him, had received most of their secondary education in publicly run lycées. What is more, almost all had secured that coveted university-entrance diploma known as the *baccalauréat* – in an era when only 1 or 2 per cent of all nineteen-year-old males were similarly successful.[43] Subsequently, as suggested by previous remarks about the deputies, most ministers went on to post-secondary education: 12 per cent in professional fields like medicine, science, pharmacy, and arts; 27 per cent at the *grandes écoles* like the Polytechnique, the École Normale Supérieure, and Saint Cyr; but 53 per cent in various law faculties across the country. In fact, most future deputies of legal background had eventually found themselves in the Paris faculty, like Barthou, although he was certainly among the minority who achieved high academic distinction. Indeed, he was among the one-third who advanced to a doctorate in law, and among the exceptionally small number – some twelve out of five to six hundred candidates – who were chosen as *secrétaires de la conférence du stage* during the post-doctorate articling period in Paris.[44] And once again the profession itself proved to be as significant as one's level of attainment within it, for men of this *formation* tended to be strong defenders of certain familiar social tenets: the emphasis on individual responsibility for individual action, the strict observance of contractual undertakings, the reaffirmation of the concept of private property, and, attendant to some degree on all of these, a corresponding lack of comprehension of working class conditions and anxieties.[45]

For once again, this was partly an elite of income as well. Almost 40 per cent of pre-war ministers came from professional bourgeois families and were sons of lawyers, professors, doctors, engineers, and middle-range public servants. Another 35 per cent were sons of highly placed public officials, industrialists, financiers, and affluent *commerçants*. By sharp contrast, it is true, men of Barthou's provenance, the sons of small shopkeepers, were in a very tiny minority, less than 1 per cent of the pre-war ministerial contingent. Nonetheless, given his own unfamiliarity with working class conditions, and given the fact that almost no ministers originated in the families of small farmers or urban workers, one can begin to appreciate the income as well as the educational disparity which separated French cabinet ministers from the majority of their fellow citizens. In turn, ministerial salaries only widened the gap. At an estimated 32,000 francs per year, a minister's salary was between three and four times that of a deputy, and between thirty and forty times the starting salary of a primary school teacher.[46] Thus elevation to ministerial rank underlined in very real terms one's arrival among a select few and, simultaneously, represented a strong economic motive for pushing one's lower middle class ambitions *à outrance*.

Educated and prosperous, in measures well above the national average, the deputy-turned-minister betrayed still other features that corresponded with his group's profile. Among those that have a special relevance to Barthou, three may be invoked at this point: region, marriage, and cultural aspiration. As for the first, several trends have been detected by Estèbe. Despite the pronounced demographic shift toward the cities in the second half of the nineteenth century, the rural communes and small towns of less than twenty thousand inhabitants continued to produce a high percentage of pre-war ministers. Nearly two-thirds, in fact, including Louis Barthou. So too he was part of another national trend, that of an increase in ministerial representation by deputies from the Midi, those thirty-two southern departments – including Basses-Pyrénées – whose linguistic roots are in the *langue d'oc*. Representing just under 26 per cent of the national population, this area nonetheless produced 30 per cent of the nation's ministers. And since more of these men were of more modest bourgeois origin than, say, the men of the Paris region, there was within this *méridionalisation* a slight but perceptible trend toward an economic democratization of French politics.[47] Son of a small hardware merchant, Barthou had slipped into this current as well. Finally, in the perception of the French, this enhanced role of men from the Midi meant as well the influx of deputies who, characteristically, were more open, less formal, than the stereotypical men of the north. Whether or not these have any substance in fact, such familiar characterizations remain very much a part of the national *mentalité*: southerners seen by those of the north as more open, hospitable but superficial; northerners seen by those of the south as solid, reliable but cold and aloof. Without question Barthou was part of this complex and, like most, both profited and suffered from these indelible stereotypes.[48]

Most ministers also married "well," which is to say that they forsook the peril of purely romantic consideration. Instead, they replaced it with economic advantage. Again, Barthou was typical. When he married in 1895, he was almost thirty-three years of age, precisely the average marriage age of the French pre-war ministers. His wife, Alice Mayeur, was ten years his junior, once more conforming to a pattern that was followed rather than prescribed. As the only child of the deceased Max Mayeur, businessman, investor, and land speculator, Alice was to bring into this union a fortune that far exceeded the resources of her husband. In this case the size of the fortune seems indeed to have been well above the average acquired by most prospective cabinet ministers, though 79 per cent of ministers had assets inferior to those of their fiancées.[49] What they lacked in financial resources, however, these bright newcomers were expected to make up for in their talent and ambition. It was in view of "future considerations," therefore, that families of financially well endowed daughters were prepared to invest in the careers of promising sons-in-law – for the sake of those daughters and, one might presume, in the hope that the investment would multiply.

Not that the returns were expected to be entirely of a pecuniary order. One could hope as well that young men like Barthou would fulfil the promise detected by these alert talent scouts and rise to positions of influence and renown – cabinet office, successive promotions in the Legion of Honour, gala events at the Elysée Palace, but also more explicit recognition of cultural achievement. Certainly

Louis Barthou seems to have entertained such ambitions from an early age, perhaps with even greater intensity once marriage had relieved him of the need to make a living. But yet once more it is difficult to distinguish between the strictly private ambition to be known as a writer and the broader social assumption that this indeed is what French cabinet ministers did whenever politics allowed for it. Nor was this mere dilettantism, at least if productivity is any gauge. Cabinet ministers who wrote books in the 1870s published, on average, fourteen works apiece, a figure that had dropped to five by the advent of this century.[50] For his part, by the time of his election to the Académie Française in 1918, Barthou had published four substantial monographs, six volumes of his own essays and speeches, another half-dozen document-laden collections, and some thirty magazine articles. Although it is true that there were other reasons for his election to the Academy, it is clear that his output was well in excess of that of his fellow ministers. So too, by the way, were his considerable successes as a collector of rare books, although again bibliophilia was a familiar preoccupation of many in political circles. He had begun collecting during his school days in Pau, but had found Paris in the 1890s to be a beehive of bibliophiles whose company he cherished as much as he coveted their books and manuscripts. In any event, Barthou the collector is yet another manifestation of a broader class-cultural-generational current.

Such, in summary, is the structure of struts and trusses which supported the stage on which Barthou embarked in the 1890s. Without it, one might see the actor in fuller relief, but the context is needed to interpret his role. In how many ways was he typical of his class of the bourgeois *dirigeant*? Well-educated, non-religious, with an industry to match his ambition, another newcomer from the south; one who would marry to form and who would achieve distinction as another articulate, literate, knowledgeable member of the ministerial class. At the same time, one ought not to confuse actors with marionettes. Undeniably a product of his society, and rarely a dissident in the face of authority, Louis Barthou was no mere transparency through which one looks in vain for personal substance. A lawyer among many, he was nonetheless an outstanding student. A bourgeois born, untypically he was the son of a small shopkeeper. A deputy elected, he was much younger than the average newcomer in 1889, and a minister appointed, he was the youngest of them all. As a suitor he married financially far better than most, and as a writer he published far more than most. A man of his times, but with talents for all seasons, Barthou is an eloquent expression of that relentless, internal negotiation that goes on between our impulse to belong and our impulse to be different.

CHAPTER THREE

In the Chamber:
Homme de centre,
1889–1910

> Nothing is as speculative as a definition, particularly
> when it comes to defining a doctrine. No matter what
> word is chosen, it cannot do justice to the range of
> complexity ... [1]

In recent years much scholarly attention has been paid to social reform in pre-war France, some of it laudatory in nature, much of it concentrated on the limitations of such reform. Two major works in particular have concerned themselves with motivation, and both have one finding in common. Faced with the growth of a politicized working class, the bourgeois governing class responded, slowly and reluctantly, to the challenges inherent in reform legislation. What they wanted was "social peace," as opposed to revolution; and that very quest helped "crystallize" a governing bloc – beginning with the captains of industry and extending across the benches of deputies and senators. Their greatest fear, more than the antirepublican opposition of the 1870s and 1880s, was a movement that was loyally republican but inspirationally socialist. To thwart its ambitions, we are told, the middle class *dirigeants* became clever counter-revolutionaries. To that end, they championed modest, piecemeal social legislation, substantial enough to draw the sting from the worst abuses, slight enough to ensure that such change guaranteed rather than imperilled social stability. [2]

In this there are few surprises, the high quality of the research notwithstanding. Indeed, those familar with Louis Barthou's *formation* might have guessed as much. But how is one to characterize practitioners of such reform – as liberals who promote change in order to preserve the social order, or as conservatives who have submitted to it for the same reason? Either way, and in contrast to the brittle rhetoric of revolutionaries or reactionaries, these are the centrists who are compelled to ponder every issue. In short, although their commitment to order is paramount, the means to that end are always under review. Each reform proposal, each demand for change, must be examined carefully. Much easier to offer a quick, conditioned, predictable response – the stock yes or no. But no more useful, or more just.

Barthou was among those who would not exchange reflection for certainty. Sometimes he endorsed reform legislation, sometimes not. Sometimes his opinion seemed to alter with circumstance, as his weight shifted from one centrist parliamentary group to another. Of surface constancy there was little; and thus his critics made him out to be the sort who trimmed his sail to the prevailing breeze, not for any destination but only for the sake of keeping afloat. This view of him was widespread, a sacred belief among his enemies, a nagging doubt even among some friends. And it does have the iron bar of simplicity on its side. Nevertheless, since historians are accustomed to detecting patterns where none has been seen before, there is no reason why Barthou's should be any different.

Robert Elegant, one of our contemporary novelists, might have been writing of Barthou when he gave us a character who "wanted the pain of the perpetual indecision which is the fate of men who are not fanatics, that perpetual indecision through which they must always choose ... the path which seems best at the moment."[3] And so often after that choice is made, it is replayed before juries determined to sharply distinguish the pure of heart from the crude opportunist. Stark choice in itself, it is made worse by too often equating principle with consistency. Barthou rejected that. Invoking Hugo, he said that to praise anyone for being faithful to the same political ideas for half a century was like congratulating "water for being stagnant, or a tree for being dead." Or, as he remarked himself, more prosaically, what is important about any change of opinion is that it be "neither the cause nor the consequence of a change in personal fortune."[4] However, some insisted on constancy above all else, to party as well as idea, for party could become the font of political truth. And that too Barthou rejected, a man who consistently found his heroes in "free spirits," men uncontainable for long by the discipline of party. This he found the most appealing quality of Danton, one who never succumbed to "the hoax ... of a theoretical absolute or of an immutable principle," and of Lamartine, who had carried the intellectual cross of being, simultaneously, a conservative and a liberal.[5] This was a governing motif in the political life of Louis Barthou, what he praised and what he tried to practise, a man who never knew the bliss of fanaticism, only the steady press of indecision.

Such was at the core of Barthou's centrism. That there were shifts in emphasis over the years goes without saying, but it was movement designed to hold fast, to principles. He was a rock-hard republican, one who believed that the future of France had no place for either monarchists or popular demagogues like Boulanger.[6] However, he had been convinced by Hugo that there could be, had been, both good and bad republics, France of the Constituent Assembly and France of the Jacobins – one of "civilisation," one of "la terreur."[7] For him, as for Hugo, the struggle continued in the present – that struggle against those on the right who, for secular and religious reasons, remained unreconciled with the Third Republic; that struggle against those on the left who defined justice and liberty solely from the perspective of the labouring classes, and who threatened to abjure patriotism in the name of international working class solidarity.

There is no mistaking the middle class character of this Republic he venerates. After all, both had matured together, moulded in the hands of bourgeois republican elders at a time when their ideals had seemed so fragile. Even in 1889 there was a lingering sense that the Republic was tenuous, vulnerable still to aristocratic resurgence or proletarian excess. Unless, of course, it were to be defended by accomplished moderates whose personal interests were compatible not only with the Republican regime but with everyone who lived under it. Or so Barthou argued; and to this was attached the belief that the Republic would be able to reconcile its legislative responsibilities to all citizens with the bourgeois expectation that government would minimize its intrusions into the marketplace. Foreign and colonial issues, national defence and education, these were legitimate, even imperative, responsibilities for a modern state. But meddling in economic matters, this demanded reflection and restraint. The economic well-being of the Republic demanded it, for was it not so entwined with the private fortunes of those who governed that Republic, and of those prominent constituents who had supported the election to parliament of men like Louis Barthou?[8]

FIFTH LEGISLATURE,
1889–1893

Barthou's first term in parliament betrayed few surprises. For the most part, he proceeded cautiously, with the kind of constraint manifest in his maiden speech of March 1890. He was unhappy, he said, about the still unclear circumstances surrounding the sudden resignation of interior minister Constans. Premier Tirard's explanation to the House remained incomplete and unsatisfactory. However, having thus complained, the fledgling deputy expressed both his desire to avoid any ministerial crisis and his gratitude to a government which was both able and responsible.[9] To be sure, less sensitive issues permitted greater openness. For instance, on the rare occasions when foreign and colonial issues were discussed in the Chamber, Barthou voted with the majority – as he did in support of French military presence in Tonkin, Annam, and Dahomey.[10] The empire, to him, was a legitimate expression of France's status as a great power and as such warranted his support. Similar was his reaction to the anarchist crisis which erupted in the early 1890s. A series of outrages with bomb, pistol, and knife provoked a wave of strict new laws aimed at silencing anarchist writers and activists. Barthou approved, a liberal among many who believed that the intolerance of fanatics could not be tolerated by men of moderation.[11]

On many other issues, however, it was his caution that was most in evidence. Ideologically inclined to free trade theory, he joined the protectionist current in parliament by voting in 1890 and 1892 for higher import duties.[12] He favoured the principle of Church-State separation, but continued to resist its implementation on the grounds that it was premature. Accordingly, while publicly excoriating the Church for political interference, as he did in August 1891, he opposed cutbacks in state funding for church schools and the anticlerical campaign to sever diplomatic relations between France and the Vatican. Greater care yet was needed for the Ralliement, that movement within the Gallican church which promoted reconciliation with the Third Republic. Barthou, like many, was cautiously circumspect, fearing a trap. He had no interest in discrediting a Catholic group which had criticized the Church's intransigence toward the Republic. Yet as a genuine disciple, as well as an electoral beneficiary, of anticlericalism in Béarn, he was determined to keep his distance from Catholics bearing gifts.[13]

He was similarly pragmatic on the complex and sensitive matter of legal reform. In November 1890 he attacked proposed cost-saving measures to eliminate the lower level judicial structure, in particular the *juges de paix* and the courts of First Instance. This, he said, was much too radical. What made sense was to eliminate only those officers and courts of demonstrated inactivity. Having thus endorsed this modified principle of economy, the deputy soon found himself on a collision course with political realities. When it transpired that courts in Oloron, Orthez, and Bayonne were to be dissolved – even by the modest criteria proposed by their local deputy – and when aggrieved constituents thus commented unkindly on that deputy's perspicacity, Barthou threw down the principle and fled. In fact, fighting a rearguard action, he managed to secure a reversal of the government's plans for Béarn. Similarly pragmatic was his stance on the issue of multiple public service posts. In June 1893 he voted with the majority to deny deputies the right to hold any other kind of salaried government position – a measure largely aimed at state-funded, politically ambitious clergy. However, he again sided with the majority to defeat an attendant proposal that such self-denial should extend to directorships in companies profiting from state contracts. Here were two cases of "conflict of interest" being interpreted quite differently by the same deputy – the first as a liberal, the second as a conservative.[14]

It was perhaps in the field of labour legislation that Louis Barthou demonstrated even more clearly the tension of one who had always to juggle reason, conscience, and electoral self-interest. In his early months at the Palais Bourbon he was cautious to a fault, mindful of his own inexperience and of the watchful gaze of the Oloron business community. He did not vote in the autumn of 1889 on the ultimately successful bill to eliminate the employment of children under the age of seven; neither did he vote on a proposal to establish equal wage rates for men and women, nor on a proposition to establish a minimum wage law. In the following year, however, he demonstrated greater assurance, and not always in ways which pleased local business circles in Béarn. He did vote against giving miners a say in the appointment of mine inspectors, and he was full of reservations about proposals for an eight-hour working day. But in May 1890 he voted with the majority to sustain a bill from 1884 which had made employers legally liable for refusing to hire unionized workers; and in July he supported legislation designed to limit to ten hours the working shift of child miners.[15]

There is some evidence, in fact, that his work on the Chamber's Labour committee was affecting his outlook – however unenlightened the latter might seem today. Confronted by volumes of testimony from those who worked the mines and factories, the sheltered lawyer from Oloron was becoming more open to the arguments of reformers, a personal awakening which also coincided with a changing mood within the Chamber. In March 1892, for example, Barthou went after employers who fired workers simply for being members of a union. In a speech much applauded on the left, he even invoked Louis Blanc to describe those who believed there could be liberty without equality. It was, he said, the "hypocrisy of oppression."[16] Of greater impact still was his role as *rapporteur* for a new law on retirement funds, although that role earned him some abuse from critics on the left who disliked any plan which relied in part on the compulsory withholding of contributions from workers' wages. The same critics were silenced, however, when he voted for an omnibus reform bill which set at ten hours the maximum working day for thirteen- to eighteen-year-olds, which recommended the abolition of employment of children under the age of thirteen, which made mandatory the physical examination of teenage workers, and which excluded women and young workers from the midnight shift and from Sunday work. Altogether, when its limitations are set beside its benefits, this bill of November 1892 has been described as the "most significant social measure" passed by the Fifth Legislature.[17]

It was in that same autumn that something occurred which was to hasten, and colour, Barthou's parliamentary reputation. Just another deputy within a republican majority, a member who spoke infrequently, a cautious reformer on a slow-moving reform current, he had yet to call much attention to himself. But this emerging reputation of one who was predictable, reliable, and uncontroversial was about to be swept away on rumours of his insatiable ambition and his political infidelity. Indeed, Louis Barthou was to be as much victim as beneficiary of the Panama scandal.

September 1892 saw the first public disclosure of the shady financial practices rampant among the directors of the Panama Canal Company. Such publicity, of course, fanned even more rumours to life, until matters were well and truly aflame in the Chamber of Deputies. Was there, members wanted to know, any substance to these allegations of financial impropriety? Was it true that some ministers, deputies, and senators had been receiving generous financial gifts from a grateful company? And for what? The government of Emile Loubet hesitated, delayed, equivocated – only to find among its indignant inquisitors the surprising figure of Louis Barthou. On 19 November he pressed the government to come clean, concluding with visible impatience: "There are some questions about which Justice remains ignorant." Suddenly, heads were turned in his direction, deputies startled by an anger addressed to a government with which Barthou was known to sympathize. There were whispers of a new Saint-Just, while Maurice Barrès, no friend of the government, honoured the young deputy by calling him a true "footsoldier."[18]

It was all rather unexpected, partly because it seemed out of character, and partly because Barthou was adding to the embarrassment of a government filled with senior republican leaders like Loubet himself, Ribot, Rouvier, and Freycinet. Whether calculated or spontaneous, his public remarks were certain to be construed as an act of disloyalty. Perhaps for that reason, to make amends for what really had been an impulsive act, Barthou was quick to return to form. While it is true that he voted with the majority to defeat Loubet

at the end of November, and that he allowed himself to be elected
to the Chamber's commission of inquiry on Panama, Barthou seemed
determined not to cause further upset. As a member of the commission, he deplored the possibility of confrontation with the new
Ribot government, argued against extending the range of the commission's investigation, and pushed for an early completion of that
commission's work.[19]

Still, the crisis continued to sputter, troubling the Ribot cabinet
and, incidentally, providing the Fifth Legislature with its most theatrical moment – incidental to the crisis, but not perhaps incidental
to the member from Oloron. He was in the Chamber that day,
20 December 1892, when the arch-patriot Paul Déroulède defied
the tongue, and worse, of the radical Georges Clemenceau, accusing
him outright of collusion with the Panama swindlers. Clemenceau
simply stood and called Déroulède a liar, a counter-charge which he
knew would provoke a duel – although not necessarily the bloodless
exchange of pistol shots that occurred at the Saint-Ouen racetrack
on 22 December. In all, Barthou later wrote, "It was the saddest
moment I ever witnessed in forty years of public life."[20]

SIXTH LEGISLATURE, 1893–1898

April 1893 brought the fall of Ribot and the installation of Charles
Dupuy's first cabinet. It was the latter, with Dupuy himself holding
the electorally important Interior portfolio, which took the country
into the general election of September 1893. The results were mixed.
The antirepublican right suffered a further decline in its popular
support, while the ranks of radical republicans and socialists enjoyed
a significant increase. The centre republicans, with whom Barthou
remained, retained their imposing bloc of some three hundred seats
in the Chamber. But the complexion of the bloc had changed perceptibly, for two reasons. On the one hand, the younger deputies
who returned to parliament in 1893 did so with a composure denied
to first-timers – the more so if, like Barthou, they were returned
with a huge majority, indeed uncontested.[21] On the other hand,
many of their republican elders had gone down to defeat, Rouvier,
Loubet, and Clemenceau among them. So it was that the galaxy of
younger talent seemed all the brighter – men like Jonnart and Barthou, both of whom had served on the Panama commission, and the
young Paul Deschanel and Raymond Poincaré. In short, the 1893
election seemed to herald the beginning of a changeover from one
partially discredited republican generation to one still unsullied by

the exercise of power. At least such was an interpretation soon furnished by men like Barrès and Charles Benoist, an interpretation which saw Panama as the occasion seized by the young to oust the republican old guard. Benoist called these young men the four musketeers — Barthou, Jonnart, Poincaré, and Deschanel, men with knives. Adrien Dansette saw cats, young tigers with big teeth and great appetites, usually agreeable but always dangerous. And when Panama happened, they clawed their way to the front.[22] They were there for the opening of the Sixth Legislature, firmly in the Progressive centre but canting slightly toward the right, in a common appreciation that the greatest threat to the Republic now presented itself from the left, among radicals and socialists, men who wanted to rework the Republic in their own image. It is this which explains why Barthou again went on record as opposing separation of Church and State, the introduction of a progressive income tax system, and the immediate introduction of a forty-hour work week, and why he was quick to attack Jean Jaurès and the socialists.[23] These were men, he said, who pretended that France was becoming more inequitable, more bitter, because wealth and land were now concentrated in even fewer hands. It was a vivid portrait, executed with "a blinding brilliance," but it was an illusion. They pretended that the legal status of unions was in jeopardy, when it was the Republic which had made them legal in 1884. They professed that the right to strike was in danger, when it was the same Republic which had enshrined that right to strike. If they were correct about the danger, he would join them in the resistance; otherwise, he would expose their "hollow words and ... futile hopes," as well as their empty theories of class antagonism and their bogey of approaching civil war. The truth was, so spoke Isidore's son, that in France there was no class system, that in France one could not tell where the bourgeoisie ended and the workers began, that in France the socialists had no monopoly on virtue.

Those who attack us ... do they imagine that we are less of the common people than they ...? Yes, we will agree with those who want to defend the worker's right to appraise his own economic value; we will agree with those who demand protection for the worker against workplace accidents; we will agree as well to realize that reform ... which will create a retirement fund for the workers. Yes, all that is possible, realizable. ...[24]

It was in May 1894 that the impression born of Panama and Barthou's energetic critiques of socialism seemed fully confirmed and vindicated. Charles Dupuy, another of Dansette's young tigers,

formed his second cabinet at the age of forty-three – this time offering portfolios to a host of younger men: Barthou, Poincaré,
Gabriel Hanotaux, Théophile Delcassé, and Georges Leygues. Only
General Mercier at the War ministry and Félix Faure at the Navy
were over fifty years of age. At thirty-two, Barthou became responsible for Public Works, the youngest cabinet minister in the Republic's history. But with that distinction came a reputation that was
made indelible by jaundiced observers. Impatient understudy, aggressive enemy, and now quick to power, Louis Barthou was made
out to be a man of unbridled ambition.[25]

There was something plausible in this, to be sure. Panama did
open the doors for younger men. But this is not to say that entry
was secured only at the price of treachery. Even Benoist, he of the
musketeer imagery, stopped at the language of treason. "The word
is dreadful and unjust. In Barthou's case, I never believed there
were betrayals."[26] And as for the charge of overweening ambition,
it too needs to be trimmed and qualified. The fact is that if Barthou
had an obsession with power, it was peculiarly sporadic. Six months
prior to joining the Dupuy government he had declined an invitation
to become under-secretary for colonial affairs in the cabinet of
Casimir-Périer. He had no experience in colonial matters, and had
simply said so, a response he was to use again in November 1895
when Léon Bourgeois offered him the Colonial ministry.[27] Furthermore, his association with Dupuy had both begun and ended
on a note seldom struck by unrestrained power-seekers. For one, he
nearly reneged on his acceptance of Dupuy's offer, suddenly overcome by doubts about his inexperience. For another, in January
1895, he actually did resign from the government, in the name of
that principle that ministers should not be implementing policies
with which they were known to personally disagree.[28]

That resignation came after only eight months of competent service at Public Works, and two days before the fall of Dupuy's once
promising government. Not everyone was impressed by his performance, of course, not those critics who had been in place before
he even assumed office. He had offended republicans of various
shades by his Panama intervention, and his assault on the socialists
in November 1893 had guaranteed him a rough ride from their
quarter. As Public Works minister he would be in endless skirmishes
with radicals and socialists, accused of ignoring workers and favouring employers – especially if the employer was a bourgeois-
directed State. Still, by his own lights he started well. Within his first
month he had rescued the miners' retirement bill from the parliamentary committee rooms, a bill which had been under discussion

since 1880. Armed with his favourite aphorism – "the best is the enemy of the good" – he fended off suggestions for still further time-consuming improvements and secured the bill's passage by June 1894. Whatever its shortcomings, and the opposition found many, here was a significant new bill which effectively rationalized into one system a host of diverse private and state arrangements designed to cover miners' health care, accident insurance, and retirement funds. At the same time, however, the minister led resistance to a series of private-member resolutions aimed at providing state-funded relief payments to strikers as well as to the jobless.[29]

Mines, and then railroads, these were the thorniest problems for Public Works ministers in the 1890s – at once a reflection of the size of the respective labour forces, of more militant unions, and of the State's financial and regulatory involvement. Barthou was quick to respond to both challenges. During the summer recess he travelled to England on a ministerial fact-finding tour, assembling information on Liverpool dock facilities and the London Underground.[30] Plans were already afoot to construct such a railway in Paris, between the Porte Maillot and Vincennes, and to have its opening coincide with the anticipated International Exhibition in 1900. It followed, therefore, that the minister responsible for such an undertaking should be as informed as possible.

Few could complain of that, but the autumn of 1894 brought a new socialist offensive against the government's entire railway policy. In November they pushed for public ownership of all French railways, and for legal action against the directors of the Northern Railway – directors whom they held personally responsible for a recent surge of train accidents. Predictably, the Dupuy government was unimpressed, a reaction which naturally intensified the left's assault on the minister responsible. Clearly, they said, he was not monitoring the working shifts and conditions of the train crews. To which he replied, calmly at first, that the government had already reduced the working hours of engine-drivers, that automatic braking was now being installed on most lines, and that everything possible was being done to improve service while reducing costs to consumer and the State. But as for the insinuation that the government was in the pocket of the rail companies, that was an insupportable travesty.[31]

Charge and counter-charge, and so it went through to the end of 1894. By then the minister was recommending to parliament a new rail convention with the Compagnie du Sud. It was an improvement over the old, he said, because it excluded the possibility of continuing to put more and more public funds into the company, while the latter increased its profits by cutting its services. Jean Jaurès was unmoved. It was a deal contrived by the minister to line the pockets of big investors, and as such should be discarded. On the contrary, Barthou retorted, it was a way of ensuring that the State had more say in the administration of the company. But it was very much a dialogue of the deaf. By December, French socialists had vowed to forestall any vote on further state subsidies for private railways, a tactic which their numbers made impractical but which did manage to charge even further the space between the minister and his most intense critics.[32]

The flashpoint came unexpectedly, and not over railways, or miners, or Madagascar – all of which had poisoned relations between the government and the left. Rather it came during a budget debate, and more precisely over a War ministry proposal to make treason in peace-time a capital offence. Coming as this did within two days of a military court martial – convened to try a certain Captain Dreyfus – this proposal seemed to be the government's way of saying that current legislation did not allow for a death sentence to have been passed on this officer. Jaurès, already exasperated by months of heated debate, detected a subterfuge, then hypocrisy, then dishonesty. Here were the bourgeois protecting Alfred Dreyfus, one of their own, from a firing squad; and when they changed the law, ordinary soldiers would be shot, and officers would still get off. It was a ruse, and a deceit, and the Public Works minister was on his feet. Livid, calling upon words he had heard once before, in the same Chamber, two years earlier almost to the day, Barthou shouted: "Monsieur Jaurès, I have but one thing to say to you. You know that you are lying!"[33]

Order was soon restored, and the debate continued. A duel, however, was unavoidable, dictated by honour and fashion both: by the latter, in that on average there was one such "prominent" duel in Paris per week; by the former, in that bourgeois republicans seemed only too eager to defend the notion of personal honour which they had appropriated from the nobility. In any event, like Clemenceau and Déroulède before them, the two antagonists met at the race-track of Saint Ouen, at 10:30 a.m. on Christmas Day. Separated by twenty-five meters, the two men responded to the umpire's commands, raised their pistols, and fired a single shot, Barthou a split second behind Jaurès. Both remained standing, untouched, no doubt both relieved that the minister's limited vision had done no harm. Ritual observed, honour satisfied, they retired with their seconds, unreconciled.[34]

Parliament proved more dangerous, particularly for a minister who risked the wrath of the railway directors by interfering in their operations, and that of the socialists by forsaking state ownership. In January 1895 Barthou announced that the companies would be made more publicly accountable, and would be held to their commitment to provide workers with reduced fares on commuter specials.[35] Moreover, he wanted the Midi and Orléans companies to desist from selling shares with false advertising. While it was true, he said, that their state-conferred franchises were in effect until 1956, their state-ensured profitability would expire in December 1914. To this, the left responded with enthusiastic cheers, the companies with incensed denials; and the Conseil d'Etat judged that both were unwarranted. The minister was incorrect. The guarantee of profits was as good as the franchise.

On 13 January Louis Barthou resigned. He would not implement a policy with which he was known to disagree and which he believed was quite contrary to parliament's original intentions. If he were mistaken, he told the Chamber, he preferred to exercise his error as a simple, independent deputy.[36] Two days later, the government fell. Dupuy had not regarded the railway issue as grounds for Barthou's resignation, let alone that of the entire cabinet. Accordingly, he allowed it to be a test of the Chamber's confidence. It was a calculated risk, and he lost. The Chamber thought the government compromised, and sent it away to follow Barthou.

It would be three years before Charles Dupuy formed another cabinet. When he did, in November 1898 and again in February 1899, Barthou was ignored. Some chalked it up to his treachery. Principle, they said, had not inspired his resignation as public works minister. Rather, he had sensed the government's imminent collapse and thus had jumped ship before it sank with him on board. Others offered even more caustic, unflattering, and groundless explanations.[37] Regardless, in the eyes of some he had been marked for life, those who felt uneasy with his blend of intellectual agility, good-natured camaraderie, and restless ambition. Not that everyone was on guard. Not the woman he married on 29 January 1895, nor apparently some prominent members of the cabinet which had replaced that of Dupuy. Premier Ribot, indeed, was a wedding guest, as were Hanotaux, Poincaré, and Leygues.[38] Nevertheless, Barthou himself was to remain out of office for some time, a condition which may have contributed to the unobtrusive role he played in parliamentary affairs right through to the summer vacation of 1895.

He returned to the Palais Bourbon that autumn, his personal life redesigned by marriage and money, and was soon reengaged in the centre's struggle against the left. In November he declined Bourgeois's offer to serve in a predominantly radical cabinet, partly on the grounds of his inexperience in colonial affairs, partly because he opposed the cabinet's resolve to introduce a progressive, sliding-scale, income tax. Indeed, three months later Barthou joined the majority which voted against this bill which would have taxed the wealthiest at five times the rate applied to the poorest taxpayer.[39] It was also in November 1895 that Barthou and Jaurès again clashed in the Chamber, this time over yet another miners' strike at Carmaux. The tone and substance were predictable – Jaurès seeing the government's pretended neutrality between miners and owners as a cruel fiction, Barthou dismissing as equally dishonest the suggestion that the workers were always right, always the aggrieved.[40]

It was only a matter of months before Barthou found himself speaking again of Carmaux, once more in the capacity of a cabinet minister. The Bourgeois government had resigned in April 1896, the victim of entrenched Senate opposition to the income tax bill and, so it was said, of the machinations of those three "jeunes Turcs," Poincaré, Leygues, and Barthou – who had been seen conspiring over a dinner table at the restaurant Durand.[41] For whatever reason, the government had retired, without provoking a dangerous confrontation between Senate and Chamber; and Jules Méline had been asked by President Faure to form an administration. He did so on 29 April 1896, a predominantly centrist cabinet which included Louis Barthou in the always sensitive Interior ministry. He was to be there until June 1898, still with Méline, one of the most enduring regimes of the Third Republic.[42]

Barthou had been an obvious choice. Méline was replacing a Radical-controlled Bourgeois cabinet, and was doing so with help from deputies on the right of the Chamber. What more natural than to place Barthou at Interior, a man who had resisted Jaurès with both words and pistol? Overall, therefore, this was not an administration from which the left could take heart. Yet this appraisal must be qualified. Méline, in fact, had done his best to recruit Radicals, including an offer of the Justice portfolio – and with it the de facto vice-premiership – to Sarrien. Unsuccessful in this bid, the premier had then assembled a centrist government with a slight tilt to the left, evidence of which came in his accord with Barthou that there would be no purge of the prefectoral corps recently appointed by the Radicals.[43] For all that, however, it was clear that this was a government committed to gradual progress, at reduced speed, and one resolved to avoid the oncoming hazards thrown up by the socialist left.

Between the socialists and the government there existed an array of barriers. Between them and Barthou as well. He saw colonial expansion as a legitimate enterprise, they generally did not. They, characteristically, were part of the centralizing tradition in France while he, as minister, became associated with certain decentralizing initiatives. The objective of his bill in May 1898, he said, was to grant greater power to the municipal and departmental councils, as a way of righting some of the imbalance created by the Revolution's great obsession with central power.[44] They differed too over the issue of rival voting systems. The socialists generally favoured the discontinued multiple-candidature method of *scrutin de liste*, insisting that this department-wide electoral sounding was a better guide to popular opinion than the existing system of one representative per *arrondissement*. Barthou responded with the argument that the latter system was a purer expression of grassroots sympathy, as voters chose a candidate, and not a party, to represent them and to be accountable to them.[45] And of course there remained between him and many members of the Chamber's left a key difference over the issue of income tax. There had been movement on his part, it is true. By the summer of 1895, if not earlier, he had reconciled himself to the necessity, or at least the inevitability, of such a tax. But he remained firmly opposed to suggestions from members of the left that the wealthy should not only pay proportionately more than their less affluent fellows, but also at a much higher tax rate.[46]

For all this, it was over the issue of labour that the government and its critics on the left clashed most often. Not without some irony. As the centre sought to undercut radicals and socialists by means of reforms designed to root out some of the worst labour abuses, the left opposition accelerated their attacks on the inadequacy of the reforms and the manipulative motives behind them. Here were the opposing grand strategies in whose interests countless battles were waged. In October 1896, Carmaux was again at explosive pitch. Jaurès held Barthou responsible for the heavy-handed police measures which, he said, had been directed against the workers in general and socialist workers in particular. Barthou retorted that it was the government's responsibility to maintain and, where necessary, to restore order. As interior minister he was indeed responsible for recent police action at Carmaux and Albi. Should the Chamber wish, it could defeat the motion to approve the government's handling of the situation. Instead, the Chamber voted strongly for the minister and the Méline administration.[47]

The reform issue was much more complex. Occasioned by a series of reform laws which it brought to the Chamber in late 1897 and early 1898, the government soon found itself under siege. To its right there were complaints about government intervention in private economic matters; to its left, there was derision over the constraints of that intervention. For his part, by the 1890s Louis Barthou had rethought the issue, troubled by the drawbacks of a too traditional liberalism. For instance, in June 1897 he defended the government's relief measures for thousands of Marseille dockworkers left jobless by an outbreak of plague. In April 1898 he was behind the bill to provide medical care for the chronically ill, and state financial contributions to existing retirement plans. He also defended a bill to provide disability insurance for workplace accidents and to make employers liable for part of the costs of such insurance.[48]

At the same time, however, he was as afraid of excess here as anywhere else. That is why he remained predisposed to the sort of "self-help" societies – now totalling over two million members – which he saw as a stimulant for individual initiative and an antidote for reliance on government-assisted programs. As he said in May 1897, the government was pledged to eliminating misery, without creating a society of servile citizens, men and women subject to the will of politically irresponsible public servants. To that end, the Méline administration hoped to collaborate, morally and financially, with the independently minded "mutual assistance societies."[49]

All of this became part of the background for the crisis that was about to break. In 1889 and 1893 national election results had suggested the emergence of two trends. Left of centre parties were making some headway; those to the right of centre, despite some aberrations, were losing ground. Accordingly, determined centrists were more likely to see the greatest danger to the Republic coming from the left, particularly from that quarter which brandished the vocabulary of revolution. Little wonder, therefore, that one such as Barthou would collide with one such as Jaurès. "Against you," Barthou once shouted, "any hesitation is inexcusable."[50] Little wonder that by the autumn of 1897 both were looking forward to the retribution which might come in the approaching spring elections.

It was at Bayonne, on 30 October, that Barthou signalled the government's electoral course. He was at his aggressive best. Although capable of malign influence, he said, monarchism in France was really a spent force, and clericalism one that was tiring. But the recalcitrant forces on the left were more threatening than ever. The government, he insisted, had a vision of the Republic "liberal and progressive"; but others looked to the Terror for their ideal, to the Republic "radical and Jacobin." Between them there was a chasm, those on one side believing in the principle of private property and the reconciliation of capital and labour, those on the other believing in collective ownership and the incompatibility of worker and employer. The latter view he summed up as a doctrine of "inventive hatred," fighting, provocative words from one whose anticlericalism was being far outstripped by his antisocialism.[51] Nevertheless, in November 1897, just after his speech in Bayonne, Barthou was forced to recalculate. Suddenly there were signs of a resurgence on the political right – a revival of fortunes which owed something to a disgraced army officer on Devil's Island, the Jew, Alfred Dreyfus.

Dreyfus had been transported from France in the spring of 1895. In mid-November 1896 the deputy, André Castelin, managed to secure a voice vote in favour of reopening the case against Dreyfus, partly on the grounds that the treason so conveniently attributed to Dreyfus seemed to have continued without him. At the very least, others had to be involved. A year later, in November 1897, the Méline cabinet issued what it hoped would be the last word on Dreyfus. Attentive as it had been to the pleas of the Dreyfusards, the government had again examined the options before it, and had again concluded there was nothing to be done. Reopening a case was exclusively the prerogative of the Justice ministry, and the minister, in this case Darlan, still maintained that there was no evidence to warrant a new trial. Implicitly, therefore, the government was saying that from the point of view of evidence, Dreyfus appeared to have been judged fairly. But to its great and subsequent regret, someone decided to advance the cabinet's position one step further. The public statement issued by Barthou in the wake of the cabinet meeting included the quite explicit statement that Dreyfus "had been duly and justly convicted by the war council."[52]

It would take a while before it was obvious how incorrect that statement had been. But the pressure on Méline mounted regardless, provoking him to the ill-judged rebuke in December 1897: "There is no Dreyfus case." That was the month in which the army court-martialled a newly uncovered traitor, Major Esterhazy. In January, however, there was an acquittal decision, arrived at as part of an ever more clumsy campaign to conceal the judicial blunders that had led to the conviction of an innocent Dreyfus. As Anatole France concluded from all this: "People do not doubt without reasons in the same way that people believe without reasons."[53] But Emile Zola doubted, and with reason. In January 1898 he placed a bombshell entitled "J'Accuse" on the front page of *L'Aurore*, an article which named names and demanded a full inquiry into the Dreyfus case. By February Zola had been convicted of a dishonourable attack on the army. By early April it was known that the Paris Appeals Court would hear his case. By mid-April the Chamber had adjourned for the general election.

By then the country's political complexion had altered considerably from what it had been at the time of Barthou's speech in Bayonne in October 1897. The socialist menace remained as disconcerting as ever, but it was now being rivalled by a renascent right which was marshalling sundry antirepublican, antiregime forces under the banner of the anti-Dreyfusards. The Jew, Dreyfus, was a traitor, they insisted; and any willingness to question the integrity of the army which had convicted him would be proof of this Republic's betrayal of all that was good in France. Barthou could not help but be moved by the emergence of this old dragon, but he resisted the urge to soften his criticisms of the left. Throughout the election campaign he stuck to the government's strategy, hammering the Radicals for their obscure and hypocritical policies, the Socialists for their efforts to restore the Terror.[54]

SEVENTH LEGISLATURE, 1898–1902

It was a particularly bitter campaign, with government forces concentrating their fire on opponents to their left. The Radicals and Socialists replied in kind, like the centrists, still assured that the right remained exhausted and discredited. For their part, those rightist deputies who had helped Méline to power, and kept him there, now chose to fight an independent electoral campaign, competing with centrists as well as with leftists and in general playing a spoiling role. It was not an entirely successful tactic, in that it did not prevent an increase in the left's share of the popular vote. Neither did it prevent a loss of seats on the part of the traditional right-wing parliamentary groups. But it did contribute to an increase in the Chamber strength of the rallié right, and to a corresponding drop in the strength of Progressives, like Barthou, in the centre.[55] In short, the country was more polarized than ever, with those most incensed by anti-Dreyfus clerical propaganda moving toward the Radicals, and those most alienated by the Dreyfusard campaigns shifting toward the reconstructed and apparently more temperate right.

On a more personal level, individuals were praised or condemned for their part in the campaign just passed. Heading the list for evaluation had to be the interior minister, whose own electoral triumph in Oloron – won in part on anti-left rhetoric – only strengthened the resolve of his parliamentary enemies. From the centre, too, there were complaints, from colleagues disappointed in the results. But disparate complaints. Some thought that Barthou had not brought down the full weight of the prefectoral administration on the government's side.[56] Others feared he had done the reverse, that he had pushed the prefects into clumsy political intrigues which ultimately disgusted many electors. On balance, the latter view enjoyed wider circulation, which, of course, neither strengthens nor weakens its credibility.[57]

In point of fact, such charges were hardly in evidence in the new Chamber. By Barthou's subsequent telling, only three things had been clear at that time. As minister he had stressed that prefects were to be above partisan electoral involvement. Second, the elections had confirmed a trend toward the left and, in that sense, away from the government. Third, the election of 556 deputies had been confirmed by the Chamber without discussion; and of nineteen cases where questions had been raised about electoral proprieties, only two inquiries had been conducted, and neither had found fault with the minister. The most that had come to light was some evidence that the sub-prefect at Narbonne had expressed some animus against the local Socialist candidate.[58] Subsequently, in 1928, Georges Lachapelle fully endorsed this, Barthou's account, dissenting only with the claim that generally the prefects had remained neutral. Too many of them had not, so Lachapelle concluded, but only because their own impulsiveness had led them to ignore the minister's appeals for restraint.[59]

Whatever explanations are invoked for the election results of 1898, the fact remains that they were not encouraging for the government or its interior minister. Returned to parliament with another huge personal majority, Barthou was worried by the disposition of pro- and anti-government forces in the Assembly. Indeed, even before parliament had reconvened he had begun to see the need for a critical readjustment. Faced with a revived moderate right, the government had to rest its hope of survival on the temper of its opponents on the left, the very ones against whom its recent electoral campaign had been directed. It made sense, therefore, to rebuild some bridges with the Radicals, an objective which Barthou may have had in mind when he initiated at parliament's recall a welfare bill for the care of the elderly and the incurably ill.[60]

But it was not that easy. However much one might credit his political acumen, there was no mistaking the appearance of political opportunism. Besides, the Radicals were unmoved by this sudden conversion or by the circumstances which seemed to have inspired it. This conclusion was reached, for different reasons, by the government as well. Several cabinet colleagues rounded on Barthou and accused him of unwarranted pessimism and of trying to turn a qualified electoral victory into an unqualified defeat. Méline, too, was in favour of putting on a bright face and going it alone, doing without the Radicals as they had earlier chosen to do without him.[61]

Perhaps nothing could have stopped the fissures from opening in any event – between moderates and extremists at either end of the spectrum, and among moderates who argued about how to contain excess from any quarter. The Dreyfus Affair continued to release its poisons, causing consternation across the centre-left benches in parliament among men who had thought antirepublicanism had all but expired. Louis Barthou became more alarmed about the government's refusal to construct a front on the left, especially with the Radicals who themselves were being jostled toward the centre by socialist forces still further to the left. Méline, however, pressed on, his government doubly vulnerable. The opposition on both flanks was gathering for the kill, while the interior minister watched in silence, refusing to defend a regime which he believed had outlived its usefulness.[62] President Faure apparently agreed. At the end of June 1898 he finally accepted Méline's resignation, and invited the Radical Henri Brisson to form a government.

Louis Barthou was in the political wilderness. He would not assume another cabinet portfolio until Sarrien called upon him in March 1906. Some said, of course, that this exclusion was richly deserved. He had embarrassed Loubet over Panama, Dupuy over railroads, and now Méline over an entente with the Radicals. At the same time, he had incurred the wrath of many Radicals, of most Socialists, and certainly of all those on the right who had been lifted by the new wave of antirepublicanism. What is more, he could deny none of it. It had happened. But why it had happened was another matter. His critics looked no further than his ambition and an alleged absence of principles. Barthou would have said precisely the reverse. He had behaved according to his principles, not despite them. He had spoken out on Panama because honesty demanded as much. He had left Dupuy rather than conduct a policy he believed was in wilful violation of parliament's intent. So with Méline: it was true that Barthou had changed his mind about the Radicals, but not for the sake of personal political advantage. Had he loved power as much as some said, he would have defended the government to his last breath. Instead, in the face of a resurgent right, excited like sharks by the sight of republican blood, he had reasoned that the centre should accommodate itself to the changed political realities. In the interests of the democratic, secular Republic to which his principles bound him.

The longer the "Affair" endured, the stronger his conviction grew. The Brisson government was no sooner in office than it learned that some of the evidence used to convict Dreyfus had been concocted. The war minister was soon forced to resign, caught between the truth as he had reported it to parliament and the truth. By the autumn of 1898 the case for revision had gathered new momentum, facilitated for the first time by the deputy Barthou. Now formally presiding over the Progressistes, he addressed the Chamber in October. The government, he said, was getting on the right track. It had properly condemned the anti-Semitic and antirepublican outbursts which long had animated the pages of the nationalist press of the French right. Similar rebuke should now be delivered to some of its own supporters on the left, who exceeded truth and taste by their criticisms of the French army. However, one fact remained. The revelation of forged evidence in Dreyfus's trial made revision mandatory.[63]

It was a balanced, conciliatory performance, distributing blame but ending on the side of the angels. And that displeased many. Deputies on the left scented the hypocrisy of a man who had been in the cabinet when an innocent Dreyfus was first court-martialled, and in another when a guilty Esterhazy had been acquitted. It had been Barthou who had issued the press statement claiming Dreyfus had been fairly tried. Furthermore, there were persistent rumours that the Méline cabinet had been told of the forged evidence – to which Barthou replied with a categorical denial. He had known nothing of Major Henry's role as forger until it became public knowledge two months after Méline's fall; and he had known nothing of the evidence assembled by Colonel Picquart on Dreyfus's behalf until the recent Zola trials had brought it all to light. Yes, he had opposed revision prior to the exposure of Major Henry. But from that moment on, from July 1898, he had accepted revision as both inevitable and indispensable.[64]

If the left greeted this testimony with scepticism, some in the centre evinced alarm. These included some Progressistes who, in principle, were more wary than their leader about the Radicals and who were doubly reluctant to see the Dreyfus business used in the interest of such collaboration. In fact, what was happening in the autumn of 1898 was a gradual reconstitution of the political centre in France, one not so much caused as conditioned by the fragmenting effects of the Affair. It happened over the space of several years, and in discrete stages. The Progressive bloc was one of the first to break, thanks in no small part to Barthou. In February 1899 he broke with his own group, and led a dissident minority of some thirty deputies into a parliamentary vote in favour of revision. That initiative was followed in turn by Barthou's decision to take his followers into a parliamentary group currently led by Raymond Poincaré and named, significantly, the Républicains de gauche.[65] The Progressive majority, for their part, slowly shifted in the opposite direction, toward the right and the defence of social order, closer than ever before to the *ralliés* and the right-wing nationalists.[66]

To the left of the Poincaré-Barthou republicans were the Radicals and Socialists, among whom further shifts and realignments would take place between 1899 and 1901. At the end of it all there emerged that perplexing creation known for a time as the Radical and Radical-Socialist party – one which was non-revolutionary, non-socialist in any collectivist sense, but rhetorically reformist to a fault. Ideologically mystifying as it was, its intent was clear enough – namely to distinguish itself from the revolutionary Marxist left while appropriating to itself the left of centre, radical-reforming tradition. Nudged toward the centre by forces on its left, it thus occupied the ground immediately adjacent to that held by the Républicains de gauche.

It was in 1901 that the latter group became part of a larger association that had been founded that year by Adolphe Carnot. Like the Radical-Socialists, this Alliance Démocratique saw itself as a force of progress; hence its conditioned suspicion of the nationalist-clerical right, and its proclaimed objective of a "liberal" Republic. But in terms of rhetorical emphasis, it was stronger on public order than the Radicals, harder on Marxist socialism, and united in its opposition to the progressive income tax. As for Barthou, he belonged there, with so many other centrists, like them having run in the same lane for the past decade, wearing the colours of the Opportunists, the Progressistes, and now the Alliance, but by and large maintaining the same field position. Moreover, it was the kind of "party" that most appealed to him, one which tolerated almost any cause, except that of disciplined conformity, and which allowed deputies to vote as they wished.[67]

Such, cryptically, was how the centre reconstituted itself in the wake of the Dreyfus Affair. Overall, there was a slight shift toward the left, as the new Radical-Socialist party and the new Alliance association constructed between them pro-capitalist, anticlerical, reformist platforms. And from that reconstitution they went on to dominate the executive branch of government right through to 1914, a fact which suggests rightly enough that the liberal-democratic-bourgeois-republican centre had held. More than that, it had revived itself by means of skilful accommodation, though not without an attendant irony. It is, after all, this period when moderate centrism is recovering its equilibrium that one finds the last great anticlerical measures against the Church and a host of stringent state actions against a rebellious labour leadership. It is also ironic that Louis Barthou, an adept centrist tactician, should be kept out of power for some years to come. He was paying a price, and he knew it, a realization that helped nurture a cynicism – a "cold and distant manner" – behind which he concealed his disappointments if not his hopes.[68]

That he was twice overlooked by Charles Dupuy is not surprising, given the legacy of Barthou's precipitate resignation in January 1895. He might have expected more from Waldeck-Rousseau, a senator with whom he had contacts through the Association nationale ré-publicaine. It was Waldeck who formed a cabinet in June 1899, following Dupuy's final effort, a cabinet which was to endure for a remarkable three-year period, until June 1902. It was a cabinet with its centre of gravity firmly fixed in the moderate centrist ranks which would soon give birth to the Alliance. Indeed, the premier himself would be instrumental in the founding of that organization. None-theless, Barthou was not approached, partly, it would seem, so as to allow Waldeck to construct a firm *bloc de gauche* by bringing in Rad-icals like Joseph Caillaux and the renegade socialist Alexandre Mil-lerand.[69] Caillaux was one thing, but Barthou certainly did not approve of the Millerand appointment. It was too much, he thought, to have a socialist running the ministry of Commerce and Industry.[70]

In general, however, he supported the government, a stance which completed his divorce from the Progressives. In particular, he backed a series of government measures designed to shore up the public education system and curb the teaching prerogatives of the Church. It was all part of the centre-left backlash to the Dreyfus Affair, as anticlericals of previously modest resolve now felt impelled to bring the Church into line. It was this mood that led to the Law on Associations of July 1901, legislation which sharply curtailed the Church's educational involvement at the secondary level by refusing the mandatory state authorization to many of the church's teaching congregations.[71] It was not the most noble of government enter-prises, or the most subtle. But historians could have warned the Church about what might happen when liberals were given an oc-casion to discriminate with a clear conscience. Barthou himself had sent some clear signals in a speech of 1903. Clericalism kept return-ing to France. In the 1870s it had been called "moral order," in the 1880s Boulangism, and now nationalism; but underneath was always clericalism, a political strategy which exploited religion as a way of undermining the Republic. As such, it had to be plucked out root and branch.[72]

EIGHTH LEGISLATURE,
1902—1906

By the time the Seventh Legislature dissolved, in March 1902, it was clear how and where the imminent general election would be fought. The reconstructed centre-left, in the form of the Radical and Alliance parties, would lead in the republican defence. The enemy now was the clerical-reactionary right, currently much invigorated by the resurgent ranks of nationalists whipped up by the Dreyfus business and the attendant assaults on the honour of the army. Barthou's own election campaign in Béarn reflected the shifts that had occurred in national politics. In 1898 he had received 95 per cent of the ballots cast in Oloron, running uncontested and with the tacit support of local *ralliés*. This was before the Dreyfus storm had fully broken, when his principal target was still Socialists and Radicals, and when he still enjoyed the prestige of a cabinet post. In 1902, by contrast, the scale of the Dreyfus disgrace was much more evident, the campaign against the right had ruptured his *modus vivendi* with the Béarnais *ralliés*, and he had lost his ministerial status.

It was a testament to his election skills that he emerged from the 1902 elections with his huge majority almost untouched. In so far as 92 per cent of the voters were concerned, any tarnish he might have acquired from the Dreyfus Affair had been cleansed by the Church-targeted Law on Associations. At the same time, however, an exceptionally high 28 per cent of registered voters had refrained from voting – a measure of the impact of recent political turbulence and strained loyalties.[73] Nationally, this mixture of uncertainty and resentment translated into more disconcerting terms. Certainly for the Alliance Démocratique, the polarization of the new Chamber was even more grave. Gains both by the Radicals and by the centre-right had been recorded at its expense; and that meant, in all probability, further confrontation between a renascent right and a pro-government left in which Radicals and Marxists outnumbered the Alliance members by two to one.[74] More ominous still, Waldeck-Rousseau of Alliance affiliation suddenly resigned the premiership, on grounds of ill health, and was promptly succeeded by the Radical and renowned anticlerical Emile Combes. The troublesome and enduring issue of Church-State relations at last was going to be faced head-on.

Like most Frenchmen, and all politicians, Louis Barthou had long contemplated this issue. He had come early to anticlericalism, encouraged by schoolboy readings of Gambetta and Ferry, as well as by the counter-productive intrusions of school chaplains. And as he entered politics, he had used that anticlerical stance to situate himself on the republican left. His anticlericalism therefore arose not because of any exceptional vision of social reform, but because he condemned priestly interference in politics. However, although he liked the principle of Separation, Barthou had never once advocated its implementation. Indeed, as befitted a temperamental moderate – and a shrewd student of Béarnais politics – he had even used anticlericalism with discretion. For instance, in the 1902 campaign he had insisted that the Law of Associations would have to be applied sensibly, with each institutional applicant for state authorization being examined on its own merits. In short, there should be no blanket denials of authorizations to religious congregations.[75] Similarly, in October 1902 he had joined the parliamentary majority in defeating an ill-prepared proposal to scrap the Concordat, separate Church and State, and sever diplomatic relations with the Vatican.[76]

Nevertheless, the still unresolved Dreyfus Affair led to a demand for a formal definition of the role religion would play in the modern state. The time for equivocation had passed. It was time for a decision, a moment announced by centrists fed up with extremists on either side of the religious divide. In March 1903, Barthou made his choice. He voted with the government to deny, with a single stroke, the applications from as many as fifty-four congregations.[77] Again, he had changed his mind, reneged on a campaign promise from the previous summer. But again, one would be hard pressed to discern any political advantage he hoped to draw from such a conversion. In the Chamber, he offended Combes's supporters by following his vote with pleas for renewed guarantees of religious liberty, and for full pension rights for elderly clergy.[78]

At home, it was even more difficult. Not surprisingly, many of his supporters had been chagrined by his vote and by the broken promise it represented. For the first time in his political career, Barthou sensed significant levels of animosity, a discovery which prompted him to change his mind again. He now decided to run for election to the departmental council, a seat of local political strength which might allow him to contain an opposition rather unexpectedly arising within a loose coalition of conservative Catholics and alienated liberals. Seriously challenged for the first time since his debut in 1889, Barthou displayed another side of his personality – something resentful and petulant. In that election campaign of 1904 he was far harder than he needed to be on his principal rival – this "nonentity," as he called him derisively. "Who is he anyway, and what has he done that he would dare compare himself with me, I who have done so much for the people of Oloron?"[79] It was true, but arrogant, and not well calculated to soften the views of those already disaffected. He won the election, to be sure, just as he was to win every other departmental election until his death in 1934. Won it handily. But the fact that the opposition polled well over a third of the votes did not escape his attention. Rather, it confirmed what he knew by instinct. Religion and politics were a volatile and unstable mixture, best kept separate.

This was as sensible as it was impractical. Both sides were too engaged to retire without some resolution. Like others, Barthou had reluctantly but firmly joined the ranks of those bent on a final settlement with the Church. Essentially, that is why he took on the local opposition with such vigour, because there was nowhere and no way for him to retreat. That is why in 1904 he supported Combes's bill to dissolve the Catholic teaching congregations over a ten-year period, and why in July of that year he voted in favour of breaking off relations with the Vatican. Finally it is why he became an outspoken advocate of Church-State Separation, and why he voted with the majority in favour of the law on Separation in July 1905. Responsibility for this action, he argued, rested firmly with the Vatican and its persistent violations of the Concordat. The French state had been left with no alternative but to follow the separation of Church from school, with the separation of Church from state.[80]

Well before then, however, the strains were evident within the governing *bloc de gauche*. Anticlericalism could hold Socialists, Radicals, and Alliance members together for a time, but the equally delicate field of labour relations dispelled any semblance of real unity among them – the more so given the wave of private- and public-sector strikes which buffeted the governments of Waldeck-Rousseau and Combes. Barthou, as a prominent member of the Chamber's labour committee, knew better than most what was happening to a France that had been trailing behind European leaders in industrial development and attendant industrial unionism. Moreover, he knew to his own satisfaction that the tenfold increase in French union membership between 1884 and 1904 had been accompanied by socialist efforts to politicize these unions and make them extra-legal political weapons for use in the cause of social revolution.[81] In the course of the Eighth Legislature, therefore, he stuck doggedly to the centrist path. He supported bills which established an eight-hour day for miners and an eleven-hour work day for most male workers, and which extended union status to more public sector employees. But he opposed the principle of compulsory union membership; and he fought against awarding collective bargaining rights to any group of public employees who shared in some way in the "public power" – those who were employed to fulfil some vital public trust, like postal and teaching services, and who then demanded the right to bargain and strike against that trust.[82] Assured of Alliance support for such positions, he knew as well that his views would receive a mixed response from the polyglot party of Radicals and Radical-Socialists, and uniform disdain from the Socialists of Jaurès and Jules Guesde.

The *bloc de gauche* had not collapsed, but it was fading. Centrists like Barthou had become estranged from Emile Combes, first offended by the sectarian zeal of General André, his war minister, and then by that of the premier himself. By early 1905 Combes had become a liability to his own cause, so personally engaged in the Separation issue that it was in risk of being trivialized as an act of personal spite. Convinced that the premier had outserved his usefulness, Barthou joined the majority which defeated the government in January.[83] It was left to the succeeding Rouvier administration to pilot the Separation bill through Chamber and Senate, a process which required most of what was left of 1905. It was just as well, for the Church issue was the most reliable of the *bloc*'s bonding agents.

It, and something called Nationalism. Patriotism, Barthou insisted, was entirely different, a willingess to sacrifice anything for the freedom, security, and dignity of one's country. Nationalism, by contrast, was the aggressive twin of clericalism, and as such a menace to the Republic.[84] On this, as well, the Alliance and Radicals could agree. So, too, the inconvenience and financial loss caused by the wave of strikes, and the defiance of the law by too many strikers, served to remind them of the shared intrinsic values which kept them in loose concert. Finally, that same concert benefited from the creation of a Marxist Socialist party in April 1905, one which only highlighted the non-collectivist nature of the Radical-Socialists. Expressly international in vision and revolutionary in objective, French socialism had done its best to unite under the banner of the Section Française de L'Internationales Ouvrières and thus distinguish itself from "bourgeois" parties.

The Sarrien ministry that emerged in mid-March 1906, on the eve of the general elections, was proof enough that the *bloc* still held. This cabinet featured Radicals like Léon Bourgeois, Albert Sarraut, and Gaston Doumergue as well as Sarrien himself, and Alliance luminaries like Poincaré, Thomson, Etienne, Leygues, and Barthou. At the same time, to accentuate the leftist cast of his administration, Sarrien brought in Georges Clemenceau, a maverick Radical, and

Aristide Briand, a renegade Socialist.[85] Barthou assumed the ministry for Public Works, where he remained when Clemenceau served as premier between October 1906 and July 1909, and from which he moved to Justice in the first Briand cabinet.

The 1906 elections therefore found Barthou secure again among the country's *dirigeants*: again a minister, and by then a vice-president of the second largest political group in the Chamber, namely the Alliance Démocratique. And once again he was unchallenged in Oloron. At forty-four years of age he seemed poised for a final assault on the summit. The conditions were propitious. Although still flying the colours of the *bloc*, he realized that, unlike the regrouped Socialists, the right was again in a state of at least temporary disarray. In short, although still defined as the principal enemy – as in 1902 – it had recently lost some of its steam. This allowed Barthou to mend fences with some of the offended liberal community in Béarn, and offer new assurances to the moderate Catholic community that the Alliance was not out to destroy all Church-run schools. Nor was it simply a matter of placing less emphasis on the clerical menace, and more on that represented by revolutionary socialism. There was another ingredient in his 1906 campaign, that of patriotism. In it he found an ideal formula for competing with the right's self-proclaimed monopoly on national pride and respect for the armed forces. But at the same time it was ideal as a means to isolate French Socialists, not simply on the grounds of their collectivist principles, but also on those of their antimilitarism and dubious national loyalty.[86]

The results of Barthou's personal campaign in Béarn were generally encouraging, as were those of the *bloc* on the whole. Uncontested, he received 83 per cent of the properly completed ballots. This time, however, a 27 per cent abstention rate had been underscored by a 17 per cent incidence of ballot spoilage, clear indications that not all had been forgiven by an electorate jaded by the degree of support he had given to Combes and Rouvier.[87] Nationally, too, there were reasons to rejoice. Some 60 seats had been lost among nationalists, progressives, and old-time conservatives. The Alliance had gained some 14 seats – bringing their total close to 130 – and the Radicals had risen to some 250 deputies with their gain of 30 seats. To be sure, the Socialists had made gains as well, picking up some 14 new seats, but their association with the *bloc* was more tenuous than ever. The recent unification of their movement under the SFIO, together with the fact that the Radicals and Alliance now controlled a majority in the Chamber, meant that the *bloc* was more thoroughly centrist than ever.

NINTH LEGISLATURE,
1906–1910

The *bloc* was centrist, but it was also reformist, partly for reasons of positive ideology, partly out of a pragmatism fired by labour dissension. As a measure of the government's position, it is instructive to see a minister like Barthou campaigning in 1906 for greater job security in the workplace, fuller legal recognition of trade and labour unions, and a progressive income tax to help float increased public expenditures.[88] As a measure of Barthou's place within this government, it is instructive to hear a fellow minister like Clemenceau condemning the fiscal irresponsibility of Socialists, or the president of the Alliance denounce "those self-serving groups which preach hatred and class struggle."[89] Both were harbingers of things to come in the Ninth Legislature, a parliament which produced some far-sighted legislation but which also resorted to stiff and repressive measures against malcontent workers. Once again, here was the plight of moderates who were prepared for change but were resolved on order. The luxury of moderates, some might say, men who had the time and resources to reflect at their leisure, men whose children had never gone hungry.

Barthou's own record in this administration contains few surprises. He voted to establish a six-day work week in July 1906, to create a full-fledged Labour ministry that autumn, to provide pension benefits for railroad workers retiring after the age of fifty, and to inaugurate a workers' pension plan which would be more fully funded by worker, employer, and state. In a similar vein, he also decreed that all discipline committees within the postal system would cease to be appointed by ministerial personnel, in favour of elections by workers.[90] But he remained a conservative when it came to many labour disputes. Maintaining his earlier distinction between public sector workers whose jobs involved an exercise of public authority, and other State employees whose jobs did not, Barthou refused to acknowledge a teacher's right to strike. He took the same stand with many post office employees. Although he reinstated most of the postal sub-agents who had gone out on a wildcat strike in April 1906, he refused to pardon those he saw as the ringleaders. These, he said, were men of revolutionary intent. They and their fellows would only see a pardon as "an act of weakness ... essentially an invitation to further revolt."[91]

The five-month postal strike of 1909 was worse, and his response comparably severe. He refused to negotiate with the strikers, replaced those who refused to return to work, and declined consideration of amnesty for those thus sacked. The strike, he told parliament, was unprovoked and illegal, an "act of sabotage" and "a national crime"; and it would be met with "very stiff and deserved disciplinary action," if parliament agreed that it and the government should run the country and not the new Confédération Générale du Travail. Not surprisingly, given the election results of 1906, the Chamber rallied to the minister, applauded his speech and ordered it to be publicly posted.[92]

Nothing better illustrates, however, the uncertainties which hide behind the labels of left and right, conservative and liberal, than the issue of the Rachat de l'Ouest. Here was the case of a government takeover of a private railway company, the Western. The government's agent was Barthou, public works minister in a cabinet now headed by Clemenceau, one which inherited rather than initiated this issue. Talks had been underway since 1904, talks which had led to a special committee report in the spring of 1906. In June Barthou approved the report, and by the end of the year the Chamber and its budget committee had endorsed the government's plan for purchasing the shares of the railroad. Thereafter, the pace slackened. While the government began investing in equipment for its anticipated new railway, the Senate dug in its collective heels. Unhappy with the principle of such state intervention, senators fell back on arguments designed to demonstrate their fiscal responsibility. This particular plan, they said, would be financially ruinous for the state. Not until December 1908 could Clemenceau get them to relent and finally follow the lead taken by the Chamber two years earlier. With that began a period known as the "Rachat provisoire," during which the convention with the railway was to be negotiated and implemented. In fact, it was not until December 1909 that final parliamentary approval was secured for the *Rachat*.[93]

In short, three years elapsed from the time the Chamber first approved the purchase. The opposition had been enduring and bifocal. To many on the centre-right benches, the intervention was provocative and unnecessary. Barthou sounded to them a radical and a turncoat. He was no collectivist, perhaps, but he had gone overboard with his public accusations that the Company was trying to inflate its share values by artificially – and dangerously – cutting back on its operating costs. Far worse, the minister had actually suggested that some opponents of the bill were trying to delay the purchase of the Western so as to drive up the values of the soon-to-be sold shares. Indeed, cheered by deputies like Jaurès, Barthou associated himself with the Western's employees – who he said would be better paid and protected by the state – and with all those consumers who could look forward to safer and more efficient rail service in western France.[94]

Having irritated many conservative deputies and senators, the minister could not have expected to escape unscathed by the left. He had affirmed that the *Rachat* was an act of expediency, not of principle, undertaken only because the state was getting too little service for its annual financial subsidies. It was a single and exceptional act, he said, thus making it sound like a contrite admission to some leftist members of the Chamber's Public Works committee. It was the summer of 1909, in the middle of the period *provisoire*. The West's share prices were rising fast as final arrangements were being made for their purchase; but controversy again erupted, this time over how long the state would be liable to pay a guaranteed minimum dividend to the new shareholders. Would it run to 1935, when the West's company structure would finally dissolve, or would it be to 1956, the terminal date set by the original concession? In 1906 Barthou had suggested the earlier date. Now, he knew that the Company would insist on the later date, and suspected that the Conseil d'État would rule as it had done in 1895. Grudgingly, enough holdouts from the left came around to ensure the convention's approval, though not without lingering convictions that the railroad and its shareholders had been treated too generously by the government.[95]

Still, the parliamentary centre and centre-left qualified their criticisms. As such, the *Rachat* issue both illustrated and reminded members of the Alliance, and those in the centre of the Radical party, of the ideas they still held in common. Faced with a mounting socialist movement to their left, and yet another consolidation to their right – one partly stimulated by the racial conservatism of the new Action Française – the governing centre-left coalition prepared for the general elections of 1910. Barthou was still in the cabinet, by now justice minister under Briand, a position to which he would return after another successful election campaign. It was this election that inaugurated the Tenth Legislature of the Third Republic, a parliamentary session which at last would take him to the summit of power.

Surveying these first decades of Barthou's career, what is it one sees, and with what assurance? The answer depends on the viewer. He may be called a man of the left, not because of a social vision but because of a consistent stand against monarchism, demagoguery, clericalism, and militant, racial nationalism. That much he shared with the Radicals and the SFIO, associations which of course confirmed his colours in the eyes of those on the right. In his own eyes as well. But today's readers are unlikely to find this enough to warrant the praise, or alternatively the opprobrium, of being on the left.

On the contrary, we might be more inclined to push him off to the right, since monarchism, clericalism, and even nationalism are no longer taken as quite the menace they once were. Like Jaurès and even some of the Radicals, we are more likely to define left and right by responses to some basic social issues, including the concept of private property. Viewed from here, Barthou is indeed catapulted toward the right – a believer in property if not in religion, a believer too in the rule of law, even when he knew it was law made by middle class legislators and interpreted by middle class judges. An unflinching opponent of socialism, it comes as no surprise that he will be seen by some not as the *homme de gauche*, which he claimed to be, but as a conservative, which he also claimed to be.[96]

But of what use are such labels, as easily removed as applied? Not that the admittedly precarious term "centrist" is definitionally superior, for it too is meaningless without some sense of the extremes. But in Barthou's case the word may have special merit, partly because it is how he saw himself, partly because of the problems associated with marking him as either of left or right, but mainly for another reason: mainly because we have seen him repeatedly relocating the centre in response to developments at either end of the political spectrum. He had changed his mind on holding more than one public office, and on the issue of Separation. He had come around to the progressive income tax and to public service unions, and was reconsidering his older resistance to the *scrutin de liste*. Some will call this opportunism, shifting according to the scent of political advantage. His friend Joseph Caillaux did, accusing him to his face of being a creature only of the moment.[97] But if such were true, it only uncovers a greater mystery. For a man reputed to be such a skilled manoeuvrer, his instinct was remarkably faulty. Too often he disqualified himself for office, or declined it, or resigned from it, and gratuitously at that. Just a little less candour, less impulsiveness, perhaps even fewer principles, was all it would have taken.

His most basic principle was to serve a liberal-democratic Republic by containing extremism, whether that of anarchist or priest, socialist or aristocrat, or, for that matter, pessimist or optimist. But what Barthou knew, and what too many ignored, was that times changed, and with them the nature, direction, and intensity of the Republic's enemies. That is what he meant when he said that "a political career cannot have the uncompromising quality of a straight line."[98] Those in the centre, those flexible enough to adjust, had to assume responsibility for combat and for reconciliation. And they would do so not by decamping, but by shifting their weight as if from one foot to another. Sometimes toward the right, as in 1893 and even 1898

– when the left seemed to be gaining ground. Sometimes toward the left, as in 1902 and 1906 – when clericalism and nationalism threatened. Moreover, if this is to be seen as essentially a holding strategy, defending the Republic against the intemperate and the woolly-minded, it should not be seen as a static defence. It required agility and balance to stay in the centre of a spectrum which stretched and contracted, elastic-like. This sometimes meant more than slight alterations in one's perspective. For Barthou it meant accepting change in his forties that as a younger man he would have resisted, particularly as it impinged on the role of the state. Like most of his generation and political allegiance, he had come to accept the case for greater state intervention in society, the idea that the State had certain responsibilities to its citizens, which would not be fulfilled by the private sector, and which could not safely be left unfulfilled. As he said in December 1905, "against the promises of utopia we must offer reforms."99

One can see this solely as the calculation of the social conservative intent on defusing revolution. Or one might be a fraction more generous, particularly if we see the paradox of praising those who are willing to learn but suspecting the motives of those who then adjust to what they have learned. Is it so implausible that this was a generation and an elite which continued to learn after they had been educated, which realized that the risks of an interventionist state could be offset by malnutrition, industrially maimed workers, and retired paupers? One might even allow for the possibility that some had been moved by the condition of too many working class families, their miseries recorded in printed testimony, press reports of mine and train disasters, and in the eloquence of too many photographs. Again, the explorations of motive are as unlimited as the explorers themselves. As for Louis Barthou personally, there are in fact few visible traces of emotional involvement in such issues, but more evidence than is needed to decipher a man persuaded of the need for reform. If not the most impressive of claims, it is a fair reflection of a man adept at using pragmatism to defend, and sometimes even to conceal, principle.

CHAPTER FOUR

Beyond the Chamber: Homme à tout faire, 1889–1910

Some claim that I love power above anything else. They have never seen my books.[1]

Barthou said that there was no recovery once politics had entered the blood. The true politician, he reckoned, "was always hoping," for the first break into executive office, or for just one more.[2] No doubt he meant it; and yet there were contradictions. Politics had brought trials as well as recognition, sometimes in the form of scathing rebukes from opponents, sometimes as the ostracism he endured between 1898 and 1906 and would again between 1910 and 1913. Frustrating too were the "sterile squabbles" of parliament, an assembly which had difficulty even following an agenda. The abuse of the *interpellation*, the impromptu calling of a minister to account, or the sometimes equally spontaneous and "urgent" opposition resolution, too often reduced the Chamber to "instant turmoil."[3] Besides, there was so much to do beyond the Chamber, to learn and to savour. As Claude Farrère was to say of him many years later, Barthou was interested in everything, a quintessential intellectual tourist.[4]

There was a link, however, between Barthou's thirst for politics and his hunger for non-political fulfilment. As it happens, in that connection is to be found the animating principle of his life, a principle which weds his calculated political centrism with his passion for self-discovery. That word is patriotism, a word that generates as much uncertainty and apprehension in today's world as it did in his. Provocative as well as inadequate, for in today's world it will take much to contain the apprehensions released by its employment.

To that end, we should be clear on his lexicon. Nationalism and patriotism were never to be confused. They were, in fact, opposite extremities. The former was politically reactionary, strident, and

ignoble; the latter was dignified and progressive, a noun which expressed a willingness to sacrifice whatever was necessary for the
country and the welfare of its citizens.[5] But this country, this
"France" to which he was committed, was not a France seen by all,
concurred in by all; for that reason it is important to see what he
saw. For him it was like a complex crystal of interlocking facets. This
crystal needs to be held to the light, in such a way as to reflect back
on his politics to 1910 and to reflect ahead to the politics of the
immediate pre-war period. In the interests of that investigation, I
will suggest at the outset that for Barthou "France" meant a reformist
Republic, a bourgeois Republic, and ultimately something far greater
than the Republic.

In 1889 Barthou praised France as an example of a modern,
centralized nation state which tolerated regionalisms at home and
colonial self-expression abroad. As a regime, the Republic was more
or less secure, as were its values: popular sovereignty, the political
equality of all male citizens, the parliamentary process, and modern
secularism. As a first-time candidate who was sympathetic to that
regime, Barthou had concentrated on the theme of republican defence and consolidation: in short, more of the same. Apart from the
specific economic measures he envisaged for Béarn, he was no obvious reformer. Indeed, in this respect he typified "les nouvelle
couches" of the lower middle class who were more interested in
"equality of status and careers open to talent" than in "equality of
condition."[6] The mission of the next generation of republicans, his
own, was seen essentially as one of raising higher the ramparts
against sullen aristocrats and priests. And little wonder. He was a
twenty-seven-year-old law graduate from Paris, one who knew something about priests and country gentry, less about peasants, less still
of the new working class which industrialization was faintly nour-
ishing in the homes of railway workers and in the mines of Cour-
rières. For him, and his family, what mattered and what was obvious
was that this third of France's Republics was benign enough, and
astute enough, to enlist talent wherever it was found, even among
the sons of shopkeepers.

By 1910, Barthou's conception of the Republic had filled out considerably. He had learned first hand of the perquisites enjoyed by
the affluent middle class. He had broadened his understanding of
the political right, partly through the instructive if disagreeable debates over the Dreyfus affair and Church prerogatives in education.
But principally, he had become more alive to the dangers of Marxist
socialism. Even that, in a sense, was the smaller portion of the lesson,
for a man of his background had needed no additional counsel on

the merits of private property. More momentous than his dislike of socialism was the realization that it had to be fought through reform. In this respect Barthou's case lends credence to those who see bourgeois reformism as an inherently conservative strategy. But again, there is considerable evidence to suggest that in the 1890s Barthou really did come to see the need for a Republic genuinely committed to social reform, one that could keep abreast of Germany, Great Britain, or the United States. To avoid revolution, to be sure, and also to ensure some unity across the non-socialist left in the Chamber, but also because it was consistent with France's international reputation for being progressive, fair-minded, and equitable.

It is much more difficult to select than to find examples of his commitment to a reformist Republic. What follows are two extended illustrations, one drawn from labour-management relations, the other from social legislation. Both, to be sure, proved to be sensitive political issues within parliament, issues on which tenuous coalitions could be unhinged. Nonetheless, by treating them here, outside the Chamber, we are reminded how arbitrary the distinction is between the political and the non-political. The Barthou who emerges in the course of these remarks is still the deputy from Oloron. But on these matters he has turned to a wider reading audience, to whom he outlines the goals as well as the constraints of his reformism. Through the device of magazine articles, public speeches, and one major book, he instructs his readers on the historical roots of current issues and, by so doing, on the need to measure up to the tradition of republican generosity and justice.

In 1904 he published *L'Action syndicale*, a book on the French union movement and the challenges which it represented to the country's legislators. It was a volume based on his own work as member and frequent *rapporteur* of the Chamber's Labour committee. Dedicated to Waldeck-Rousseau, this book addressed a range of union-related issues and drew liberally from a large corpus of international literature. Simply put, it helped establish two points. First, it confirmed Barthou's considerable sympathy for the union movement. Unions, he said, "have the potential to render the greatest possible service to French workers," principally by allowing the individual to break out of the isolation too long imposed on him. Second, it also confirmed Barthou's opposition to any attempts by the socialist left to politicize the union movement. Unions ought not to become tools in the hands of social revolutionaries, those who believed that destruction had to precede creation.[7]

He was also uncomfortable with the idea of compulsory union membership, for reasons which he presented as progressive. First, the union movement required liberation, not captivation. Historically, he said, reformers had been inclined to combat excess with excess. The revolutionaries of 1791 had been so successful in shattering the monopolistic practices of the ancien régime's great *corporations* that they had released every worker into what became a condition of self-governed bondage, each cut off from the other by the prohibition against any form of organized labour. The Third Republic had done much to rectify that condition, notably by its 1884 law opening doors for collective bargaining. Now, it too needed to be revised and expanded. Of that there was no question – but not in such a way as to allow proponents of compulsory union membership to restore some of the old restrictive practices of the Bourbon regime. Second, compulsory membership also had to be considered in the light of social Catholicism. There were among these Catholic proponents of social reform some who wished to secure control of the union leadership and then, on behalf of the Church, turn the workers against the Republic. Allow union membership to become compulsory, and you would only multiply the numbers of those who might fall further under the spell of priests. In short, and to his own satisfaction, Louis Barthou had uncovered the familiar hand of clericalism. For that reason alone, he argued, the cause of compulsory union membership was suspect from the start and had to be resisted.[8]

He was equally opposed to one other aspect of the union movement, that which involved certain groups of public service personnel. These were the *fonctionnaires*, men and women whose responsibilities could only be fulfilled through the exercise of the state's public authority. These were not the ordinary, authority-free *employés* who were paid by salaries set on the free market, but those who benefited from remunerative *traitements* prescribed by parliament. For this reason – the prestige of their office and their superior financial security – they ought not to be granted union status. Interestingly, *L'Action syndicale* did not include teachers among those so defined, but by 1906 he had done some rethinking. By then he had concluded that the ongoing efforts among certain primary school teachers to acquire union status were inappropriate. No, they were a challenge to the authority of the state. Quoting from one manifesto which maintained that teachers were *not* agents of the public authority, Barthou retorted: "They are appointed, in the name of the State, by a government which is the agent of the people."[9] Moreover, not only was this tiny minority of troublemakers pushing for exceptional professional autonomy under the guise of this coveted union status, but some were intent on going much further. Some wanted to use the classroom as a cradle for the proletarian revolution, and thus to prepare "their combat position in the army of the revolutionary proletariat, against the very society which has hired them."[10]

In other respects, however, Barthou did justify his growing, pro-
union reputation. Apart from offering general applause for the
movement, his book praised those unions which had fought their
way into the private sector, and gently rebuked employers who had
opposed that intrusion all the way. He supported as well the union
status accorded in 1892 to the so-called liberal professions like medicine, dentistry, and midwifery.[11] And he had no problem with the
unionization of public service *employés* in railroad and postal-tele-
graphic service. On another labour matter he took an unusually
advanced position. He wanted any revision of the 1884 legislation
to include the elimination of two particular articles which invoked
legal penalties for any wilful obstruction of trade. As long as they
were there, he said, there was a shadow over the whole union movement, and an unnecessary shadow, since the common law afforded
ample protection for society against really destructive economic behaviour. All the more provocative for being redundant, the articles
were no more than a gratuitous insult to "working-class democracy."[12] Finally, he argued in favour of extending the financial and
legal existence of unions, an idea contained in Millerand's proposals
of November 1899. Yes, he knew that some unionists saw in this a
trap, designed to make them more legally liable. But Barthou replied
that it was time the union movement came of age. Enough, he said,
of treating unions "like baffled minors." Make them responsible,
legally and financially, and thus make them "the masters of their
own destiny."[13]

A second illustration of Barthou's carefully defined commitment
to a reformist Republic may be drawn from the vast expanse of social
reform – specifically, that relating to the condition of women. There
is no mistaking that he would have disappointed even a moderate
feminist of today. One case in point would be his association of
national defence with women as child-bearers, begetters of soldiers.
It was an ancient enough theme, long before his day; and the din
from the patriotic breakers of 1911 had caused people to shout some
rather silly things. Nevertheless, we have a right to expose the silly
and, in this case, the tasteless. Unmistakably, too, though none but
the naive would admit surprise, there is in this French Edwardian
an attitude toward women which would be described today as pa-
tronizing. This is especially true of working class women, some of
whom he once visited in their "cute little homes" surrounded by their
equally cute "tiny gardens."[14]

But he also had other things to say about the condition of women,
some of them pedestrian to today's readers, others less so. But significantly, he uttered them in the spirit of reform. For instance, from

1897 onward he actively associated himself with a number of groups concerned about France's depopulation. The nation's productive resources, he feared, were faltering, certainly in comparison with other major European powers. The Republic had to discourage the trend toward smaller families. It was in this cause that as justice minister in 1910 he stiffened the penalties for abortion soliciting, and promoted legislation first for unpaid and eventually for paid maternity leave from employment, as well as for state assistance to financially distressed families of more than three children.[15]

In other respects he was even more sympathetic to the plight of women, a sympathy not least expressed through his publicized efforts to hire women for stenographic positions at the Justice ministry.[16] But it was on some very sensitive social issues that he spoke out with a passionate candour. Of all the crimes he could imagine, he said, none was more "abominable" than that of the man who fathered a child out of wedlock and then abandoned the prospective mother "like some useless burden."[17] He was similarly outspoken on the subject of divorce, particularly as it affected women. In an article of 1902 in the *Nouvelle Revue* he added his voice to this, one of the most contentious issues of the day. Some advocates of reform, he said, wanted to see divorce made possible either on the grounds of mutual consent, or on those of one partner's resolute insistence. Personally, he feared the latter, especially on behalf of women who were likely to be reduced to a "concubinage légal," subject to a husband's caprice. Divorce by mutual consent he accepted, even desired, although he thought it was still a long way off.[18] In the interval, in 1902 he initiated a parliamentary motion to modify the Civil Code by excising article 298 – that which prohibited an adulterer from ever marrying his or her lover. Mindful that this might be regarded as a masculine ruse, Barthou hastened to pitch his case to women readers. Adultery, he said, was either an affair of the heart or it was merely one of the moment. If the former, the law condemned two lovers to the perpetual "shame of a common-law arrangement," in fact perpetuating the illegitimacy of their relationship. If the latter, the law only offered haven to those who "practised adultery like some sport." Indeed, until it were reformed, the law actually protected a married man from ever having to consider making a subsequent marriage with a pregnant lover. In short, he wrote, "as always, ... owing to selfish male interests, the woman is sacrificed to the man."[19]

The preceding illustrations of Barthou's approach to certain social issues of his day also serve as a measure of his belief that reform was in the nature of this bourgeois Republic. It had taken this Republic to rectify in 1884 some of the worst labour abuses from the nineteenth century, and then to appreciate little more than a decade later that even more reform was essential. The same was true for legislation on divorce, abortion, maternity leaves, and family assistance. As the compassionate Diderot had long ago observed to an attentive Barthou, the principal duty of the state was to safeguard the welfare of all its citizens, including the swollen majority of peasants and workers.[20] But a state governed by whom? For Barthou, the answer was transparent – the state as it was, as it had been since he had brought home the news of Sedan in 1870. Since then, and with mounting assurance, France had become for Barthou the France of the bourgeois *foyer*: guided by its values, inspired by its ideals, led hesitantly by its elite toward a greater responsibility for the less educated, the less secure, and the less nourished. It had taken effort and discipline for these *hommes de gouvernement* to confront directly the problems which surfaced from the nether worlds explored by the novels of Emile Zola. It had only taken time for them to accustom themselves to the banquet life of the prosperous and privileged bourgeoisie.

Louis Barthou married in January 1895, at thirty-two years of age, a month after his Christmas Day duel with Jean Jaurès. His bride was the twenty-two-year-old Alice Mayeur, sole child of Marguerite (née Amiel) and the late Max Mayeur. Unlike her husband-to-be, who still resided in the student quarter of the Left Bank, Alice lived at 49 rue Cambon, a wealthy corner of the Right Bank, near the still fashionable Place Vendôme. Her father had enjoyed great success in business and investment, and had added to these financial triumphs the laurels of a departmental councillor for Seine et Oise.[21] Without question, he had died a very wealthy man, one with a bulging portfolio of shares in the principal railway companies and in those of Paris tramways and gas utility companies. Additionally, he had invested heavily in what was already choice garden property in the suburb of Vésinet. Indeed, as these properties were slowly sold off between 1896 and 1927, they brought to the married couple an accumulated revenue of over twelve million francs. In turn, the mobile assets which were included in Alice's part of the formal marriage contract were given an estimated value at the time of her death in 1930 of nearly five million francs. Even allowing for the effects of inflation over the span of their thirty-five-year marriage, her financial resources were many times greater than those of her husband. In fact, his total contribution of seventy thousand francs in 1895 was roughly equivalent to the additional cash and bond monies furnished by Alice – that is, quite beyond her share and real estate assets. Louis Barthou, in short, married into a small fortune.[22]

The civil marriage contract, prepared by Maître Dauchez, was concluded in the town halls of the fifth and first *arrondissements* on 26 January 1895. It was witnessed by the deputy, Léon Say, and senator Etienne Goujon, for the groom, and for the bride, by her grandfather, Emile Amiel, and her uncle by marriage, Charles Philippon.[23] There followed, on the 29th, a society wedding in Alice's parish church of the Madeleine – at which Marie Barthou earned a few looks for her unfashionable country bonnet – and a reception at the Continental Hotel.[24] Thereafter, with plans made for a summer honeymoon in Switzerland, the couple took up residence in a spacious apartment, on the fourth floor, at 7 avenue d'Antin, now named the avenue Franklin-Roosevelt. There, two hunded yards from the Seine, and a block from the Champs Elysée, the Barthou couple settled into a life that was a universe removed from the apprehensions of postal workers, miners' widows, and primary school teachers. Financially secure, attended by a small domestic staff, and further consoled by their country residence at Le Vésinet, they mixed with those most blessed in the Republic and shared with them that strong, optimistic pulse of Paris. And what could be more fitting for this promising match and its prosperous setting than the arrival in 1896 of their first and only child, Max Emile?[25]

The World Fair scheduled for Paris in 1900 was already a subject of much discussion as Barthou entered his first year of married life. Buoyed by memories of the 1889 extravaganza, those with time and money to spend and invest were eagerly bracing themselves for the turn of the century. There was simply so much to do and see, as one followed the frantic efforts of the capital's newspapers to keep up with all that was novel. Just at the end of 1895 *Le Figaro* became the first Parisian daily to expand to a six-page edition. By then, the three-year-old *Le Journal* had already carved out a substantial market for itself among modest-income bourgeois, many of whom were first introduced in its pages to great contemporaries like the poet François Coppée and the popular dramatist Octave Mirbeau.[26] Cycling continued its energetic course. The craze had diminished, but in its place was the dedication of the specialists and the enthusiastic journalism of *Le Cycle* and *La Bicyclette*. And where cycles went, automobiles were close behind, as was evidenced by the inauguration of the Paris-Marseille return auto-race in October 1896. Indeed, in less than a decade Paris was to become familiar with all the controversy surrounding the steady appearance of motor taxis and buses, the steady departure of horse-drawn transit vehicles, the steady intrusions of impatient telephones.[27]

Amid all the gains, some losses were unavoidable, but among those who could afford much more than good food and accommodation the sense of progress was compelling. Progress on all fronts: technological progress, social progress, cultural progress. Far below the summit of Eiffel's tower, these were the Parisians who might drop in at the Café Napolitaine to catch a glimpse of Feydeau or Courteline, take a stroll in the Champs Elysée quarter past the headquarters of Pierre Lafitte where the fashionable *Fémina*, *Musica*, and *Fermes et châteaux* were published, or attend a performance by the divine Bernhardt, or – Barthou's favourite – Mme Bartet, at the Théâtre Français. And for someone like him, the city's musical offerings were a source of endless delight: the compositions of a Debussy or Saint-Saëns brought to new heights under the baton of Pasdeloup, Calonne, or Vincent d'Indy; a new opera from Massenet or, from 1909, the frequent visits of the *ballets russes* to the Châtelet. Everywhere there seemed movement, whether expressed by the metropolitan underground that had started to run in the autumn of 1899, the rising up of the Grand and Petit Palais in time for the World Fair, the passage in parliament of pension plan legislation and accident insurance legislation, or the musical explorations of Gabriel Fauré.

Not that it was all bright. The anarchist terrorists were falling to the guillotine, but the more lethal cholera of 1894 could not be contained so easily. As it proved in 1910, the Seine could still overspill its banks and send its neighbours scurrying for higher ground – including the families of cabinet ministers.[28] Tragedy, like the fire in the rue Goujon in May 1897, could still consume a hundred lives in an hour; and singular deaths like those of Gounod and Maupassant in 1893, de Lesseps in 1894, Pasteur in 1895, and Verlaine in 1896 reminded even the affluent that some things never changed. Nevertheless, even the steadily escalating strike figures could not dispel the mood of middle class confidence, bolstered as it was by the cynical wit of Victorien Sardou's *Madame Sans-Gêne*, the compassionate wit of Rostand's *Cyrano de Bergerac*, the generosity that created the Académie Goncourt, or that which bequeathed to the nation the estate and art treasures of Chantilly.[29]

For Barthou personally, it was a new age of discovery. With an assured source of wealth – which more than levelled out the income fluctuations that came with entering and leaving cabinet posts – and with both predictable and self-regulated periods of leisure, he was able to follow closely the latest innovations. He did so partly out of a natural interest, partly out of a financial ability to indulge that interest, and partly out of a belief that a French patriot ought to be abreast of his country's progress. Even here, in interests such as these, Barthou detected the larger interests of France. Not that the experience was always reassuring. In 1907, for instance, he was obliged to offer ministerial congratulations to the Italian victor of a motor race at Dieppe. Gratuitously, he added his personal hope that the French auto industry would be able to redeem itself the following year.[30] On other occasions, too, the automobile proved of little amusement. It was bad enough, as justice minister in 1909, to have to be among the first to devise laws capable of restraining the suicidal tendencies of the capital's drivers, tendencies most clearly expressed in their flagrant indifference to posted speed-limits. But it had been worse the year before, at the Rond-Point, where the errant taxi in which he was riding collided with an innocent lamp post. The driver had been thrown from the vehicle, and the minister was found bleeding profusely from facial cuts inflicted by glass fragments.[31]

Like most, he had better luck with airplanes, another interest cultivated by money and a patriot's eye for military potential. Indeed, he knew a great deal of the nation's air history, and took pride in pursuing Hugo's interest in the development of heavier-than-air machines.[32] In the more active sense, it had all begun in the skies over Brussels in 1887. Soon after that first ascent he had made contact with aviation enthusiasts in Béarn and Paris. Before long, he was making periodic flights, many of them organized by his even more engaged brother, Léon. In June 1907, for instance, the popular weekly *L'Illustration* carried a photograph and short report bearing on the brothers' flight from the Saint-Cloud airfield. The flight, in Léon's own *Excelsior*, did much to underscore the association between aviation and the French state, for the entire crew included Louis Barthou as public works minister, Léon Barthou and Georges Lamirault, respectively *directeur* and *chef* of the minister's personal cabinet, and M. Grosdidier, parliamentary deputy for the Meuse.[33] A few years later there was a less publicized flight, this time with the young naval officer and future Academician Claude Farrère. In this case it turned out to be an unexpected night flight from Saint-Cloud to Cabourg in Normandy. Barthou was immediately keen on the idea of the flight, but seemed visibly less enthusiastic about the destination. When gently probed by an apprehensive Farrère, the minister explained with a smile: "I like Normandy, it's just that we'll have to come home on the Western Railway."[34]

Clearly, a problem-plagued railway was no competition for a minister who loved to fly and who marvelled at the exceptional progress being made in the area of powered flights. A keen balloonist, he soon became known for his even more energetic championing of the airplane. In September 1908 he drew the attention of the London *Times* by his dawn visits to the airfields at Issy-les-Moulineaux and his remarks on the link between aviation and patriotism.[35] A few months later he had the distinction of being taken up by the American air pioneer Wilbur Wright. It was in December 1908, at Le Mans, that he was accorded that first short flight of just under four minutes, following which the American assured him that he was safer in the air than he would be on one of the state railroads. Such perspicacity, and humour, obviously sealed the accord between the two, and as a result they flew again in February 1909, this time in Pau. It was a longer flight, the memory of which Barthou kept alive by reminding audiences of his own pioneering efforts and by reminding them, with a pun, that he had been the first French minister "who had *volé* (flown/stolen) ... in the air!"[36] Prouder still, perhaps, was the moment that summer when he had awarded a *croix de chevalier* to Louis Blériot, a few days after the latter's twenty-seven-minute flight from Calais to Dover.[37]

Also symptomatic of the times, as well as of bourgeois girth, was Barthou's new-found passion for physical exercise. In part it was fashion, for sport and exercise had become big business by the first decade of this century. In part it was patriotism, as Barthou, like many others, argued the case for building a strong soldiery from a fit and energetic civilian population.[38] In part, too, it was recognition of some ten years of comfortable married life and the rich fares of countless political banquets. Together, they provided a strong enough incentive for his self-devised, religiously observed personal regimen: an early rising toward 5 a.m., twenty-five minutes of rigorous exercise – comprising calisthenics and a workout on his home-installed rowing machine – and a bracing cold shower or bath. The benefits of such a plan were simply incalculable, or so he often lectured guests and hosts. To be sure, such routine could produce some awkward moments. Once in Bordeaux he had been surprised in his hotel room by a *valet de chambre*, thoughtfully despatched to the minister by the local prefect. There he was, he recalled, flat on his stomach, exercising in his pyjamas, unaware that the servant had returned to the prefecture convinced that the minister had lost his senses. But the minister did not care, for he had his own reasons. Fashion and patriotism were surely part of it, but so too was the discovery through his reading that vigorous, accomplished men, like Bismarck and Gladstone, Gambetta and Hugo, had all observed physical training programs.[39] Also, and perhaps ultimately, he saw his regimen as a daily test of personal discipline against the temptations to defer until tomorrow. He knew them all, he said, all of them specious – laziness, apathy, a fondness for warm beds – but none more so than that of time. "Même le temps!" That was the weakest of them all, for people could always find time to do the things that they really wanted to do.[40]

None could deny that exercise compensated him royally. He might have been short in stature, and short-sighted, but he conveyed the impression of great physical vigour. It was more than the agility of mind and body; there was also a sense of physical strength. The friendly journalist Louis Latzarus described his hands as broad and muscled, two natural, heavy fists. A less friendly Léon Daudet, recalling those "hands of steel," reported how his own nearly two-hundred-pound frame had once been picked up from behind, unceremoniously, and actually carried through the corridors of the Palais Bourbon. Underneath, and chuckling, was "little Barthou ... muscled like some athlete."[41] It was done with little visible effort, Daudet thought, though with more vanity. Charles Benoist noted this latter quality, an egotism more obvious than the muscles. Barthou, he remembered, had a rather annoying habit of reminding everyone of how he had been the youngest cabinet minister in the Republic's history.[42] He could also be guilty of petulance – as witnessed earlier in the case of his displeasure over Combes's failure to promote Barthou's prefectoral candidates – and of arrogance, of the sort contained in his remarks about his electoral rival in 1904.[43] Whether or not such behaviour was in some way compensation for his diminutive physical stature, the fact is that here was one who had learned to exploit his own energy, will power, and ambition – the very combination which some found so disconcerting.)

There were others, those who knew him well, who saw the disguise. The flinty, sharp-tongued Barthou, they knew full well, was as quick to be touched as to be angered. In his effervescence there was always the risk of impulsiveness; in his enthusiasm, always the risk of hurting or being hurt. He magnified certain inherent characteristics – from humour to hedonism – so as to camouflage what in fact was an emotionally vulnerable, sensitive nature. Pierre Benoit, an old friend, likened him to a veteran soldier who only laid down his arms in the company of his intimates. Louis Vitalis, one of Barthou's closest collaborators, saw a man who darted back and forth from banter to brusqueness, again like a soldier moving from cover to cover.[44] Frankly, it is not clear how much of this was apparent before 1914, that halcyon period when, for Barthou, ephemeral political disappointments were assuaged by success and recognition elsewhere. Nevertheless, it is clear enough that Barthou, the passional man, was in place well before the tragedy of the approaching war. For evidence of this, one may turn to still other forums, although as always they are those frequented by the affluent middle class into whose circles marriage had taken him.

The coexistence of sensitivity and abrasiveness is perhaps best illustrated with reference to another of his great passions: music. Of all the arts, he reckoned that none could claim a more exalted place. It was doubly unique. Masterpieces on canvas or of stone were reproductions of things perceived by the artist. In this sense, music was the more original. Second, the tangible *chef d'oeuvre* had to be visited, seen exclusively in its final form. Music, however, came from any direction and carried infinite interpretations, thanks to the talents of the performing artists as well as the receptiveness of each listener.[45] But for that very reason, it demanded intense concentration and attentiveness. Few breaches of social convention bothered him more, therefore, than those committed by concert-goers who whispered or shuffled their way through a musical performance. In their presence, he lost all patience, and turned mean. At best they were there only to hear, rather than listen; at worst, they were there to be seen. He would not, could not, tolerate them. Enraged by their whispering, their toe-tapping, their belated discovery of the concert program in their laps, he would command their silence with an angry, imperious "Chut!" It was no act. He was angry. And it was not to teach anyone a lesson. Why he exploded was more simple. It was, he confessed, a matter of "defending something that gives me so much pleasure."[46]

He meant it. Music moved him deeply. In a public lecture on Beethoven in 1911 he admitted that he had never listened to the *Missa solemnis* without being moved to tears. It was quite true. Jacqueline Souchère saw it for herself, as did the poet Armand Godoy.[47] It is speculative, of course, but it is also possible that this sensitive man, cut off from religious observance by politics, found in music an outlet for a profoundly emotional, indeed mystical spirit. Repeatedly, he kept finding in Beethoven something that was not of this world – the Ninth Symphony as an "immortal sigh," the Mass in D as "unearthly" but a gift for the world from "one of humanity's greatest benefactors." Pity those who could not feel his genius, those to whom "Crucifixus" brought no tears, those who could not take the step from admiring to adoring Beethoven.[48] Such was the language employed by a man in his forties. Thirty years later, elderly and alone, he would speak of Beethoven and Wagner both, in the language of souls, sacrilege, and miracles.[49]

By then, he had been going regularly to the Bayreuth festival for over four decades, making that trip both as the Wagnerphile he was and as an amply financed bourgeois. Wherever he was, concerts drew him, in Vienna, or Rome, or Berlin. So too did these cities' art galleries, their museums and architectural masterpieces, just as they had done when he had travelled in his twenties. The fact is that Louis Barthou loved to travel, because of his curiosity, because his pleasure expanded with his knowledge, because he had the money and the time to do so. Through the principal accounts of his travels, we can see an at once energetic and leisured bourgeois at play, a man absorbing worlds that remained unseen by most of his compatriots and, in that one sense, perhaps accentuating the differences between his sense of France and theirs. But at the same time we also see more of that boyish exuberance and emotional receptivity which is central to our understanding of Barthou and Barthou's understanding of France.

Just as he travelled so often to Bayreuth, from the 1890s through to the end of his life, so too did he create a summer vacation regimen in Switzerland. Indeed, so dear to him did this become – "his Bürgenstock" on Lucerne's Lac des Quatre Cantons – that we must make provision to return later to this special refuge. For the moment all that need be said is that he and Alice started vacationing there in 1895, a few months after their wedding. It was a choice no doubt dictated by any number of private reasons but also, in all likelihood, because Swiss vacations had become fashionable in the 1890s, because hiking was a current rage, and because the combination of the two publicized the health-giving properties of mountains.[50] For Barthou there was something else. This was paradise, this Bürgenstock, high above the waters of the lake, yet surrounded by the peaks of neighbouring mountains, that corner of the world to which he had been drawn by descriptions left by Chateaubriand, Dumas père, Hugo, and Wagner. Indeed, it was a place fashioned for romantics – lively water, jagged peaks, mist, fog, and mountain clouds.

The trips he made to Germany and Austria in 1901 and 1902 provided inspiration of another sort, some of which will invite later comment. What may be said now is that these trips were yet further confirmation of the pleasure he drew from the galleries and opera houses of France's Germanic neighbours. It is true that by then he was having even more difficulty than he had in 1887 reconciling the genius of the German masters with their quarrelsome descendants. Nevertheless, he could not say enough about the exceptionally rich offerings of the Vienna Opera – *Fidelio, Faust, Aida*, Léoncavallo, Strauss, Wagner – or the comparably superb collections in the art museums of Dresden. Moreover, he found two other sources of immense gratification. First, Germans and Austrians could enjoy the finest music at very cheap prices, unlike Paris where he knew that music was "a high-priced luxury." Second, unlike many of his subjects, Kaiser Wilhelm did not like Wagner, a condition which confirmed for Barthou his judgment of the king and his hopes for the German people.[51]

In December 1910 Alice and Louis Barthou decided upon a Christmas holiday in Egypt and the Sudan, destinations which appealed to their mutual taste for restrained adventure and exotic novelty. Louis went armed with a travel diary, excerpts from which soon appeared in *Illustration*. Little escaped his attention, from the careful ministrations of a local military doctor in the port of Suez to the Christmas crackers which appeared on a table in Khartoum, to the delight of some remarkably plain English women. He marvelled at the heat, the blueness of the sky, the biblical-like Arab dress, the sound of a train whistle in the middle of a desert night. Everything was new, striking one chord of excitement after another within this forty-eight-year-old politician who had just resigned the Justice portfolio of the French Republic. Recalling what Flaubert had said about the difficulty of imitating a camel's bleat, Barthou was not too proud either to try, or to admit failure. And the crocodiles: "There it is, long and lithe, a crocodile, a real crocodile, a wild one!" It took longer than the others to disappear off the river bank, allowing those on board Barthou's vessel to have a close look. "We have actually seen crocodiles on the White Nile! And the satisfaction of being able to say so ... will be as great as the sight itself. There is always something of a child's vanity left in every man and woman."[52]

But as much as anything, it was the landscape which so stirred a romanticist nursed from another culture on Hugo, Beethoven, and Wagner.

Palm-trees ... extend their supple elegance up toward the cloudless sky ... The setting sun illuminates the homes of Suez with blues and purples, colours delicately mixed with an infinite softness to leave a violet glow. It's enchanting ... The mountains, too, ... take on a range of indescribably soft purple hues.[53]

Not in the kind of language common to the Ministry of Public Works, these were nonetheless the responses of one who had been several times minister. On the surface, the dichotomy between official and private expression could hardly be more striking; and yet beneath the form there is a bond that would yield to nothing. Although each of these vacations was purely private and unofficial, Barthou went nowhere without a sense of being French – an articulate, cultured, French bourgeois whose duty it was to see that the Republic kept France at the head of the civilized and progressive nations of the world.

There was, therefore, beneath the gravel bed of republicanism, class affiliation, and personal self-fulfilment, a bedrock which was solid and impermeable. In a word, it was France, older and greater than republics or empires, rendering minuscule and ephemeral the day-to-day exchanges in the Chamber of Deputies. Louis Barthou, a man excited by concerts and crocodiles, believed in this France with a passion comparable to that of General De Gaulle. Both were moved by the Ideal of France. In the long run, politics were of little account. What mattered, solely, was the service one provided to the renown of France. Barthou did not admire the politics of Robespierre, or Napoleon, or Jaurès. But he recognized that each brought to his country – republic or empire, liberal or socialist – a distinction based on sincerity and genius. What did it matter, ultimately, whether Corneille and Racine, Stendhal and Verlaine, had written under the Bourbons, the Bonapartes, or one of the Republics? If not strictly true in a musical sense, at least in a broad cultural sense Lully was a predecessor of Fauré, just as in science Courvoisier had led Pasteur, or in literature Loti had followed Bossuct. All this to Louis Barthou was part of his personal patrimony, as real to him and infinitely more substantial than anything he would receive from Isidor's estate in Pau. Until one grasps this, there will be no understanding of either Barthou the man or Barthou the statesman. Both will remain elusive and incomplete.[54]

His France, in sum, was far more than the prodigy of political encounters. That much he knew even in 1887, during a vacation abroad, when he had learned how deeply rooted was his cultural patriotism. But by the turn of the twentieth century that awareness had multiplied, partly it would seem because his status as a French deputy automatically conferred the unofficial status of government representative. Attending an international exhibition in Dresden in May 1901, he could not conceal his pride in the acclaim and prizes earned by French artists – Bonnot, Duran and Carrière, Bartholomé, the sculptor, and, for his *Samson et Dalila*, Saint-Saëns, the composer.[55] The following year it was Vienna, a capital which he greatly admired, but in which he found himself reminded of home. Sometimes it was in some bookshop, where he was appalled once more by the unmerited publishing success of the most mediocre French writers, especially those who were sullying the reputation of French literature by exploiting the licentious. By 1902 Barthou was even regretting the passing of those days when Zola had been so admired abroad. Personally, he had not cared much for Zola's "realism," and still believed him guilty of literary excess, but he now freely granted that he deserved to be recognized as "a force in contemporary literature." As for the splendours of Vienna's museums, he was still awestruck, but now thoroughly convinced as well that nothing could

really compare with the Louvre. "I don't know whether other collections have more works of great art, but I do know that other
collections are less complete."[56]

This was not, he hastened to explain, a judgment derived from
some "obligatory expression of chauvinism." Rather it was a considered opinion based on visits to many galleries and museums in many
countries. But, on balance, still a half truth. It is true that patriotic
allegiance did not always qualify his aestheticism, as his often rev-
erent appreciations of German, Dutch, and Austrian art make clear.
At the same time, there is no question but that he saw France as an
unsurpassed cultural entity whose future achievements had to be
facilitated and applauded by those entrusted to govern her. The
state had to place itself in the service of art, an axiom for which
there was one corollary. Art should be employed in the service of
the state. That *is* what he believed, however quickly that belief can
be turned into something ugly and vicious by minds smaller than
his. Apart from wartime, when he indeed countenanced the use of
art as propaganda, he was thinking of service, mutual service – the
state to serve artists, artists to serve the state by earning international
acclaim. That there could be manipulation on either side goes without saying; that there could be personal interests involved will also
become evident. But at base, when he thought of art serving France,
he was thinking of art untainted by political consideration, an art of
truth and beauty illuminating a fair and pleasant France.

In order to appreciate his meaning, one had best start with what
he said. Necessarily this must be brief and selective, only enough to
capture that note of pride and adoration. First, some writers past:
Corneille, whom he held to be the greatest poet of old France, was
also one of the great guardians of the human conscience. La Bruyère
remained unrivalled as a reader of "the human character," unless it
be by another French genius like Pascal. Diderot, despite momentary
lapses, expressed within his own person the essence of what was
meant to be French: "incisiveness and clarity of mind ... quickness
of comprehension and judgement."[57] Napoleon, writer, soldier, gov-
ernor, was "a national treasure ... who belongs to us all," still attract-
ing generations he had not even tried to deceive. That Napoleon
had his dark side was hardly at issue. Neither was the venom of
Sainte-Beuve, nor the partisanship that had caused Chateaubriand
to forget that being French demanded a certain *mesure*.[58] And yet
it was this, the fact that they were French, and men of genius, that
so impressed Barthou and impelled him to enlist in the service of
this exceptional culture.

It stood to reason that his own contemporaries had a role to play
in Barthou's conception of France, and were certainly as enlistable

as those long since dead. As a statesmen of considerable influence he would serve their interests, as they would serve art, as together they would contribute to the greater glory of France. Again, if there is an element of calculated exploitation – again from both sides – it is worth repeating that he really did admire the art itself and indeed was widely recognized as both literary expert and artistic connoisseur. What is more, he turned himself into one of the foremost authorities on three of his favourite pre-war writers: Edmond Rostand, Anatole France, and Pierre Loti. Rostand he admired as artist and person, an unpretentious man whose talents were made greater by his modesty. Reckoned by Barthou a genius, the shy and introspective Rostand was all the more special because he was a Béarnais by adoption and a patriot of proven resolution. He had never overcome the humiliation he felt for the 1870 defeat and, for that reason, had built into his theatre – *Cyrano, L'Aiglon, Chantecler* – the ideals of patriotic devotion, courage, and sacrifice. An artist of distinction, he never ceased to believe "in the soul of France."[59] For both reasons, art and patriotism, Barthou considered him a national resource and maintained close relations with him until the writer's death in 1918. Conversely, it was Rostand who conferred upon Barthou that fitting republican title: "the minister of poets."[60]

Anatole France he first met in August 1890. There began a friendship which lasted until the writer's death in 1924. For much of the time the two did not see eye to eye politically, France being attracted to the ideals of socialism, Barthou being repelled by them. Nevertheless, the deputy believed that he could recognize genius when he saw it, and of Anatole France there was no doubt. "As a scholar, he had read everything; as a psychologist, he had deduced everything; as an intellect, he had understood everything."[61] But more striking still, Barthou thought that he saw in France an example of the rich cultural inheritance with which he himself was so fascinated. Because he knew so much, France was a living beneficiary of the styles, techniques, and insights of respected predecessors like Pascal, Voltaire, Courier, and Renan.[62] Even if he were partially blind to the genius of Victor Hugo, Anatole France was prepared to act as French literary partisan, adopting the possessive "notre" when discussing de Musset, and ranking Racine above Shakespeare when it came to female characterization.[63] All this Barthou took to be confirmation, however redundant, of France's towering status within the pantheon of contemporary French writers.

Barthou and Pierre Loti first met in the autumn of 1906, an encounter which grew into an exceptionally intimate relationship – despite a poor beginning. Barthou's ministerial status had proven a liability, introducing a title which only reminded the writer of how little he liked politicians of any sort. Barthou and, more important, Alice were determined to overcome all obstacles and win over the unusually glacial genius whose writings they so admired. Admired, in Louis's case, for his descriptive powers of nature, powers which Barthou held to be without precedent in the whole of French literature. Indeed, to one of Barthou's romanticist leanings, Loti was the quintessential example of genius that could be neither attributed nor explained. In fact, he was the very reverse of Anatole France in that he was no reader, and knew little about previous French masters. What he had learned to do came from inside, and thus was the more mysterious. Loti, Barthou would say, "had no parentage and his sudden bursting out on the literary scene represented a kind of miracle."[64] And to his literary greatness he added another, that of patriotism. Indeed, as war approached Loti was keen to come out of retirement as a naval officer or, by second choice, serve his country as a wartime writer and public speaker from the Académie Française.[65]

These were not, and were never imagined to be, one-sided relationships. Barthou did put himself at the disposition of artists of all sorts – running interference for them against the defending side of state bureaucrats, hastening official recognition of their achievements, even promoting the careers of the artists' friends. Years before, he had learned from the Pau municipal council the importance of being *serviable*, and now he developed that native talent into his own consummate art for artists. He went into their service, and his own – skilfully manipulating the great patronage engine of the state in their interests, then relishing the autographed letters of thanks acknowledging his support or, more splendid still, gifts of original manuscripts for his private collection. As he once remarked in a private jest bordering on the serious: "Whenever I accept a cabinet portfolio, I think first of my library. The fact is that each of my ministerial appointments has allowed me to expand my collection."[66]

Donations mounted with services rendered, and those seemed never-ending. In 1896 and again in 1898 the poet Coppée pressed Barthou to find public service positions for friends. In 1906 it was the composer Camille Erlanger, who had been advised to ask Barthou, "a passionate music-lover," for help in securing a "croix" in the Legion of Honour.[67] That was the same year that the dramatist Georges de Porto-Riche invoked assistance in securing a coveted post at the Bibliothèque Mazarine, while in the following year it was the turn of the writer Victor du Bled to appeal to Barthou for aid in some approaching competition.[68] In 1908, amid the requests for services, were one from Pierre Loti and another from Claude Debussy – the former in a bid to secure for a friend a post in the telegraph service at Caen, the latter in an attempt to protect his brother's threatened job as assistant inspector of the trouble-plagued Western railway.[69]

Art and politics mixed in still other ways, at least two more of which command immediate attention. The one, bibliophilia, was a logical extension of Barthou's appreciation of French literature, a further manifestation of his affluence and still another mark of his association with a fashionable activity. The other, his own work as an author, takes us out on to new ground, only to lead us back full-circle. Writer, or collector of other writers, Barthou saw the history and culture of France as a single tapestry which had been woven together only after centuries of patient and inspired craftsmanship.

He had started his book collection before he left Pau in 1889, the first major purchase – and a bargain – being the collected works of Taine. Before long a desultory interest had become a passion, one of the most enduring of his life. On arriving in Paris he had found the establishment of Rouquette in the *passage* Choiseul. New doors opened thereafter, one leading to the publisher-dealer Edouard Pelletan, another to the corner of the rue de Seine and the rue Toustain where he found the inspired engraver and binder Marius Michel. These two mentors together, Barthou later recalled, had taught him the cardinal lesson of book collecting. It had to start with a love of the literature itself, the language of the text, not with the embellishments that might come later from illustrations or bindings. Collectors who did not begin there, they told him, were like wine connoisseurs who never opened a bottle. Ignorant and pretentious, they confused outward form, however pretty, with what was truly precious within.[70]

In Barthou's case, however, there was something else as well. His aestheticism responded to text and format both, but his patriotism too was nourished in a book-lined study glowing with French masterpieces. From the 1890s until his final days in 1934, Louis Barthou built a personal library that was a monument to his country's literature, from the seventeenth to the twentieth centuries, superbly illustrated by French engravers, bound by French artist-binders, and personally appropriated through the device of his own *ex libris*: Truth, in the form of a nude female, emerging from a well, and being confronted by the alarm raised by honking geese (Ignorance) and barking dogs (Outrage).[71]

Barthou's principal, pre-war work of literature was his lengthy biography of Mirabeau. It appeared in 1913, and as such would be better suited chronologically to a later discussion. Thematically, however, it is more appropriate here, partly because it sets us on a return path to formal politics. A further word of explanation is in order. This is not the place to undertake a careful appraisal of Barthou as historian. But if one were obliged to render a summary verdict, it would have to present *Mirabeau* as the work of an enthusiastic, well-informed amateur. The book can make some claim to analysis, and demonstrates his grasp of contemporary historical perspectives; but it is also characterized by the author's personal asides, by a predilection for lengthy quotations, by temporal uncertainty, and by a succession of unexplained references to people or events. Indeed, though written with verve, even eagerness, it would not even qualify today as "popular" history, for it presumes too much upon a reader's knowledge.[72]

That said, *Mirabeau* is an important source for students of Barthou. It is yet another reflection of Barthou the patriot, and it offers as well further insight into Barthou the man. As for the first, there is no mistaking the fact that Barthou saw Mirabeau as one of France's greatest glories. A liberal, for one who was both aristocrat and monarchist, he had died in April 1791 before being able to effect the desired reconciliation between committed republicans and committed monarchists. In short, he had found himself in the middle, attacked by extremists in one camp for defending the monarchy and by those in the other for flirting with the contagious ideal of liberty. Barthou trembled with excitement before the eloquence of this great centrist who, while yet a monarchist, could stand with the Third Estate and defy the bayonets of the king. Because Mirabeau aspired to engineer a "rénovation nationale," and because those aspirations were conveyed in such impassioned, majestic prose, the republican Barthou ranked this monarchist among France's finest patriots.[73]

But there was more to it than that. There was something in Mirabeau, book and man, that was strikingly reminiscent of Barthou's own political travails. He never once alludes to this, although it is inconceivable that he was unaware of the parallels. True, time would make them even more evident – the personal tragedy, the allegations about the use of ghost-writers, the rumours of moral lapses. But even in 1913 they were there, too patent to support any doubts that *Mirabeau* was in part a *cri de coeur*. It was more than the two men's mutual love of music and the attendant impatience with churlish concert-goers; more too than their appreciation of eloquence, their prodigious memories, their mercurial temperaments. Indeed, so numerous were the similarities that it is a wonder Barthou did not thoroughly confuse historical and contemporary circumstance. Which of them was accused of a "an irrepressible fondness for intrigue," and perceived as a "victim of his own excessive shrewdness"? Was it Mirabeau, or Barthou, who had clung to "a centrist course" and who had resolved to struggle "against both despotism and anarchy"?[74] Was it Barthou, or Mirabeau, who had faced the incensed idealists and their accusations of inconstancy and opportunism? Ostensibly in defence of Mirabeau, Barthou surveyed the road that had to be followed by practical men of action. In so doing, he struck again that chord with which the previous chapter opened and closed.

It's Machiavellianism, the unbending moralist will say, he who does not concern himself with adapting the means to an end. On the contrary, reply experienced politicians across the ages, man must be led according to men's wishes. ... The philosopher and the statesman do not observe either the same method or the same goals. The former uses a featureless wall map, where there are no impediments. The latter has his feet on the ground where he stumbles on all sort of obstacles.[75]

Perhaps it is already clear that Louis Barthou had never outgrown the hero-worship of his boyhood. Rather, he had cultivated it, extending his vision of France by adding to it more and more heroes from the pages of French history. Although it seldom occurred to him to make the case, he was convinced that history was in large part the work of great individuals. It was imperative, therefore, that this historical awareness be passed securely from one generation to the next. This was a responsibility, an obligation, for all those in public life and, more broadly, for the educated bourgeois elite upon whom the state now drew for leadership in every field. Informed and articulate, it was they who had to keep alive the flame of a reformist, progressive Republic and to celebrate those heroes who had led the way – men of the centre, like Ferry and Waldeck-Rousseau, as well as those like Jaurès, a conscience of the left, or Albert de Mun, a conscience of the right.[76] So too it was this bourgeois elite who would remember the cultural heroes of the past and who would shower recognition upon those still in service. Always, for Barthou, France's history was a single fabric of tightly woven fibres – Jeanne d'Arc and Gambetta, Bossuet and Baudelaire, Lully and Saint-Saëns, Pascal and Curie – a mystical, unfinished tapestry at the foot of which ran the stream of ephemeral events.

CHAPTER FIVE

To the Summit, 1910–1913

Unlike the hands of a well-adjusted watch, which gives the exact time, the motions of men are not always a very good indication of their feelings or their character.[1]

General elections in the spring of 1910 strengthened considerably Barthou's chances of forming his own cabinet in the foreseeable future. For one thing, his local power base in Béarn seemed virtually unassailable. There were problems, undeniably, mainly related to divisions within the Oloron republican community over the burgeoning local union movement. But there were still other issues, notably the replacement of the old seminary by a state-run secondary school, which divided his Béarnais political opponents just as badly.[2] The net result was that in September 1909 he resecured his seat and chairmanship on the departmental council, and in April 1910 trampled his opposition in the legislative elections. This time, running against a sole opponent from the right, Barthou was able to leave his campaign in the hands of local organizers. He spent but four days electioneering, appearing only in the larger villages of his Oloron riding, but excusing his absence by invoking pressing ministerial duties. The issues were familiar enough in any event: defence of the Briand government's efforts to expand secular education, advocacy of the very long heralded progressive income tax, new promises for improvements in the pension plans of workers and peasants, and new undertakings to curtail the political activities of trade unions. These, together with the customary plea for faster progress in the construction of the Pau-Canfranc railway, were at the core of his low-key electoral campaign. And it worked. He drew the support of 83 per cent of those who cast votes, compared to the 10 per cent who rallied to his opponent. From Louis Barthou's vantage point, the Tenth Legislature could hardly have begun more auspiciously.[3]

Happily, too, his local electoral security had been abetted by his fortunes as a cabinet minister. By the spring of 1910 he had served for four years in three consecutive cabinets: in those of Sarrien and Clemenceau, at Public Works, and, since July 1909, in that of Aristide Briand, as justice minister and de facto vice-premier. Moreover, each was a regime associated in Chamber politics with the left, regimes which had enlisted names like Caillaux, Viviani, and Millerand, regimes committed to anticlericalism, the principle of a progressive income tax, and reformist labour legislation. At the same time, however, the paradox they represented was also becoming over-large. Progressive and reformist by conviction as well as by rhetoric, these were all governments which held public order to be indispensable to progressive development. Hence, when confronted by a crescendo of strikes and labour disturbances aimed at the public authority as well as the public service, these were administrations which applied the full weight of the law – including police and army units – against what they held to be apprehended subversion. From the socialist perspective, of course, this was further if redundant proof of bourgeois hypocrisy. And to the extent that Barthou – already resented and distrusted – was in the service of such regimes, he too was said to be of that same deceitful stamp, faulted for failing to do what the right accused him of having done already.

The autumn of 1910 brought matters to a head. Having campaigned on a familiar left-centre platform in the spring, and having backed the electoral collaboration of Alliance and Radicals in the second *scrutin*, Barthou returned to the Palais Bourbon as a prominent *homme de gauche*. In that sense, he was very much in the mainstream that had carried the Briand government to victory. However, it soon transpired that he and his premier disagreed on the temper of the new House and, in particular, of the more than two hundred first-time deputies. Briand did what Barthou certainly had done before. Conscious of socialist gains, and the drop in the numbers of conservative deputies, the premier shifted slightly toward his right, compensating as it were for the hazards of popular suffrage. This time, however, Barthou declined the adjustment and insisted on inscribing himself as a member of the Chamber's *groupe de la gauche radicale*.[4]

Such was symptomatic of the difference in emphases between the premier and vice-premier in October 1910, when the national railway union called for a country-wide strike. Briand, the former socialist, went straight for the throat. The very day of the national strike call, he announced his intention of drafting strikers for short-term hitches with the army. The cabinet went along with this dramatic and intimidating measure, fully aware of the supportive public mood though less confident of the Chamber's response. Only three ministers dissented, tried to dissuade the premier, and indeed even offered to resign – the socialist labour minister, Viviani, the former socialist, Millerand, at Public Works, and the expressly antisocialist minister of justice, Louis Barthou.[5] It was a surprising division, but not one without reason. Two principles were at stake for Barthou. First, he considered the measure much too severe to serve the interests of a government and country interested in class reconciliation. Second, as Clemenceau's minister of public works, he had personally conceded the railway workers union the right to strike. He could not now deviate from that publicly announced position;[6] nor did he, despite the discomfort he must have felt when the Chamber endorsed Briand's action. It presumably came as no surprise, therefore, when he learned one month later that his ministerial service had been terminated. Recalling with some understatement his falling-out with Briand that autumn, Barthou later admitted that there had been "a cooling in our relations."[7] Arguing that the government needed to be reworked in the more centrist image of this receptive Chamber, Briand formally resigned his first government and then promptly offered President Fallières a refurbished second. Many ministers, of course, retained their posts; but prominent among the casualties were René Viviani, Alexandre Millerand, and Louis Barthou.

Dropped by a premier intent on leaning marginally to the right, the discarded minister clearly relished the extra time that suddenly was at his disposal. For instance, had it not been for the rude political fortunes of November 1910, he would not have been able to make the Christmas trip to Egypt and the Sudan, in the company of Alice and their good friends, Joseph Caillaux and his soon-to-be-second wife, Henriette Raynouard. At the time, relations between the two men were excellent. Apart from sharing the tenuous bond of being out of office, they also seemed to enjoy the sometimes deceptive intimacy implied by the *tutoiement* and the even more dubious unity conferred by their vice-presidentships in the ideologically sprawling Alliance Républicaine Démocratique. More telling perhaps was the sympathy exchanged between the two women, Alice having first introduced Henriette to Caillaux during a reception at the Barthou residence.

In January 1911, therefore, upon their return from Egypt, there was still no sign of the crisis that would soon beset them all. Not even that uneasy moment on the banks of the Nile when Caillaux,

by his own telling, had drawn a not so friendly stiletto. He had told
his travelling companion, there and then, that what Barthou really
lacked was character, that he was temperamentally an opportunist
who would do anything for power. To which, reportedly, Barthou
said nothing, and by so doing tacitly confessed in Caillaux's eyes.
What Caillaux apparently forgot to include in this unfriendly verdict
was the fact that Barthou had just been dumped from a cabinet for
speaking his mind on a matter of principle. What he chose not to
say was that Barthou's social origins were against him in any event,
that he could never be expected to escape "the lower class blood in
his veins."[8]

Upon returning to France, Barthou promptly resumed his writing
career, taking this opportunity to begin work on his *Mirabeau*. He
also contributed two articles in 1911 to literary magazines, both
pieces clearly designed with public instruction in mind. As a former
interior minister, he thought it appropriate to argue the case for
abandoning one current practice. Premiers should not assume the
Interior portfolio. These days, he said, this ministry was simply too
important to have anyone but a full-time minister in charge. Because
of the legislation already passed, or under consideration, the state
was sure to be increasing its role in society even further. The Interior
ministry was certain to be part of that continued expansion, with its
involvement in public assistance programs, including health care, as
well as national police services and public administration. Indeed,
as a measure of its multiplying tasks, Barthou recommended the
attribution of a permanent secretary-general to this ministry, as well
as a change of name to that of Administration Intérieure.[9]

No less interesting, but more entertaining, was his article for *Revue
bleue*.[10] On the surface, this celebrates the freedom of those who are
not cabinet ministers, for life is tedious and rigorous for those who
are. What goes on in parliament, on the floor of the Chamber, or
in committees is only a small part of it. Even cabinet meetings had
been made more supportable, at least under the impatient hand of
Clemenceau. He had discontinued the convention of two meetings
per week at the Elysée palace and one at the premier's own ministry,
and replaced that formula with one of meetings being held on the
basis of need alone. Moreover, by informally designating an inner
cabinet, and by calling for ministerial attendance on the basis of
agenda items relevant to their portfolios, he had increased the ef-
ficiency of cabinet deliberations. But other things had not changed.
There remained, for example, the familiar Sunday occasions when
ministers were expected to launch everything from ships to tramways, bridges, tunnels, canals and schools. Not to mention the un-

veilings inspired by "the statuemania which clashes with our not very egalitarian democracy." Even worse were the insufferable demands of the whole patronage system, all the hours that had to go to meeting wave upon wave of supplicants, each intent on securing some form of special consideration.

The system, Barthou argued, was inefficient at best and insidious at worst. Ministers who had important jobs to do were spending too much time oiling the wheels of patronage and too often getting caught up in the gears shifted by expectant political clients. Just as serious, if it did not lead to that, it led to misunderstanding and resentment. He cited the case of one senator who had tried to use his influence on a local judge and who, failing that, had expected justice minister Barthou to bring the judge into line. The senator seemed to think that such efforts on the part of his own client were quite appropriate, and never understood why neither judge nor minister had acceded to his request. Conduct of the sort expected by the senator, Barthou wrote, had nothing to do with justice. All it succeeded in doing was debasing the entire system.[11]

Given its provenance, this was a strong indictment indeed, the more so as it was treated with wit as well as candour; and yet, for all that, a strange piece for him to write. No longer a tyro, at nearly fifty years of age, and an accomplished patron himself, whom among the politicians and their beneficiaries did he hope to sway? At first blush it sounds about as sincere as a brothel-keeper disparaging sex. There was no hope of effecting any significant change, particularly on the force of a single article which remained without sequel. All that would come of it would be stuffy denials and the resentment borne by hypocrisy. There was nothing to win, a certain amount to lose. Why do it? The likeliest answer is that Barthou did not always weigh in advance the consequences of speaking his mind. This does not prove, of course, that he always spoke the truth, but it is another indication that his candour was not always under the rein of personal political advantage.

Whatever its motivation, this article appeared in the very month that Joseph Caillaux became premier of France. For the preceding six months, events had been unfolding along lines advantageous to this, one of Barthou's closest friends. Briand had fallen in early March 1911, to be replaced by the Radical, Monis, who had invited Caillaux to be his finance minister. Barely three months later, in June, that regime was being replaced by one led by Caillaux himself. Like so many, the new cabinet was a mix of things old and novel. Roughly half of the cabinet posts changed hands, a renovation grand enough to have accommodated a friend and ally like Barthou. But that did not happen. Eventually, the premier got around to explaining this oversight, by which time he realized that Barthou was smarting from this deliberate act of exclusion. The explanation was hardly calculated to make him feel better. With questionable tact and logic both, Caillaux claimed that Barthou was still too closely associated with the conservative stance of the first Briand government – a claim which ignored the fact that Barthou was a primary casualty of that administration.[12] It would have been more credible, perhaps even more true, simply to recall the dynamics of coalition politics according to which cabinets were as much exercises in bridging differences as in uniting like minds. Friends might remain friends, and vote accordingly, but ministries that did not reflect a sufficient cross-section of differences within the Chamber were in for a short ride.

As late as October 1911 the relations between Caillaux and Barthou remained unaffected, at least on the surface. The premier still termed Barthou "one of my best friends."[13] But the strains were developing underneath, policy differences aggravated no doubt by personal pique on both sides. Barthou was worried by the government's apparent readiness to take the state further into railroad ownership and administration, and to introduce a radically new income tax law purportedly designed to soak the rich; and he was perturbed as well by what he saw as Caillaux's too patient handling of the ongoing strike in the armament industries.[14] Nonetheless, his confrontation with the government was to develop in an unexpected quarter.

Foreign policy, at least ostensibly, was to prove the sticking point. At first glance, this was indeed unexpected, particularly as Barthou had been slow to evince an interest in international relations. For that very reason, two interpretive possibilities suggest themselves. The first, simultaneously more subtle and more speculative, argues that foreign policy in this quarrel was mere pretence, that what expressed itself in matters diplomatic was only the alienation of Caillaux from the Alliance. In short, Barthou's differences with Caillaux were mainly of a domestic order, related in particular to the pace and degree of reform contemplated by the Caillaux government. For some, therefore, what we have in the approaching crisis is but a thinly veiled conservative manoeuvre to use complaints about foreign policy as a device to attack a government detested for other reasons.[15]

The second interpretation works with what was apparent, namely the sudden international crisis prompted by competing French and German interests in Morocco. It is true that Barthou had expressed limited interest in international politics during his first two decades in parliament. However, it is also true that from 1905 onward Barthou had been a principal force within the Alliance in promoting patriotic cause and vocabulary. Mindful of the way in which conservative politicians had tried to present themselves as sole guardians of the patriotic flame – with twisted versions of the collision between Dreyfus and the Republic – Barthou had pushed the ARD to reaffirm its commitment to the army and to national defence.[16] Accordingly, it was perhaps not so surprising – or so suspicious – that Barthou figured prominently among critics of the government's handling of foreign policy; in particular, of its handling of the Agadir incident, or what is often called the second Moroccan crisis, in July 1911.

He did not criticize Caillaux's determination to avoid an open confrontation with Germany. What disturbed him was the fear that in this admirable desire to avoid conflict the government had conceded more than it ought by the terms of the Treaty of Frankfurt. By November 1911, when the substance of this accord with Germany became public, Barthou had become an outspoken critic. The settlement, he told the ARD, was too loosely worded, and as such opened the doors for solid French concessions in the Congo in exchange for only putative recognition of a French protectorate over Morocco.[17] The accord also might be construed as one which France had been intimidated into signing – an interpretation which he found disturbing. Finally, the entire arrangement had been worked out with absolutely no reference to parliamentary advice or opinion. However, and for that very reason, Barthou maintained that parliament had no choice but to go along with the treaty – unless it wished to create a major domestic crisis on top of an international one. That, he said, was unthinkable. But no more of this secret diplomacy! There had been too much of it already, and in its shadows parliament carried on in blissful ignorance, unaware of deals with Germany or, for that matter, England. After all, he observed, it had been the same story with the Anglo-French agreement of April 1904. Such behaviour had to stop, for it was inimical to the ideals and the interests of a democratic regime. "This secret diplomacy ... presents a shocking contrast with the idea of a democratic regime which thinks it is free to determine its own directions. France has the right to be aware of the affairs of France."[18]

How little France knew of such affairs became clear in January 1912. Caillaux's treaty had been approved by the Chamber in December, one vote for it having been cast by Barthou. But contrary to the latter's advice – which was to close the books on the matter – the Chamber decided to examine the now confirmed treaty by means of a special commission. This commission, on which Barthou did agree to serve, soon discovered that the manner of the premier's diplomacy had been as questionable as its substance. It did not take long to discover that the foreign minister, de Selves, had been kept in the dark by Caillaux. In short, the government's secret diplomacy had been very secret indeed. However, rather than directly contradict his premier – who continued to deny that he had played any significant role in this covert diplomacy – de Selves now announced his resignation from the cabinet. Predictably, of course, this action precipitated the very cabinet crisis which the minister said he wished to avert. Thereafter, the premier's own days in office were numbered as apprehensions about his judgment and integrity mounted. His treaty with Germany was destined to win Senate approval in February 1912, but by then he was out of office. Several weeks earlier, following his own appearance before the commission and the resignation of his minister, he had been obliged to resign. To the end, he remained convinced – quite beyond reason – that he had been betrayed by envious friends rather than by mistakes of his own making.[19]

It was no consolation to Caillaux that he had been replaced by Poincaré, a member of the investigative commission. Neither was it solace enough that Barthou had been excluded from this cabinet as well. For indeed it had happened once more: another of Barthou's old friends had managed to form a cabinet without calling upon his services. Presumably he was hurt again, as Caillaux reported him the year before; but he would have denied it, claiming to understand, promising to support the new government in the Chamber and across the country.[20] Poincaré, for his part, would have explained his decision by drawing upon the familiar imperatives of coalition politics, leaving unsaid the fact that he still considered Barthou a doubtful asset when it came to working with Radicals and Radical Socialists. All things considered, it was better to have him as a prominent and forceful voice in the ARD and the Chamber than a potentially divisive force within a cabinet that still needed Radical support.[21]

Once more excluded by this curious "republic of pals," Barthou resumed his pursuit of everything else that interested him. There was no withdrawal from political life, which continued to exercise its fascination undiminished, but his interventions in the Chamber lessened perceptibly throughout the course of 1912. Part of this, one suspects, owed something to the bitter misgiving that too often he was paying the price of other men's ambitions. Part of it, too, derived from a reluctance to make more than was necessary of his lingering reservations about the government's contemplated return to some form of proportional representation through the *scrutin de liste*.[22] Moreover, from May 1912 when he was elected to chair the Chamber's Foreign Affairs committee, much more of his time had to go to the preparation of committee meetings.

Here was a position of considerable prestige, the acceptance of which bespoke not only a sharpened interest in international affairs on Barthou's part but also parliament's mounting concern about European peace. Circumstances thus lent to the office an importance which guaranteed the incumbent nation-wide attention; and in a sense, the less frequent his addresses the greater their weight. This certainly was true of his much applauded speech of 1 July, which played a key role in securing Chamber approval of another recent treaty, this one recognizing France's protectorate over Morocco. This treaty, he affirmed, was a model of clarity, and posed no difficulties for members of his committee. It was typical, he ventured, of Premier Poincaré's ability to frame accords which were both precise and flexible. Furthermore, this excellent text found its complement in the talents of the soldier-governor who would implement the accord with the sultan's government. France, he predicted, could not be in better hands than those of Lyautey, "this humane and gifted general." Thus assured by its committee chairman, as well as by Poincaré – premier and foreign minister combined – the Chamber voted overwhelmingly to ratify the protectorate treaty.[23]

There were other reasons, it is true, why Barthou's activity in the Chamber seemed to lessen during the course of this, Poincaré's first government. Much of the time he was busy writing, for personal satisfaction but also – one might be forgiven for suggesting – for the kind of recognition that might some day take him to a chair in the Académie Française. *Mirabeau* was already nearing completion, ahead of schedule, thanks to a rain-soaked holiday in the summer of 1912 which had allowed him to double the four hours of writing originally budgeted per day.[24] That in turn had allowed him to start assembling a collection of shorter pieces under the title *Impressions et essais*. And on top of this there had been a lecture on the role of the legal profession in the French theatrical tradition, an article on Lamartine's private life, and another on Hugo's skill at proof-reading – both laden with lengthy quotations from previously unpublished manuscripts – and another article on the delights and rewards of manuscript and book collectors.[25] All this pleased him, absorbed him, furnished him with subjects to discuss as well as write about. Addressing the Académie years later, Pierre Benoit recalled a short stint as Barthou's secretary in 1912, when Maurice Reclus had taken a brief holiday. We began, he said, not by talking about Oloron's municipal finances, or the police barracks in Arudy, but rather of de Musset and de Vigny.[26]

Writing and collecting for Barthou were like twin sisters, distinctively two, but at times close enough to be one. Both offered refuge and release, inspiration for patriotism and for aestheticism. Surrounded by books and drafts of his own manuscripts, he could relax, alone or in the presence of people he could trust, Béarnais particularly. His old school acquaintance Jules Bertaut remembered the jubilation and unconcealed pride with which Barthou would show a friend his latest acquisition, unable to control the triumph in his eyes and voice. Louis Latzarus, a journalist from the friendly *Figaro*, and a Béarnais in the bargain, described him caressing the leather-bound volumes and gently blowing away some particle of dust before returning this beloved object to its shelf. So too the journalist, P.B. Gheusi, writing of the same pre-war epoch, fondly recalled Barthou slowly turning the pages of Victor Hugo's diaries, the originals, his hands literally "trembling with emotion."[27]

Passionate and gratifying as it was, this calling demanded tremendous effort and application. It was an enterprise which demanded as much time as money, the kind of persistent effort which was only likely to be appreciated by the other great bibliophiles and connoisseurs of his day. There were dealers to keep in touch with, as well as contemporary authors, engravers, and binders. There were fellow collectors to be cajoled into parting with some treasure in their possession, or families who retained original works from some celebrated antecedent, or executors of estates left by yet other deceased authors. And there were, too, the demands, however pleasant, imposed by membership in several leading bibliophilic societies, the most important of which for Barthou was Le Livre Contemporain. Present at its creation in December 1903, Barthou was to become its president in 1913, a post which he would retain until his death twenty-one years later. It was from this office that he would direct the publication of the society's annual deluxe editions, playing an active role in the society's preference for French authors and, in particular, for the works of his personal favourites like Hugo, Loti, France, and de Vigny.[28]

Travel, too, was part of Barthou's busy agenda in 1912. Little more than a year after his trip to the Nile, he found himself embarked on the longest voyage of his life – this time, to the United States and Canada, where he was to see duty as a delegate of the Comité France-Amérique. The occasion was to celebrate the three hundredth anniversary of Samuel de Champlain's voyage to the New World. More particularly, the delegation was to accompany a representative statue of France by the sculptor Rodin, a commissioned work which was to be incorporated into a new monument to Champlain on the shores of the lake which had been given his name. Included in the prestigious delegation was Gabriel Hanotaux, official leader of the group, Louis and Léon Barthou – the latter identified as delegate of the Aéro-Club de France – two members of the Académie Française, namely the painter F. Cormon and the geographer Vidal de la Blache, the flyer Louis Blériot, the journalist Gaston Deschamps, and the Count and Countess de Rochambeau. In short, a delegation studded with political, cultural, and scientific celebrities.[29]

As befitted station and occasion, the delegation travelled first class, beginning their voyage from Le Havre on the new luxury liner *France*. They departed on 20 April 1912, to the strains of a quayside band playing the "Marseillaise," passengers straining to see the last of the fluttering flags and pocket handkerchiefs and wondering about the wisdom of leaving land. The *Titanic* had gone down only five days earlier, with the loss of over one thousand lives. Like that doomed ship, the *France* was on her maiden transatlantic voyage. Gaston Deschamps confirmed how often they had thought of the recent disaster, listening for several days to the inquiries of the ship's foghorn, watching the captain test the water for iceberg – cooled temperatures and in fact suddenly order a more southerly course on their fifth day at sea. It was with some relief, he admitted, that they glimpsed the coast of Long Island and arrived in New York on 28 April.[30]

Their itinerary was demanding: two weeks of land travel, taking them on a circuit from New York, Washington, Philadelphia, Boston – including Harvard and Yale – to Lake Champlain. Then they were to proceed across the border to Canada: Montréal, Québec, Toronto, Niagara Falls, and back to New York, from which they would return to France in mid-May on the steamship *La Provence*. Regrettably, Barthou published no account of this trip; however, through the detailed reports left by Deschamps we know that he was singled out to accompany Hanotaux inside the crypt which held Washington's remains at Mount Vernon and in which the two men left a commemorative wreath. We also know that to him fell the honour of introducing Louis Blériot to several thousand Montrealers who had been drawn to see the celebrated aviator. What is more, if the past indeed be prologue, we know intuitively that Barthou shared with Deschamps a profound patriotic reaction to this "return" to North

America. The more so for its being a patriotism rooted in historical tradition and cultural achievement: pride in the battle of Ticonderoga of 1758 where Montcalm and grenadiers from Béarn had acquitted themselves well against English arms, or pride in Rodin's *France*, unveiled on the shores of Champlain's lake to the strains of the French national anthem. Here, in Deschamps's words, was France recognizable – "the power and the tenderness of the mother-country ... the nobility of her generous aspirations." And years later, Louis Barthou would still speak affectionately of the Canadian visit, of the "family community" which he had discovered there. He still remembered the crowds at Saint-Jean, Québec shouting "Vive la France," the revelation that the old Norman tale of La Claire Fontaine was still woven into the culture of French Canada, the sight of a Québec architecture which instantly recalled the rooftops of La Rochelle and Saint Malo, the first glimpse of that province's sobering device: "Je me souviens."[31]

Poincaré, too, had a long memory. In January 1913 he was elected president of the Republic, succeeding Fallières, and being succeeded himself in the premier's office by Aristide Briand. The latter called Barthou back to office, again as justice minister. But once more his tenure proved brief. On 22 March the government fell apart, leaving Poincaré acutely uneasy. Very much alive to the unstable international situation, and to recent German rearmament measures, the cabinet had just resolved on an important national defence initiative. Having met only weeks before with senior military advisers on the Conseil Supérieur de la Guerre, the Briand cabinet had decided upon an extension of military service from two to three years. But now, the lingering, forever controversial issue of electoral reform had led to this same government's resignation. To whom should Poincaré turn, in the higher interests of national security?

The choice of Barthou was obvious, on personal and ideological grounds, but more so if one exaggerates the room for friendship in politics. In fact, Poincaré proceeded very cautiously. Barthou was bright, urbane, a patriot, and a proponent of the three-year law. Moreover, he had distanced himself from the fallen government's electoral reform proposals without having broken cabinet ranks. In short, he had minimized his own liabilities in the Chamber as a member of the just-resigned cabinet. Besides, Briand now backed him for the premiership, as did Dubost, president of the Senate, while Paul Deschanel, president of the Chamber, had included his name on a list of three potential premiers. But the question remained in Poincaré's mind as to whether the left had ever put aside their old grievances from the days of Méline. Accordingly, he turned first to Léon Bourgeois, who declined on the grounds of poor health. Only then did Poincaré call Barthou who, he recalled with a slight sniff of disapproval, could not contain his eagerness.[32]

Before formally accepting this long-awaited charge, even before completing discussions with his potential ministers, Barthou issued a series of public undertakings. He would not assume the Interior portfolio, a self-denial which was consistent with his previously published views, and which also had the merit of undercutting anyone intent on bringing up his service under Méline. What he wanted, he said, was a "ministry of détente, union, and republican conciliation." Nevertheless, his ministry would not include anyone opposed to the proposed three-year military service law. On that, there was no room for equivocation.[33]

That said, he then proceeded to form another centre-left coalition cabinet, a rather nondescript administration which boasted few of the leading republican personalities of the past decade. Indeed, there was not a former premier among them, and of the twelve ministerial portfolios, three were occupied by men of no ministerial experience whatever. That in itself was cause for some alarm, but there was more. Barthou had asked Jean Dupuy to stay on at Public Works and Charles Jonnart at the Foreign ministry. Both declined. Bienvenu-Martin was invited to join the new cabinet. He declined, as did Paul-Boncour, Viviani, and Doumergue, and, possibly, Bourgeois, Ribot, Clemenceau, and Caillaux. Accordingly, in the face of such difficulties, it was deemed expedient to shift Klotz from Finance, where he had served Briand, to the Interior ministry, while the intended public works minister, the Radical Socialist Charles Dumont, was abruptly shunted to Finance at the last moment. This was not the stuff of which confidence is made, and it is remarkable that the government actually survived its opening vote on 25 March, survived by a margin of only twenty-five votes and over two hundred abstentions. Just as telling in its own way, however, was the response this vote implied toward the government's platform. Despite all that Barthou had done to streamline his program and minimize his liabilities, he had only just made it through the first vote. It looked therefore as if this was a Chamber resolved, or almost resolved, to resist the three-year service proposal and the attendant acceleration of financial contributions for rearmament.[34]

The arguments deployed by the bill's opponents were predictable enough, two of which can be canvassed quickly at this point. The first had the sort of ideological cast most likely to be favoured, and proffered, by socialists. This proposed escalation of military preparations, they argued, was as inimical to the cause of Europe's peace as it was self-serving for reactionary military circles and weapons manufacturers. Given his previous confrontations with French socialists, Barthou was easily held up as the willing tool of a manipulative bourgeois regime. The second, usable independently or in conjunction with the first, was what might be called the technical argument. It alleged that, whether or not one supported the intent of the bill, the fact was that the legislation itself was conceptually flawed. One was not going to defend the security of France by simply increasing the size of the standing army. Rather, the government needed to spend its money elsewhere, on the upgrading of the reserves (an argument advanced by Jaurès and the Socialists), or on better heavy artillery and mobilization procedures (arguments which seemed particularly compelling to many on the Radical Socialist benches).[35]

In the debates which flared sporadically in the Chamber between March and July 1913, the government responded with observations of its own. Short on experience and prestige as it was, the cabinet did have in General Etienne a seasoned war minister, and in Pichon a man accustomed to service at the Foreign ministry. Nonetheless, it was the premier himself who was repeatedly called upon to intervene in these debates, backing and filling for less adroit colleagues while steadily advancing the bill under the guns of his critics. The technical criticisms were more easily contained, principally by drawing upon the statistics furnished by the Conseil Supérieur de la Guerre and upon the expertise of the serving officers who had been brought together on a special commission specifically to advise the War ministry. Advice from such a quarter, together with the endorsation of the Chamber's Army committee, enabled the government to argue that there simply was no effective alternative to the legislation now before parliament. Indeed, years later Barthou credited passage of the three-year law to General Joffre, then chief of the general staff. Prevailed upon by the premier to address parliament, the general had overcome much of the resistance with an arid, unmoving, but profoundly sincere description of the worsening military imbalance between France and Germany.[36] At the same time, kinship and accord with soldiers could not be pushed too far, given the conditioned response of the socialist benches. Instead, Barthou was at pains to stress that, while accepting the analyses of the military experts, his government had fashioned its own policy in keeping with advice rendered by deputies on the Army committee.[37]

Overt ideological opposition, some of it at any rate, could be met head-on with comparable directness. Certainly after April 1913, when two separate border incidents had threatened to inflame Franco-German relations – one at Lunéville, where a German Zeppelin had landed by error in France, and the other at Nancy, where there had been an unpleasant clash between local residents and two different groups of German tourists. For a government desperate for support of a major defence bill, here was a gift straight from Mars. But it was sent back, undisturbed. The fact was, so Barthou later testified, "I had no need whatever to 'whip-up' the national conscience."[38] Instead, the government quietly and expeditiously resolved both incidents, defusing them with peaceful assurances to the German government and with disciplinary action against a handful of its own local agents whose handling of the two disturbances had been judged clumsy and dilatory.[39] No hysteria, no provocation, no exploitation. By such behaviour the Barthou government countered the accusations of those who saw it bent on confrontation.

In May, however, it opened itself to another charge, the third on an expanding list. Recognizing that the bill's passage was going to take time, and that the army had to know what would happen in October when the 1911 class of conscripts was scheduled for release, the government acted and then held its collective breath.[40] All those young men who had been anticipating their return to civilian life in October were suddenly informed that their tour of duty had been extended, perhaps for up to another year. The opposition, led by the press of *Aurore* and *Humanité*, redoubled its attack on the bill. There were incidents of insubordination in the barracks of Toul, Mâcon, and Rodez. The Confédération Général du Travail spoke out on behalf of workers and soldiers, and soon found itself facing legal action launched by a government which thought it detected sedition.[41] In the Chamber there was a new surge of hostility, still inspired by the old reasons, but now refuelled with a third. Now the government was acting unconstitutionally, it was said, by acting on the provisions of a bill not yet enacted in law. And if further proof were needed of its reactionary tendencies, so the argument continued, having defied parliament this government now had the temerity to try to gag labour critics and to forbid public demonstrations against the bill. In reply, the Barthou ministry carefully explained the reasons for the timing of its decision, and vigorously affirmed its constitutional right to so act. According to its legal advisers, article 33 of the 1905 military law expressly permitted the government to extend the period of military service at a time of perceived emergency. Such was its perception, such was its decision. Moreover, those who disturbed the public peace as a way of drawing attention to their dislike of the government's lawful measures were themselves in violation of the law and could not expect to act with impunity.[42]

Having weathered that storm, and with its parliamentary position actually improving, the government had no choice but to set its course toward yet another crisis. This time it was over money. How were its measures to be financed? The first step was to secure immediate funding for the increased costs of keeping the 1911 class with the colours until the end of the budget year. This the government achieved on 27 May, following a particularly well timed and artful intervention by its premier.[43] The second step was to agree upon the means by which the entire package of expenditures would be financed over the ensuing years. To that end, finance minister Dumont announced that the government would borrow the requisite amount – estimated at 1,300 million francs – and service the debt with a progressively based income tax. An income tax! Banal as it appears today, in 1913 these were words more explosive than priest or anarchist. Senate opinion, generally stout on the military law itself, was certain to waver over the contemplated financing. On the other flank, the Radical Socialists and the Socialists were equally certain to see the scheme as another conspiracy of the rich.

So it was that differing ideological, technical, constitutional, and financial perspectives separated the government from its critics, most of whom sat on the left of the Chamber; separated them, and possibly also obscured another reason for the determined resistance. In fact, government supporters believed that the arguments used publicly against them were only cosmetics to conceal the real issue: the base but familiar jockeying for power. In their eyes, the so-called Unified Socialists of Jaurès were less guilty of this than the Radical Socialists. The former, it was thought, were so ideologically programmed that they were largely oblivious to the parliamentary and public groundswell of support for the government's bill. The latter, however, with their new *de facto* leader, Joseph Caillaux, were something else. As the editors of *Le Temps* saw it, Caillaux was engaged in a subtle, indirect campaign to return himself to power – the first step of which had to be the toppling of Barthou. Accepting the government's contention that current French strength was inadequate for the circumstances, Caillaux nonetheless withheld support for the present bill, endorsed the technical objections of his colleague General Messimy, and aggravated parliamentary doubts about the government's plans for financing a strengthened army. Worse, in the eyes of those with whom he had worked in the ARD and, since 1910, in the premier's own *gauche radical*, Caillaux was not above associating this government with sabre-rattling tactics and, the final affront, with the politics of "reactionary nationalism."[44]

As for the funding issue, Caillaux disparaged Dumont's plan to borrow and, taking advantage of the minister's undeniably vague proposals, cast doubts on the government's determination to implement a serious, progressively scaled income tax. Instead, this new darling of the left recommended much stiffer measures – a sharply graduated income tax and an independent tax on capital.[45] Tersely put, the government had it all wrong, a conclusion which opened the way for Caillaux to some kind of parliamentary alliance with Jaurès and to hopes of bringing Barthou down. Such at least is how *Le Temps* saw it, from a perspective which, while clearly sympathetic to Barthou, is also reminiscent of an earlier observation about lawyers in politics.[46] Trained to argue for their client, right or wrong, too often they contemplate issues in the light of tactical advantage rather than of society's welfare – precisely, of course, the rebuke administered to Barthou by Caillaux himself. Thus, denied the luxury of fighting over profoundly held differences, lawyers are animated by antagonism based on personality and rival ambition.

In the case of these two, Caillaux and Barthou, the former was clearly trying to write the latter's political obituary, in advance. This, despite the reiterated and reciprocal assurances of friendship recorded by Caillaux. Indeed, by his own telling, he remained loyal to Barthou, for as long as he could, refraining from vigorous attack in the hope that Barthou would see the light, but all the time fearing that Poincaré would replace a defeated Barthou with some other lieutenant and so scotch Caillaux's own hopes of a comeback with the Radical Socialists.[47]

Yet another source of apprehension for the opposition was Barthou's own surprisingly strong performance in the Chamber. Indeed, the government was now winning votes by majorities far greater than what it had put together at the time of its debut. Time and time again the premier himself had turned an opposition flank by saying the right thing, in the right way, at just the right moment. His personal and parliamentary talents were proving impressive. Not that everything was visible. It was just as well, for instance, that he had kept in excellent physical shape, for five months of intense parliamentary pressure could take a heavy toll. Indeed, it obviously did so. Writing to Loti in June, he admitted that he was carrying a "crushing burden," and Alice commented to a friend on her husband's worsening eye strain.[48] Neither will anyone ever know, amid the voluminous record of all he said in 1913, all the things he was tempted to say but did not. So much was falling on his shoulders that it was asking a lot for him to keep his own temper while trying to compensate for ministers who had lost theirs.

On one occasion in May, he had been obliged to deliver a hasty, improvised yet calming speech, following a near fight on the floor of the Chamber between his war minister, Etienne, and a vocal Radical deputy.[49] The next month he had to deal with a skittish and disgusted General Pau, an old soldier who was serving on Etienne's special advisory commission. Required to be in the Chamber, Pau was making little effort to conceal his anger at comments made by a series of Socialist and Radical Socialist speakers. Patience soon exhausted, he was in the process of making a stormy exit when Jaurès seized on the opportunity to accuse the government of trying to unsettle parliament with menacing old generals.[50] Barthou arrived in the Chamber at that moment, just in the nick of time. Apprised of the situation by anxious aides, he went straight to the tribune. Unsure of what he was going to say, he fell back on desperation. He appealed to common sense. What had happened was unfortunate, unwelcome, ill advised; but it was no more than the impulsive gesture of a frustrated man who had given forty years of his life in service to France. The general's behaviour had nothing whatever to do with the government's wishes or its bill. Fortunately, Jaurès was pacified, but not before Barthou had resolved never to be late for another sitting of the Chamber. Indeed, if any reminder were necessary, General Pau promptly obliged. Hardly had the premier regained his bench than he overheard Pau whisper to General Legrand that he would not be coming back the next day. With a smile set in angry disbelief, Barthou leaned over and whispered: "But of course you will, mon général, particularly after what I have just said, and even without me having to give you an order."[51]

Less audible still was the contract he had made with himself as a device for confronting red-faced, angry, deliberately provocative critics. The trick was not to be provoked, a trick learned only after years of political experience and – in his case – never fully mastered.

When I was a minister under Méline, they called me a reactionary; I was very young then, and the charge upset me. When I was a minister under Clemenceau, I heard them say that even he was an instrument of reaction. It was then I realized what such epithets were worth.[52]

Sustained by that realization, and driven by a patriot's conviction that the three-year law was essential to the security of France, Louis Barthou embarked on the most demanding and the most public performance of his political career. Appropriately, it was at the tribune, which had enthralled him in September 1889 when he had first entered the Chamber. At the tribune where Mirabeau had made his name, he whose eloquence had been extolled at such length in the premier's own recently released book with the publisher Hachette.

Eloquence, Barthou believed, was almost as difficult to define as to achieve. It was not the mark of those "who speak so as to say nothing," or those who mistook it for verbal acrobatics.[53] He agreed that it was in part "a natural aptitude" and in part "a shortcoming overcome," but knew there was something more. Not surprisingly, he sensed a kinship between speech and music, praising Mirabeau's ability to achieve harmony and rhythm by tuning each word in a sentence and attributing that talent to his "musical ear."[54] Was it emulation, or something more natural still, which made his own speech suggestive of some musical quality? Jules Bertaut, for instance, remarked on Barthou's musically phrased speech, and Ignotus commented on his "lilting voice."[55] Other musical associations were also suggested. Barthou himself was fascinated by the fine line that needed to be followed between improvised and rehearsed, between spontaneity – where one gambled on inspiration and against something maladroit – and calculation – where one risked boredom for the sake of precision. He strove to find the middle, as so befitted him. He would read formal, official declarations from the tribune, but little else; and yet the ease with which he improvised was more apparent than real. An acknowledged workhorse, he laboured for hours on the data and documents upon which he intended to draw. Then, typically, he walked, across Paris, into the Bois de Boulogne, along the quais, working out in his head the speech he would deliver. On such occasions he was known to dart across the street in order to avoid interruption from some approaching acquaintance.[56]

The moment having arrived, he approached the tribune, mindful of the gravity of the place and of Floquet's rebuke to one onrushing deputy: "Monsieur, you are not in a mill."[57] Often he appeared nervous, and admitted privately to a queasy stomach.[58] That there was an inner tension was clear enough to those who knew him. On the one hand, there was Barthou marshalling fact and figure with the lawyer's composure, often calling them up from memory; intimidating with his command of the data, but eschewing declamation, deliberately informal, with hands customarily plunged into trouser pockets. On the other hand, just below the surface there was a thick bed of spontaneity, what even friendly witnesses called a "southern impulsiveness." He was capable of resisting provocation, when and if he tried, but his instincts went the other way, like those of the hunting dog to which Paul Flat likened him. No doubt there were encounters to be won by the direct approach, but there were pitfalls too. Despite his attempts at self-restraint, he could be carried away, trading taunts and accusations, often betraying by facial grimace when opponents were hitting home.[59]

But Barthou at his most visible, certainly in 1913, was the speaker in oratorical flight, complementing all this body language with the vocabulary of an alarmed patriot. For men, as for books, it was not the embellishments that counted, but rather what they stood for. And in the summer of 1913, the premier impressed parliament and country with what he had to say. Some of it, indeed much of it, was statistical, focused on Germany's mounting military advantage – the sort of data that contrasted France's 70 per cent increase in military expenditures over the past thirty years with a corresponding 227 per cent increase by Germany. Some of it was as rigid as the statistics he drew upon, particularly as he pledged himself to go "jusqu'au bout" when it came to defending France's interests in the world. But this he followed with notes of conciliation, indeed reconciliation, stressing his desire to make war less rather than more likely, projecting some future opportunity to revise downward the provisions of the very bill now under consideration, even in gentle humour linking himself with Jaurès – by invoking their shared memories of past disagreements. Finally, there was throughout his much applauded, subsequently *affiched*, speech of 4 July 1913 an element of unabashed passion. He was a patriot, he said, not a nationalist, not – as critics suggested – one who was a political reactionary. Indeed, as one who had fought clericalism and antirepublicanism all of his life, he found thoroughly offensive the attempts to link him to nationalism. "I am no nationalist ... It's to your patriotism that I appeal!"[60]

By the time of the summer recess, the premier was exhausted. He had weathered the storm. Parliament had approved the three-year military service bill, but the struggle had taken all of his energy. True, there had been moments of reprieve, snatched from the jaws of politics. Anna de Noailles had sent him her new *Les Vivants et les morts*, signed and inscribed "To Monsieur Louis Barthou, so that this volume can belong to the best Host that poets have in France." But the binder had taken longer than expected; and so, even amid the fireworks of the Chamber debates, he had asked his aide, Louis Vitalis, to put on some pressure. When could the work come home?[61] In May, despite the clamour surrounding the military service bill, he had attended a memorable anniversary dinner for the *Revue hebdomadaire*, where he had relished the company of distinguished writers and journalists; and in July he had taken pleasure in announcing to the Société des Gens de Lettres that one of their brightest stars, Paul Hervieu, was to be given a higher rank in the Legion of Honour. How he treasured those occasions among great writers, great patriots!

Abroad, you are the ambassadors of the French language. You know enough not to write the kinds of books which risk our being put in a bad light by our rivals. You are animated by the will to render to France the homage due to her.[62]

And of course, as he acknowledged to the journalist Jean Lefranc, there had been the domestic refuge too, Alice and Max, who had bucked up his spirits and teased him about being difficult to live with, laughing to themselves as he retired to his library and Rabelais, or Montaigne, Verlaine, or Moréas.[63]

Whatever the few moments of relaxation in Paris, the family had looked forward to their vacation at Bürgenstock in August of 1913, more or less liberated from telephones, ministerial assistants, newspapers, and school books. Max, at seventeen, had just completed his baccalauréat, and Alice was visibly delighted to have her two men more relaxed. It was here, at the Grand Hotel, that Lefranc found them, and dined with them that August. The premier was in excellent form, already revived by the long hikes which had been added to his religiously observed morning exercise, and soothed by the company of three favourite travelling companions: one Racine, one Chénier, one La Bruyère. In sum, he was in the best of spirits, enjoying the jokes about his exercises, an indulgent father who happily suffered interruption from a playful son who would not be overawed by the premier of France.[64] This open bond of affection caught the eye of another journalist, not long after their return to Paris. Barthou had given a public lecture on Victor Hugo, following which a young man had approached him and, "with a touching playfulness," had awarded the distinguished speaker a high mark for his speech. It was Max, of course, whom a beaming Barthou introduced simply as "Mon fils."[65]

The Bürgenstock idyll had soon given way to renewed political turmoil. Some of it had little to do with the new military legislation, at least not directly. Just before the summer recess, it is true, Barthou had managed to put another cat among the pigeons, this time in his dual capacity as premier and education minister. In accord with his own sentiments, as well as those expressed by vocal parents, he had tried to reaffirm the rights of the latter to comment on the choice of school textbooks. Though he never said so directly, it was clear that he hoped parental pressures might help restrain the pacifistic and antipatriotic pedagogy of some classrooms. Predictably, reaction was mixed. Those whose politics stretched from the centre to the right generally applauded. Those inclined in the opposite direction tended to be more critical, partly in defence of teachers' prerogatives but mainly out of an appreciation that those teachers who most feared "militarism" were also likely to be the strongest defenders of secular republicanism.

No one was more alive to this than Louis Barthou, for he had long appreciated the role played by the teaching profession in underpinning republican democracy. Thus, while he sought to isolate those teachers who, in his view, really did confuse nationalism and patriotism, he had to defend himself against charges from the socialist left that, by opening the doors to more parental influence, he was surreptitiously bringing back clerical influence. In Barthou's case, given his past record, the charge seemed patently disingenuous; however, like all indictments based on future commission, there was nothing to disprove. Denial was all there was left, firm and passionate. "I am of a secular mind. Deeply so, because of my educational background, my whole past, and all I believe in."[66] Nonetheless, given both his personal convictions and the frail position of his government in the Chamber, he also made it clear that he would lead no new offensive against the educational prerogatives of the Church. In a speech of late November, the minister assured an audience of the Ligue de l'Enseignement that he opposed a state monopoly in education. This was not solely for financial reasons, he said, not even primarily. Rather, he subscribed to the ideal of freedom of education, an ideal which would be snuffed out in the absence of private schools.[67]

By the end of that month the government's ability to survive was very much in doubt. Reconvened in early November, after a three-month recess, the Chamber was soon restless. The ministry had done better than anyone had expected. In particular, it had actually managed to secure passage of a controversial law in the face of organized and tenacious resistance. Indeed, it would prove to be enduring resistance, for three year service was going to disrupt the lives of hundreds of thousands of conscripts and their families, and was going to have heavy financial implications for the public treasury. Therefore, although approved by parliament, the bill was anything but forgotten. Instead, its critics returned to the Chamber determined to renew the struggle, embarrassing the government on every possible front. And there were many.

There was, of course, that campaign of innuendo which made out the government to be some occult friend of clericalism. This, together with the chauvinism said to be latent in the three-year law, was enough to colour Barthou and colleagues as a troop of right-wing reactionaries. Less grave, though present, was the lingering issue of electoral reform. Here was something which was so spectacularly divisive that it could be used with great effect against almost any government – but only if the opposition were sufficiently united. In fact, they were not. Socialists and Radical Socialists agreed, for the most part, on the iniquities of the three-year law. They did not agree on electoral reform, the Socialists generally favouring some form of return to the *scrutin de liste* and proportional representation, Caillaux's forces generally opposing such a measure. Accordingly, Barthou's opponents were not especially exercised to hear him say, at the beginning of the new session, that the current possibilities of electoral reform were just about nil. The Senate and Chamber, he observed, were simply too far apart. Moreover, as Caillaux and his allies appreciated, since the government had not made electoral reform central to its program of action, it was unlikely ground on which to engineer its defeat.[68]

Far more promising were the financial provisions for the new service law. All told, the three-year law was expected to increase the national deficit by as much as eight hundred million francs. The question remained as to how this debt was going to be serviced. It was a good question, because the government was boxed in. To cover such expenditures solely by means of tax increases violated every tenet of good sense, or so argued Barthou and Dumont. First, it was unfair to ask current taxpayers to assume the entire financial burden of legislation designed to protect present and future generations. Second, the government was now convinced that the country was not ready to pay for its defence by resorting to the controversial device of a personal income tax. However much the cabinet remained committed to the principle of such a tax, progressively scaled – as Barthou rather loosely reaffirmed in November – it was also sensitive to fears that this tax would require disclosure of all revenue income from investments as well as salaries.[69]

With that admission, the government exposed a soft underbelly. The critics howled that it was just another case of reform if necessary but not necessarily reform. With some accuracy, it should be said, Caillaux claimed the government had no will to make the rich pay, and thus was really only "walking on the spot." To which Barthou replied, "But precisely like you! I am only repeating precisely what you said!" Following which he proceeded to quote Caillaux, and thus himself, on the threats to personal privacy which were likely to accompany income tax legislation, ending with a smiling reproach, "I am but a pupil paying close attention to the lessons of his teacher."[70] There was, in short, some hypocrisy about.

There was another way to raise the revenues required for the new law, and in the government's estimation the only way. This was to raise money through a special bond issue. That is to say, instead of requiring heavy contributions from taxpayers, the government would attract contributions from investors. To do so, and quickly, the bond would offer a guaranteed annual return of 3 per cent for up to thirty years, tax free. The business community generally ap-

plauded, as was evinced by the welcome Barthou received from the
Comité républicain du commerce et de l'industrie.[71] The Budget
committee of the Chamber, dominated by Radicals, was much less
enthusiastic. Instead, it tried both to reduce the size of the target
figure and to delay the entire loan proposal by weighing it down
with ideas for a capital tax and for stiffer succession duties.[72] Caillaux's forces, in and outside the Budget committee, were picking up
the scent of crisis, and thus redoubled their efforts to portray the
government as an arm of wealthy investors.

On 19 November the committee finally accepted the principle of
the public loan, but continued to balk at raising the full 1.3-billion-
franc package.[73] The government persevered, refusing to budge
either on this or the increasingly sensitive tax-free provision. Indeed,
Barthou now proclaimed that this tax incentive would stand as a
point of confidence in his government. He nearly made it. On
1 December the Chamber approved both the principle of the public
loan and the amount targeted by the Finance ministry.[74] There
remained only the issue of the tax benefit. Here things began to
unravel, for there had been too many reservations about it from the
start. Yes, it would certainly attract investors, but it was seen by almost
the entire French left as a flagrant example of the state toadying
to private wealth – a charge which of course had been levelled at
Barthou over the *Rachat* of the Western railway. Furthermore, this
provision came under attack from those who feared the precedent-
setting nature of the benefit, and from those who claimed that the
taxing rights of future parliaments were being constrained by such
an undertaking. Caillaux said he had tried to warn Barthou that he
could never bring this provision through; and Poincaré, probably
with greater sincerity, had done the same thing. By the president's
reading, the mood of the Budget committee and of the Chamber
made it madness to insist on this one final measure. But Barthou
could not change direction, or would not.[75]

Poincaré was nervous as he watched the Chamber assemble on
2 December. The premier, a friend since their student days, was
inviting trouble, though with remarkable diffidence. Barthou "gives
me the impression that he does not care very much about retaining
power, indeed that he is not much disturbed by the fact that there
may be opening before him ... a way out which might preclude
disaster."[76] There was a lot to say for Poincaré's appraisal. The premier seemed to be experiencing a disgust-induced fatigue. Two
weeks earlier he had expressed some of it publicly.

Ah! Gentlemen, this government had an exceptionally difficult time of it
from the beginning. Some had pronounced it dead even before I had tried

to deliver it. They have given us a rough time, even through the recess; they have misrepresented our intentions, they have come close to accusing us of being political reactionaries, of betraying the Republic.[77]

This he found intolerable, but what magnified the affront was the opposition's refusal to risk a parliamentary vote on the government's overall program. Even the day before, he had challenged the Radicals and the Socialists to introduce an *interpellation* on the administration's general policy, instead of harassing it by clause and codicil.[78] He had not forgotten, of course, that this was the way of parliament and the role of the opposition. He simply wanted to have done with it, to put them down or be put down. As evidence of his state of mind, he told one audience that he had taken to reminding himself, daily, that "misfortune happens quickly."[79]

Such was his mood on the night of 2 December, prior to the Chamber's vote on the tax-free provision. Here was the last, and therefore the most formidable, hurdle. It was also Caillaux's last chance. The government, he said, was about to breach an act of parliament of 1908 by which revenues derived from such bond issues were in fact to be taxed. Moreover, if allowed to continue, the government's measure would effectively break faith with all previous investors who either had paid, or would be expected to pay, tax on similar investment income. Dumont replied that the measure was peculiar to this bond issue alone, and was intended to have no precedent-setting implications whatever. Moreover, he pointed out, this new wave of investors would not be exempt from the income tax legislation which parliament was still in the process of considering.[80]

It was not enough. The opposition wanted the premier. Barthou advanced slowly to the tribune, knowing full well that his cabinet was "in the lap of the gods." But there was no mood of resignation. It was the Barthou of Paul Flat, bristling and pugnacious. Repeating all the arguments yet again, he insisted that this benefit was essential for investor confidence and thus for the rapid sale of the bond issue. The Socialists laughed. Who, someone yelled, was threatening their confidence? To which a visibly irritated premier shot back: "Who? The budget committee." As *Le Temps* reported, it was at this moment that the government's cause was undone. Barthou knew it as well as anyone. Indeed, he added expressly that he accepted in advance the consequences of this remark. "One of those who interrupts me now, reproached me yesterday for only being concerned about political survival." On the contrary, "I care so little about surviving that I will not agree to anything equivocal, anything which could weigh down with uncertainty the intentions of this Government."[81] It was far from the discreet and judicious response that survival called for; and the Chamber sent him packing with a slim deficit of twenty-seven votes. Poincaré, when it was all over, shook Barthou's hand but could not help saying that it was really an act of suicide.[82]

It was no way to defend a government. That much is clear. But why, after waiting so long for the chance to be premier, had he let it slip so quickly? Blinded by those who have seen him as someone maddened by a thirst for power, we might grope forever in search of an explanation. But for those more familiar with his career, with his temperament, there is a perceptible consistency between his conduct in December 1913 and that under Dupuy, Méline, and Briand, premiers whom he had refused to back when he thought they were in the wrong. Such behaviour, of course, does much to explain his reputation for betrayal, but it disturbs the image of him as a man out for power at any price. Instead, if anything, his erratic ministerial fortunes are less suggestive of the power seeker than of one whose temperament demanded more freedom of expression than politics alone would allow and more opportunities for other forms of fulfilment. Thus, although probably unwelcome, his fall from political grace was not the tragedy it might have been for others, not when there were books to write, to buy and read, and something inside which could only be satisfied by literature and the company of writers. Louis Barthou needed the inspiration and, as he admitted, the consolation which these could bring to one so buffeted by political turbulence. It is therefore in no sense a *non sequitur* to record here his triumph as well as his defeat of December 1913. Sponsored by Paul Hervieu and Edmond Rostand, Barthou was unanimously elected to the Société des Gens de Lettres. And certainly for two reasons. He was, to cite Hervieu, an "eminent writer," notably the author of *Mirabeau*. Charles Le Goffic, the officer presiding over this election, went further, recalling Barthou's *L'Action syndicale* and his forthcoming *Impressions et essais*, and calling them models of their genre, impartial, well researched and skilfully written. But below the literary accomplishment, which was undeniable, there was present, unstressed, an appreciation of his recent political role and the suggestion that to him belonged "the gratitude ... of his fellow citizens."[83]

CHAPTER SIX

Collapse and Recovery, 1914–1919

My son does not belong to me, but to the Republic; it is She who will determine his responsibilities so that he can serve her well. [Danton][1]

The new year arrived and, at its debut, seemed likely to sustain the recent momentum in Barthou's political career. Within weeks of his fall from office he became involved in a new political initiative, one designed to prepare the republican centre for the spring general elections and, in the interim, to resist the anticipated follies of the new government. The latter was led by the Radical Socialist Gaston Doumergue, whom wags had quietly dubbed "La Joconde" in tribute to his smiling countenance.[2] He was smiling now, so it was said, because he was premier and Caillaux was only his finance minister – despite the normal convention of asking the principal slayer of one regime to form the succeeding administration. But President Poincaré had not been able to stomach having Caillaux in such an office, not because of any attachment to the toppled Barthou but because he feared giving Caillaux a free hand with either the three-year service law or the long-bruited income tax legislation. Doumergue, at least, had voted for the new military law, and had undertaken to honour the parliamentary vote of July 1913.

Prominent among those who opposed this Doumergue-Caillaux administration was a new Fédération des Gauches at the head of which were Louis Barthou and Aristide Briand. It was they, principally, who had fashioned this umbrella organization under which functioned their own Parti républicain démocratique, itself a reworked format of the old Alliance. And as such continuity might suggest, the Fédération was an attempt to revive less the substance than the image of the republican centre in time for the general elections. The substance was only too familiar: defence of the three-year law; support for the principle of public-secular education, without abolition of private-religious institutions; support in principle for the return of *scrutin de liste*, but only with provisions for minority representation; support in principle for a progressively based income tax, but only with adequate assurances for financial privacy; support in principle for further progressive social legislation, but only in ways consistent with maintaining a balanced budget.[3]

Little wonder the Radicals scoffed at this program of the federated "left." It was indeed a conservative platform, not so much because of its component planks – which had the right sound when hammered into place – but because of the spirit of the builders themselves. At the Fédération's core were some 130 deputies and senators, virtually all of whom had taken alarm at the return to power of the Radical Socialists – partly because this was a more uniformly Radical administration than ever before, partly because these were men who had allied with Jaurès, the Socialist, to fight the three-year law, and partly because of the personal factor that was Joseph Caillaux. Self-seen patriots feared him because of his secret dealings with Germany in 1911 and because of the way he had intrigued against Barthou and the three-year law. Others dreaded him more for his income tax ideas – the very principle itself, its association with the socialist virus, and the personal impetuosity with which the minister was expected to plough right ahead. Still others resented his sudden, recent, departure from the Parti républicain démocratique in order to assume leadership of the Radical Socialists. For a variety of reasons, therefore, the Fédération had every appearance of a bulwark designed to prevent Doumergue and Caillaux from doing anything reckless.

For this, Louis Barthou was an obvious leader. Here was a role consistent with the man that temperament and education had made of him. But there was more to his taking this role than the ideology of moderation. There was also something personal in the attempts to contain Caillaux, something which would play no small part in one of the tragedies toward which he was heading. Precisely how this happened is a matter of conjecture, an uncertainty underlined by the dogmatic but disparate verdicts of his own contemporaries. The fact was, and this does seem clear enough, that there had developed between him and Caillaux a deep, personal animus. Caillaux's published reflections expressly denied this, while affirming it implicitly. Barthou denied it as well, but it was a denial that was unconvincing from someone whom politics had left remarkably thin-skinned. Besides, it was evident to all that he had a score to settle with Caillaux for having brought down his government – so evident, in fact, that few bothered to look beyond the factor of revenge.

Barthou was certainly unhappy with Caillaux's behaviour in late 1913, a reaction fanned by the draught of a collapsing friendship. Yet the premier's own performance suggests that, consciously or otherwise, he was ready to leave office. Caillaux's role as a facilitator, while central to the fall, should perhaps not be overstressed. What seems to have enraged Barthou was less the betrayal – if indeed he so viewed it – than the hypocrisy to which it gave rise. Having man-oeuvred against the three-year law and pledged himself to restore the two-year service, Caillaux agreed to enter a government com-mitted to retaining the new military law. Having fought the principle of the financing loan, he was soon implementing it, indeed even increasing the amount targeted; and by February 1914 it looked very much as if he were going to retain the very tax-free *rente* on which he had felled the Barthou government. Indeed, it was Bar-thou's turn to accuse the government of encouraging speculation on government bonds – precisely because it now looked as if the tax-free provision might even be extended.[4] As for the much-heralded income tax, where was it, and in what form? Having excoriated his predecessor for failing to act promptly, why had Caillaux not pro-posed a solution, and why were his cabinet colleagues busy offering the same kinds of assurances to the business community which had been made by Dumont and Barthou himself? Incensed by what he took to be duplicity, Barthou reminded an audience in Le Havre of that stinging couplet from Racine's *Athalie*:

O promesse! ô menace! ô ténébreux mystère! Que de maux, que de biens sont prédits tour à tour![5]

The confrontation between government and leading spokesmen of the Fédération received close press attention, not the least aspect of which was Caillaux's alleged infidelity to his own "fiscal cate-chism."[6] Given the imminence of the spring elections, that was to be expected. What was unexpected was the escalation of a particular press campaign against Caillaux by the centrist-conservative *Le Figaro* and its editor, Gaston Calmette. Several features of that campaign are worthy of note, though none more so than the pattern which can be traced by the very sequence in which one chooses to present them.

First, the campaign was aimed directly at Caillaux and at certain aspects of his personal behaviour, past and current. He was accused of financial impropriety – personal, professional and political – and of flagrant deceit. Second, his accuser was a professional journalist, respected hitherto for his moderation and sense of journalistic responsibility; no guttersnipe. Here was a Calmette unseen before, engaged in some kind of personal vendetta against the country's finance minister.[7] Third, his campaign began at the end of December 1913 and continued sporadically until mid-March 1914, thus coinciding with the fall of Barthou, the rise of the Fédération des gauches, and its attendant offensive against the government. Thus assembled, this circumstantial evidence suggested a compelling link between the Fédération and *Figaro*. Moreover, the link was further strengthened by two additional facts. Calmette and Barthou were close personal friends, and, since mid-February 1914, Barthou had assumed responsibility for the propaganda efforts of the Parti républicain démocratique.[8] Tersely put, therefore, Louis Barthou was suspected of having been one of Calmette's principal animators and, in time, the most culpable of his executioners.

To this point, the general outline of what happened is clear enough. Having previously concentrated on Caillaux's alleged financial indiscretions, around mid-January Calmette was rumoured to be about to change the thrust of his attacks. Now, he was said to be ready to bring up the issue of Caillaux's clandestine dealings with Germany in 1911, and to do so with evidence drawn from secret government documents. The problem was that these documents, decoded German telegrams from 1911, would reveal at a stroke the cryptographic successes of French counter-intelligence services, and thus explain how Caillaux's covert manoeuvring had been discovered. The cost of exposing Caillaux, therefore, would include provoking an unpleasant diplomatic incident between France and Germany, and just at a time when reasonable men were trying to resolve a host of international apprehensions. For this reason, Louis Barthou, personal friend of Calmette, had undertaken to dissuade the journalist from publishing these decoded telegrams, the so-called *documents verts*. He spoke to Calmette on 14 January, secured the editor's assurance, and then relayed the good news back to a relieved government and a very much relieved Joseph Caillaux.[9]

But Calmette, it seems, had merely agreed to change weapons. By 19 January he had resumed his campaign in *Figaro*, with an emphasis upon other alleged transgressions by Caillaux. This literary onslaught continued sporadically through February 1914, and took new fire in the second week of March. On 10 March Calmette implicated the current finance minister in an old and apparently forgotten scandal from 1911, one which had taken on the appellation of the Rochette affair. In brief, Caillaux was now accused of having sought to obstruct the path of justice when he had been finance minister in the cabinet of Ernest Monis. According to Calmette, an ambitious but clumsy swindler by the name of Rochette had enjoyed protracted delays in the state's judicial proceedings against him – thanks to the protective intervention of powerful people in the cabinet, notably Caillaux.

Having rocked political and judicial circles with this sudden charge, Calmette then looked for something heavier still. On 13 March he published a private letter which Caillaux had penned to his first wife, currently referred to as Mme Guyedan. Although not embarrassing in any personal sense, it was to twice discomfit Joseph Caillaux. First, this letter of 1901 appeared to reveal him as a deputy who, while publicly backing the advent of an income tax, was really trying to impede proposals then being considered. In short, it suggested a duplicity that had a particular wounding relevance to the income tax advocacy of the finance minister of 1914. Second, the now public letter had been of a private character, and as such raised the question of its provenance. Who had supplied it to Calmette, and how many more were in the editor's possession? Caillaux had to live with the uncertainty of the latter, but he was convinced that the letter had gone from a bitter Mme Guyedan, to Calmette, through the conduit of a now uncertain friend and confirmed political opponent, namely Louis Barthou. They, Mme Guyedan and Barthou, had been seen one night in 1912, under a lamppost, examining a small package of letters.[10] Such, at least, was the version reported by Caillaux and his wife, Henriette. Who, they asked, was better placed than Barthou subsequently to place such ammunition in the hands of his friend the journalist?

By 14 March Caillaux was visibly unnerved. His tactic of retaining a dignified and disdainful silence seemed only to have quickened Calmette's audacity. The minister went to see President Poincaré, in the hope that this friend of long standing could do something to quell the campaign. Rattled by the barrage of public criticism, Caillaux was particularly disturbed by one rumour of Calmette's intent. The journalist was said to be ready to publish an official letter, written in March 1911 by the public prosecutor, M. Fabre, in which he had formally complained that his efforts to proceed against Rochette had been thwarted by the intrigues of Premier Monis and finance minister Caillaux. Caillaux hotly denied this accusation to Poincaré and said it was all the more reason to stop publication of this damning, untrue letter. Moreover, he added, as former justice ministers themselves, both Briand and Barthou would be hard pressed to explain how such a letter had found its way out of the Justice ministry. Given that consideration, together with the personal and political affinity which existed between the *Figaro*'s editor and Briand and Barthou, the president and finance minister reached an accord. Poincaré would ask Briand and Barthou to intervene with Calmette, expressly to stop publication of Fabre's letter.[11]

Continuing with Poincaré's detailed version of events — for Caillaux's memoirs say nothing of the preceding conversation — the president was unable to see Briand, who was out of Paris for the weekend. He did see Barthou, on the Saturday the 14th, but did not actually request an intervention with Calmette. Rather, when the issue of the Fabre letter was raised, Barthou said that he had discussed all this with Calmette on his own initiative and was satisfied that the letter would not be published. But Monday, 16 March, brought a new crisis. Calmette merely hinted that day that more revelations were imminent. Caillaux and Doumergue sought out Poincaré, urging him to stop Calmette from publishing the Fabre note by calling on the services of Briand and Barthou. The president did so, after 4 p.m. that afternoon, and received assurances — according to his version of events — that they would dissuade Calmette.[12]

Whether they actually had time to do so, late that afternoon, seems doubtful.[13] Whether Henriette Caillaux knew of any of these intended *démarches* is also uncertain. Neither is it known whether she was more upset by the political implications that might accompany revelation of the Fabre note, or by the rumours that Calmette had also acquired, through the same source, copies of personal letters exchanged between her and Caillaux prior to their marriage. But intent as she appeared on defending her husband, and on saving them both from the ignominy of further public inquiry into their private lives, Mme Caillaux resolved to act. How rational, or how distracted, she was at the time also remains controversial. The fact remains, however, that she went out, acquired a handgun and ammunition, took a taxi to the offices of *Figaro* at around 6 p.m., asked to see Calmette, and upon entering his office emptied her revolver into the hapless editor.

Unremarkably, she was charged with murder. Her husband, whose career some suspected had been the real reason for her action, promptly resigned from the government. Premier Doumergue reshuffled his cabinet and waited to see what might transpire in the Chamber. On 17 March it was apparent that the cause of the murdered editor would be taken up by others. There was little hope that the once almost forgotten Rochette affair would dissolve a second time, the more so as Calmette had died with a copy of the Fabre letter in his pocket. But only a copy. Doumergue denied any previous knowledge of this document and did what he could to cast doubt on the authenticity of the recovered copy. "What value has this mere copy?" Without the original letter, signed by Fabre, if such ever existed, all the country had were "baseless accusations." At this point Barthou approached the tribune and, following some controlled, introductory remarks, calmly read the original Fabre letter into the record of the Chamber.[14] Before he had finished, it was clear to all deputies that the original Rochette commission of inquiry would have to be reconvened in the light of this new evidence.

Much of this story has been told before, and more thoroughly.[15] Those accounts, like this, have relied heavily upon the versions supplied by the press, Poincaré, and Caillaux. None, of course, has sought to highlight Barthou's involvement, and yet no account of this affair would be possible without invoking his role in some way. The fact remains that Louis Barthou either was, or was made to be, central to the tragedy that befell Gaston Calmette. Part of the circumstantial case against him has already been made, touching first upon motive – disgust at Caillaux's hypocrisy as well as a desire for revenge – and second upon opportunity – his political and personal ties to Calmette. To this may be added the indictments furnished over time by Caillaux and Poincaré, indictments which are very much part of their own defensive positions.

On balance, Caillaux seemed convinced that Poincaré had been more instrumental in Calmette's campaign than had Barthou. Not that it was easy for him to think that either friend had conspired against him. Indeed, his memoirs try to keep afloat the figure of a man far too innocent and naive to think such thoughts. By his telling, it took him over two months to even suspect that Calmette was only someone's valet. Slowly too did it dawn on him that the president, to whom he had turned, was distressingly composed about this ongoing wave of crises – "dry as a pumice-stone." Even then, it took some years for Caillaux to translate Poincaré's detachment into evidence that the president had actively plotted against him. From that moment, Caillaux never wavered in that conviction, never reconciled with Poincaré.[16]

He was kinder on Barthou, possibly because he thought him less substantial than Poincaré. Barthou, he was sure, had schemed with Calmette and Mme Gueydan. That was his style, a southerner, often impulsive, always a schemer, but not up to designing the kind of sustained campaign conducted by *Figaro*. Barthou, he convinced himself, was simply used by Poincaré to play a larger and a dirtier game than he would have envisaged on his own. Apart from his assessments of their personalities, Caillaux drew on two other points.

First, it had been Barthou who had intervened with Calmette in January to prevent publication of the *documents verts*. Second, following that intervention, on meeting and thanking Barthou, Caillaux had detected no hint of personal bitterness, nothing of the sort that it would take to deform legitimate political differences into a highly public and personal vendetta. In short, Caillaux was satisfied that Louis Barthou had played but a secondary role in this personal and political crisis. Accordingly, he did effect a reconciliation with Barthou in the 1920s, and seemed genuinely moved when Barthou died in the autumn of 1934.[17]

Caillaux's chief suspect, Raymond Poincaré, was much tougher on Barthou – perhaps justifiably. But the fact is that, as a suspect himself, there was an advantage in having some credible alternative. Put simply, Poincaré mounted a kind of triple defence against Caillaux's growing suspicions, Clemenceau's public accusations, and anyone in the future who might repeat either. Prior to the publication of his personal diary in 1927, Poincaré let it be known that he considered Barthou's role in the Calmette business "inexcusable," and seems deliberately to have leaked a story to the effect that Barthou had indeed confessed to having furnished the letters with which Calmette had paid with his life.[18] The published diary added to the effect with a satisfying combination of direct and indirect remarks. Among the former were the repeated protestations of his own innocence in the *Figaro* campaign, and his repeated regrets about "poor Calmette." Among the latter was his well-timed and subtly expressed regret that the journalist had become involved in the campaign of Caillaux's political enemies, a campaign which he obliquely attributed to Barthou with the claim that the Béarnais knew more about that campaign than any man alive.[19] The image gets sharper still (at least such was Poincaré's intent) when one adds to this the impression of how he had helped Caillaux by calling on Barthou's influence with Calmette: in mid-January over the German telegrams, an intervention which Barthou attributed to Doumergue and not Poincaré; on 14 March, when Barthou assured the president that he had already secured Calmette's cooperation, on his own initiative; on 16 March, when it appears the only intervention initiated by Poincaré was made extraneous by the actions of Mme Caillaux.

The president's third line of defence was a master stroke. Having sent circulating the rumour of Barthou's confession, Poincaré declined to publish a full version of his entry for 17 March – the gist of which is as follows. Barthou arrived in the president's office, full of remorse, and admitted that he had fed Calmette the Fabre letter, though only after having secured the journalist's assurance that the letter would not be published in full. In all likelihood, there would be a new commission of inquiry, before which he intended to tell the truth. He had discussed the whole business with his brother and his wife, and this is what they had advised. Indeed, Alice had even threatened to leave him if he did not tell the commission everything he knew.[20] In summary, by this unpublished version – to which Barthou obviously had no opportunity to reply – Poincaré established two things. Barthou had been behind Calmette, and all Barthou's denials of this had been lies.

It may be that Poincaré was as close to the truth as we are likely to come. In short, he was not involved in the campaign to discredit Caillaux, despite his own very close ties with Calmette; Barthou and Briand were; and Barthou lied when he denied having given the Fabre letter to Calmette.[21] It may also be that Caillaux's reading of the situation, based on his knowledge of Poincaré and Barthou, was fundamentally accurate. Namely, that Poincaré's detached behaviour prior to 16 March, and his passionate professions of innocence thereafter, were symptomatic of someone with a guilty conscience.[22] Caught between the allegations of Poincaré and the contrary suspicions of Caillaux, a reader will not be heartened to hear of Aristide Briand. Predictably, he denied having had any role in the Calmette campaign, and admitted only to having passed on the original Fabre note in January 1913 to his successor in the justice ministry, Louis Barthou. When he discovered that Calmette had acquired a copy of that note, from an unknown source, he had advised the editor not to publish it. That is all. Or rather, that is essentially all Briand ever said on the matter – a testimony which his most recent biographer admits to being incomplete and thus unpersuasive.[23] And then there is the deposition and testimony of Louis Barthou to the second Rochette commission and the evidence which he gave in connection with the trial of Mme Caillaux.

Barthou's defence rested, like those of the other principals, on denial and custom-designed arguments. Among the first was the necessity of denying any role in Calmette's press campaign. Although he and the murdered editor had been friends for twenty-five years, "Neither at close-hand nor from afar, neither directly nor indirectly, was I involved in the campaign waged by M. Calmette against M. Caillaux."[24] Next, and in keeping with that categoric statement, he specifically denied having conveyed any of the letters once in Mme Guyedan's possession to the offices of Le Figaro. He knew nothing of such letters, had never seen them, never passed them on to anyone; indeed, he had not even known of Caillaux's letter on the income tax – that signed "Ton Jo" – until Calmette had published it.

I have never seen them, I have never read them, I know nothing about them, I do not even know if they exist and, if so, what they contain.[25]

Finally, he had retained the original Fabre note – received from Briand in January 1913 – but had refused to show it to anyone, including Calmette and other journalists who had asked to see the document which rumour had already made famous.[26] Only one thing in this connection would he admit. On 9 March, when he realized that Calmette had acquired a copy of the Fabre note – from some unidentified source – he had verbally confirmed for the editor that his acquired text was authentic.[27] For those interested in such subtleties, it is this admission which takes us as close as Barthou's testimony will allow to Poincaré's unpublished report of Barthou's confession on 17 March.

The arguments which Barthou invoked to support his assertions can be reduced to the following, in ascending order of importance. First, although he alone had the original letter signed by Fabre, he claimed that copies of that document had been seen by others, well before Calmette. Specifically, he testified that Jules Sauerwein of *Le Matin* had acquired a copy sometime in 1913. In other words, the copy found on Calmette need not have come directly – and by Barthou's testimony did not come – from the Fabre original.[28] Second, Barthou argued that the strongest proof of his innocence lay in the fact that he had not used the Fabre weapon in 1913 to silence Caillaux before he had undermined the Barthou administration. He had received the letter from Briand in January 1913 – by their telling, an exchange conducted privately in deference to the political sensitivity of the document – and yet had never used it to restrain Caillaux's attacks on the three-year law and its attendant financing. Having thus acted in 1913, when his own government was at stake, why, he asked, would he have pulled it out for use in 1914?[29] Third, far from having intrigued against Caillaux, he had several times intervened on the finance minister's behalf, and earned the minister's thanks. On two occasions, in January, he had so acted, first at Doumergue's behest – and without reference to Poincaré – by securing Calmette's promise not to publish the *documents verts*, second by warning Caillaux that his ex-wife, Mme Gueydan, seemed intent on revenge.[30] Then on 9 March, Barthou testified, he and Briand had talked to Calmette entirely on their own initiative. It was then they had learned that the editor had acquired a copy of the Fabre letter, then that Barthou had confirmed the general accuracy of that copy, and then that they had secured the journalist's undertaking not to publish that document.[31] Finally, though this was not made in any way central to Barthou's own testimony, we know from Poincaré's account that Barthou and Briand had agreed to undertake yet another *démarche* to Calmette on 16 March, an intention preempted by Calmette's death two hours later. In sum, this was not the action of one bent on destroying Joseph Caillaux.

Not everyone was, or will be, convinced. It is clear that some members of the second Rochette commission were troubled by Barthou's failure to explain why he had kept the Fabre document at all. If he had not intended to use it for some political purpose, then why not return it to the Justice ministry, even destroy it? To which he replied, lamely, that he had received it as a personal charge from Briand and felt honour-bound to keep it safe and secure. Perhaps more difficult to explain than why he had kept it secret was the explanation for why he had revealed it to parliament on 17 March. It seemed hardly in his own best interests. Poincaré had urged him to tell the whole truth, except for saying anything about the Fabre note – which he expressly counselled him to forget. Not perhaps laudable, but definitely logical.[32] To the president's considerable irritation, Barthou took candour to extremes. He acknowledged that he had taken from the Justice ministry a document, handed to him by a cabinet minister, and that this very document – or rather a copy – might have been the reason for a man's death. In short, by reading the Fabre note from the tribune of the Chamber, he had connected himself to a murder.

To this conundrum another may be added. Many on the political left explained his action as being demonstrative proof of his obsession with being revenged on Caillaux. Even at the price of discrediting himself, he was prepared to do anything to discredit Caillaux; again, not a laudable action, but one which had a certain twisted logic. However, this is not the remorseful, guilt-ridden Barthou whom Poincaré described on 17 March, hours before the Chamber debate. Nor was it the man whom Caillaux himself detected, a friend to whom intrigue was natural but to whom a pathological hatred was not. Just as compelling an explanation, therefore, is Barthou's own account, one which is consistent with the personality of a man whom we have followed with some care. Before leaving for the Chamber that afternoon, he had asked a younger colleague, Léon Bérard, whether he should take the Fabre note with him, in the event that he should face questions from the floor. They decided between them that it was unlikely the need would arise, but that it would not hurt to have it with him. He did not *intend*, he said, to reveal it; but as he listened to the debate, the opposition's questions, the premier's responses, he suddenly decided that he had no choice but to read the letter. As he saw it, Calmette's honour as a journalist, and as a friend, was in danger of being compromised by suggestions that his campaign against Caillaux had been based on spurious documents.[33]

Not everyone was convinced, certainly not the jury which rallied to the defence of Mme Caillaux in July 1914 and acquitted this confessed murderess of both premeditated and unpremeditated homicide. The other principals fared less well. Calmette, her victim, had had his name dragged through the mud as one of the imperatives of her defence. Caillaux was out of office again, and in for even rougher times ahead. Barthou, Briand, and Poincaré were left alone with their consciences – a deserved fate in the eyes of the self-righteous. Such a one was Maurice Barrès, a member of the Rochette commission of inquiry, but a deputy of the right who had absolutely no brief to make for any of those called to testify in March 1914. Nonetheless, he acknowledged considerable admiration for Barthou's plucky performance. The little Béarnais had come into a commission full of hostile Radical Socialists and taken them all on. If looks could kill, Barrès said, Barthou would have followed Calmette there and then. But he attacked instead. He testified that Caillaux had once told him that he had indeed tried to get Rochette off in 1911, out of fear of blackmail. It was not what the Radicals wanted to hear, though it amused Barrès. What was it, he wondered, which had brought men to these depths? Considering the likes of Barthou, or Caillaux, or Briand, there was no grand clash of idea or ideal. In fact, if anything they were too much alike, like three young dogs in the parliamentary kennel, perfectly accommodating until food – or power – arrived under their noses. Then came the noisy squabbles, touched off by the tussle for purely personal advantage.[34]

The indelible image of *les trois chiens* is amusing, disagreeable, and, in this context at least, more than a little warranted. There is nothing very redeeming about the Caillaux-Calmette affair, and no wand to turn it into something worthy. Nevertheless, those interested in Barthou will know now, or will quickly discover, that he too was one of the principal political casualties of this unbecoming affair, and not always for reasons of evidence. After all, no empirical evidence was ever produced to prove Barthou's complicity in Calmette's campaign. Indeed, when it comes to evidence there is a savage irony in the fact that Calmette died either because of one letter, which he never did publish, or because of a cache of private letters, which were never found. For this reason, it may be appropriate to offer some final impressions of this incident, impressions which themselves have only a partial evidentiary basis.

We know, on the basis of his account, confirmed by others, that Barthou did several times intercede on Caillaux's behalf. We also know that Alice Barthou did not carry out the threat to leave her husband if he did not answer with the truth, a fact which is as eligible to defend Barthou as it is – in Poincaré's account – to belittle him. More striking still, indeed remarkable, is Barthou's consistent refusal to speculate on the guilt of others. Before the Rochette commission, and during the pre-trial and trial proceedings for Mme Caillaux, he made no attempt to defend himself by implicating others. He did not blame Briand, or Poincaré, or anyone else for Calmette's campaign; and he did not suggest that the journalist had really brought it on his own head, any more than he implied Caillaux had all this coming to him.[35] Indeed, in the face of a particularly nasty verbal attack by Caillaux's friend, the deputy Ceccaldi, Barthou told the silent courtroom that, while deeply resenting the remarks, he had to admire the spirit of friendship which had triggered them. There is a dignity here, an admittedly angry dignity, which seems very much to his credit.[36] Finally, and more subjectively still, the avowedly sympathetic listener may detect in Barthou's formal declarations a candour and directness which are consistent with our previous constructions of his earlier political career. But let the reader judge.

Addressing a friendly audience in April 1914, Barthou evoked the memory of the fallen Calmette, in whose name he had exposed the Fabre original in parliament.

That much I did. I don't regret having done so. Now, as always, today like yesterday, tomorrow like today, in the Chamber, in public meetings, in the face of parliamentary colleagues, before the electors of Oloron whom I have represented for twenty-five years, I will stick to what I have said, and I will accept responsibility for what I have done. Whatever they may do, whatever they try to do, whatever doubt they try to create, I will say, I will shout, that in my conscience I am absolutely certain that I did my duty, my whole duty, and nothing but my duty.

At which point a voice from the audience congratulated him on the courage he had shown.

No, citizen, you are mistaken. It takes no courage to speak one's mind, or to assume responsibility for what one has done. ... I have twenty-five years of parliamentary life behind me ... I have been involved in a lot of things, and certainly I would not pretend to think, or have the presumption to suggest, that I have always been right. But there are some times when you know in your heart that you have done the right thing.[37]

However he may now be judged, the voters of Oloron remained as loyal as ever. They were unmoved by the accusations of the Parisian left and conversely attracted by his shift toward the centre in the form of the new Fédération. Clearly, they liked his self-styled description, "neither a backward conservative, nor a reckless revolutionary," and gave him their enthusiastic electoral support in 1914. He received 84 per cent of the ballots cast, as opposed to 7 per cent for a socialist opponent and just under 9 per cent for his rival on the right.[38] The Fédération, however, did less well. The Socialists and the Radical Socialists had campaigned effectively against what they said were the two greatest failures of the previous legislature – the passing of the three-year service law, and the continued refusal to pass an income tax bill. Their reward was an increase of some thirty seats in the Chamber for the Socialists and another dozen for the Radicals, bringing the former to over one hundred deputies and the latter to over two hundred. Between them, whenever accord could be reached, they could more or less ensure a solid working majority in the Chamber of Deputies.[39] That is why the Doumergue regime lasted until June, and why it succeeded first, and briefly, by that of the Radical Alexandre Ribot, and then by that of the independent socialist, René Viviani. It was the latter, with Doumergue at the Quai d'Orsay and Messimy at the War ministry, who supervised France's halting entry into war with Germany in August 1914.

Europe's tragedy had begun, that of Louis Barthou was just beginning. The preceding year and a half had brought unprecedented vituperation, but also unaccustomed acclaim. As a politician he had been instrumental in securing passage of the three-year military service law – the importance of which had become more obvious with the approach of war – and had remained a leading figure in the campaign to see that the new Chamber did not rescind what had been accomplished. As a writer he had entered the fold of the Société des Gens de Lettres, become president of the Livre Contemporain, and submitted in July 1914 his candidacy for Henry Roujon's vacant chair at the Académie Française.[40]

Nevertheless, when war came he was out of office; and when Viviani reconstructed his cabinet at the end of August, intent on placing prominent men in roles of national leadership, Barthou received no call to service. Briand was brought back, and Delcassé; so too Millerand, and Ribot. Even the Socialist Jules Guesde was included. But there was no room for Barthou, not even in a cabinet expressly built on the themes of patriotism and national unity. Once too often he had offended the left; and the Calmette-Caillaux affair, for all of its unproven allegations, was the freshest and most egregious cut of all. His undermining of Caillaux through the exposure of the Fabre note had set the entire left against him, Viviani noted, and thus precluded any possibility of his being brought into a government pledged to unity.[41]

There was another price to pay. On 3 August, when war was declared, Max Barthou found his father in the library. "Papa, I'm here to ask your permission to enlist." Alarmed by the gravity of such a request on the part of an eighteen-year-old, Barthou questioned whether this was a carefully considered step. The reply was instant and unequivocal. "Yes, I've given it a lot of thought. And surely you, who have asked France to sacrifice so much, cannot honestly deny me."[42] His father reluctantly agreed. His mother only consented, for the bond between her and this only child had been strengthened by the frequent absences imposed by Louis's public life. Pierre Loti later recalled that bond, picturing as he did this young Max seated on the floor, at his mother's knee, playing with the family's old Siamese cat; and Yvonne Sarcey said she always thought of him as "your Max, Madame," an engaging young man who was keen on literature, music, art, indeed everything except – as he teased his father – politics![43]

But jokes were put aside with the war. Max left for his basic training and was subsequently posted to General Joffre's headquarters well behind the front lines. He was safe there, but restless. For her part, Alice too engaged in service. Armed with a new Red Cross diploma, she became head nurse in a military hospital at Larressore near Bayonne in the south-west.[44] As for her husband, he was soon involved in a variety of state-administered services. In August he considered taking up a proposal from Messimy that he actually be commissioned in the eastern army as a patriotic writer and tub-thumper. Instead, he opted to assist the War ministry in Paris with its efforts to reorganize the entire military health service. Meeting in the Invalides, under the chairmanship of Paul Doumer, the organization was called the Commission de co-ordination des secours volontaires.[45] It may have been in that capacity that Barthou was able to visit Max toward the end of November 1914, when he discovered his son's latest resolve.

Here, I'm just too safe; with my name, it doesn't seem right. Should I not be setting an example? Papa, as the "son" of the three-year service law, I think I should be doing three times what others are doing![46]

He wanted to be transferred to the Alsatian front, and asked his father to back the request for such a posting. Some days later, in a letter of 5 December to Georges Cain, Barthou reported that he was hard at work on *Lamartine orateur*, that Alice was still at Larressore, and that Max was due to be shipped to Thann in a few days.[47]

Max Barthou arrived in Alsace on Saturday, 12 December, having been able to work in a twenty-four-hour leave with his parents two days before. On Sunday he wrote to his father, thanking him for having supported his transfer to the front, within earshot of the German guns. On Monday, while walking in the streets of Thann, he was killed outright by a German artillery shell. His letter arrived in Paris the following day, only moments before the lawyer and family friend, M. Lescouvé, arrived to break the news of his death. Poincaré, too, went immediately to the grief-stricken parents. Barthou was unable to converse. He sat repeating his son's words: "With your name, papa, I owe it to the country."[48]

The grief in the father's voice was unmistakable, but was there not as well some chord of guilt? The three-year law, the consent for Max to enlist, the support for his transfer to the front, each now took on the form of an accusation that could never be withdrawn. But even worse, there is some suggestion that Alice may have reinforced this special anguish. Utterly devastated by this loss, she is said to have begun some kind of withdrawal from the routine of her former life, and exhibited a new-found piety as she searched for consolation within the Church. More telling still, she is said sometimes to have expressed her grief in verbal recrimination against her husband, being particularly outraged by any possibility that he could draw political benefit from their son's sacrifice.[49] Here, it must be stressed that the evidence, if it can be so called, is indeed thin; however, it is consistent with some of the familiar patterns detected by those who study grief. It also seems to be in a kind of loose accord with Alice Barthou's own perplexing, passionate relationship with Pierre Loti. And since conjugal relations may be said to have some bearing on the human condition, Alice's interest in Loti may offer up something to those primarily concerned with her husband.

For those unfamiliar with Loti, it may be said that his works are redolent of exotic places and romantic athleticism – and all putatively autobiographical. Sixty-four years of age in 1914, he still cut a dashing figure and surrounded himself in alias-abetted mystery. One of those men whom women were said to find irresistible, he had something childlike in his manner, something that demanded attention and pampering – but strictly on his own terms, and at his own time. We know less of Alice Barthou, and indeed very little of her life before World War One. We do know, however, that she was smitten by Loti when still a schoolgirl and carried that devotion to her first meeting with the famous writer in 1906. It was a meeting which she initiated and arranged for herself and her husband. From this, it seems safe to suggest that the romanticism of Pierre Loti, man and writer, struck very deep chords within Mme Barthou.

Judging from what she would later write about the exotic delights of Morocco, and recalling her complaints about the forced rhythm of Paris where she led the custom-disciplined life of a prominent *bourgeoise*, Loti's books were an escape for her, to the South Seas, the Orient, the Near East. His presence was a more complete release. With Max's death, and Loti's own genuine grief, the writer became supremely important to the recovery of Alice Barthou. By 1916 they had agreed between themselves that she would be his *marraine de guerre*, the wartime mother who "adopted" some soldier in need of care packages and affectionate correspondence. Loti, like thousands of much younger Frenchmen, would be the *filleul*, the adopted child or godson.

It was a wartime custom, but there was an intensity on the part of this forty-three-year-old woman that could not have been common to many *marraines*. No longer did she address her letters "Cher Monsieur ... et Ami," as she had done in 1909. Now, there was something more familiar.

Tenderly, so tenderly, I embrace you my dearest friend, oh so dear! Tell me at least that you know how much I love you, and that you also love me a little – however little – ... Let me come back, to be right beside you ... to hold your hand in mine, gently and with untold tenderness.[50]

Even with allowances for the carefully observed *vouvoiement*, these are surely the outpourings of an exceptionally attentive friend. Indeed, as her husband wrote to Loti: "I think she is falling in love with her godson!"[51]

More than ever convinced that underneath the Loti exterior there was a "delightful, if cultivated, childlike quality," Alice found a new outlet for her maternal needs.[52] When time permitted, and Loti allowed, she would slip away from Larressore, or later from Paris, to visit him at his country residence at Hendaye or his principal home at Rochefort. His health was failing, a condition which brought out all the caring qualities of mother and nurse. Together, these ensured the most attentive medical care, but often a care conveyed in a brusque and peremptory manner. There were times when it seemed as if his medical needs were only a pretext for Alice to take charge of his whole life.[53] More than once he took umbrage, on one

occasion upbraiding her for her "bossy manner," describing her behaviour as "cutting" and her personality as "abrasive and arrogant"
– the product, he ventured to suggest, "of all the attention you get
as the wife of one of our famous politicians."[54] She surely found it
no easier, admitting on occasion to some difficult moments brought
on by this cosseted writer. But Loti was Loti, a man of genius who
needed the adoration of surrogate mothers and who, in return,
promised escape. Escape from Paris, "the intolerable, vile Paris," to
the deserts of North Africa or to Loti's own "maison enchantée" in
Rochefort where she could dress in veil and *haïc*, and sit with him
on pillows, in his private mosque, before the *stèle* of Ahziyadé. Here
on the shores of the Atlantic, they would share visions of men in
flying bournous, giant palm trees and camel caravans, while fending
off what she called the "cruel realities of life."[55]

Reality was equally cruel for her husband. He was crushed by
Max's death, and was never strong enough or artful enough to conceal it. A year and a half after the tragedy at Thann he could still
be reduced to tears by some unexpected reminder of his son.[56] Seven
years later, when as war minister he had to lay a wreath at the tomb
of the Unknown Soldier, observers noticed the tears coursing down
his cheeks as he thought, yet again, of Max. Even a decade after
Thann, any reference to those who had fallen in the name of their
country was enough to bring tears rushing to his eyes.[57] Moreover,
Louis Barthou never forgot that this was a shared tragedy. In June
1916 some innocent remark at a restaurant table touched off more
tears. When a companion tried to explain to an onlooker that he
was thinking of his son, from behind those tears Barthou managed
a choked correction – "of my son, and of my wife."[58]

That October, he included in one letter a thinly veiled reference
to Alice, who was still serving as a wartime nurse.

Her white uniform covers her mourning clothes. All the tenderness of her
mother's heart, still bleeding from an unclosable wound, goes to the
wounded young men in her care.[59]

Yet again, in a letter of March 1919 to Marshal Lyautey, projecting
a visit to Morocco the following month, Barthou expressed the hope
that this visit would serve "as a much-needed distraction for her
shattered emotions."[60] Therefore, if it is in the context of personal
tragedy that one can appreciate Alice's intense attachment to Loti,
that same context also offers evidence of her husband's understanding and compassion. He too became increasingly close to Loti as he
realized, however wryly, that the writer was helping to hold Alice

together. Thus it was that he joked about the jealousy she betrayed of anyone who came too close to her *filleul*, including her own husband.[61]

For him there were only three roads to recovery, and one of them was still sealed. Several times throughout the course of 1915, in May, July, and October, Poincaré's diary refers to some talk of bringing Barthou into the Viviani cabinet. The premier wanted to do so, but again and again he encountered stubborn resistance from socialist colleagues who threatened to resign. Whether or not there was more to it than this, the crucial sticking point always proved to be the incident of the Fabre note, although Barthou himself preferred to think that he was paying a price for the three-year law.[62] In late October, Aristide Briand became the new premier, with an expanded cabinet designed to include every cross-section of political allegiance. But Barthou remained out, the problem unchanged. Instead of a portfolio he was offered missions to Spain or Roumania. He declined both, principally on the grounds that he could not leave Alice, who, at last, was finding some consolation in her ministrations to the wounded in Paris.[63]

A second avenue was one he had been on since the outbreak of the war: state service in the form of various commissions, most relating to the medical treatment and rehabilitation of wounded soldiers. In January 1915, at the behest of war minister Millerand, he agreed to serve as vice-president of the Commission supérieure consultative de santé militaire and, in this capacity, to liaise with the Fédération Nationale d'Assistance aux Mutilés.[64] In some quite different role, he and Pichon had been behind a special Franco-Italian conference in September 1915, the ostensible purpose of which had been to liberate from German influence the Banca Commerciale Italiana. More broadly, however, there was some hope that out of this small beginning could grow a strategy for the economic encirclement of Germany.[65]

The year 1916 brought more state service, although still nothing at cabinet level. In the spring there were rumours that the Briand government was going to fall, predictions that gave rise to speculation about a possible replacement. Some thought that Barthou was in for a portfolio, despite socialist objections; others thought that he might even be asked to form a government. Indeed, there were signs at the beginning of June that he, too, believed that his moment had come.[66] It had not. Briand weathered the crisis, and Barthou remained on the outside. By the end of the year he was more frustrated than ever. Mme Sainsère, an old friend of Barthou, reported his disgust to Poincaré: "To think that they will simply have left energy like mine go to waste instead of using it in the war effort!" Poincaré understood, despairing about a political world too finite to make room for a man of Barthou's capacities.[67]

To his credit, the outcast continued to serve where they would let him. Increasingly, this was leading him into more visible roles. In November 1916, for instance, he prepared a piece for *Le Monde illustré* in which he described the work of the military health commission, and pleaded for cooperation from the vast governmental bureaucracy which too often got in the way. Some of it was necessary, even useful, he granted, but much was obstructive and irrelevant. The new motto for the war, he suggested, ought to be "Less paper and more action."[68] Earlier in the year his work for the commission had taken him to the Italian front, a visit which allowed for a few exhilarating moments high above Venice in a French military aircraft. And in July he had visited wounded French prisoners interned by international agreement in Switzerland. No pleasure this, to walk amid the rows of wounded, marvelling at the dedication of Red Cross workers but barely able to contain his hatred of the interned Germans he encountered, "specimens of a lesser breed, cowed themselves by force, now out to rule by it."[69]

This kind of hate-filled, publicly delivered judgment, genuine as it surely was, was also suggestive of a new role which Barthou assumed in 1916, alongside his service on the military health commission. Early that year he was enlisted in a government effort to combat pacifist propaganda with the writings and speeches of prominent patriots.[70] In that cause, Barthou published three volumes of collected letters, articles, and speeches between 1916 and 1917, all designed in their way to combat defeatism and inspire public confidence in the war effort. This is not the place to examine these writings in detail; however, some consideration of them is warranted here in the interest of appreciating his wartime role and, inferentially, his wartime state of mind.[71]

By his telling, the European tragedy had begun with the creation of Germany by Prussia in its own image – "brutal, violent and hypocritical." Then, in 1914, in "the most vile national crime which has ever bloodied and stained human history," Germany had attacked Belgium and France. By so doing, she proved for all time that her race stood only for "barbarity, perfidy and treachery."[72] Comparing French and Germans now was like confusing men and machines, for a German, "in my eyes, is no longer a man." One could not think of negotiating a peace with them, people who had started the war and were now rightly afraid of losing it. For France it was strictly a matter of going "jusqu'au bout," right to the bitter end, no peace talks, no compromises. Indeed, not even defeating Germany would be enough. "We must level her, reduce her to impotence and hate her still." Yes, he repeated, "Hate the Germans with all the intensity ensured by our claims against them. Hate them bitterly, violently, relentlessly. Between them and us, it is a struggle to the death." And when it was over, when Germany was defeated, she would have visited upon her a punishment – "implacable, inexorable, without pity ... on the bandit kings ... on the army of thieves, arsonists and killers and ... yes, on the German people, stupidly misled by their masters or cravenly intimidated." How mindless were those who thought it could be otherwise, those who still, still entertained visions of future reconciliation! People like this, who believe forgiveness is the best guarantee for a lasting peace, "will never have me under their banner. I will rely on hatred."[73]

But one could not penetrate the dark German recesses without the light cast by the sacred cause to which France and her allies had rallied. That light now burned brighter still, he maintained, because of the national reconciliation which the German outlaws had effected among Frenchmen. They thought we were divided, Barthou said, but they were wrong. He had seen in the trenches French Catholics and French Jews minister to each other's wounds, French privates *tutoient* their officers, peasant soldiers march beside students of the Ecole des Beaux Arts, all of them caught up in the momentum of a just cause. And at home, among *les civlos*, this national unity was finding other forms of expression, including the inauguration of the "Union Française," to whom he spoke in October 1916. Postal workers and railway men, he observed, were raising funds for the war effort, and their example was being followed by others. In a moving appeal by a bereaved father, Barthou addressed those whose loved ones were still at the front. It was up to those at home to support their men in uniform by subscribing generously to the war bond program.

People of France, you are now of but one opinion: that of France. Your old divisions have been erased, your old quarrels vanished, the old differences among you discarded. ... To invest in war bonds is to fight. To invest is to vanquish.[74]

German perfidy, French national unity and sacrifice, confidence in victory, such were the themes to which Barthou perpetually returned in 1916–17. These, and one more, the personal side of which required no embellishment. This was the heroic role played by the women of France, by *les vaillantes*. In a speech delivered at the Sorbonne in April 1917, to an association called L'Effort de la France et de ses Alliés, Barthou recalled the extraordinary services of the French Red Cross, an umbrella organization which comprised the Société de secours aux blessés militaires, the Union des Femmes de France, and the Association des Dames Françaises, each of which had representatives on his own military health commission. These women, over 375,000 of whom were at work in the civilian sector alone, had rendered precious service to the war effort, whether through their care of the wounded, the blind, orphans, widows, or refugees. Moreover, women were at work in countless other ways, in banks, the public service, industry, and transport. France, he predicted, was embarked on a new industrial and social revolution, the coming of which he applauded. By her service, by meeting men on equal terms in this great national defence effort, the French woman was making an irrefutable case for equal rights with male citizens. From her sacrifice, happiness was sure to follow. But for the moment, he recognized there was little enough happiness for the women of France. Their current work only provided consolation at best, especially for those who had been destined to outlive their sons, those for whom living now required more courage than dying. And then, in a covert reference to Alice, Louis Barthou recalled some lines from Pierre Loti, in which the celebrated author had expressed thanks for the comfort he had drawn from strong and noble women "who have just lost what to them was the closest and dearest, an only son."[75]

The following month, in May 1917, Barthou again found himself on a podium, this time to give a public lecture on physical fitness to the Université des Annales. Called at very short notice to fill in for a speaker who was either "sick, dead, or a minister," Barthou made light of the fact that he had not succumbed to any of "these three mishaps."[76] But he was much more anxious than he appeared, anxious about the war effort and therefore about his enforced exile from government. He found the Russian situation very worrisome: "I am very gloomy." And the home front in France was "bad, very bad," where "pacifism and defeatism went unchecked."[77] In September, Alexandre Ribot, premier since March, was trying to save his government. A cabinet shuffle was in order. Again, Barthou's name came up, and again it was dropped after soundings among the Socialists.[78] Not until Ribot's efforts failed, and Paul Painlevé was asked to form a cabinet, was Barthou made a minister of state, that is, a minister without portfolio. After almost four years of exile Barthou was back, "smiling and playful," as Poincaré found him.[79] Happier still was he when, in late October, he was able to replace a resigning

Ribot as foreign minister. It was his first appointment to the Quai d'Orsay. It also proved to be one of his briefest tenures as cabinet minister, for the misfortunes which had dogged his ministerial career were far from over.

What happened to him is easily enough explained. Why it happened is a question of another order, the more so because we are even more dependent than usual on the impressions left by everyone except Barthou himself. Having just acquired its new foreign minister on 23 October 1917, the Painlevé cabinet very quickly gave way, on 16 November, to a Clemenceau administration. The incoming premier did not want Barthou, judging him, as was relayed by Poincaré, "pas sûr," or not solid enough.[80] Majestically ambiguous, this short phrase invites interpretations, two of which are most apparent, although neither seems fully compelling.

Nineteen-seventeen had been the "année terrible" of the French war effort, an effort eroded by military reversals, a debilitating pacifist campaign, instances of mutinuous behaviour in the army, and an endless succession of rumours about clandestine attempts to negotiate an end to the war with Germany. Caillaux was thought to be among those so disposed, and Briand, and on occasion Painlevé himself.[81] The first two, of course, had long enjoyed close relations with Louis Barthou – at least until 1913 – and Painlevé currently presided over the only wartime cabinet to include Barthou among its ranks. There is a suggestion, therefore, that in Clemenceau's eyes, the eyes of one who had declined to join the Painlevé cabinet and who was fiercely *jusqu'auboutiste*, Barthou kept bad company. For this reason, so it is argued, Clemenceau judged Barthou unsuitable for a position in a cabinet which was there to "faire la guerre."[82]

If Clemenceau believed this, he was sorely mistaken.[83] There is, it is true, a private letter of September 1917 in which Barthou recounted to Anatole France the rumours about secret peace initiatives across Europe, including some concerning the Russians. But although France himself seemed to think that Barthou was now prepared to wait for the Germans to "surrender to us and our mercy," there is nothing in this letter which testifies to a lack of resolve on Barthou's part to prosecute the war as vigorously as ever.[84] Indeed, the weight of the evidence is decisively on the other side.

In the first place, in private conversations with Poincaré, and in the course of cabinet discussions, Barthou completely divorced himself from the secret peace initiatives with which Caillaux and Briand were said to be involved.[85] This was unsurprising, consistent as it was with all of his utterances throughout the year. In late May, for instance, he had told an audience that it would be "almost criminally irresponsible" to speak too soon of peace. France had to be freed first, along with all the other martyred peoples of Europe. On 1 October he published a piece in *Lectures pour tous* in which he reported Germany's latest strategy – "a peace offensive" by which she hope to disturb the unity of the French war effort. Some in France, he said, were silly enough to take the bait, and to counsel negotiations just when the Germans were tiring. "But let us stand united, unmoved by the calls of these misguided shepherds." At the end of the month, speaking as minister to the Chamber, he called all citizens to rally to "our strict and pressing duty to persevere to the end, *jusqu'au bout.*"[86]

The following month, in a speech at the Sorbonne, he said that the living had to keep faith with the dead by waging war to final victory, "jusqu'au bout."[87] Two weeks later, and but days before Clemenceau formed his ministry, foreign minister Barthou appeared before the Senate's Foreign Affairs committee, a committee chaired by Clemenceau. What interested the members were all the rumours of some negotiated end to the war. The minister's reply could not have been more explicit. He had recently assured the Russian government that France would never negotiate a separate peace, and had even used his powers as censor to forbid publication of an article in France which attributed to Alexander Kerensky an interest in a negotiated peace. In so far as the government was concerned, "We think, in fact, that the war must be waged *jusqu'au bout.*"[88]

In the light of such pronouncements, it must be clear that Clemenceau and Barthou agreed on the subject of a negotiated peace. If, therefore, the new premier believed otherwise, that belief was grandly, even peculiarly, mistaken; and as a result, Louis Barthou once again became victim of false but demonstrably effective innuendo. There is, however, a second possible explanation for his exclusion from Clemenceau's war cabinet. This too carries with it a terrible irony, although it may have the redeeming quality of making Barthou somewhat more a master of his own fate.

We have in Poincaré's diary-memoir a work of considerable importance as far as Barthou is concerned. Stretching for eleven thick volumes, this massive document renders a mixed impression of the president's long-time acquaintance. To begin with, he says astonishingly little about a man who had been, ostensibly, a close friend and colleague for some thirty years. Then, when he does recall the name, it is designed either to illustrate his own efforts to get Barthou into a cabinet or to comment in passing on this same candidate's more obvious shortcomings. This judgment, however, is not offered here with a view to discrediting the president's reading of Barthou. Indeed, the direction in which we are heading requires us to assume the general accuracy of Poincaré's impressions. Briefly put, they amount to a sketch of Barthou as a man who, in the autumn of 1917, was manoeuvring to the inside with all the tricks of a veteran jockey. Against a full field.

By mid-October 1917, Alexandre Ribot was coming under heavy pressure in parliament. Premier between March and September, and foreign minister since, he was being pulled and pushed toward resignation from the Painlevé cabinet. Some members of the administration thought that Barthou should replace him, as he eventually did. Barthou, though finding the incumbent chronically indecisive, at first disagreed. Rather, as he said to both Poincaré and Ribot, he thought the government should stand or fall together. If it fell, he would present himself as the only credible alternative to a government headed by Clemenceau, and a better one since the Socialists in parliament detested him less than they detested Clemenceau.[89] It was brash and self-serving. Poincaré did not like it; neither did Ribot. But by now Barthou had his reasons for thinking that, in the president's line of vision, old friends were more difficult to discern than old enemies. He was right. Poincaré had already decided that Barthou's time had not come. Indeed, despite a hearty personal dislike of Georges Clemenceau, the president knew that Clemenceau's hour was almost at hand.[90] Almost, for the Painlevé cabinet still limped along, partly by having Barthou replace Ribot at the foreign ministry.

By accepting the premier's offer, Barthou improved his chances in the race for the premiership, the more so as the socialist *L'Humanité* made no particular point of condemning his promotion in the cabinet. The old resentments had not disappeared – Albert Thomas led the socialists to vote against the motion of confidence in the refashioned cabinet – but the intensity of the criticism seemed less acute. Thus encouraged, Barthou was again suggesting to Poincaré that he had a good chance of forming a ministry with Socialist support.[91] That a new regime was inevitable seemed the more clear by the beginning of the second week of November. Again Barthou asked the president to clarify his intentions, ostensibly because both Viviani and Clemenceau were already constructing prospective cabinets. The former had made overtures to him, and he was scheduled to meet with Clemenceau as well.[92] By 14 November the Painlevé cabinet had decided to resign; and thus the jockeying intensified in this the last furlong.

There was another, less friendly, chat between Barthou and the president, Poincaré now irritated by the open self-promotion: "Barthou can only speak of himself." Nevertheless, by then it was apparent that Barthou had given up on his own chances and was now hoping to stay at the Foreign ministry under Clemenceau, whose cause he now endorsed.[93] That same day, however, Poincaré was advised by Thomas that the parliamentary socialists would fight a Clemenceau appointment. His own advice was to replace Painlevé with a cabinet built around himself, Viviani, and Louis Barthou. Later that afternoon, when Poincaré invited Clemenceau to the premiership, he learned two points of interest. Thomas would not be in the new cabinet, because he had refused a post. Barthou would not be offered one, because he was, again, not sufficiently "sûr."[94]

Hence, we can derive the two possibilities for explaining Barthou's exclusion from the government which went on to win the war against Germany. The first has him barred because of doubts about his commitment to prosecute the war to the end – despite a surfeit of public statements to the contrary. The second has him barred for one of two other reasons. As a leading contender for the post of premier, Barthou was a rival whom Clemenceau may not have wished to have had within his cabinet – the more so given the Béarnais's reputation, however questionably founded, for betraying cabinets of which he was part. At the same time, November 1917 had brought an ironic twist, in the form of rumours about a purported entente between Barthou and the Socialists. Given the latter's animosity toward Clemenceau, Barthou may have disqualified himself in the new premier's eyes by a momentary association with a group he had spent his career resisting. None of this absolves him from the subtle but adhesive charges of shameless political manoeuvring in the autumn of 1917, or eliminates the possibility that he was isolated not so much because of what he had done as because of the kind of person he was seen to be. After all, whether from the memoirs of "friends" like Poincaré and Caillaux, or from those more removed, like Benoist or Hanotaux, or from those further still, like Maurice Barrès, there emerges the impression of a brash, impulsive man whose ambitions had been whetted, not dulled, by several periods of political ostracism. Yet while this over-eagerness helped to harden his reputation as a manoeuvrer, it also neutralized the effectiveness of those manoeuvres, and thus prepared the way for the final irony. Portrayed as one with a natural taste for intrigue and manipulation, he was not, it seems, especially good at either. Thus portrayed, by men perhaps more knowing and more skilled, Louis

Barthou described his own fate when he wrote in 1923 of the otherwise unidentified Léronensius: "there is nothing worse than a reputation for being *habile*, that is, shrewd or cunning. *Léronensius* is hurt by his, a reputation awarded to him by those more cunning still, those whose *subtlety at one moment becomes deceit at the next.*"[95]

Again out of office, in November 1917, Barthou was soon re-engaged in a host of familiar preoccupations. He continued to follow the course of the military campaigns with the eye of a patriot. In February 1918 he wrote to Anatole France, a letter of conflicting sentiments. Events of these "tragic times," he feared, were getting well beyond human control or comprehension. "We don't know what is going on." But rallying from this momentary despair, he ended more confidently: "I won't hazard a guess that this will be the end of the war, but I do think that we are at the beginning of the peace."[96] A similar note was sounded in an ensuing letter of early April, Barthou expressing the belief that there was less danger now of a German surprise attack. Moreover, he was delighted to have Foch in charge of the allied command. Pétain, he reckoned, "is a little too inclined to the defensive, which can quickly lead to retreats"; but Foch "has an appreciation and a taste for action."[97]

That reassurance came at the right moment, for Alice became ill that spring. In March she had suffered an attack of appendicitis, and by April the doctors had decided to operate in the face of a rapidly rising temperature. Her condition, on which Barthou reported to Loti and to France, had been more serious than the doctors had cared to admit. Still, her recovery was rapid enough. Within a month she was back at work at the Necker hospital where, in May, she insisted on attending the appendix operation of her own maid.[98]

With domestic order restored, Barthou could concentrate on the course of the war and his contribution to it. Although publicly he continued to buoy up spirits with confident predictions of victory, and with assurances that the Germans were already disabused of their pre-war belief in the decadence of France, privately he was anguishing over the latest German offensive.[99] To Loti he confided doubts about the future. America could save France from defeat, if she could hold on long enough. "But can we hold? I have a troubled heart ..."[100] In this connection, he was also alarmed by the "peace-now" currents which were sweeping through some of the regiments, and expressed the hope to Poincaré that Clemenceau would take decisive action to quell them. Indeed, though absent, he became part of a row between the president and the premier when the latter tried to associate Poincaré with Barthou's criticisms of the current government and his latest attempts to get back into office.[101] Not even the breaking of the German offensive that summer, and therefore of the crisis atmosphere it had created, was enough to harmonize relations between Barthou and the premier. They several times clashed over the matter of government prerogatives as opposed to those invested in parliament – most notably in the Chamber's Foreign Affairs committee.[102] As Barthou saw it, the premier's strength in one capacity was his weakness in another. A natural fighter, Clemenceau relied on courage and intimidation. "Perfectly able to win over and seduce, he would rather snap." Even in front of the parliamentary committees, Barthou recalled, Clemenceau was short on "patience, flexibility, and that shrewd capacity to charm. Haughty and overbearing, witty to the point of cruelty, he didn't spare anyone."[103]

Given this reading from a member of the Foreign Affairs committee, one might assume that all firing would not stop simply because the war had ended. The armistice which was concluded in November 1918 did indeed halt the fighting on the military front, but merely signalled a new stage of struggle as politics and diplomacy became extensions of the war. A peace treaty, indeed a collection of peace treaties, had to be negotiated in ways consistent with the needs and interests of all victors. That being impossible, a peace settlement would have to be contrived which, like the Republic itself, divided the least. In that endeavour, Clemenceau would play the single most prominent role, in some respects assisted, in others not, by the pen and tongue of Louis Barthou.

His pen was to achieve a very special distinction in 1918, one which would help to restore him to emotional health following the personal tragedy of Max's death and the political tragedy of his cabinet exclusion. He had been writing a lot, of course, during the entire war, in the interests of what he called "truth propaganda."[104] But he had also continued to write extensively on what generally might be called the history of literature. It is this which constituted what was earlier referred to as the third avenue for his recovery from Max's death. This was a continuation of his pre-war career as writer, one who had entered the ranks of the Société des Gens de Lettres and who had applied for the Roujon chair at the Académie Française.

The war had delayed many of the Academy's proceedings, and thus had given Barthou more time to strengthen his candidacy. Despite a travel- and speech-filled wartime agenda, he also found time to write on literature. Between 1914 and the spring of 1918, he produced over a half-dozen literature-addressed articles, including those on the youth and early romance of Victor Hugo, on the publisher Edouard Pelletan, and, especially, on the life and career of Lamartine. Of particular note, given the circumstances of his own candidacy, was a piece published in 1916 by *Revue de Paris* on Lamartine's election to the Académie Française. Surely, too, there was something personal in the lines from Lamartine with which he opened one public lecture, something that reminded him of Thann.

Un seul être vous manque ... Qu'importe le soleil? je n'attends rien des jours ... Il n'est rien de commun entre la terre et moi.[105]

It was to this same poet-politician that Barthou addressed his next major book, *Lamartine orateur*. Published in 1916 by Hachette, the book was dedicated "To the fond memory of my son Max." It was the more fitting when his readers discovered that Lamartine, too, had suffered the loss of his only child. Indeed, though the book is much less a biography than a monograph on Lamartine as public speaker, the parallels between historian and subject are obvious – so much so that it is this feature which is most instructive to the student of Louis Barthou. In his treatment of Lamartine, there are echoes of himself; and they *are* echoes, sounds repeated, for what we find here basically confirms our sense of Barthou the man. For that reason, brevity recommends itself.

Barthou was drawn to Lamartine by an admiration bordering on affection. As in the case of Mirabeau, he never commented on such personal similarities, but there is no doubt that he admired the combination of letters and politics, the talent of a celebrated public speaker, the formidable memory, even the habit of early rising. He also admired, indeed he practised, Lamartine's independence from political party – although he judged excessive his hero's remark: "Parties, whether white, red or blue, are only interested in stirring up political passions ... hateful, shameful passions."[106] But it was Lamartine's personal ideology which Barthou found as commendable to the twentieth century as it had been to the nineteenth: freedom of the press, of religion, and of private property; greater decentralization of the political process; and yet state-regulated compulsory education and state-initiated legislation designed for the political and social enfranchisement of the masses. Such were the ideals of Lamartine, and of Barthou who followed him. So too they were in harmony when it came to the grand strategy with which these objectives were to be realized. They both praised gradualism, slow and steady progress which demanded consensus-building in advance, and which was sure to draw the fire of critics on both flanks. As was true of *Mirabeau*, where the language and sentiment of the historian ran together with those of his subject, so here we have Lamartine speaking for Barthou.

One has to ask oneself: am I, or am I not, a man who believes in steady progress, one who wants the political, moral and social world to be constantly changing for the better? Well! I say to myself, yes, yes, I am one of those! ... Yes, I am a simple worker in this enterprise of nations and of centuries, an enterprise which consists of replacing the old ... slowly, painstakingly, prudently... Don't mistake me on that, Gentlemen, it is because I am such a progressive that I see myself as a conservative as well.[107]

On 2 May 1918 Louis Barthou was elected to the Académie Française, partly on the strength of this recent *Lamartine*. At fifty-six years of age, this new "immortal" was overjoyed.[108] Not even the long delay in his formal reception could diminish the honour and the pleasure accorded him by this eminent body. Sponsored by Loti and the enigmatic Poincaré, Barthou took his place "under the Dome" in February 1919, expressing when he did his gratitude. "For my part, I owe you the one joy that life had yet to give me. This recognition has flattered my pride but, more so, it has moved me to the bottom of my heart."[109]

Replying by custom, Maurice Donnay turned to the new member's list of credentials. They were considerable. Louis Barthou had accumulated a substantial list of books, volumes of collected essays and speeches, and periodical articles from the principal literary reviews as well as the popular magazines. Given the obvious fact that he was not a writer by profession, his literary pretensions were not lacking in substance. At the same time, Donnay rightly refrained from claiming that this was a corpus of fine literature. It would have been inappropriate for him to suggest that the historical work, though enthusiastic and informed, was naive in analysis and methodology, or to comment on Barthou's propensity for document reproduction; and surely it would have been dwelling on the obvious to say that the compilations of wartime propaganda lacked objectivity and *mesure*. But they were outspokenly patriotic; and this the Académie did not forget, any more than when it had welcomed Clemenceau, and Foch, and Joffre, and Jules Cambon in 1918.

Donnay made it clear that he was speaking of a patriot as well as a writer. He invoked Barthou's service to France as the father of the three-year law, a measure which so many now believed had saved the country from disaster in 1914. He recalled, in fact, a note which Barthou had written to him at the height of the 1913 debates, in a hand which betrayed the strain, the haste and fatigue of the moment. And then there had been the wartime role, writing and speaking, in and out of France, exposing German lies and atrocities. Not once, he said to Barthou, did you sound "those horrible trumpets of doubt and defeatism, only those glorious sounds of the victory you sensed was certain."[110] Because it was true, it was an especially fitting tribute to a man whose commitment to literature was as profound as his commitment to France, and vice versa. More eloquent still, for being silent, was the design Barthou had worked out for his academician's ceremonial sword. Ornamental though it was, it carried in its engravings and inscriptions a summary of his life thus far. Its ivory handle was given over to two delicate engravings, one of Calliope, the muse of eloquence, the other of the tribune at the Palais Bourbon, around which was carved the familiar device: "Si vis pacem, para bellum." Above the handle, on the gold pommel, he had placed in tribute the portraits of his heroes, boy and man – Mirabeau, Lamartine, Hugo – while below the handle, toward the blade, there was inscribed in gold the shields of Oloron and Béarn, complete with a racing *gave* and the mountain peak of Midi d'Ossau. On the opposite face, the reverse side, he had made provision for two other cherished memories. One, inscribed on a raised golden oval, was the discernible figure of Truth from his *ex libris*. The other, etched in ivory, was a partially unfurled French flag, on either border of which could be read a miniature monument to a cherished eighteen-year-old: Max Barthou. Thann. 1914.

CHAPTER SEVEN

The 1920s: Patriotism and International Diplomacy

A negotiation is not like tracing the path of a straight
line. It has its pauses, its detours, and its reprises.
... A negotiation is one continuous process in which
firmness does not exclude flexibility. There is more
than one route and more than one means to get to
one's goal. [1]

Prior to World War One, Barthou's association with international
politics had been minimal. Although accustomed to foreign travel,
he seldom intervened in parliament's episodic considerations of foreign policy and wrote little on international problems. Even after
1905, when he tried to steer the Alliance Démocratique Républicaine
clear of the shoals formed by the Dreyfus affair and the clerical
question, and toward the high ground of republican unity and patriotism, he took his bearings from the landmarks of domestic politics. Not until 1911 and the Agadir crisis did he seem much absorbed
by the threat which international instability could represent to the
Republic. Typically, he had supported the general lines of French
foreign policy in the 1890s and the first decade of the twentieth
century – voting for the reinforcement of French imperial interests,
for the continuation of the alliance and military convention with
czarist Russia, and, of more recent origin, for the burgeoning entente
which Delcassé had engineered with Great Britain. Germany, for
him, remained the principal threat to European peace, as aggressive
in design as in the days of his boyhood when she had wrested from
France the eastern provinces of Alsace and Lorraine.

Nevertheless, even in 1911 when he had spoken critically of Caillaux's treaty with Germany over Morocco, he had offered more than
involuntary chauvinism. He had two concerns. First, and in a way
which anticipated his subsequent criticism of the negotiations in
1919, he complained of the lack of guarantees. France, he said, had
made immediate concessions in exchange for only future considerations from Germany. Second, in yet another preview of his concerns in 1919, he criticized the occult way in which recent diplomacy

had been conducted, including that which had led to the entente
with England. He did not mean, of course, that diplomacy had to
be conducted in public places, where flexibility might have to be
surrendered in the interests of appearance. Rather, he wanted it to
be handled through traditional, professionally maintained channels
– and with adequate reference to the committee system upon which
a democratic parliament was expected to work. The following year,
in 1912, Barthou became chairman of the Chamber's Foreign Affairs
committee, just in time to render service to the new premier,
Raymond Poincaré. As lavish in his praise of the latter as he had
been critical of Caillaux, Barthou played an important role in securing parliamentary approval of the negotiated Moroccan protectorate.[2] By the following spring, he found himself prime minister,
invited to that office by the newly elected President Poincaré. Foreign
policy was now the number one issue.

Premier from March to December of 1913, Barthou was largely
absorbed by the issue of the three-year service law and the attendant
controversy over its financing. Accordingly, his direct involvement
in the conduct of foreign policy was very limited, greatly overshadowed by that of Stephen Pichon, to whom he had entrusted the
Foreign ministry, and by that of Poincaré, to whom he willingly
accorded presidential prerogative. For the rest, and given the outbreak of two successive wars in the Balkans, he was fully agreed on
the need to stabilize that theatre before conflicting Great Power
interests led to a confrontation between France and Germany and
their respective allies. While freely admitting that he was no expert
in eastern affairs, he knew by instinct that a catastrophe was in sight
unless cool heads prevailed.[3] His own contribution to peace, as he
saw it, was bilateral, the centrist's reliance on deterrence and conciliation.

First, it was up to him to increase the size and resources of the
French armed forces, to a level grand enough to dissuade Germany
from launching a surprise attack. Couching their explanations in
exclusively defensive terms – the need to respond to German rearmament – Barthou and General Etienne refused to admit that
French military strategy, like the German, was pitched to the offensive.[4] Some would say they lied to parliament and the country, others
that they did not tell the truth. Had they been more candid, however,
recognizing General Joffre's offensive preparations and their relationship to the Russian alliance, it is unclear how they would have
better served the interests of European peace. Candour of that order
would have furnished Berlin with more reason, or pretext, for intimidating behaviour, just as it would have doubled resistance to the

military law among the government's critics on the left. Thus, from the premier's point of view, complete candour carried with it the double liability of playing into German hands while delaying efforts to strengthen France's military capacity. Too much the pragmatist for that, Barthou not only stressed the reactive character of the government's bill but misrepresented the defensive role which the army intended to play in the event of a German attack.

Second, just as there was nothing sinister in the government's reluctance to tell the whole truth about the high command's strategic planning, there was nothing provocative in its direct dealings with the German government. Quite the contrary, and Barthou was right to reject allegations that he had whipped up anti-German sentiment in France for the sake of passing the military bill. His speeches, while referring to the German arms buildup – sometimes directly, often very indirectly – were not inflammatory in either rhetoric or tone; and his government's handling of the border incidents in April 1913 betrayed a commendable restraint. Any suggestion that he had been party to a militarist policy, he said, was as stupid as it was infamous.[5]

Not until 1914 and his role as propagandist did the moderate Barthou give way to the rabid. Aggrieved patriot and grieving father, he plunged into the war effort as writer and speaker, condemning Germany and Germans, promising their chastisement. Periodically afflicted by private uncertainty, Louis Barthou admitted no public doubts about the inevitability of France's triumph. By the time he became foreign minister in 1917, he had repeatedly proven his reputation as an inspired patriot. A *jusqu'auboutiste*, he condemned those circles – sometimes dubbed pacifist, sometimes defeatist – which called for an immediate halt to the military slaughter. For him, not until Germany had sued for peace unconditionally could any thought be given to ending the war, and then only if it ensured an unequivocal allied victory. Until then, what he called "the holy cause" would continue against "the barbarism" of Germany and Germans.[6]

Clemenceau had not included Barthou in his cabinet, ostensibly because of doubts about his resolve to prosecute the war. By the summer of 1918 the two were again at odds, although again what separated them seems to have derived largely from the premier's misunderstanding. He complained to Poincaré that Barthou was using the Foreign Affairs committee to make trouble for the government. In particular, he believed that Barthou had exploited rumours that the French government had several times ignored serious peace initiatives from the enemy, initiatives which might have permitted an earlier end to the war. Clemenceau wanted the parliamentary committee to issue a public denial of those allegations, and seemed to believe that Barthou was the principal obstacle to that wish.[7] Why he thought so is again quite unclear. In fact, Barthou supported the premier's position on this issue – partly, it should be said, so as to exonerate himself from a similar charge relating to his period as foreign minister in the autumn of 1917.[8] Moreover, far from impeding the government, Barthou was remarkably solicitous toward it. In the summer of 1918, for instance, while sharing in committee criticism of the government's ambiguous policy toward the new Soviet state, "a wait-and-see policy," he led the resistance to making these criticisms public. This was not the time for a public debate on such an issue, he said, not at this difficult moment of the war. Far better, he advised, to communicate these concerns discreetly, recognizing that ultimately the government "bore sole responsibility."[9]

By the early autumn, however, relations between the government and the committee were experiencing new strains. Barthou, it may be said, both heightened and assuaged those tensions, for if he defended the consultative right of parliament against a government ill disposed to listen, he also defended the executive's right to fulfil all of its responsibilities. Thus, whereas in late October he began by supporting committee demands for some role in the anticipated armistice negotiations, he quickly bowed to the government's argument that the imperatives of secrecy made such consultation impractical. Having so conceded the point, however, he was as quick to insist on a role for the committee when the time came for negotiating an actual peace settlement. "We must be kept informed by means of close conversations with the government ... Victory will begin a critical new stage; the challenges posed by the peace are even more formidable than those presented by the war."[10] Through November and December he continued to walk the same fine line, admitting to the government the authority which went with its responsibilities, while insisting on the rights and responsibilities which parliament had conferred on its Foreign Affairs committee. By the end of January 1919 his impatience had been pricked by consternation. Clemenceau, despite assurances of his regard for the committee, had not appeared before it since early May of 1918. Now, with the peace conference underway in Paris, there were already rumblings that France's interests were being compromised. "Without hysteria, but with intensity," Barthou told his colleagues, "I say that this cannot continue." Moreover, it would be intolerable if this committee were to have dumped in its lap, at the last moment, a treaty already negotiated. "We must not ... content ourselves with commenting on decisions which we only know about through the press."[11]

In early February a handful of deputies reported to the full committee on a recent meeting with the premier. Barthou, among this select few, offered his impressions at some length. It proved to be his last major intervention in the work of the committee, for it seemed clear to him by then that the battle was indeed lost. Clemenceau, again, had made all the right sounds, but his undertakings to involve the committee in any serious form had been severely qualified. He simply did not intend to restrict the government's freedom of action in any way, or to run the risk of premature disclosures. He had agreed in principle to meet with the committee, but refused to speculate on the timing of such contact. All told, Barthou ventured, it was evident that the peace negotiations would not be conducted with any very active reference to parliament. At best, it would be told however much, or little, the government reckoned consistent with the interests of confidentiality and the wishes of France's allies. Neither caveat, Barthou granted, was without force, and he reminded his committee colleagues that their role was indeed a lesser one than that assumed by the government. "Criticism is easy; the art of government is difficult."[12]

The parliamentary process of assessing Clemenceau's work as peacemaker began in early July, a week after Germany's reluctant acceptance of the Treaty of Versailles. For that purpose, the Chamber had constituted a special Commission des Traités de Paix, by which Louis Barthou was unanimously elected *rapporteur-général* for the treaty with Germany. To him, therefore, fell the broad responsibility of analysing the treaty prior to the Chamber's vote on ratification. However, before turning to that analysis, it may be useful to remind the reader of the atmosphere in which Barthou and his compatriots found themselves in 1919.

Eight years of age when Alsace and Lorraine had passed to German hands, Barthou was able to celebrate their return at the age of fifty-seven. That, at least, was some compensation for five years of destruction and slaughter. But could anything, any benefit however large, be an adequate return on such a terrible investment? Northern France had been left a prostrate *mutilé de guerre*, so many of her villages erased by the work of artillery shells and replaced only by hundreds of new cemeteries. Monuments to the war were everywhere, long before the survivors thought of erecting them in bronze, marble, and granite: railway lines torn up for miles, mines flooded, schools and hospitals flattened, farmland churned by shrapnel and polluted with toxic chemicals, forests reduced to stands of shredded matchsticks, hills levelled and craters fashioned with the same indifferent ease.

It was here, in the mud of the western trenches, on the duckboards or on the barbed wire, or in fragile aircraft above, that France lost nearly a million and a half young combatants. A million and a half, without counting those who survived their wounds, mainly younger men, who deprived one generation of sons and another of fathers, young men lost to the economy, to the arts, to learning, to government, and, perversely, even to the armies of the future. Little wonder that the survivors were in no rush to fix precisely the costs to be charged to an enemy judged responsible for this carnage. By anyone's reckoning, the figures were astronomical and would mean inconceivable levels of public indebtedness once the direct costs of the war – including loans from the United States – were multiplied by the costs involved in the reconstruction of civilian areas. Clemenceau's government spoke for this battered society and negotiated on its behalf in 1919. Barthou spoke from it, and from a parliament already too familiar with the financial and emotional cost represented by every war orphan and widow, every grieving parent and mutilated veteran. We forget this at our peril, for no one in 1919 was capable of forgetting.

Paris was still intact, largely. But it had known the ravages of artillery bombardment, air raids, and the accompanying deaths of civilians, in their homes, churches, hospitals, and hastily contrived shelters. It was a marred and in places blackened capital, a far cry from the glittering, confident city which Alice and Louis Barthou had enjoyed at the time of their marriage twenty some years earlier. Certainly it was badly equipped to host the huge international peace conference that was under way within two months of the armistice. The order, so painstakingly imposed on the chaos which had come with the war, now dissolved in the disorder which as surely accompanied the outbreak of peace. Unsurprisingly, in a society accustomed to rationing, there were shortages of everything, from petrol to writing paper, just as there were shortages in translators, cartographers, stenographers. Telephonic service was unpredictable, and telegraphic facilities overburdened by the needs of international delegations installed in Paris for some six months. Early evidence of the influenza bug which was to sweep the continent in 1919 only added to the discomfort of a capital still in mourning and newly apprehensive about the peace objectives of France's allies. Few felt this more than members of parliament, who knew full well that they would be among the first to appraise a peace settlement to which they had been allowed to contribute so little. Among them were men like Barthou, who had lost one son for this peace, and Paul Doumer, who had lost four.[13]

Even by late January Barthou had sensed how dangerous the peace could prove for France's long-term security interests, and he said so to the members of the Foreign Affairs committee. Two months later he went public, suggesting in a subsequently published address that Germany was insufficiently disarmed, that the peacemakers had been too slow in formally attributing responsibility for the war to Germany and her allies, that her war criminals – including the exiled Kaiser – should be brought to justice, that the left bank of the Rhine should be permanently demilitarized and the Saar basin turned over to France with Alsace and Lorraine. As for reparations, there was no question but that Germany should pay. She had, he said, "chosen this war, she had lost it, she must pay for it." Not that she could pay all of the costs, for that was inconceivable, even a dangerous delusion. But certainly she should be obliged to pay everything within her legitimate means before a sou was raised from French taxpayers.[14]

Opinions like these doubtless contributed to his election to the Committee on Peace Treaties, and to his subsequent election as *rapporteur*. In a war-torn capital of a war-torn country, Barthou was recognized as a patriot of impeccable credentials – not the least of which was his association with the three-year law. But there was more to his election than that. He was seen as he wished to be seen, as the moderate centrist who could restrain dogmatists on either flank. On the Foreign Affairs committee, for example, he had upbraided colleagues on the left and the right – censuring socialist members for speaking too freely with journalists of *L'Humanité*, or rebuking the right-wing Jules Delahaye for calling Ignace Paderewski a mere "piano-player." Defending the Polish statesman as a musical artist and a refined mind, Barthou asked why no one was surprised when many countries found their leaders among pedestrian lawyers.[15] More broadly, and as already witnessed, Barthou had been careful to defend the interests of parliament – in the form of its standing committees – without insisting on hobbling the executive branch. Critical though he was of Clemenceau's methods, and at least some of their apparent results, he took pains to remind committee colleagues that the government's task was exceptionally difficult.

It was for this reason that he insisted, from the outset, that his job and that of the committee was to ensure ratification of the Versailles treaty. So too was it their responsibility to identify to parliament the perceived weaknesses of that treaty. And therein lay the challenge:

to demonstrate that the government, overall, had defended the country's interests, and yet to suggest where it had agreed to hazardous concessions. Nor was this simply to assuage the resentments harboured by the current Clemenceau administration; more important was the need to contain already circulating fears that France, though victorious, was now more in peril than she had been in 1914. While every effort should be made to ensure further German disarmament, it served no useful purpose to play upon the anxieties of the French people.[16] Finally, Barthou also stressed from the beginning of these meetings that the committee should not be tempted to solicit the views of Marshal Foch. Everyone knew that the marshal had argued against some of the treaty provisions, that he was in basic disagreement with the government. Nevertheless, as Barthou had argued during his own premiership in 1913, no government was bound to accept the counsels of its experts, military or civilian. Besides, Foch had not been party to the negotiations and therefore never had to contend with the complexities of negotiating among allies.[17]

That said, Barthou also emphasized that there would be nothing casual in the committee's appraisal of this giant *fait accompli*. He intended, with their consent, to demonstrate that the government would have strengthened its bargaining hand immeasurably had it turned for support to its parliamentary committees. And he would have none of the lame arguments which attributed the government's behaviour to expectations set by the British prime minister, David Lloyd George, or by the American president, Woodrow Wilson. This situation was entirely of the government's own making, and he intended to say so. Moreover, whereas his report would try to avoid pointless criticism, it would have to locate the median between fanning the flame of anxieties about the nation's security and implying falsely that such anxieties were baseless. If the premier had done about as well as he could on reparations, he had done less well on the security provisions.[18] In particular, as Barthou said directly to Clemenceau on 17 July, there were grave doubts about the efficacy of the Anglo-American guarantee to French security. How long would it take such powers to rescue a France victimized by a surprise German attack, particularly if those same powers refused to countenance preliminary military conventions? Although the choice had been made between those guarantees and Foch's proposed military regime for the left bank of the Rhine, Barthou was among those worried by the military situation. Indeed, he said that he agreed with Foch that, with the disappearance of the Russian alliance,

France now faced a Germany whose potential for aggression in fact had multiplied. And he disagreed, apparently, with Clemenceau's retort that the combination of new states like Poland, Czechoslovakia, and Yugoslavia represented a potential for resistance even greater than that once exhibited by czarist Russia.[19]

There was little the committee could do, however, about whatever weak spots it detected. Barthou could ask why Foch's arguments had been rejected in favour of American and British proposals. He could lament the fact that the infant League of Nations had not been born with teeth, that each of Germany's federated states had not been compelled to sign the Versailles treaty, and that the first financial payments from Germany had been postponed until May 1921. But the treaty remained, as signed; and a recommendation for ratification remained the committee's only recourse. Or almost the only one. On 1 August Louis Marin moved that a decision on ratification be deferred until the American Senate had accepted the guarantee to French security and until the Chamber was fully apprised of the treaties concluded with Austria, Hungary, Bulgaria, and Turkey. Louis Barthou spoke passionately against the motion, and threatened to resign his functions if it were passed. Instead, having defeated Marin's motion, the committee proceeded to vote, overwhelmingly, in favour of ratification.[20]

Throughout the month of September 1919, in the course of four extended parliamentary sessions, the committee, the government, and the Assembly thrashed out the arguments for and against ratification. Throughout it all, Barthou remained a central figure, sometimes incurring the wrath of the premier, sometimes that of the premier's most inveterate critics. Some on the socialist left said the treaty was too harsh and too vindictive to serve the cause of a lasting peace. There were conservatives who said the opposite, that it was too generous toward Germany. The cabinet, predictably, cared for neither appraisal; nor did it appear to appreciate the more nuanced remarks of Barthou. That he was critical was unmistakable, for his report opened with a sharp rebuke of the government's studied disregard of parliament. "Parliament finds itself confronted by a *fait accompli*, to which it has been a complete stranger." It ended with an equally sharp judgment on the imprecise wording employed by the treaty's architects, who, he asserted, would have been better off to have used French as the primary language.

Born of disparate ideals and sometimes conflicting interests, the treaty tries to reconcile all, but without erasing the traces of contradiction. Its substance lacks unity and, too often, its form lacks clarity. There is no sense of one governing ideal; rather it looks too much like the pieces of a mosaic that have been separately cast and then ineptly assembled.[21]

Between prologue and conclusion Barthou offered a mixture of praise and muted criticism. The committee subscribed completely to the treaty's formal indictment of Germany. France had been the victim of a war "criminally unleashed." It was fitting, therefore, that Germany should be stripped of her colonies, denied initial right of membership in the League of Nations, made to pay for the damages she had inflicted on allied civilian populations, and be restricted to a small, long-service army. Similarly, it was appropriate that Alsace-Lorraine be restored to France, that Poland be re-created amid the ruins of eastern Europe, and that the allies retain control of the Rhine bridgeheads for the specified minimum of fifteen years. Nevertheless, it was also fair to say that the treaty rested on a collection of uncertainties. The League of Nations, Barthou observed, had been authorized but not empowered to ensure adherence to the disarmament provisions. The problem represented by bolshevik Russia remained so unresolved that Germany's presence in central Europe had suffered no diminution. But most grave, France had given up her earlier demand for a permanent, allied occupation of the Rhine's left bank in favour of as yet unratified guarantees of support from the United States and Britain. Granted, Clemenceau had little alternative but to compromise, for rigidity would have engendered among the allies "such dissension the implications of which do not need to be recalled." But it remained a risky, untested, indeed as yet unfinished business.[22]

One measure of the discretion Barthou had exercised in his written report is to be found in the verbal exchanges which followed its formal submission. Speaking with less restraint in the ensuing debate, he reiterated his reservations about the putative guarantees to French security. The United States might not ratify the treaty at all, or it might deny approval to the clauses pertaining to the League of Nations. But if Washington rejected the League, in the context of which the guarantee to France had been framed, then the guarantee itself evaporated; and with it would disappear British assurances of aid which had been pegged expressly to those from the Americans. Where then, he asked, was France's security? The committee had asked foreign minister Pichon, but without result. It had asked the government's special adviser, M. Tardieu, whom Barthou privately regarded as "the evil genius of the peace." Now it was time for the premier to answer the "critical, agonizing question that I have posed."[23]

It was certainly the greatest of all the unanswered questions in 1919. But Clemenceau had heard it many times before. The problem was that it was unanswerable until the American Senate had decided on its course, and thus had either justified or only confirmed Clemenceau's calculated gamble. Given this, Barthou served no useful purpose by taking an extra tug at the Tiger's tail, unless it was to demonstrate that his committee was not at the beck and call of an irascible premier. Irascible he was, however, and fatigue was turning him malicious. He stood and accused Barthou of trying to undermine the treaty by delaying the vote. Stung by the charge, Barthou replied in kind. He did not refer to his fight against the Marin motion. He simply rejected the allegation with disdain, again challenged Clemenceau to answer the question, and this time – to the applause of the socialist left – needled the old man by referring to his "parody of negotiations." Still no direct reply, and nothing very audible from a muttering premier. But Barthou, who had exceptional hearing – "too good an ear" – was too angry to quit.[24] He spoke aloud Clemenceau's guttural aside, one which suggested Barthou was in the employ of the left. Drawn up to his full height, Barthou addressed the man who had first christened him "petit Barthou." He found intolerable this aspersion cast on his independence, and protested that his own love of France was every bit as great as that of the premier.[25]

Altogether, this clash was not especially remarkable, another instance of unbecoming parliamentary behaviour from both parties. Nevertheless, since it is not always the agreeable which is instructive, this particular exchange does have an illustrative function. If it demonstrates, for example, the combative, sometimes mercurial temperament of Louis Barthou, it also speaks to the personal sensitivity which age had done little to diminish. More than that, he was most easily bruised by the rebukes of people he admired, Clemenceau among them. So it was that he was hurt by the Tiger's refusal to appreciate the delicate task assumed by the treaty committee and, in particular, by its *rapporteur*. Clemenceau, he knew, was a difficult man, brusque, impatient, trenchant, indeed often unjust – as Barthou regarded his once scathing remarks about Gambetta and Ferry. He was also prey to flattery, and discouraged independent thinking among his entourage of advisers. And yet he had agreeable qualities in abundance, from the lesser to the great. Among the former, he was a paragon of personal industry and punctuality, and an absolute stickler for French grammar. Among the latter, he was a patriot whose love of France was unbounded. In that love, Barthou suggested, was the explanation for Clemenceau's exceptional service during the war – when "no one else could have done what he did" – and during the trying peace negotiations – when he had to work with an American president whose ignorance of Europe was lamentable.[26]

By the spring of 1920, six months following the Chamber's ratification of the Versailles treaty, Barthou was convinced that the peace had been poisoned at the well. In the course of an interpellation of the Millerand government in March of that year, he surveyed the ground already lost. Identifying two features of the peace settlement on which he had personally placed much emphasis, he bemoaned the fact that this settlement had led to a Germany more unified than she had been in 1914, and he again criticized the failure to prosecute all German war criminals. Such concessions, he said, the product of indecision and irresolution, were contributing to a general devaluation of the peace settlement, from which Germany could only draw benefit. Indeed, a widespread lack of faith in the treaties was actually spurring on German efforts to have the Versailles provisions relaxed. Hence she persistently avoided her treaty obligations, "by lying," whether it was in connection with her requisite coal deliveries to France or the conditions of her disarmament. Moreover, London often seemed to go along with such violations, demonstrating the permissiveness of an English government which had attended to its own security concerns by the destruction of the German fleet and the abolition of the German air force. Thus, with the confirmed American failure to ratify Versailles – and the consequent collapse of the Anglo-American guarantees to France – there was already discernible "a crisis among the allies." This, he ventured, would get far worse as long as the word *révision* seemed only to operate "at the expense of France."[27]

It was here that Barthou expanded the scope of his inquiry into government foreign policy. He might have stopped where he was, on the simple message that Germany had to be brought into line. "I could have won an easy victory, but the truth is more important than such success." Germany was only part of the problem; another was the grand uncertainty that was the new bolshevik Russia. It was time, he admonished, for the government to admit that French policy toward Russia had been maladroit and unproductive. It was clear by now that Generals Koltchak, Youdénitch, and Denikine were not what parliament had been told they were. These were not democrats, but essentially monarchists, and their attempts to destroy the soviet state by force had ended in an unmitigated failure. No more forth-coming had been the policy of isolating the bolshevik bacillus behind a purely metaphorical *cordon sanitaire.* What was needed was a clear and coherent policy toward the Soviet Union, one that would come to grips with the new realities, and one that would be especially mindful of the dangers inherent in some future Russo-German com-bination.[28]

For the remainder of the year Barthou intervened rarely in Cham-ber debates on foreign policy. But this in no sense signalled indif-ference. He was again presiding over the Foreign Affairs committee, an office from which he supported the Millerand government's de-cision in April 1920 to occupy Frankfurt temporarily – in response to German arms violations. He also adopted a firm if temperately expressed stand against further revision of Versailles. In particular, he alerted his colleagues against British-backed German attempts to relax the reparations provisions, and against the apparent acquies-cence of the current French government. The Reparations Com-mission, he said was more and more inclined to simply record German violations instead of ensuring enforcement of the treaty.[29]

In the public forum, he published a weekly column entitled "La Situation" for *Les Annales,* a column principally addressed to ques-tions of international politics. Although this is not the place for a detailed analysis of the views he there expressed, it is possible to indicate the tenor of his public commentaries and thus to situate him in relation to some of the continent's more perplexing problems. While repeatedly recalling the difficulties encountered by the French delegation in 1919, he was growing ever more critical of the Ver-sailles treaty and of the subsequent failure to enforce even its too generous terms. The peace, he observed, had been imperfectly as-sured and thus the coals of confrontation, far from extinguished, had continued to glow just below the surface ash.[30] Essentially, Cle-menceau's failure at peace had been as considerable as his triumph at war, caught as he had been between Lloyd George, whose instincts were perpetually attuned to the best interests of the United King-dom, and Woodrow Wilson, with his "magnanimous but utopian abstractions."[31]

From the original mistakes, Barthou believed, had arisen the sub-sequent problems of implementation. Flawed as it was, Versailles was still "the law ... which lays down Germany's obligations." Never-theless, Germany seemed able to break her reparations obligations with impunity, delivering less than half the promised coal payments to France and watching the allies at Spa – doubtless with amusement – take heart from new German undertakings to pay more than they had been doing. Instead, so he told his readers, Germany should be forced to pay precisely according to the terms set out in Versailles and by those of the subsequent London conference.[32] So too on disarmament. The treaty allowed for a one-hundred-thousand-man German army, in place by the end of March 1920. Yet in June, the actual figures were still twice that, and even further delays in the process of troop reduction had been accorded by conferences at San Remo and Spa, the latter effectively moving the target date to January 1921. Unhappy with the delays, Barthou was the more upset when in January 1921 those conditions still had not been fulfilled. If Germany's standing army were now at the agreed-upon level, there were as yet many more men still under arms in clumsily disguised police and paramilitary formations. In short, the arms violations were continuing, unchallenged by the allies, and further proof that the Germans "understand ... only the law of force."[33]

He was less certain about the Russians, or rather what to do with them. Predictably, he did not like the Soviet regime, presenting Lenin as a "terrorist" and Trotsky as a tool of a "blood-covered dictatorship"; and Chicherin, the foreign minister, he wrote, was as dishonest as the Germans. Their house, he predicted, would crumble under the weight of its own excesses. But not from without. Just as France's earlier support for Denikine had proven misguided, so too would that accorded by Millerand to General Wrangel. If any solution were to be found, Barthou wrote in November 1920, it would have to come from a united allied policy, rather than from independent and disparate policies generated in Paris, London, and Rome.[34] In the interim, every effort was needed to realize one of the key ideas from 1919, namely the designing of a "corset" around Germany, a defensive apparatus fashioned through cooperation between the western entente and the hoped-for combination of Poland, Czechoslovakia, Roumania, and Yugoslavia. The Czechs, in particular, he saw as being close to France, animated by the same principles of republican democracy. And Poland, whose reappearance he had applauded in his report on Versailles, was similarly indispensable to an eastern block which might constrain Germany from expanding to the east and Russia to the west.[35]

The most vexatious international difficulty for Barthou was the "English problem," precisely because it was the complement to that which was most grave, the "German problem." He was neither anglophobe nor anglophile. Although well acquainted with English literature, including Shakespeare, Milton, and Kipling, and although often moved to quote Herbert Spencer, he seems not to have been at home in England, never travelling there strictly for pleasure, and never making much of an effort to learn the language. Whether or not this had something to do with resentments nourished from his youth in that "ville anglaise" of Pau, it is safe to say that he had no special affinity for the English.[36] This did not impair, however, his appreciation of England's contribution to parliamentary democracy, or the stability afforded by her party system. Neither did it blind him to Britain's heroic military efforts in the last war, nor to the skill of her negotiators in 1919. Indeed, he wrote just a little later in the decade, the English government was singularly good at looking after its own interests, good enough to be a model for France. It was, of course, a complaint delivered as a compliment, for he now thought that Clemenceau had been gulled and his successors bluffed. The fact was, Barthou finally admitted, he really did not care for Ramsay MacDonald, Curzon, or Lloyd George, and believed the feeling was mutual. Indeed, in a sketch reminiscent of the famous portrait by Keynes, Barthou wrote of David Lloyd George:

He is no humanist. He reads little. The Bible is his bedside reading. He likes to draw upon it: he preaches. But it is not because he is a one-book man that he is so formidable. Charming and mercurial, clever and shifty, bold and malign, in any discussion he is a first-class jouster. Far from discomfiting him, his ignorance comes in handy since, being free of principle, he retains all the flexibility he needs.[37]

At base, and like many of his compatriots, Barthou resented the ease with which English spokesmen quietly subscribed to the view that France was the principal impediment to lasting peace. The offence was the more grave, as seen from Paris, when the charges of obstructionism were followed by allegations of France's desire to secure some kind of continental hegemony. And then there were myriad policy differences, each widening further the divide between London and Paris – the British generally softer on German reparations, disarmament, and Soviet Russia, but harder than France on Poland and Turkey. The last position was especially trying for Louis Barthou, who had become a proponent of the revision of the Treaty of Sèvres. In accord with his outspoken literary friend, Pierre Loti – whose passionate defence of the Turks was well known – Barthou argued that Turkey had been unfairly dealt with in the treaty and that the nationalistic rebellion of Kemal Ataturk had been triggered by the clumsy Greek occupation of Smyrna. But Lloyd George would have none of it, supporting Greece despite the return of the unpopular King Constantine. By the autumn of 1920 Barthou was writing privately to Lyautey of Lloyd George's "perfidie" and by the spring to Loti of "the frightful egotism of our ... English friends."[38] Although exaggerated *ad absurdum*, the charge that Barthou was courting war with England came out of this tense atmosphere. He rightly denied it as a complete "lie," but he must have known where his critical candour had led him.[39]

So it was that by the end of 1920 Louis Barthou personified the impatience of a country grown impatient. And worried: worried about some war of revenge initiated by a Germany which still denied its defeat, which rejected the constraints imposed upon her, and which for a while would no longer have a Russian colossus to contend with in the east. Worried about war thrust upon a France which had forsaken a permanent occupation of the Rhine in exchange for guarantees that had not come to pass. Worried too by the tension between the desire to be secure and the desire to limit the costs – financial, social, and psychological – of maintaining a large standing army of peacetime conscripts. Expressing all of this to parliament in December 1920, Barthou said he did not share in Premier Leygues's optimism. France was continually giving ground on the Versailles provisions while German officials continued to disparage the treaty, and in "insolent language." Reparations were not paid on time or in the stipulated amounts; Germany was in a chronic state of disarmament violation; yet it was France who was made out to be aggressive and the main roadblock to peace. Little wonder that he faced the new year with a mixture of apprehension and hope. "1920 has become History. I don't regret it: it was perplexing, uncertain and spineless."[40]

The next year opened on a more promising note. A week after becoming war minister in Briand's cabinet of January 1921, Barthou replied to a letter from Loti: "Am I happy? Because I'm a minister? Hardly. To be in this ministry, yes, because, apart from the foreign office, I wouldn't have wanted or accepted any other post."[41] Even then he knew it would be a "heavy task," but by the time he wrote to Lyautey, in May, he could say just how onerous was his burden. Since almost nothing had been done for two years, all that remained were "pieces of an army." Hence, compared to this task of rebuilding the army for an effective, peacetime role, that of getting the three-year law passed had been "child's play."[42] Speaking to the Army committee in February, he freely admitted in camera what he would have been loath to say publicly: some regiments were so disorganized, and the morale of the officers and men so low, that even the basic training of new recruits was proving impossible. Conversely, he warned the Senate's committee two days later, the German army was already taking advantage of its small professional force by designing it as an army of cadres, that is, one organized to provide the leadership nucleus for a forbidden army of conscripts.[43]

That was why, so he told the senators, the government was considering measures to halt this hopeless policy of drift. Germany's treaty violations were legion, and she now had been warned – with the reluctant consent of France's allies – that her conduct might provoke another occupation of German cities in the Ruhr. As he put it, if he were asked to meet with the premier, and Marshals Foch and Pétain, it would not be to talk of the weather or "the cycles of the moon." Indeed, he made it clear that a decision in principle had already been taken to send in French troops, an action which would be closely coordinated with Belgium under the terms of their mutual military convention.[44] Accordingly, it came as no surprise when in March the French army, under Barthou's orders, moved to occupy Dusseldorf, Duisburg, and Ruhrort in response to German arms violations and reparations defaults. Satisfied to find himself part of a government prepared to act with vigour, Barthou admitted to Loti that, though he was overcome with fatigue, the labour had been worth it. "We've got hold of the Boche and won't let him go."[45]

There was something of a new look to Louis Barthou in 1921, the year of his first post-war cabinet portfolio. Physically, there was no marked change. He remained as energetic as ever, although there were unmistakable flecks of grey in his manicured beard and moustache, and further evidence of a receding hairline. But there was now something in his deportment which spoke of a strengthened personal authority. It was not pomposity, but rather the outward signs of a senior statesman, approaching sixty years of age, who had been prime minister and become an Academician, and whose public appraisals of the Versailles treaty seemed unhappily well founded. Lengthy and distinguished service had thus raised him to the status of a senior republican consul, as Serge Berstein has put it; and it is this which is evident during his auditions as minister before the parliamentary committees.[46]

There was more to it than his measured intolerance of interruptions from deputies too impatient to await answers to their own questions; more to it than his by now familiar insistence that ministers, while obliged to listen to military and civilian experts, were not obliged to follow the advice tendered.[47] Similarly, while as insistent as ever on the rights of parliament's committees – "I am one of those who have insisted ... on the authority of parliament" – he had no doubts about the rights of the minister. For instance, being a member of the Army committee gave no one the right of direct access to officers or soldiers. Such contact, he stressed, was up to the minister to control, as he saw fit.[48]

When it came to policy generation and implementation, the need for active ministerial direction varied with the gravity of the issue. A case in point was the proposed legislation on military service. He told the Chamber, as he had told its Army committee, that while he agreed with those who wanted to see the current three-year service reduced, he simply would not consider anything less than eighteen months in the present circumstances. He could also be "unmovable" on budgetary matters, even in the face of pressure from the powerful Finance committee. Speaking on the budgetary provision for the training of military pilots, for example, Barthou said categorically that he would accept no further cuts in an area so important to French security.[49] Neither was he inclined to manoeuvre his way through difficult auditions by making promises he was unlikely to keep. Confronted in July 1921 with a request that he slow the pace of layoffs in the armaments industry – an upheaval necessitated by efforts to rationalize artillery construction in France – Barthou replied with characteristic directness. He would be a poor minister if he agreed to that, he said, and a poor excuse for a man if he promised things he could not deliver. "I don't want to be a poor minister, at least to the extent that it depends on me, and I particularly don't want to be a dishonest man."[50]

The same candour was evident in public, when it came to speaking of old friends and old enemies. Just as he defended the remarks he had made to the Chamber in March 1920 about England's pursuit of self-interest – with the argument that frankness was essential to cordiality – so he seized upon a formal occasion in August 1921 to repudiate certain rumblings from the Anglo-Saxon world. It was a pure calumny, he said, for anyone to attribute to France a spirit of conquest. Such an allegation was like the venom secreted by reptiles.[51] As for Germany, nothing appreciable had changed. She now claimed to be inspired by democratic ideals, and to have laid to rest the spirit of militarism; but only time would tell whether German words were matched by German deeds. France was ready to be convinced of these professions of peace, but she could not afford to stand on faith alone. Germany would have to honour her disarmament and reparations commitments. "Such implementation alone ... will furnish proof of her good faith."[52] At base, however, he had seen too much, written too much, suffered too much of Germany's work in France. Struggling, or so he said, to keep an open mind, he could not help reminding his audience of Germany's continued bad faith and insolence. And no one who had noticed the tears could have doubted there was something personal behind the minister's address to the Unknown Soldier.

Poor, young, unnamed soldier who sleeps here your last sleep, warrior of France, unknown yet celebrated, dearest child of this beloved country, your sacrifice will not have been in vain.[53]

Given his insistence on the need to enforce Versailles to the letter, it was understandable that Barthou was identified as one of the hardliners in the Briand cabinet. Natural too that his name should have been linked with those – in and out of the cabinet – who had become anxious about the premier's agreement to attend yet another international conference, this time at Cannes, in January 1922. Barthou had not opposed French participation in a succession of previous conferences – San Remo, Boulogne, Brussels, Spa – but he had expressed his despair that each conference seemed to have lessened France's rights while multiplying those of Germany.[54] And as suggested by his recent performance as war minister, his mood had hardened in the light of continued German arms violations. That he was nervous about his premier's meeting at Cannes with Lloyd George, the "Welsh witch," is virtually certain – the more so as he was in a position to know the acute reservations then being expressed by President Millerand and by Raymond Poincaré, former President and currently chairman of the Senate's Foreign Affairs committee. That he was personally involved in the ultimately successful bid to unseat his own premier is quite another matter.

Some have said that he was, with the kind of unqualified assurance that is required when evidence is lacking. Barthou, so it is said, leaked to the press President Millerand's perturbed and critical communications with Briand at Cannes. Faced with an organized and vocal resistance in and out of parliament, the premier returned to Paris and promptly resigned – another leader betrayed, for another thirty pieces of silver, to recall the allusion which Briand is said to have used to Barthou.[55] Others, while fingering Millerand, Poincaré, and Doumer, the finance minister, have not included Barthou among the conspirators.[56]

The truth in every detail is likely to remain unknown. What can be said with some assurance is that Barthou, at least in 1921–22, remained an opponent of further concessions to Germany, whether or not they had the support of the English government. Had he thought Briand was going too far – and it now seems clear that the premier was not disposed to make concessions, especially on repa-

rations – Barthou might well have welcomed the collapse of a cabinet
to which he belonged. What, if any, initiative he would have taken
is more open to dispute. The underhanded tactic of a press leak is
certainly consistent with the reputation of a man to whom betrayal
came easily. But it is less consistent with the man portrayed here.
Far from the intriguer who worked from the shadows, Barthou
seems rather to have preferred to meet the opposition head-on,
sometimes indignantly, not always with great tact. So he had behaved
in 1910 over the handling of the national rail strike, under the same
Premier Briand. Having thus acted, directly and in the open, and
at a time when he had much less experience and stature than he
now enjoyed, he would not likely have felt in 1922 a stronger need
for subterfuge and treachery.

In the face of Briand's precipitate decision to resign, Millerand
asked Poincaré to form a government. The former president did so,
retaining, however, most of Briand's ministers, including Barthou.
On request, the latter moved to the Justice ministry and thus to the
de facto position of deputy premier. All told, Briand's replacement
by Poincaré thus amounted to a slight shift of cabinet personnel, a
marginal hardening of tone, but no sea change when it came to
policy. The problems, too, remained as defiant as ever. Poincaré had
no answers, other than that of reiterating the need to enforce the
Versailles treaty; and thus his preference was to postpone the follow-
up conference to which Briand had agreed, and which was now
scheduled for Genoa. Though any discussion of reparations and a
possible moratorium for Germany was to be excluded from Genoa,
on Briand's insistence, there was still the thorny problem of re-
admitting Russia to the European community and an assortment of
deep traps on the path to any new British undertaking for French
security. Knowing that it would be difficult to reaffirm the primacy
of the German problem without discussing reparations and treaty
revision, Poincaré delayed the conference for as long as he could.
Moreover, having assumed the foreign ministry portfolio himself,
he nonetheless resisted arguments from both Barthou and Lloyd
George that he should attend the conference in person.[57] Instead,
he resolved to send his deputy premier to Genoa, with a firm mandate to agree to nothing.

If ever there were a diplomatic Everest, Barthou stood before it
at Genoa, equipped only with a short rope provided by a premier
primarily interested in damage control. Under the instructions of
one such as this, Barthou had little but his own native skills with
which to resist the sometimes seductive, sometimes intimidating
Lloyd George. The fact was that France had every reason to covet

a new British commitment to French security. At the same time, however, the French delegation were to make no concessions to the Germans or Russians until the former started to comply on reparations and the latter agreed to compensate French investors for the millions of francs which had been poured into pre-war, pre-revolutionary Russia. In short, Barthou was expected to be recalcitrant toward the two powers upon whom Lloyd George had constructed his personal vision for a pacified Europe. From the outset, therefore, while it was improbable that Genoa would ever succeed, there seemed every likelihood that to France would go the blame if it failed. Poincaré, the "gentleman in Paris" spurred on by a strong press campaign, was prepared to take that risk. Barthou, the gentleman in Genoa, was assuredly less keen on acting as a lightning rod for all the ill tempers in France and those gathered in Genoa.

But he had little choice. From the outset he complained that his instructions were either too restrictive or too vague, qualities which he warned Poincaré were likely to embarrass the French delegation. The only advantage which their sometimes imprecise nature offered – and he seized upon it when he could – was to give him a chance to exercise his own judgment.[58] Imprecision was of little use, however, when it came to dealing with Lloyd George, whom Barthou in Genoa found to be quite conciliatory, while Poincaré fumed over the critical assessments of the Welshman which were carried in the Paris press.[59] Nor was this the sole divergence between the premier and his deputy. Barthou did not like Poincaré's suggestion that the French delegation should threaten to pull out of the conference if Russia and Germany did not immediately renounce their just-concluded Rapallo accord. He liked no better the idea that he should draw formal attention to German violations of the Versailles arms provisions, fearing as he did that such a reference might bring the whole of the treaty back to the negotiating table.[60]

Poincaré remained unmoved. He continued to urge Barthou to threaten withdrawal from the conference, and now began – on 22 April – to raise the possibility of bringing his delegate back to Paris for a briefing. But his delegate was wary, declining to make such a threat unless he had in hand very precise instructions to do so, and adding purposefully, with an edge, that he knew how difficult it must be to send appropriate instructions to those who had to make decisions on the spot.[61] Several days later Barthou stalled again. He now argued that for him to come to Paris at this difficult moment might look as if he were being recalled, as if there were discord between himself and his government. He would leave as soon as he could, once he had allayed misgivings that France was actually withdrawing from the conference.[62] In short, he was deliberately mis-construing his chief's wishes, as well as ignoring them, a tactic to which Poincaré replied in kind. Once again he informed Barthou that, however preposterous and ill founded, reports in the British and American press continued to speak of disagreements between himself and his delegate in Genoa. Indeed, some reports even had the temerity to suggest that such notions had come from Barthou's own entourage. To which Barthou replied from Genoa that anyone who believed he had been behind such malicious articles would likely be foolish enough to think that he, Poincaré, had lent credence to them in Paris.[63]

This verbal duelling with Poincaré characterized Barthou's com-munications from Genoa. It is, however, only symptomatic of the role which he had devised for himself after arriving in Italy, devised out of temperament and pragmatism both. Either, of course, can be framed positively or negatively, and were by contemporary observ-ers. As for temperament, or character, one can subscribe to the informed, unsympathetic witness Louise Weiss of L'Europe nouvelle, or the informed, sympathetic Jean de Pierrefeu of Illustration. The former did not like Poincaré, "Raymond de Mon Droit," as her friend Briand called him, and did not much care for Louis Barthou, "a puppet" and a man of "dubious character." "Louis the charming," she dubbed him, without apparent appreciation of what she called his "conciliatory attitude."[64] Pierrefeu watched the same man, but read him differently. Barthou, he said, was one who needed to get along with others. To be protesting all the time was intensely dis-agreeable for this "genial southerner." Instead, he preferred to smooth over differences, where possible to conciliate. Symptomatic of his disposition was his masterful dealing with a sometimes difficult French press corps, a role for which he was especially suited as current president of the Association des journalistes parisiens. He knew just how to woo them, Pierrefeu reported, like some masculine "Sarah Bernhardt," knew how and when to reprove gently or to ingratiate with flattery. As a natural diplomat, he had mastered "the weapons of seduction."[65]

But to what end? Weiss saw only one. Barthou was a pragmatist in the base sense, a man only interested in power. Having dumped her friend Briand, as she believed, he was out to do the same to Poincaré, in the hope of replacing him. Thus he played up to Lloyd George by complaining of the premier's intransigence. Thus he ig-nored instructions to return to Paris until word arrived that Poincaré was about to fall. Thus he returned from Paris, having reread Machiavelli, to further his career by preventing Lloyd George from wrecking Anglo-French relations. Nothing, in short, was enough to appease the indomitable Mme Weiss.[66] Pierrefeu, too, recognized the strength of Barthou's political instincts. Discovering Barthou alone in the Villa Raggio on 29 April – almost a week after Poincaré had begun calling him back to Paris – the journalist observed a surprisingly morose figure, even a little dishevelled. He was feeling depressed, isolated by the public criticism he had been enduring. Suddenly, news arrived that Paris was buzzing with rumours of some new ministry; and just as suddenly Barthou was on his feet, animated, as if called by a dinner bell, "cured of his upset and ready to eat."[67] Still, there was no rush to Paris. He delayed his departure from Genoa for four more days, alternatively put upon by Lloyd George, at hand, and by Poincaré, at a distance.

It is not what one would have expected from a man intent on manoeuvring Poincaré from office. Nor is the man who returns to Genoa anything like Weiss's consummate Machiavellian. Indeed, he returns belled by Poincaré, with instructions carefully fashioned so as to "constrain somewhat your freedom of manoeuvre."[68] If, however, some doubt is allowed on this score of personal power as his *idée fixe*, there is room to develop Pierrefeu's understanding of Barthou's pragmatism. This journalist admired the way Barthou responded to the challenges of a conference which required a spirit of conciliation to stay alive. This is not to say that the hawk had taken on the plumage of the dove. Rather, here was a statesman who had spoken many times of the importance of the entente with England, and of the need to work out a sensible, allied policy toward soviet Russia. No friend of the latter, he cared little for the Russian delegates at Genoa – Chicherin with his shifty eyes, Litvinov with his impenetrable dogmatism, both with their common "penchant for chicanery."[69] It was they who had engineered the surprise Russo-German agreement known as the Rapallo accord, and who had announced its conclusion during the first week of the Genoa conference, much to the consternation of the British, French, Italian, and Belgian delegations. Nonetheless, he personally leaned toward Lloyd George's view that the Russians, now more than ever, had to be accorded a prominent place at Genoa and had to be reconciled with the rest of Europe. Speaking to that belief, he first offended Poincaré and the Belgians, and then, bowing to a rush of contrary-minded instructions from Paris, he further offended Lloyd George.

Here was the heart of the problem for a pragmatist worthy of the name. In one way or another, France's hopes for strengthened security against a renascent Germany still rested heavily on the possibility of restoring a meaningful Anglo-French alliance. Poincaré knew this as well as anyone, but he had chosen to send Barthou to Genoa with the task of securing British cooperation, while resisting Britain's conciliatory mood toward Germany and, to a lesser extent, toward Russia. If it were not quite a mission impossible, it was near enough. Thus, to present Barthou's relations with Lloyd George as those between pigmy and titan is surely a case of exaggeration flirting with error. For the better part of six weeks Barthou withstood intense pressure from Poincaré, who upbraided him for being too conciliatory and too independent-minded, and from Lloyd George, who found him neither sufficiently one nor the other. And predictably, when he did give ground to either, too often he was held up in the British and French press as a man of little independent authority – which was true – and of a weak and pliable character – which was not. Indeed, rather than remarking negatively on his eventual submission to his premier, one might instead remark on his resistance to instructions which he thought might bring down on France all the opprobrium for the conference's failure.[70]

Similarly pragmatic was his sometimes applauded, sometimes regretted, rescue of Lloyd George in May 1922, toward the end of the conference. The prime minister had been indiscreet, again, this time hinting to Barthou and the French press that Poincaré was essentially wrecking the chances for a revived Anglo-French accord. Though these hints were calculated to pressure Paris, the tables were soon turned when a journalist from *The Times* fingered Lloyd George himself as the chief threat to the entente – if, that is, he actually had said what had been attributed to him.[71] Discomfited by domestic reaction, Lloyd George pressed Barthou to deny that these things had been said. With considerable grace, and before Poincaré could interfere, France's chief delegate did so, immediately incurring the wrath of those like Mme Weiss who accused him of rescuing France's nemesis in order to court domestic opinion in France.[72] But for those unmoved by this bewildering display of logic, there is a more obvious explanation for Barthou's action, one which speaks more positively of his pragmatism in international politics. Good relations with Britain were an imperative for French foreign policy, no less so when they were in fact troubled. To lend credence to a possible rupture made very little sense. Accordingly, Barthou denied the prime minister's threat, relieved the pressure on a man he had no personal reason for exonerating, and welcomed the outpourings of officially expressed amity from both sides of the Channel.

Because Genoa is commonly seen more as a failure than a success, there is no question of returning a triumphant Barthou to Paris. Nevertheless, his accomplishments were substantial. By displaying

more conciliation and flexibility than anyone had imagined likely –
including Poincaré – he had helped defer the collapse of the conference by several weeks. By so doing, he had blunted some of the
criticism of France, and dispersed some of it to the other delegations.
In a sense he had played Poincaré's game, but not always by Poincaré's rules. For eventually, sometimes with regret, he had adopted
the government's line. Indeed, he failed Poincaré only in being unable to have the Rapallo accord nullified, a failure of course which
was broadly collective rather than personal. The premier, therefore,
had reason to be satisfied with his delegate's performance. Once
again, Louis Barthou had served him well, ultimately having resisted
his natural inclination to compromise, that element in his makeup
which made Poincaré nervous. But kept in close check, he had
proven again his resolve as a patriot and his loyalty as a friend. For
both reasons, Poincaré welcomed him back to the cabinet. For a
short time: by the autumn of 1922 he had found another highly
demanding mission for his deputy premier, this time as head of the
French delegation to the International Reparations Commission.[73]

It was in October 1922 that Poincaré announced the cabinet
change. Louis Dubois, currently the French delegate to the Reparations Commission, was resigning for reasons of health. As a consequence, Louis Barthou would replace Dubois, while Maurice Col-
rat, a member of the recent delegation to Genoa, would assume the
duties of the justice minister. Reporting the change to his English
readers, *The Times*'s correspondent in Paris was broadly reassuring.
President Millerand and the Poincaré cabinet were grateful that
Barthou had accepted this difficult assignment. He was, the journalist continued, a "master of the language of diplomacy," as he had
so ably demonstrated in Genoa where he had "compelled the respect
of Tchitcherin and conciliated Mr. Lloyd George."[74] At the same
time, there was no reason to question Barthou's personal attachment
to Poincaré's ideas on the enforcement of Versailles. Nothing at
Genoa had suggested a rethinking on matters such as reparations.
Indeed, he had required no prodding from Paris to insist that reparations remain strictly the responsibility of the Reparations Commission. All that remained unclear was what the Commission might
now do in the face of Weimar Germany's repeated failures to honour
the payments schedule.

Elected chairman of the Commission at his first meeting on
10 October – an office accorded by statute to the head of the French
delegation – Barthou did his best to strike the right opening note.
He wanted to see the treaty respected and enforced to the letter,
but he was also anxious to avoid a policy of vexatious, counter-

productive pinpricks.[75] For the next three months he was true to his word, at least in the sense of ensuring that reparations were not trivialized. Within a month, he was pressing the Commission toward making a formal declaration of default on German wood and coal deliveries to France. Sometimes speaking expressly as head of the French delegation, and sometimes as an openly partial chairman of the Commission, he resisted attempts by various German missions to secure reductions in the payments and delays in the delivery schedules. He listened to them and then, on their departure, he rejected what he had heard. Again and again he countered German complaints and pleas with the rights of France and Belgium to receive compensation for the wartime damages inflicted by Germany. Convinced as ever of Germany's "ill will," he was soon engaged in a protracted battle with the head of the British delegation, Sir John Bradbury.[76]

What was at issue was an open secret. Rumours were rife that the Poincaré government was preparing to occupy Germany's industrial Ruhr basin, preparations which followed a decision in principle of 27 November 1922.[77] What was essential, however, was to have in advance a formal judgment of default by the Reparations Commission headquartered in Paris. As Poincaré put it, Barthou had to "get to the heart of the matter," for there was no point in having a Commission which sat idly by while Germany engaged in flagrant violations of her treaty obligations. Barthou understood perfectly. His job was to provide the government with the means of implementing "a seizure of certain securities in the Ruhr, within a satisfactory legal framework."[78] Bradbury, on the other hand, was determined to be uncooperative. Alluding to French preparations for a "certain eventuality," he confronted Barthou during a meeting in late December, appropriately on Boxing Day. Bradbury complained, disingenuously, that the move to declare Germany in default was too sudden and unexpected to warrant an immediate decision by the Commission. Barthou denied, disingenuously, any connection between the non-political deliberations of the Commission and the political responsibilities assumed by the French cabinet – adding gratuitously that he would refrain from mentioning the cloud of contradictions which obscured British policy on reparations.[79] Debate ended, and despite Bradbury's none too veiled threats of resignation, the chairman succeeded in securing a three-to-one vote in favour of declaring Germany's default in timber payments.

Writing shortly thereafter to Lyautey, Barthou expressed regret about the strains in Anglo-French relations. The only thing that had surprised him, however, was the surprise evinced by the British delegation over the intensity of French anxieties.[80] That they were intense became the more obvious when he proceeded to push for a second declaration of default, this time with regard to the even more critical subject of coal payments. Having entertained another group of German emissaries on 8 January 1923, Barthou promptly re-opened the Commission's deliberations by saying that nothing he had heard had made him change his mind in the slightest. The fact was that in 1922 Germany had managed to satisfy 80 per cent of her own needs in coking coal, but barely 50 per cent of those required by France.

From a strictly moral point of view, it is inadmissible that the defeated country, that which owes reparations, is flourishing while industry in the victorious but ruined country grinds to a halt because it is not getting the essential deliveries owing to it.[81]

Sir John Bradbury fought a rearguard action, but on 9 January the French, Belgian, and Italian delegations recorded another German default. Two days later, the French government ordered its troops into the Ruhr, in yet one more attempt to ensure Germany's complete compliance with her reparations obligations.

Directly associated with the military intervention of March 1921, Louis Barthou was only indirectly linked with the more dramatic move of January 1923. Nevertheless, he had accomplished, whole-heartedly, what Poincaré had expected of him, and eventually decided that it was appropriate for him to comment publicly on the government's decision. In April he assured the departmental council of Basses-Pyrénées – over which he had presided since 1904 – that the occupation had been necessary and that Poincaré merited praise for his decision. Reparations defaults, together with incessant arms violations, had made the step imperative.[82] In January 1924, he offered an even more public defence of that action, and at a time when doubts about the efficacy of the measure had been multiplied by Germany's passive resistance.

It was the right thing to have done, he claimed, because it was the only step France could have taken to ensure that she received at least some of the reparations owing to her. Moreover, as he had told his earlier audience in Pau, the move into the Ruhr had also enhanced France's military security in the face of repeated German arms violations. The occupation, for however long it lasted – and clearly he was no partisan of early withdrawal – was no solution to the basic problems of reparations, any more than it was a solution to French security. But for him, it was better than whatever was in second place. For the time being, France was more secure for being in the Ruhr, and could afford to be optimistic now that more reparations were being paid in full and on time.[83]

Although this public address of January 1924 amounted to a fully-fledged defence of Poincaré and the occupation, it was not long before there were signs of a softening on Barthou's part. It was not a complete surprise. The crisis had been weathered without an interruption of peace or of France's relations with Great Britain; however, it was manifest that coercion was no long-term answer. Doubtless this was why, in April, he welcomed the new approaches recommended in the report submitted by the Commission's Committee of Experts – the committee chaired by General Charles G. Dawes. As one who long ago had refuted the idea of France ever getting everything that Germany would owe her, Barthou saw the possibilities of some new accord which, if based on genuine German concurrence, might in fact secure more for France. Even if concessions had to be made on final amounts and payment schedules. Certainly there is evident by April a tiny glimmer of conciliation on his part, notably when he said the language of victors and vanquished had to give way to the less value-laden vocabulary of debtors and creditors.[84]

Poincaré, however, remained obdurate, displaying again the luxuries and liabilities of removing himself from international conferences and the knavish tricks of foreigners. He was unhappy with Barthou's positive receipt of the Dawes report, and unmoved by advice that France had to give on some diplomatic front if she were going to dispel rumours that the Ruhr occupation was the first step toward annexation.[85] As Poincaré saw it, Barthou had acted precipitately. Now what he wanted was to see from his friend some of the old "insightful firmness and shrewdness," in the cause of slowing down the Dawes initiatives. As Barthou saw it, there was again a problem of communication. He had acted not out of impulse or presumption, but rather because he wanted to ensure that France was not diplomatically isolated. As for his "shrewdness," and unsure whether the premier was serving up charge or compliment, Barthou accepted the word as meaning only that he had been "irreproachably clear."[86] As Edouard Herriot saw it, there was no doubt that the gap between Poincaré and Barthou was widening, principally because the latter feared the isolating effects of the government's policy. Significantly, therefore, when the Radical Herriot succeeded Poincaré as premier and foreign minister in June 1924, he chose to leave Louis Barthou at the Reparations Commission.[87]

His remaining years at the Commission, between the summers of 1924 and 1926, were relatively tranquil, in keeping with the conciliatory mood which in 1925 was christened the "Locarno spirit." Having again demonstrated a measure of independence from Poincaré, Barthou was accepted as an appropriate agent for the at least rhetorically redressed foreign policy of Herriot and the Cartel des Gauches. By August he was speaking more openly of his hopes for new beginnings in the relations between the Commission and Germany; and as a measure of those hopes, in September he took it upon himself to agree to a 10 per cent reduction in German coal payments for that month.[88] At the same time, however, he made it clear that his was far from a complete conversion. He wanted to be convinced of Germany's good faith, so he told the Commission, but there were still too many grounds for doubt. Time alone would tell whether the language of reconciliation would be matched by Germany's honest fulfilment of her treaty obligations.[89]

Thus having survived the crisis of 1923, defended Poincaré's decision, and perceived its limitations, Barthou held on to what he could of the Versailles conditions by alternating between firmness and tractability. The latter may have done little to impress the German government, but it did seem to patch up part of the quarrel with Sir John Bradbury and his successor, Lord Blanesburgh. Indeed, by August 1926, when he took leave of the Commission, Barthou had the satisfaction of knowing that relations within the Commission now reflected the more conciliatory spirit that was coming to prevail among their respective governments. Blanesburgh praised the retiring chairman for his statesmanship and for the way he had been able to "secure the confidence of our former enemies." The Belgian delegate, M. Delacroix, praised his candour and his rectitude, while the Italian and American spokesmen – dutifully shelving some memories – praised his impartiality and "absolute fairness." Everyone agreed and, with a genuiness confirmed by the records of their proceedings, said more. Barthou had been an extremely competent, well-prepared chairman, one who had expedited discussion and decision-making over the course of some seventy meetings, one who had done so with a cultivated humour and civility.[90]

On this note Barthou left the Commission and returned to the Justice ministry in yet another Poincaré cabinet. By so doing, he curtailed his direct involvement in French foreign policy, an area of responsibility which had preoccupied him for the better part of a decade. And with considerable distinction, or so we might now argue.

Circumstances had first entrusted him with a critic's role, beginning with his membership in the Foreign Affairs committee and
extending to the Committee on the Peace Treaties. On both he had
led in the criticism of the Clemenceau government's refusal to solicit
parliament's views on the armistice or on the Versailles treaty. By
the same token, he had also led in the reluctant acceptance of the
government's methods, partly because he appreciated its concerns
about ensuring confidentiality, partly because too persistent complaint about the *fait accompli* was certain to crack the surface of the
united front which France had to adopt in the face of its former
enemies and allies. As for the treaty itself, his appraisal was a mixture
of open commendation and carefully nuanced reproof, consciously
designed to bolster the nation's sense of earned victory without fos-
tering a degree of over-confidence. Thus, while focusing on the
uncertain, and soon illusory, Anglo-French guarantees, Barthou acknowledged the severe constraints under which the government had
been obliged to work. For his part, Clemenceau ignored the restraint
of parliament's *rapporteur*, and resented the criticism. Some deputies,
principally those on the socialist left, ignored the criticism and resented the restraint. But the Chamber as a whole approved the
Committee's analysis and ratified the treaty it recommended, but
continued to articulate the insecurity still felt by this victorious
France.

For a time, in parliament and press, Louis Barthou had himself
expressed those concerns. Then in 1921, as war minister under
Briand, he was officially engaged in addressing the German problem,
both in the form of public and private addresses, and in his efforts
to remould a demobilized and at times disheartened French army.
It was this combined service, including his part in dispatching army
units across the Rhine in 1921, which led to his enlistment by Poincaré in 1922, briefly as delegate to Genoa and subsequently as delegate to the Reparations Commission. Both were delicate missions,
for both required intransigence and conciliation in just the right
measure. In a post-war world which was experiencing acute difficulty
in arriving at peace, and where success came in small draughts, Louis
Barthou's performance was certainly creditable enough. Placed by
temperament at the centre of a controversy, he was by now a veteran
at reconciling the soft flanks of either extreme. Thus at Genoa he
showed enough independence from Poincaré to make an impression
on the British, and enough compliance to prevent Poincaré from
wrecking the conference with a public disavowal of his delegate. As
for the Reparations Commission, Barthou supported Poincaré until
whatever was to be gained by intransigence seemed less than what

might come with greater flexibility. Although this long-rehearsed ability to shift from one foot to the other did attract criticism from some, others recognized that this agility was the mark of one who had never been partial to dogmatists. His only dogma, in this instance, was the enhancement of French security, upon which he believed – and with much justice – the peace of Europe depended. In the interest of this, he shrugged off the familiar accusations about lack of principle or weak character, and advanced patiently toward the same unchanged goal, secure in his belief that there was always "more than one route and more than one means to get to one's goal."[91]

CHAPTER EIGHT

The 1920s: Political Turmoil and Private Pursuits

In my library I spend the most peaceful, the most illuminating, hours of my life. It is there that I am happy to lose touch with the mortal passage of time.[1]

Barthou professed that his four years on the Reparations Commission had been among the best of his life.[2] Doubtless it was gratifying to listen to the warm testimonials from fellow commissioners, but his remark was one of the moment. The 1920s had been difficult years for him, as well as for France. They had brought much new recognition and prestige, it is true, but also a measure of political disenchantment, more personal bereavement and anxiety, and plenty of criticism from home and abroad. And if, in this testimonial glow, his memory had spared him some of his recent travails, his prescience also faltered. For the next three years as minister, and for some time thereafter, he would face a campaign of personal vilification that would make the Caillaux affair of 1914 seem like a minor domestic spat.

Just as the end of the war required nations to adjust as radically as they had done in 1914, so it required individual men and women. Louis Barthou was no exception. For him personally, ratification of the Versailles treaty meant accepting that Max would not return with the peace. Neither would his father, dead in 1915, nor his mother, who had died in 1919. There was, in short, a sense of a chapter coming to an end, a sense further sharpened by events in parliament.

Having recently acquired celebrity status by virtue of his report on Versailles, and yet another sweeping victory in the general elections of November 1919, Louis Barthou returned to a Chamber full of deputies he did not know. Rather than retaining roughly two-thirds of the members of the previous Assembly, as was normally the case, this election had returned only a third. The majority of deputies, therefore, were new to him in appearance, younger in age, and different in outlook. Added to this, there was an associated sense of isolation and impotence. Having kept his distance from the victorious Bloc National and its member parties, Barthou now sat with a small centrist group called the Gauche Républicaine et Démocratique, observing from their benches over the next fourteen months the ebb and flow of cabinets – Clemenceau, Millerand, Leygues.[3] Thus, disconcerted by foreign political problems, Barthou was also distressed by what he saw around him. Denied any cabinet portfolio with which to defend himself, Barthou thought that he was being viewed as a man over the hill, rushed to the status of greybeard as the first step toward benign oblivion. He did not like it. Pricked by amour-propre, he fought back by offering sage advice to anyone prepared to listen, but without ever subduing the traces of generational alienation.

Writing of this new and largely untried Chamber, Barthou admitted to feelings of resentment. Too often, he said, the old guard like himself were seen as men pushed by personal ambition and drawn to the tactics of intrigue.[4] Coming in the wake of the war and its attendant sacrifices, such accusations bit very deeply, the more so as they were seldom explicit enough to refute. Forgetting what had been said of the young "kids" of his own generation, men earlier accused of an eagerness to discard their elders, he now found quite unseemly the impatience of younger men. But there was more to it than this, or so he argued. "Professional" politicians like himself, who had given their lives to politics, were now objects of distrust among newcomers who had first made their mark in commerce, engineering, aviation, or automobiles. These new technocrats were men accustomed to measuring competence in expressly non-political terms. More than that, they added to their disdain of men with no particular expertise an irritating sanctimony. Barthou resented their slighting remarks about the shadowy, corrupt, unprincipled intrigues of pre-war politics – sensing perhaps his own reputation in the Chamber for manoeuvre and betrayal.[5] But however it was expressed, for whatever motives, the message was clear enough. "Make room for the young!"[6]

Clear on what they wanted, Barthou was in no hurry to oblige. Sounding more elderly than his physical energy suggested, he disparaged the impatience of his juniors, and judged unseemly their expectation of a cabinet post after but the briefest political apprenticeship. In his own day, he said – with some measure of personal authenticity – it was as common to decline office as to chase after it. Instead, now cabinet portfolios were sought more as rewards for party loyalty than for sustained and competent service. There was something undignified about it all, he contended, and depressing, when one considered that not even all the heroism and sacrifice induced by the war had been sufficient to stop this scramble for favours and personal advancement.[7] He had had enough. Piqued by the conduct of younger men who behaved with too little decorum, or so he perceived them, in 1922 Louis Barthou decided to run for the Senate. After some thirty years as a deputy for Basses-Pyrénées, he presented himself as candidate in a senatorial by-election occasioned by the death of Henri Faisans. It was another coronation. On the first *scrutin* of July 1922, Louis Barthou had amassed 913 of the 999 votes cast in the electoral college.[8] Henceforth, it was Senator Barthou.

Generational disgruntlement seems to have played its part in this decision to run for a seat in the upper Chamber, where members tended to be both older and more conservative than their colleagues in the lower Chamber. There was also a feeling on his part that the actual system was malfunctioning. He was much concerned with the problem of ministerial instability, the frequency with which one cabinet gave way to another, and another. This, he told the Académie Française, was a national scourge, for it continually confounded efforts at long-term planning.[9] There was as well the problem of an undeveloped prime ministerial office. Indeed, unless a premier assumed an additional cabinet portfolio, he had no office at all, and no secretariat or archive. It was like a military commander trying to operate without a headquarters.[10] This in turn was symptomatic of something more fundamental still, namely the crisis of executive authority. So zealous had been the deputies' attempts to ensure parliament's authority that too often a government's power of decision-making was dangerously eroded. Thus, and again, cabinets were overthrown with disturbing rapidity, sometimes because one minister had shown too much initiative, sometimes because another had been too cautious, sometimes merely because another had run afoul of a parliamentary committee full of aspirants for his job. And even if the crisis were averted, and the cabinet upheld, too often the minister had to spend a disproportionate amount of his time answering inquiries from the Chamber and Senate instead of developing the requisite expertise for his portfolio and the requisite personal authority over his permanent civil service. Finally, the powers of the presidency were also too constrained by custom to allow the incumbent to play the kind of role that was expected of him. Although Barthou was still no advocate of constitutional revision on this score, he did argue that the powers constitutionally accorded to the president ought to be employed in the interests of reaffirmed executive authority and greater ministerial stability.[11]

There was yet another dimension to Barthou's immediate post-war anxiety. Broadly expressed, he was preoccupied with threats to national unity, conscious as he was of the tragic possibility that France could emerge from a united war effort only to succumb to a host of internal divisions. This had been one of his central concerns at the time of his report on Versailles, a report tailored to accommodate both supporters and critics of the government; and it remained his objective in the wake of the report as he sought to forge a parliamentary consensus on post-war foreign policy. The fact that unity was elusive is reflected in his repeated emphasis on the need for it. It was this that characterized his public treatment of the sensitive election for president in the autumn of 1920, that which ultimately elevated Alexandre Millerand.

Mindful of the divisions which surrounded a possible candidacy from Clemenceau – though without addressing them openly – Barthou repeatedly enjoined readers of *Les Annales* to look for a president who could personify national unity. "France has too much to do to be able to afford the luxury of useless quarrels and internal divisions."[12] Central to his concern about Clemenceau, whose election he privately considered would be "a public misfortune,"[13] was the predictable resistance of the socialist left. Not that he was any more disposed toward them than in the past. Nevertheless, he reasoned that nothing ought to be done that might offend or weaken a party already under acute pressure – both from indigenous communist elements, and from the revolutionary "bolshevik contagion" of the Communist International in Moscow. French socialists, however ideologically misguided, had shown themselves prepared to respect the verdict of universal manhood suffrage and, for the most part, the laws of France. They were, therefore, a lesser threat to national unity than those of bolshevik persuasion – those "brigands ... assassins ... thieves" who had already declared war on the French state.[14]

There was one final dimension to Barthou's general unease in the early 1920s, one which accentuated his concern about national unity, political stability, and the bumptious ingratitude of the next generation. Indeed, this too is to some extent an expression of generation, for it speaks to time-related changes in personal relationships. Simply put, in the period up to the summer of 1926 when he rejoined Poincaré as justice minister, Louis Barthou suffered the loss and the approaching loss of people especially dear to him.

Four years after the death of his mother came that of Alice's peculiar godson, Pierre Loti. He died in June 1923, at the age of seventy-three, still mysteriously childlike to his grieving friends in Paris. For nearly two decades they had been close to him, husband

and wife, finding in him something deeply moving, especially after the death of their Max. It was more than the genius they detected, it was the melancholy that underlay the genius, the sense of suffering, the fear of death, the dignity with which he sought to combat that fear. Although the relationship between the two men was certainly based in part on respective appreciations of self-interest – the statesman lobbying in the writer's many causes, the writer reciprocating with gifts of manuscripts – it would do neither justice to exclude the presence of genuine and mutual affection. Apart from serving as executor for Loti's estate, Barthou was to keep his friend's memory alive in a succession of books, articles, and public addresses, each of them expressive of an affectionate fascination for the grand "magicien" Pierre Loti.[15]

He did the same for Anatole France, another close friend who died in 1924. Again, as in the case of Loti, there was something in France which Barthou never fathomed. As a consequence, there had been some awkward moments, particularly when the writer had sided with the likes of Jaurès and Caillaux over the three-year military service law.[16] However, Barthou subsequently recalled how relations had been repaired with the coming of the war and the ensuing death of Max. In the first instance, according to Barthou, France had written the War ministry in September 1914, offering his services with the line, "Make a soldier out of me." In the second, he had written to the bereaved parents, saying that his memory of Max would never permit him again to look without tears on the tombs of Athens's fallen warriors.[17] Both gestures moved Barthou deeply, strengthening all the more his admiration of France as literary genius. Indeed, it had to have been that appraisal and that gratitude which were behind Barthou's persistent defence of Anatole France as a great patriot – even when it meant overlooking the writer's renewed attraction to international socialism in the last years of the war. Instead, Barthou remained unshaken in his conviction that France had been too independent a mind to become a vassal to any party or dogma. Even if he had been "an apostle of internationalism," he had never renounced the idea of his country. A patriot then, in Barthou's book, France had thus excelled as an artist of France, to whose people he had confided the precious *Les Dieux ont soif*, better than Taine as history, better than Flaubert as novel.[18]

The death of France in 1924 was accompanied by renewed anxiety for Barthou. His wife's health was deteriorating. It had been uncertain since the summer of 1922, a condition unremedied by their vacation in Bürgenstock. Two years later they discovered she was terminally ill. The only value of the operation performed in the summer of 1924 had been to prove its futility, or so Barthou confided to Marshal Lyautey.[19] At the same time France's death led to a contest for his chair at the Académie Française, between Paul Valéry and Léon Bérard. On first reflection, one might well take Barthou's vote for granted. Bérard was a Béarnais and a political colleague of similarly centrist persuasion, while Valéry was already known to have scoffed at both the artistry and the patriotism of Anatole France. Nevertheless, Barthou supported Valéry and so "betrayed" again, this time Bérard. Why he did so never generated much speculation, thanks to the force of assumptions. The first of these assumptions was that Barthou was indifferent to the modern poetry of Valéry – an assumption which should be re-examined in the light of the many autographed first editions of Valéry in the Barthou library.[20] Nevertheless, there has been an obvious preference for less aesthetically informed explanations.

Certainly it would be a mistake to exaggerate the natural affinity between Barthou and Bérard. There is, it is true, the story of Barthou's promotion of Bérard's early career, and his persuading him to accept his first cabinet post in the Poincaré government of 1912. There is as well Barthou's account of his disclosure of the Fabre report in 1914, just prior to which Bérard had served as a confidante of sorts.[21] There were, however, pronounced differences in their character: Bérard, fourteen years younger, pious Catholic, Jesuit-educated, more introverted, possibly more introspective, a man of greater natural refinement than Barthou – so it is said – but likely too of greater natural conservatism. They were not kindred spirits, a fact which became more apparent in the immediate post-war period. Although they ran on the same ticket in 1919, when the country briefly returned to the *scrutin de liste*, by 1924 there were suspicions that Barthou was conspiring against Bérard's re-election.[22] Hence, there was some background to the ill will which became more public with Barthou's support for Valéry in 1925. But background, like belief, is not evidence; the evidence is frankly uncertain, but not so the belief. The belief is that Barthou, unable to forget Max's sacrifice, was unable to forgive Bérard's sedentary and safe military service. Fairly or otherwise, it was an issue in Béarn after the war; and without visible involvement from Barthou, Bérard was called to account publicly for his wartime service in the face of organized hecklers.[23]

Given the nature of this ambiguous relationship, it is difficult to gauge the impact on Barthou of this quiet drifting apart. Bérard was never to Barthou what Loti or France had been; and yet we know by now that Barthou's own nature was too sensitive to support broken friendships with indifference. Moreover, he was astute enough to know that some kind of political price would have to be paid in Béarn for appearing to have scotched, if temporarily, Bérard's hopes for the Académie. Indeed, doubtless he was soon made aware of those rumours which explained his vote for Valéry as nothing more than a vain wish to remain not only the first but the sole Béarnais in the Académie Française.[24] Accordingly, coming as this did on the heels of his other political and personal tribulations, the Bérard affair could only have added to the emotional burdens which Barthou carried with him into Poincaré's government of 1926.

Three years earlier Barthou had written that the Justice ministry was the most dangerous of all portfolios. One minute all was tranquil, the next there was some explosion.[25] It was a judgment based on previous experience, but ensuing events might have suggested premonition. He was on the brink of the Daudet affair. In June 1927 he carefully traced the tragedy which had befallen the star royalist in the Chamber, Léon Daudet, and did so with a sensitivity which befitted one who himself had suffered the death of a son. In November 1923, Daudet's own teenaged son, Philippe, had died under very mysterious circumstances. The official verdict was one of suicide.[26] The grief-stricken father said it was murder, a politically inspired assassination executed by the Republic's police. Their motive, he claimed, was to punish the monarchist-inspired movement, Action Française, for whom he himself served as a chief polemicist. That public allegation against the public security forces had led to a defamation suit against him, which he lost, and to an appeal, which he also lost.

In June 1926, prior to Barthou's return to the Justice ministry, a special commission had reviewed Daudet's arguments for a second appeal – this time based on a claim of new evidence – but had delivered another ruling against him. As a result, he faced a fine and immediate imprisonment for seven months. It was at this point that Barthou, newly returned, personally intervened in Daudet's favour. Having discussed the matter with Poincaré, though expressly not with the cabinet as a whole, the minister granted a new appeal on his own initiative. He had done so, he told the Chamber, solely out of appreciation of Daudet's courage and the magnitude of his loss.[27] Nonetheless, the second appeal to the Court of Cassation met the same fate as the first, a judicial decision which left the minister with little choice but to enforce Daudet's sentence. In June 1927 the deputy-journalist entered the Santé prison. In July he escaped, took refuge in Belgium and escalated his press campaign against the hated Republic and its especially contemptible justice minister.

Because this campaign of vilification proved so effective, because it did so much to colour what little is now remembered of Louis Barthou, it must be approached with caution. At its centre is a perplexing professional, even moral, dilemma for the historian. To repeat the charges against him is to risk adding to a tissue of lies. To ignore them is to risk charges of a cover-up. Either way, the biographer will be a lesser victim than his subject; and from that comes the belief that candour will be more disarming than silence. At the same time, the reader must be warned at the outset that no one can be certain how true or untrue were Daudet's allegations against Barthou. Moreover, even allowing for their authenticity, one may well ask how telling they are when it comes to appraising the work of a public servant. Compared to those exposed in our own day, when the private transgressions of public figures lack nothing in imagination, those levied against Barthou may pale into insignificance. What is common to past and present, however, the substance of the issue, is not so much the specific peccadillo as the questionable judgment behind it. In short, infidelity in marriage or belief is one thing; the assumption that one can get away with it, and if necessary lie about it, is another. The former may or may not invite moral censure, but the latter warrants unease and even distrust. Lack of judgment of this sort, lapses of integrity of this sort, must be seen as legitimate issues for biographers to address, even those who would willingly surrender their right to pass moral judgments. There is, therefore, at least potentially, something worthwhile to be drawn from Daudet's characterization of Louis Barthou.

There is also another word of direction to be offered to readers unfamiliar with Daudet and those who collided with him. Like many talented polemicists, he made a virtue of excess. It was his stock in trade, and rare was the senior republican politician who did not know it. Poincaré became "the little dwarf," Briand "the wandering gutter-snipe," Herriot "this dreadful dumbbell," Steeg the "son of a Boche," Paul-Boncour "the Don Juan of the lavatory." As one police report put it, Daudet invariably attacked the Republic by subjecting its chief spokesmen to systematic character assassination. "No one is safe when Daudet has marked him out as a target."[28] That Barthou should have come under his guns was wholly unremarkable, except for one detail of importance. Until the mid-1920s the two had been friendly, at least to a point consistent with the politics of one republican and one royalist. Daudet respected Barthou's patriotism, his wit, and his credentials as a literary connoisseur. In particular, they shared an admiration for the work of Daudet's father, Alphonse, and of Victor Hugo, whose granddaughter had become

Léon's first wife. Writing in 1925, after Philippe's death but before Barthou's return to the Justice ministry, Daudet was relatively tender with Barthou. While acknowledging that this Béarnais still remained an enigma to him, Daudet admitted that he found his company amusing and agreeable.[29]

Everything changed with the collapse of Daudet's final appeal and his passage to the Santé prison. Suddenly, Barthou became the chief target of abuse for Daudet and his equally acerbic colleague, Charles Maurras. Long convinced that the Republic was an affront to France, the writers of the *Action française* now focused on a justice system which, so they alleged, protected murderers behind false witnesses and pliant judges. Symbolic of this rot, its personification, was the minister himself. By August 1927 everything had been said that was going to be said, relentlessly, over the next four years. Stripped to their essentials, there were three principal accusations. Barthou was a liar, a thief, and a pervert.

First, his literary achievements, crowned by a gullible Academy, were the works of ghost-writers. Not given to understatement, the royalists proclaimed that, of *Mirabeau* and *Lamartine* and all the other books and articles, Barthou "never wrote a single word."[30] Second, his famous library of manuscripts and first editions was the product of extortion and theft. From the vulnerable he extorted gifts, from the ignorant he purchased at bargain prices, and from the others, he stole.[31] These alone would have been enough to inspire the new appellations "Médor" (or Fido) Barthou, the "chien" Barthou – epithets Daudet liked so much that he had tried them on other enemies before reserving them especially for Louis Barthou.[32]

But it was the third charge that proved truly inspired, so much so that people who now recall almost nothing of Barthou are sure that he was either aggressively homosexual or heterosexual. What Daudet actually said was that Barthou had become the plaything of a Mlle Jacqueline, a lady who kept rooms on the rue de Furstemberg – conveniently close to the Institut de France – and who specialized in whip-enhanced sexual gratification. By Daudet's telling, it was to this sordid world of pimps and flagellation and "unspeakable practices" that France's minister of justice repaired, when he was not sending innocent men and women into penal servitude. And therein lay the explanation for Daudet's own fate. Though not personally responsible for Philippe's death, or for the miscarriage of justice at his father's trial, Barthou had come to accept the police version of the "suicide" because his private vices made him their tool. Next to this strictly personal consideration, it mattered little to the minister that he should be lending himself to the communist network within the French police force, and behaving altogether like some "little doggie which the 'gentlemen' of the national police force kept on a leash." All told, by Daudet's construction, Barthou was the lowest form of life, a minister who protected killers, thieves, and black-mailers, because he was no better than they, because he was a "drinker of pus and an eater of unmentionable filth."[33]

To all this, Barthou responded with silence. He did not attempt to reply, either in parliament or in press. Knowing that as a Daudet target he was in the best of republican company, knowing too that confrontation was the polemicist's objective as well as his métier, the minister said nothing publicly and offered no forum to the *Action française* by way of court action.[34] By silence he conveyed contempt. By jest he sought to make light of the work undertaken by deadly serious men. The latter tactic was observed by Maurice Martin du Gard following a luncheon at the Hôtel Continental in December 1928. Taking leave of his friends, Barthou asked the coat-check attendant to hurry, adding loudly and with a grin, "I'm in a rush to get to the rue de Furstemberg."[35] But silence remained the principal defence, a tactic advised by personal observation as well as instinct. Long ago, he had watched his old mentor, Emile Garet, refuse to be drawn by unjust criticism, and through his readings he had come to admire Baudelaire and Renan for their similarly dignified and shrewd restraint in the face of critics. So it would continue through-out the ensuing years of Daudet's assaults, the minister frequently singling out for special praise the silent fortitude of other men he admired, Méline, Ferry, Joffre.[36]

Dignified and shrewd though it may well have been, Barthou's tactic has its limitations for a biographer. On the one hand, there are strict and precise indictments. On the other, a defence based on silence. Hence we are left to our own devices to make what we can of the truth. Given the fact that this is an inquiry into unsubstantiated allegations, no apology need be made for admitting its speculative character.

As for the first charge, that of the ghost-writers, one can conclude that this was wildly overdrawn. That he may have used research assistants for basic tasks could be conceded without protest, even though there is no evidence even for this. It is, however, plausible. But for the rest, the work may be safely attributed to Barthou him-self, a judgment based on the following considerations. First, much of his work had as its archival base his own library collection of unpublished manuscripts, a considerable resource, near at hand, that did not require external aid. Second, much of his written work was characterized by extensive quotation, verbatim reproduction of documents, and, to be frank, a considerable degree of repetition and overlap. Thus, forthcoming book chapters often first appeared in magazine publications, or the content of one article would be slightly reworked in order to form the basis for another. In short, and without disparaging his industry, the volume of Barthou's literary production should not be taken as an absolute measure of original work or thought. Third, his industry was indeed very impressive, employed as it was over days that started at 5 a.m. and years which offered intermittent release from the burdens of ministerial responsibility. Finally, one can only endorse two recent assessments of the stylistic unity in Barthou's corpus of work.[37] In a word, it is the work of a single author. For these reasons, combined, there is little reason to accept Daudet's charges in any appreciable way, and none at all to believe his claim that not a single word was that of Barthou.

The charges of extortion and theft are more difficult to assay, the more so given the failure of any plaintiff to take legal action against him. Accordingly, the authenticity of those charges must not be exaggerated. Thus qualified, the accusation may not have to be dismissed in every particular. Doubtless, Barthou was a very zealous collector who was prepared to use his influence to secure promotions and honours for those who might show their gratitude with gifts of books and manuscripts. There is no evidence to suggest that such arrangements were ever spelled out quite so crassly, but plenty to indicate how they worked. As he said publicly, a serious collector had to be bold and persistent, qualities which may have resulted in some potential benefactor feeling under siege.[38] Then again, bibliophiles and their commercial agents know well the passions sometimes unleashed by particularly cherished items, and recognize that some among their midst are capable of walking off, apparently distracted, without having remembered to pay for the newly found treasure. Distracted, or merely teased by the possibility of a truly exceptional bargain, they are at risk of doing something unlawful – until gently reminded by alert and understanding proprietors. There were times, it seems, when Barthou was capable of such oversights, but quasi-appropriations of this sort hardly constitute the kind of behaviour attributed to him by Daudet and Maurras.[39]

The third charge, predictably, is even more fraught with difficulty. It is also, at one and the same time, the least and the most grave. It is the least because, among the French political elite of the Third Republic, extra-marital liaisons were extremely common.[40] Accordingly, public revelations of this sort, while probably unwelcome, were likely to have been less damaging than they might be today, when connections are often drawn between public and private trust. But Daudet's charges, couched in the language of dogs and whips, were especially grave in quite another sense. If the story of Jacqueline, true or false, has but slight historical significance, the same could not be said of its personal import. Not when one thinks of the way this public campaign must have affected Alice Barthou, a woman dying of cancer. It is with her in mind, as much as her husband, that one is obliged to press further into matters so long and indelicately raised.

Three observations are called for. First, the campaign against Barthou had no precedent before 1927, before Daudet was on his way to prison bent on personal vengeance. Hence the entire slough of allegations about the minister's personal conduct appeared only in the last decade of his life, just before his sixty-fifth birthday. Until then, as was expressly pointed out in a study of 1922, although his politics had been much attacked, his "private morality" had never been in question.[41] Second, not only is it certain that Alice Barthou's health was failing from 1922 on, and that her religious piety was becoming increasingly intense, but there is the rumour that relations between husband and wife had never fully recovered from the death of Max, a son who in a sense had died because of the name he carried. Third, only in the post-war period do contemporaries start to remark on two facets of Barthou's personality for which there is virtually no pre-war evidence. One apparently new predilection was for erotic verse and art, the other for off-colour, risqué humour. Daudet, for instance, picked up on Barthou's sometimes rather crude table talk, but so too did a range of other observers, from the critical Octave Homberg to the more restrained Léon Noel and the overtly sympathetic Geneviève Tabouis.[42]

Taken together, observations of this sort, speculatively assembled, may add up to something distantly reminiscent of Daudet's gibes. But if so, they would also soften the lines of his caricature, leaving Barthou as he was, a physically vigorous man, under acute public and private stress, who may have found some measure of sexual release through language, art, and – possibly – the charms of some Jacqueline.[43] Again if so, one must decide for oneself whether there is anything vile here and, if so, how it measures against the journalism of the *Action française*.

Implausible though it may seem, the reader still cannot appreciate the full range of stress under which Barthou laboured in the late 1920s. For precisely at a time when royalists were attributing vices to him of every description, including that of being a communist stooge, the French communist party launched its own withering

attack on the minister of justice. In this case, however, the polemical
battle rarely spread to the swamp of personal invective occupied by
the royalists, and did owe part of its outbreak to Barthou's own
capacity for inflammatory language. Daudet's innuendo notwithstanding, Barthou had never professed any love for communism or
for the Soviet Union. On the contrary, he had long been a public
critic of the bolshevik revolution, of its leadership, and of those
misguided French compatriots who had been caught up in their web.
As war minister in 1921 he had condemned the circulation of communist propaganda in the barracks, and had presented *Humanité*'s
ensuing outrage as proof of his resolve to defend the social order
at any cost.[44] By the spring of 1927, as Poincaré's justice minister,
he was under full sail against the communist leadership in parliament
and its lieutenants in the offices of *Humanité*. Jacques Doriot he
accused of waging a "criminal campaign" against France, Vaillant-
Couturier of trying to incite civil rebellion, and Marcel Cachin of
encouraging soldiers to shoot their officers.[45] Three amnesties for
political offences had been passed since 1919, he said, thus freeing
communists in particular from the legal consequences of their behaviour; and yet such gestures on the part of the state seemed only
to have incited further outrages and been interpreted as evidence
of bourgeois weakness. Enough was enough. The Poincaré government would do no more. Indeed, it would stand or fall on its resolution not to grant a new amnesty. Parliament, Barthou warned,
simply had to be aware that the country was again in danger, this
time from men who wanted nothing less than the overthrow of the
French state.[46]

Challenged by this diminutive warrior, the communist press waded
eagerly into the fray. Aroused by the minister's uncompromising
references to crimes, perfidy, calumny, and mindless obeisance to
Moscow, *Humanité* branded Barthou "a consummate reactionary"
and a mouthpiece for the far right.[47] For the next two years, until
November 1929 when Barthou relinquished the Justice portfolio,
the rhetorical and judicial battles between the government and the
communists raged in full force. And Barthou was in the thick of it,
speaking out with a passion he was never to use against the royalists
– a difference which the communists were quick to see as evidence
of their case against the minister. In June 1928 Barthou warned the
Chamber again that the communists were committed to a "merciless"
struggle against parliament and the entire social order, in the face
of which he pledged never to abdicate his responsibility to suppress
insurrection.[48] Indeed, he was not above using threats. On one occasion, for instance, he lost patience with a communist deputy on

the Chamber's Commission de la Législation Civile et Criminelle. Having reaffirmed the government's determination to root out all those who conspired to subvert the social order, he reminded the deputy that there were still judges and prisons in France. "You have heard me? You do know what I mean?"[49]

With this final stress factor in place, it becomes possible to understand more fully still the connection between Barthou's political and non-political life.[50] No decade had been more turbulent for him than this of the 1920s, and yet neither was there one more productive in terms of his leisure pursuits. Far from feeling a tension between politics and books, Barthou saw in the latter a kind of private refuge that was essential to one who could not long resist the hurly-burly of the political circus. In this sense, therefore, everything derived from the sanctuary which was his library – renewed political energy, as well as more reflections on the history of France, the literary genius of Montaigne or de Musset, the theatrical genius of Rachel, the musical genius of Wagner. Here in a world of his own design, he could shake off the taunts of a Daudet or a Cachin, and reflect upon the loss of old friends or, no doubt, on the anxieties associated with his wife's precarious health.

By the late 1920s this personal retreat had also become a sanctuary for some of the finest editions in the history of French literature. Accommodated in a special room on the Avenue Victor Emmanuel III – as the Avenue d'Antin had been renamed following Italy's intervention in the war – Barthou's collection was concentrated in four tall glass-fronted *armoires*. Here, above the gardens of the Grand Palais, in a library gilded by the light of the late-afternoon sun, Barthou fretted over and fondled his latest acquisitions – in the company of two marble busts, one of Lamartine by David Angers, the other of the young Max Barthou. By then, his collection was approaching two thousand volumes, the works of several hundred authors. In the 1890s he had entered the mainstream of French bibliophilia, developed conventional tastes, and accordingly targeted the classical works of the sixteenth, seventeenth, and eighteenth centuries, some two hundred original editions of which he managed to acquire in the course of his lifetime. But well before the war, he became part of a vanguard of French collectors who shifted their interests to the nineteenth century, to those whose stature had grown with the passage of time: Hugo, Lamartine, Vigny, Stendhal. And these in turn had their ranks increased by the works of the ensuing generation: Baudelaire, Flaubert, Maupassant, and, later still, Rimbaud and Verlaine. More notably still, Barthou soon became even more of a trend-setter with his growing interest in the works of his

own contemporaries – Rostand, France, Loti, to be sure, but also
Barrès, Noailles, Colette, Valéry – two successive generations which
placed another six hundred volumes on the shelves of the Barthou
library.[51]

It was, altogether, a highly personalized collection, no simple hos-
tage to the tastes of others. If he pursued Hugo, he paid less attention
to Balzac; if he collected Loti and the sensual verse of Pierre Louÿs,
he did not much bother with Apollinaire, Gide, or Proust, the new
wave of the 1920s. One may, as a result, question his taste, even his
prescience, but it changes nothing. As he wrote to Seymour de Ricci
in 1927:

I have made my own library, not that of others. I have never claimed that
my tastes have set the fashion, but fashion has never determined my tastes.
I am aware of the gaps in my "bookshop": they are not all inadvertent.[52]

His tastes and society's fashion were perhaps more in accord when
it came to his choice of bookbinders and illustrators. Set on the
acquisition of first editions, he was less interested in retaining their
original bindings, preferring instead to clothe his purchases according to the tastes of his own day. Though ever insistent that the
exterior was subordinate to the text inside, he had a passion, a mania,
as he put it, for exquisitely designed and embossed bindings, many
executed by his pre-war favourite Marius Michel, or by the post-war
art-déco specialist Pierre Legrain.[53] And finally, there was his own
particular speciality, the *truffage*, the unique artifact which he ordered bound in with the literary text – a letter by Stendhal, a pencil
sketch by Hugo, a page of original manuscript in Loti's hand. Rare
editions, complemented by the coloured engravings of artists like
Pierre Bouchet, sumptuous leather bindings, the special *truffage*,
such was the artistry with which Barthou adorned his private temple,
his "sanctuary."[54]

It was not, of course, entirely private. Although he often spoke
publicly about his treasures, and made no attempt to conceal their
existence, he was simply cautious about those he allowed into this
inner sanctum. Speaking to an audience in 1920, he recalled his
horror at what had happened one day when he had been pressed
by Alice to show his library to two of her friends. Having carefully
extracted from its protective sheath a volume by Anatole France, he
had placed it in the hands of one visitor before turning to search
out a second item. No sooner was his back turned than the first
intruder began to leaf through the pages, without having removed
her evidently soiled gloves. In an instant the damage was done, some

mark left behind. Determined that this should never happen again, Barthou resolved not to have the volume cleaned. Instead, he kept it close at hand, a display piece which could be pulled out to instruct and, no doubt, intimidate future guests.[55] Some, happily, required no such instruction, that charmed circle of fellow bibliophiles whom he admitted as a mark of friendship and shared passion. It is they who have left us with those glimpses of the minister, sparkling-eyed, showing off his latest acquisition, or gently blowing away some offending speck of dust from one of the treasured tomes, or sitting at his large writing desk dashing off notes of request, or of thanks, to those whose works he still wanted for his shelves.

Surrounded by genius, it was here that he wrote of it, in his public addresses and in his articles. For him, as for Carlyle, history was mainly the work of great individuals. There were exceptions, he knew, times when events and circumstances essentially conditioned human responses, but for the most part he was drawn to the view, temperamentally as much as intellectually, that history was indeed the story of great men and women.[56] For that reason he was captivated by the notion of genius, upon which his faith in France was founded. Accordingly, between the peace conference and Genoa, he contributed lectures and articles on La Fontaine, Hugo, Maupassant, Lyautey, Napoleon, Diderot, and the naturalized Greek poet Jean Moréas. During his years on the Reparations commission he turned to Lamennais, Chénier, Samain, France, Lamartine, and again to Diderot and Hugo. And from then until the end of the decade, isolated from the insults of royalists and communists alike, he devoted his leisure moments to the poets de Musset and Lamartine, the historian Thiers, the actress Rachel, the statesman Deschanel, and the soldier Lyautey.

Lectures and articles apart, Barthou also published another half-dozen book-format works in the decade between 1919 and 1929. Each, unsurprisingly, is addressed to a single genius – Lyautey, Lamartine, Hugo, Wagner, Rachel, and Robespierre. Several are slight in content or at least in their instructive value for Barthou as subject, but the last three are more substantial in both respects.

In the case of the composer and the actress, if it is their genius which attracts, it is their humanity which holds Louis Barthou. Having acknowledged that special quality which sets them apart, he does not engage in treatises on their talent from any technical point of view, as certainly befits a man who was neither musician nor actor. Neither does he much concern himself with the internal psychology or motivation which might rest below their surface behaviour. Rather, it is the Romanticism inherent in the stories of Wagner and

Rachel which is the real source of Barthou's fascination, and of which genius is but one part. More obvious is his attention to their personal relations, their highly publicized private lives. In particular, he is preoccupied by their turbulent, not to say physically demanding, romantic attachments. Clearly, he is absorbed by their passions, their legendary sensuality, in which he seems to detect some association with artistic genius. But he is no voyeur, at least in any vulgar sense, for he refuses to find anything raw or distasteful in their succession of infidelities. Before any court of conventional virtue, he remarks, Rachel would be a lost cause. But if he will not defend her, neither will he judge her, for he is too moved by her emotional vulnerability, too respectful of her rags-to-riches ascent, much too admiring of an actress who did not pretend to be something she was not. Her success never went to her head, never made her forget her humble origins, a quality applauded by this son of a hardware merchant, grandson of a smith.[57]

Barthou found something deeply moving in Rachel's desperate search for love, as he did in the case of Richard Wagner. The composer, he knew, was moody, overbearing, and proud to a fault; and he was hard on the women who adored him, not out of malice but because of that surfeit of energy which was at the source of his genius. Again the genius. If Wagner shared in all of the defects of human nature, humanity was compensated in full measure by the gift of his music, "his all-powerful music."[58] Moreover, Barthou's notion of genius was conditioned by his notion of suffering. As he was to say of Loti – "you have to have suffered in order to move others" – so he believed of Rachel and Wagner.[59] Barthou was especially touched by romantic suffering, a response made the more poignant by his wife's health – to whom he dedicated *La Vie amoureuse de Richard Wagner*. In a passage written by a man coming to grips with private sorrow, Barthou describes Wagner's unspoken farewell to the beloved Mathilde.

As the sun rose behind the mountains, he looked "for a last time, *over there*" ... The arrival of a radiant early morning was in such contrast to his spirits that it only worsened the heartache of this pitiful great man. He walked away, like a blind man, eyes dry, fixed straight ahead. ...[60]

Barthou was less moved by Maximilien Robespierre, whose fall from power in 1794 he traced in *Le Neuf Thermidor* of 1926. Dedicated to Poincaré, this is a work about one of France's most famous revolutionary figures, written by a man who had spent a career defending the political and social order. Readers might have expected an unsympathetic portrait, but what they got was much more measured. Determined to be no "apologist" of Robespierre, Barthou pulled no punches about the excesses committed by the radicals who had profited from the death of Mirabeau. "Never, at any time or any place, has justice been reduced to such a cruel parody.[61] Intoxicated by power and good intentions both, and no longer able to distinguish between resistance and mere reluctance, Robespierre accelerated the pace of state executions. Nevertheless, vain though he may have been, and arrogant, he was not by nature a sadistic or even cruel man. His problem, as Barthou judged, was that he was too much the ideologue and not enough the man of action. Power not only corrupted him, it confounded him, a condition signalled by Robespierre's remark: "I was born to combat evil, not to preside over it." Not a genuine hero in Barthou's eyes, Robespierre was himself a victim, of events not of his making, of other men worse than he. There is tragedy, therefore, in this tale of human frailty and failing; and in that there was the link between the abstemious tyrant, the profligate composer, and the mercurial actress.

As works of history, these are not of enduring quality. Written for a popular audience, they are essentially stories told by an enthusiastic raconteur, strong on narrative, weak on analysis. Quite apart from his surprising lack of interest in the motivation of his subjects, there is little attempt to place them either within the social context of their day or even within their artistic-political tradition. Beside these, the familiar problems pale in comparison: the imprecise references to dates and to sources, the heavy reliance on quotations. Still, it is futile if not unfair to judge the popular historian by standards to which he does not aspire. Barthou's work is that of a serious dilettante who obviously enjoyed research – in the National Library and Archives as well as in his own collection – who was inherently drawn to the talent of great men and women, and who simply accepted without comment the didactic function of history. Wagner apart, all of his major works were addressed to French figures of past or present, the knowledge of whose genius, he believed, should be imparted to all French citizens.

This connection between the French public and his private cloister was expressed in still other ways. For the fact was that his literary career was in no sense akin to solitary confinement. If it brought its quiet moments, respite from the clamour of politics, it also brought an often intense schedule of literature-related activity.

There was the work of the Académie Française, where every Thursday the select "forty" were expected to pursue their work on the national Dictionary. It was a task for which Barthou was admi-

rably suited, given his reputation as a linguistic purist and, accord
ingly, his horror of acronyms.[62] There was also the occasional three-
months' tour of duty as *directeur* of the Academy, the elections of
new members and the subsequent receptions for the successful candidates – the latter providing Barthou with opportunities to formally
welcome Joseph Bédier to Rostand's chair in 1921, Henri Robert to
Ribot's in 1924, and Albert Besnard to that of Loti in 1926. On top
of this there was the work of the prize committees and the public
ceremonies to which, in the 1920s, he contributed addresses on
Ernest Renan, Virgil, Paul Deschanel, Robert de Flers, and Paul
Déroulède; and finally, there were the luncheon meetings with select
Academy colleagues – those self-styled on the "left" – which convened monthly at the restaurant Ledoyen.[63] As befitted a man who
considered his own election to be the single greatest honour of his
life, Barthou spared no effort when it came to the Académie Française, and acquired within its precincts the reputation of a diligent
attender, always punctual, keen to contribute.[64]

Elsewhere in the literary arts he was a highly visible patron and
participant: presiding over banquets held to honour men of letters,
participating in the fortnightly meeting of writers who assembled
for the Déjeuner Hervieu or the annual banquet of the *Revue des
deux mondes*, serving as jury member for literary prizes like that of
the Prix Gringoire or of Siècle Médical, lecturing to the mainly female audience gathered by Yvonne Sarcey for the Université des
Annales.[65] Public as well, by definition, was his weekly column in
1920 for *Les Annales*, and the pieces he sent off to popular magazines
like *Lectures pour tous* or *Le Monde illustré*, as well as his contributions
to a range of more expressly literary and bibliophilic periodicals.
Indeed, Barthou was always careful to see that politics did not come
between him and the French press, that world which he had entered
in the 1880s and never really left. It was more, therefore, than a
link with book and magazine publishers. He was particularly well
connected to the newspaper press of the republican centre. It helped
considerably to occupy a post as vice-president of the steering committee of the Associations de la presse française, a post which he
owed to yet another high office. President since 1918 of the Association des journalistes parisiens – among whose nearly four
hundred members the influence of *Le Temps* and *Agence Havas* was
very evident – Barthou was extremely well placed to cultivate his
image as a deft and multi-talented public figure.[66] Even a fair-
minded one, for he polished his relations with the press by acknowledging its right to be not only critical but unfair. Describing the press
as "Gutenberg's terrible instrument," for good or for evil, Barthou

maintained that the truth certainly would be no better served if there were only one newspaper, no matter what its political or ideological perspective. Later, following the collision with Daudet, he reaffirmed his belief that people in public life simply had to be prepared to "let the dogs bark, even the vipers to hiss."[67]

There were still other ways in which private literary activity spilled over into his public life, heightening his profile and disarming at least some of his potential critics. In a word it was patronage, that art which he had begun to master as a member of the Pau municipal council. Although the form varied, Barthou was prepared to lend his name to others' causes. He had done so for years, and often been handsomely compensated by donations to his library, but the fact remained that he had earned the gratitude of many. Sometimes, it was no more than a short preface, prepared for some friend with an exemplary grace – "As old and profound as is my affection for you, I want you to know that my praise owes less to my friendship than to the pleasure your book has given me."[68] Sometimes, his service was enlisted to help secure preferment for a Justice ministry official, on Maurice Donnay's behest; sometimes for one of Jules Cambon's candidates for admittance to the Légion d'honneur, or for one of Lyautey's friends who was hoping for a post in Public Instruction. Even the partially reconciled Joseph Caillaux was submitting requests – again under the cachet of the *tutoiement* – on behalf of judges and functionaries in the Justice ministry.[69] The arts, too, remained well represented among Barthou's grateful clientele. It was he, for instance, who helped secure in 1927 the Academy's Prix Coppée for the Béarnais poet Tristan Derème and a government commission for the local sculptor Lucien Pallez, just as it was he who was called upon in 1928 to help obtain a "croix" for a senior director of *Mercure de France*.[70]

Favours of another order were reserved for fellow bibliophiles, in whose society he found both pleasure and recognition. He gave unstintingly to the society of Le Livre Contemporain, the presidency of which he had assumed in 1913. His executive committee met regularly either at his home or in the offices of whatever ministry he had come to occupy, for a time even in the headquarters of the Reparations commission on the rue de Tilsitt.[71] From whatever venue, it was Barthou who was the chief animator, selecting which works would be earmarked for one of the society's special collector's editions, often personally contributing portions of manuscripts destined for inclusion in one of these limited editions. Indeed, avid collector as he was known to be, he was also known for his generosity. In 1924 he basically gave to the *Revue de France* a valuable, unpublished, autobiographical manuscript by Anatole France; and outright gifts of autographs and manuscripts went to many others, including Derème, André Gaudelette de La Morlière, Emile Henriot, the banker Horace Finaly, and the Académie Française.[72]

Thus, in so many ways, the connections were made between public and private pursuits, between the serenity promised by his library and the notoriety promised outside its walls. Far from being mutually exclusive, the worlds of politics and letters converged at the doors of his book-lined domain. It is from there that any understanding of Louis Barthou must eventually emerge, any understanding of the complete man, with his sense of the French body politic and of France's cultural identity – historical, literary, theatrical, artistic, musical. Indeed, even with respect to the latter, his library had something important to offer. For thanks to the radio there installed, he was able to enjoy the concerts from the Conservatoire, when time or circumstances made attendance impossible.[73]

By 1929 circumstances too frequently intruded. Politically, the energies of the Poincaré government were failing, a condition symbolized by the premier's worsening health. By July, his cabinet had run its course as Briand added to his duties at the Foreign ministry those of the premier's office. Barthou stayed on at Justice, but seemed relieved when, in November, this administration also collapsed. The new premier, André Tardieu, asked him to retain his dual position as justice minister and deputy premier, but the sixty-seven-year-old politician had had enough. Still harassed by the vicious press campaign of *Action française*, perhaps unnerved by the police security measures which had been imposed in response to threats to his life, Barthou declined Tardieu's offer in favour of returning to the serenity of his own residence.[74] It was just as well, for he was on the eve of another personal crisis. His wife was in the final stage of her illness.

Alice Barthou died on 15 January 1930, at the age of fifty-seven. Ten days later *Illustration* published her photograph above a short article which called her a woman "au grand coeur," reminding readers of her work for charity over the years and her wartime service as a headnurse.[75] That was all, for hers had not been a very public life, overshadowed as it had been by the honours and abuse accorded to her husband. Later, others remembered her for her own interest in literature and her own passion as a collector of Marinot glassware.[76] Slightly taller and more heavily built than her husband, she spoke slowly and sparingly, again in contrast to her animated and voluble spouse. She appears to have been a wife who had never pushed her husband up the political ladder, but rather one of the majority of political wives – as Barthou perceived them – who resigned themselves to the inconvenience of marriage to a public figure and who paid more attention to school curricula than to political debates.[77] Nevertheless, it is clear that she had been a woman of considerable strength of character, as well as an inherent romanticist like her husband. A nurse-administrator who enjoyed travel and books, a sometime writer and a constant collector, and one who could chasten the erratic Pierre Loti, Alice Barthou was much more a personality in her own right than outward, certainly initial, appearances would allow. A woman who spoke her mind, and who insisted on being more than a marital appendage, she provided incalculable service to her husband's career by ensuring a domestic and a social milieu infinitely more refined than that from which he had come.[78]

Incomplete as our impression of her must be, fragments such as these are a small reminder of what, whom, Louis Barthou lost in January 1930. After thirty-five years of marriage, he was alone. That was how Pierre Benoit found him, alone, in the library, the day the tomb at Père Lachaise was to be opened so that the remains of Alice could join those of Max. Barthou sat at his desk, Benoit recalled, *lorgnons* for once removed, while the tears coursed down his cheeks into the greying goatee. Gazing around at the books before him, a passion of his life, he choked out the words: "Nothing is of any interest now. Everything's finished."[79] It was not, of course, not quite, but for months thereafter he made no effort to conceal his grief from those whom he trusted and to whom he could confide his sense of loss and vulnerability. Such a one was Suzanne Cappiello, wife of the artist Leonetto, to whom he wrote a short note cancelling a luncheon date. He had accepted the invitation, he said, because he thought he was ready to see old friends. But "I presumed too much on my courage." The fact was that friends constituted the greatest difficulty, for it was they whose very presence recalled so many memories still too painful to face.[80]

It was those memories which lay behind the decision to change residence, leaving the apartment which he had occupied since his marriage in 1895 in favour of one on the fourth floor at 34 avenue Marceau. He moved there later that year, with Laure and Gustave Baty, his faithful housekeeper and *valet de chambre*, and with his mother-in-law, Madame Mayeur. At sixty-eight years of age, and now caring for a woman of eighty-two, Louis Barthou may well have believed that his ministerial career was finished. Not necessarily by choice, but at an end all the same. Certainly he resolved never to move again. So terrified was he that his bust of Lamartine would be damaged in transit to the avenue Marceau, and so relieved that it was not, that he told a friend: "That's the last time. It won't leave here again until after I'm gone."[81]

CHAPTER NINE

Private Healing and Re-engagement, 1930–1934

Nineteen thirty-four will witness some delicate, difficult, even dangerous negotiations. France ... will be pressured, even by her friends, to agree to new concessions. ... When our statesmen, though resolved to treat no one as an enemy, have responded to the world with the requisite *no*. ... far from having compromised that peace, we will be one step closer to it.[1]

In December 1929 Louis Barthou resumed his part-time journalistic career, barely a month after the fall of Briand's last administration. Throughout 1930 he would contribute a column entitled "Propos Libres" to the bimonthly magazine *Les Annales*, an association which he maintained for the three ensuing years, albeit on a more occasional basis. In part, it was a way of coping with the grief that accompanied Alice's illness, and with the loneliness that arrived with her death. In fact, the first piece he wrote following the funeral was addressed to her memory.[2] Thereafter, for the next few months, his attention was focused principally on domestic politics. Parliament was once more in crisis. André Tardieu he praised as an excellent chief executive, but one who had faltered badly when it came to Chamber politics. When the premier fell victim to the flu in mid-February, and Chéron, the finance minister, was left in charge, the government suddenly found itself under attack by deputies who were still smarting over their exclusion from Tardieu's expanded cabinet. Hence, after less than four months in power, the government fell. Camille Chautemps became premier, for three weeks; and then Tardieu returned with his second administration. It was all too much, Barthou wrote, this coming and going of ministries, all of them ephemeral creations of loosely knit parliamentary groups which refused to submit to the discipline of real political parties. What was needed was a reaffirmed sense of national unity – for him a familiar plea – so that the near anarchy of the Chamber might give way to a higher national good. Until such a time, the best that could be hoped for was the emergence of some leader who had the requisite skills to contain all of this centrifugal energy. Such a man, he prescribed, would have to combine just the right measure of firmness and flexibility, and understand the difference between conciliation and abdication.[3]

He said that he would not envy the man who dared to accept such a challenge, but there is little doubt that he considered himself up to it. It came as no surprise, therefore, when his own candidacy for the premiership became the subject of discussion in late November 1930. Tardieu was again in political trouble. Barthou outlined the cabinet's difficulties for readers of *Annales* and acknowledged, while denying, the current suspicions about his eagerness to see the government fall. Some make me out to be "an intriguer, thirsty with ambition," he admitted publicly, but that only shows that they "know little of my life, which I have turned to other things."[4] Neither, perhaps, were they entirely mistaken. For in the first week of December 1930 Louis Barthou accepted President Doumergue's invitation to form a cabinet.

But the problems which had plagued parliament in general, and the Tardieu government in particular, were not susceptible to easy solutions. The split between Tardieu's forces on the centre-right and those of the Radical-Socialists on the centre-left remained unbridgeable. A broad-based coalition thus proved impossible; and Barthou's own support from among the modest ranks of the Union Démocratique Républicaine was far too slight to command a majority in the Chamber. Faced with Poincaré's health-related refusal to come out of retirement, and with the enduring enmity between Tardieu and the Radicals, Barthou had to inform Doumergue that his efforts had been in vain.[5] Instead, he accepted the War ministry under the very short-lived cabinet of Théodore Steeg, and then retired with it in January 1931. Retired to the life of an ordinary senator, and to the world of books and journalism.[6]

History continued to preoccupy him, always the history of France and of her great men. Sometimes it was the history of his own contemporaries: Marshal Joffre, for example, on the occasion of whose death in January 1931 war minister Barthou delivered the official eulogy on the great esplanade of the Invalides. Marshal Lyautey was also well served by this friend of long standing, served in the sense that he was still alive to read Barthou's public homage to him as a man of genius. Lyautey's work in Morocco, Barthou wrote, was one of the greatest contributions ever made by a single individual to France's national interests.[7] Sometimes it was the history of a more distant past, principally addressed to the dramatic events and figures of the French Revolution. Mirabeau, for instance, remained a favourite hero, but now it was another revolutionary figure who most "excited" him, as he confided in a letter to Lyautey.[8] *Danton* was published in 1932 by Albin Michel. It was to be the last and, in some respects, the most substantial of Louis Barthou's work as historian.

Methodologically, this is a more interesting work than his earlier volumes. To be sure, many of the familiar weaknesses are still evident, but so too is an enhanced sophistication. Less dependent upon the sources of his own library, Barthou draws more heavily here upon documentation from the national archives, from the pages of *Le Moniteur*, and from the works of professional scholars like Aulard, Mathiez, and Madelin; and he is more attentive as well to the problems of source reliability and to what constitutes sound evidence.[9] Perhaps this is related in some way to the fact that he generally is less concerned with the private life of Danton – in contrast to his handling of Rachel, Wagner, even Mirabeau – and more with the historical controversy surrounding Danton's alleged role in the September massacres of 1792 and his involvement with the English government. Finally, if he is not appreciably more successful in this respect, Barthou certainly would like to convince his readers that he is fulfilling the mandate of the impartial historian.

Impartial, of course, he is not. Robespierre, for one, is in for a much rougher hand than was accorded him in *Le Neuf Thermidor* – perhaps because it is he who is responsible for Danton's execution, an act which Barthou condemns as a betrayal of justice and friendship both. For his part, Danton emerges as an attractive figure, with qualities long praised by his historian. Apart from his inherent laziness and diffidence, Danton is said to have had all the qualities of a great leader. An astute judge of men, strong-willed and courageous, he was a natural *chef*, a man of action, yet a talented, intuitive orator. Though capable of misjudgment, he eschewed both deceit and hypocrisy in favour of a sometimes brutal candour. And, though sometimes also crude in manner and speech, even a woman-chaser, his "nature rabelaisienne" only added to the rich, spontaneous personality which captured the affection of so many followers. More than this, however, Danton combined three other salutary qualities. He was a pragmatist, dogma-free, one who could adapt to changing circumstances. Second, and accordingly, he was ever the moderate, suspended between two rival currents, anxious to make them one. In that desire, Barthou wrote, was "the tragic side of his destiny." Finally, in this resolve to unify Frenchmen against an external enemy, he was the quintessential patriot. Recalling Danton's rebuke that angry words within the Convention would not kill a single Prussian, Barthou reckoned, in 1932: "There is not a single line from all of Mirabeau which, in eloquent simplicity, outdoes this one appeal."[10]

Music was another subject on which he continued to write during his semi-retirement from politics. In August 1930, in an article written from Bayreuth, he described the "sublime," when the house lights dimmed and Arturo Toscanini took up the baton for *Buhnenleitung*. This maestro, he judged, was himself a man of genius. Just as he had smoothed over some of the uneven passages of Debussy's *La Mer*, during a performance at the Paris Opera in the spring, so he was now doing with some of the rougher sections of Wagner's *Parsifal* – yet without ever forgetting that he remained in the service of still another genius. Were it not for his own long memory, one which took him back to 1899 when Hans Richter had conducted Wagner, Barthou said that he could imagine no one else ever attaining the artistic heights of Toscanini; and so he concluded his article for *Annales*, with a personal word to the conductor: "It's not enough to say that you have given me pleasure. You have done me good."[11] For that is what music, sensitively interpreted, did for him, just as interruptions of any sort still irritated him beyond measure. Indeed, he thought that concert-goers should receive formal instructions about not desecrating symphonies and sonatas with applause between movements. Until they did, there was at least some advantage to attending concerts by radio, a medium to which he contributed by helping create a national radiophonic orchestra and a Comité national de propagande pour la musique. The fact was, or so he believed, that French citizens needed to be schooled in music appreciation, especially in the artistic achievements of their own compatriots like Berlioz, Fauré, d'Indy, and Franck.[12]

Next to the pleasure afforded him by music, there was but one equal, literature, ideally presented in bindings worthy of the writers' art. And on such subjects Barthou upheld the traditions of a lifetime by continuing to instruct French audiences and readers. Retirement simply gave him more time to point out anew the relationship between books and civilization in the broadest sense. They spoke, he believed, to the aesthetic essence of a national culture, embracing visual beauty as well as the verbally expressed ideas that have "haunted the human spirit." They were even allies of the humanist ideal, in a world troubled by unrest at home and by war talk abroad. Thanks to great literature, pitched as it was to a universal human condition, there was some hope that men and women of all nations could be reconciled one with another. That is why, in 1933, he coined a new device, different from that inscribed on his Academician's sword: *Si vis pacem, para ... librum*.[13] Books, like music, could soothe anxiety and constrain anger, whether in the form of Lamartine's poetry, Loti's evocation of nature, or France's enduring optimism: "Slowly, but inexorably, humanity is realizing the dreams of wise men." And lest hope should give way to complacency, he might have added to a lecture in 1933 – delivered only months after Adolf Hitler had come to power in Germany – that *Les Dieux ont soif* had much to say about men who thought they had a monopoly on absolute truth.[14]

All of this writing and speaking, though public in the obvious sense, was private in quite another. It was more than the fact that the texts themselves were prepared in the solitude of his own library. More telling was the way these texts reflected a range of Barthou's own emotions, attitudes, and values. Often, he is explicit, obviating the need for inference of any kind. Sometimes when it is called for, as in the case of *Danton*, the connections between author and subject are sufficiently self-evident that inference seems fully warranted. There is, however, still another body of material from which can be extracted further insights into a man approaching retirement and beginning to reflect back on some fifty years of public life. In 1931, for instance, he wrote a piece on his boyhood in Oloron, one which called up memories of parents and playmates, the village store-keepers, the first encounter with the work of Victor Hugo. Two years later he wrote a preface for Pierre Daguerre, in which he again recalled his youth in Béarn and surmised that it had been the re-membered roar of its streams and waterfalls which explained his affinity for the turbulent music of Richard Wagner. But it was at Bürgenstock in August 1932, at seventy years of age, that Barthou sat down to write a series of letters to an old school chum from Pau. These he published the following year as *Promenades autour de ma vie*, equipped with a preface which affirmed that every particular in these informal memoirs was exact – except for those which were invented.[15]

Given this tongue-in-cheek remark, it was just as well that these were not intended as political memoirs, at least in any conventional sense. He said that he had no desire to write that kind of history, describing the works of such a genre as too often "dressed-up, trumped-up and misleading."[16] Instead, *Promenades* took the form of a stroll among memories which to him were the most dear, whether of school days, or his first political campaign in 1889, or of great men like Briand, Foch, Clemenceau, or Joffre. But apart from a few pages on the three-year service debates of 1913 – in which Joffre and General Legrand, even General Pau, are given much credit for the bill's passage – there is little more to be found on his own political career. It was as if all of this had much less importance in his own mind than the privilege of meeting Hugo, or seeing on stage the legendary Mme Bartet, or befriending Anatole France,

Rostand, Loti, and Coppée. Music and musicians, too, he paused over, indulging himself in memories of concerts by Françis Planté, or Paderewski, keyboard artists who could capture a composer's every emotion, from the sorrowful to the jubilant, the tender to the sinister. Under their touch the piano took on the textures of an entire orchestra, revealing the single truth of all great music. "It alone can express everything, since only it can convey the inexpressible."[17]

Unlike his political career, which seemed at an end, here was a part of his life which still retained its richness. Every morning he walked for well over an hour, often along the Felsenweg which traces the contours of the cliffs high above the shores of the Lac des Quatre Cantons. The afternoons were spent reading or, more accurately, rereading, for he had taken as company that summer a favourite edition of Baudelaire's *Fleurs du mal*, a new edition of *Les Liaisons dangereuses*, and a volume by Diderot – "my Diderot, ... so understanding, so good, so generous of spirit, so profoundly human."[18] Then there were the evenings, often spent in the concert room of the Hotel Bürgenstock where Horowitz was playing Chopin that August of 1932. All of this was set in the isolated splendour of the Bürgenstock estate, where the mists still settle in rich green valleys, and the cable car still makes its run to the water's edge at Kehrsiten, and Pilatus still towers in the distance. "My Bürgenstock," he called it, because of its exceptional beauty, because too for him it was so much a part of happier times. Watching couples dancing on the terrace – offending him slightly by their public embrace – he clung to memories accumulated since 1895 when he and Alice had first arrived at the Hotel Bürgenstock shortly after their marriage. Here, he said, were the memories most precious to him, of Alice and Max. Here, "so very alone ... I have rediscovered ... some part of my soul."[19]

It was here, and now, that Louis Barthou completed arrangements for his own funeral and for the disposition of his estate. Having prepared a new will in March 1930, two months after his wife's death, he now stipulated that his funeral was to be strictly private and observed with the greatest possible simplicity. Although there was to be a church service, in deference to Alice's wishes, there would be no procession, no wreath, no speeches, not even a public announcement about the time of the funeral. The estate was to be left in the hands of three executors, with the Académie Française designated as executor in perpetuity.[20] In return, that institution – membership in which was to be the sole honour inscribed on his tomb at Père Lachaise – was to receive the Lamartine bust by David

Angers, and monies for the creation of three literary prizes in the name of Louis, Alice, and Max Barthou. Apart from a handful of private beneficiaries, other corporate bodies designated to receive money or art works from the estate included the Louvre, the Carnavalet, the Victor Hugo and Decorative Arts museums, the Oloron town council, and the Paris Journalists Association. The autograph collection and the library were to be sold, dispersed for all time.[21] He expressly did not want to see his collection going to the State and its repositories. So dear was every item to him that he could not bear to think of them being in the hands of anyone who did not want them badly enough to pay small fortunes for each. Having thus settled his estate, Barthou typed a letter to Mme Mayeur, at six in the morning. "Bonjour Maman, I am so at rest here, and in such serenity, that I have been getting my affairs in order. ... Do you know, Maman, how much I love you? I'll say it again, with a tender embrace."[22]

The morning before, he had begun to write the series of letters later published as his *Promenades*. In the first letter, before turning to the security of the past, he cast a glance at the present: only briefly, but long enough to express some optimism about the state of international politics. Clouds, he acknowledged, were certainly gathering on the horizon, and yet some comfort could be drawn from the fact that almost everyone, everywhere, was appalled by the thought of a new war.[23] It was wishful thinking, to be sure, but there was substance as well. Indeed, there had been a number of signs in recent years that Barthou had been attracted to the conciliatory gestures and underlying vision of Aristide Briand, to that passionate conviction that war could never more be tolerated. In October 1930 he had supported Briand's vision of a European federation; and in June 1931 he had urged the minister to stay on at the Quai d'Orsay, since his was the only policy that made sense for France.[24] Less than a year later, when Briand died, Barthou prepared a moving eulogy for readers of *Les Annales*. Not only was Briand a brilliant speaker, he wrote, of quick and deadly wit, but he had become an apostle of peace, a sceptic when it came to religion but a true believer when he addressed the challenge of international reconciliation. Though neglectful of data and dossiers, and a reader whose tastes were confined to adventure novels, here was a man who had mastered the one book that really mattered – "that of peace among mankind."[25]

In a certain sense, Barthou was admirably placed to appreciate the difficulties encountered by Briand. For if he believed that the ultimate solution to French security lay in a reconciled European community, he remained sceptical about Germany's professions of good faith. Periodically, for the past two years, he had reminded French readers of Germany's constant violations of the Versailles treaty, and of the revanchist sentiments deliberately being inculcated into German school children. He still saw red whenever the exiled Kaiser made any public statement, for he continued to hold the fallen emperor personally responsible for the deaths of millions. "This miserable creature," he called him. "Cursed be this scourge of humanity!"[26] As for the nationalist leaders in the Weimar Republic, the Hugenburgs and the Hitlers, they were gaining momentum on a wave of revenge talk inspired by lies and false propaganda. Indeed, the fact was that all German political groups were committed to treaty revision and refused to accept the French contention that peace could be assured only by respecting the treaties of 1919.

This stalemate, he argued, could be broken in one of only two ways. Either the policy of concessions should be continued, with the Germans complaining more with every gain they made, or France had to say, in a word, *Non!* It was the latter course he recommended to the staggering Tardieu government in late 1930. He did not regret, so he said, any of the concessions that had been made at Locarno, at La Haye, at Geneva. Hitler would have risen more quickly still had France been intransigent. But now it was time to say "enough!" and "non!" if necessary. France would have to assure the security of her frontiers "by her own means," just as she now had to combat the efforts of some to whitewash Germany's part in the coming of war in 1914. Such a suggestion, he fumed, was simply an affront to the truth.[27]

There was little, of course, that he could do about any of this. Indeed, given the apparent discrepancy between his praise of Briand's internationalism and his distrust of Germany, there was no sign that a solution to France's primary foreign anxiety was any more obvious to him than anyone else. As it was, he could content himself with very occasional interventions in Senate debates, and with a steady stream of lectures and articles. By 1933, when *Promenades* appeared, he had been out of power for three years. That fact, together with his age, gave every appearance that a distinguished political career was all but over. Lingering ambition was all that was left. That, and a rather silly sounding prophecy. One night he had found himself at the home of his cousins, the Gilbert family, on the rue de l'Estrapade. There, a woman friend of Mme Gilbert had read his palm and pronounced that he was destined to return to power, and in a particularly important office. Barthou dismissed the idea with a laugh, proclaiming his career was already at an end. More solemn was his response when she added that he was going to die a violent death. If true, he replied, best that it be while in service to his country.[28]

If it were to be, 1933 presented neither opportunity nor risk. Instead, he continued to busy himself with writing, opening one article just at the end of the year with the remark: "I don't care for prophecies." He was not thinking of himself, rather of the foreign and domestic uncertainties which awaited France in 1934. Once again invoking his favourite line from Herbert Spencer – "it's only the unexpected that happens" – he expressed a faith that war was not imminent and that the League of Nations, though "forgotten and half-dead," still had a role to play in preserving the peace. Domestically, too, the problems were great, disorder and division still rampant. But if national discipline could be re-established, and with it new confidence, the French parliament could demonstrate to all that the country's capacity for revival was far from exhausted.[29]

For a while, his distrust of prophecy seemed amply justified, as the country plunged into the turbulence of February 1934. Three governments had taken office in 1933, the last of which fell in January of the new year. There followed a cabinet led by Edouard Daladier, for less than two weeks, which collapsed in the face of street riots and ideologically inspired rumours of imminent *coups d'état* and civil war. Accusations about financial corruption, the prostitution of justice, and staggering ministerial incompetence, were flung around with abandon, as deputies of all stripes found themselves the butt of reckless press campaigns and targets of physical menace. For several days in the second week of February it looked as if the Republic might collapse, crushed by the weight of domestic divisions. It was at that point that President Lebrun prevailed upon one of his predecessors, Gaston Doumergue, to come out of retirement and put together a new government.

Given the current crisis, which none could deny, the moment at last seemed opportune to construct a more broadly based coalition, one that could cover the spectrum between centre-right and centre-left, and that could recruit as a result an array of experienced leaders for the cabinet. With this in mind, Doumergue brought in Herriot, Tardieu, Sarraut, Laval, former premiers to a man, as well as seasoned former ministers like Chéron and Germain-Martin. For further prestige and authority, he installed the air chief of staff, General Denain, at the Air ministry, and Marshal Pétain at the War ministry. It was an ambition fulfilled for Louis Barthou as well. Not only had he lived to see the kind of centrist coalition he had been counselling for several years, but to him fell the prestigious if trouble-ridden portfolio of the minister for foreign affairs.

For readers familiar with Barthou's state of mind in the early 1930s, there would be no surprises in the policy he tried to implement in 1934. Consistent in every respect with his character, and his distrust of dogmatism, he wanted to keep his options open in the belief that French interests and French security required a good measure of flexibility. This was not, as he had said for years, simply giving in to German demands for treaty revision. Those demands now had to be resisted, the policy of concessions retarded, *but* in ways that did not further inflame Germany or reinforce the image of France as the major obstacle to international harmony. Such thinking had been central to his behaviour at Genoa in 1922, and was now to resurface as he returned to office at the Quai d'Orsay. Indeed, only two days before the Doumergue government was installed, Barthou had reminded his fellows on the Senate's Foreign Affairs committee that French foreign policy had to be developed with a threefold strategy – alert armed forces, international cooperation within the framework of the League of Nations, and improved bilateral relations with current and potential allies.[30] Neither hawk nor dove, by more contemporary parlance, Barthou continued to subscribe to the ideals cherished by Briand and to the realities contained in every German treaty violation.

That sounded, one deputy remarked, as if the Doumergue government was only going to offer more of the same. Was the new minister likely to do anything different from the policy of his predecessor, M. Paul-Boncour? Probably not, Barthou replied, not in substance, but there might well be significant differences of nuance.[31] For instance, the recent French note on disarmament, of 14 February, was being recognized as different in tone from the responses previously adopted by the Daladier and Chautemps governments. As the ambassador in Berlin had put it, this note was regarded in Germany as being appreciably more firm in language and spirit, not belligerent but much more forthright. In particular, the French government was now speaking openly of German rearmament under the Nazi regime, speaking of it and identifying it as unlawful and inimical to the cause of peace.[32]

Addressing the Chamber's Foreign Affairs committee on 2 March, the minister justified the note with the observation that genuine dialogue among nations – as among people – demanded that both sides should speak their minds. Indeed, it was essential for France to speak out, to expose publicly the clandestine activities of the German arms industries and the growth of Germany's proscribed air force. "I had the great honour to be a friend of Briand. Apart from a few points of detail, I renounce neither his attitude nor his policy."

However, the peace would never be well served by simply ignoring, or denying, the truth of Germany's military revival.[33]

Neither was it well served, he argued, by gratuitously aggravating relations with friendly powers. The United States had been alienated by France's failure to honour her undertakings on the payment of war debts. Efforts had to be made to correct this situation and repair an important friendship. Relations with England had been similarly compromised, partly, and again, because France had not fulfilled her promise to revise certain import restrictions deemed offensive by British business circles, partly because Whitehall thought the French government was being obstreperous on the disarmament issue. Entente with England, he reminded his audience, was simply too important to permit such differences to survive. More sound, he suggested, had been France's insistence on the continued independence of Austria, but French diplomats now had to ensure that Czech, Yugoslav, and Roumanian fears of a Hapsburg restoration in Vienna did not translate into tacit acceptance of a German take-over of Austria. As for Austria herself, new efforts already were being made to dissuade Chancellor Dollfuss from continuing his repression of Austrian socialists and trade unionists, measures which had so offended parties on the French and British left. Finally, France had to take seriously the current malaise in her relations with Poland. Marshal Pilsudski, the aging Polish head of state, continued to reaffirm his fidelity to the French alliance of 1921, but further and strengthened assurances would have to be forthcoming before the air was fully cleared.[34]

For the moment, there was but one sign of any marked improvement in France's position abroad. That was with respect to Italy. Mussolini, the minister advised the committee, could be counted on to support France's policy of Austrian independence, and there were larger possibilities still for effecting further Franco-Italian cooperation. New initiatives were also in the offing on a number of other fronts, including his own projected personal visit to Warsaw and Prague. As for Germany, however, he foresaw no dramatic departure from the policy pursued by his predecessors. Though faithful to the ideals of Briand, he had no intention of encouraging the kind of summit diplomacy which had led to the disappointments of Locarno. Premier Doumergue would not be going to Berlin, nor Hitler coming to Paris. Instead, Franco-German dialogue would be conducted through the normal, professional channels, those served by the respective foreign ministers and their diplomatic representatives in Paris and Berlin.[35]

By April 1934 the disarmament issue had become the focal point for French continental diplomacy. Here was the great divide, real and symbolic, between France and Germany. And if, in addition, it was a principal irritant in Anglo-French relations, so too it was for the eastern allies a weathervane of France's resolution to accommodate or contain a renascent Germany. As the minister was to put it, there were four options before the Doumergue government. The first was to uphold the principle of a general, multilateral disarmament, that with which the Geneva Disarmament Conference had opened in 1932 but which had been eroded by Germany's departure from the Conference the following year. The second was for France to disarm further, down to approximate parity with Germany, as the British seemed to prefer. The third was for Germany to rearm to parity with France, as the Italians advised; and the fourth was for France to call a halt to these unproductive talks about disarmament and instead reaffirm her commitment to a strict enforcement of the Versailles arms provisions.[36] There was but one problem in Barthou's list of options: none, it seemed, was very promising.

The first was an ideal that had gradually been sapped of its credibility. The second and third, given the risks they contained for French security, were certain to have a very difficult time securing majority support in parliament. The fourth would only confirm the current, and dangerous, stalemate. Such, at any rate, was his considered analysis, the sort of lucid overview he might well have presented as a journalist writing for readers of *Les Annales*. In April 1934, however, it was not enough for him to outline the alternatives. As minister responsible, it was up to him to recommend some course to the Doumergue cabinet.

He reached his decision within the week of 9–16 April, following a series of conversations with his senior officials. A minister known for his careful minuting of the diplomatic documents, and for his attentiveness as a listener, Barthou was impressed by what these advisers had to say.[37] On 9 April he received André François-Poncet and Jules Laroche, France's ambassadors in Berlin and Warsaw respectively. He had already absorbed their written appraisals and, following this personal encounter with them both, appeared to have made up his mind. On balance, the best course of action would be to take the initiative – propose a new arms convention which would concede Germany's right to rearm but which would also include mutually agreeable constraints on production levels and types of weaponry. If not ideal, such a proposal had two merits. It would not play into German hands by allowing Hitler to continue in his role of hapless victim of French obstructionism. Second, properly introduced as something constructive, it might help to break down the diplomatic isolation into which the disarmament issue had condemned France.

Writing to Lyautey on 15 April, Barthou acknowledged that he faced a tearful responsibility, but expressed confidence that he was clear on what he had to do.[38] There was, however, one early obstacle to clear: Gaston Doumergue. The premier had already evinced a special interest in the conduct of his government's foreign policy, partly by insisting on monitoring the ministry's diplomatic traffic, partly by installing his personal offices at the Quai d'Orsay, on the floor directly above those of Barthou. It was to this that the minister alluded when, gesturing upwards, he told François-Poncet that everything would depend on how the premier reacted to the kind of initiative they were proposing to take.[39]

Concerned about Doumergue's response and, one might allow, about the risks that were inherent in the course he was contemplating, Barthou continued to solicit the views of his permanant advisers. What would Briand have done? he asked Alexis Léger, the experienced secretary-general at the Foreign ministry.[40] Indeed, he even asked Léger to drive him out to Cocherel, Briand's country residence and the site of his grave, as if such a pilgrimage might afford some moment of insight. It was there, at Cocherel, that Léger had the opportunity to sketch out his own vision of a continent made safe for France. What was needed, he told his minister, was a regional security pact for eastern Europe, what some already were calling an eastern Locarno. What he had in mind was an international convention which would guarantee the existing frontiers of eastern Europe and which, at the same time, could be used as an entrée for bringing the Soviet Union into the League of Nations. By inscribing Russia, as well as Germany, in such an eastern pact, it might be possible to contain the volatile potential of frontier revisionism in the greater security interests of all signatories. Additionally, by constructing some separate Franco-Soviet accord within the framework of the League Covenant, France might acquire a new ally, without running the risks inherent in a strictly bilateral agreement unrestrained by other international conventions.

Barthou listened attentively, as was his custom, and then declared that the key to such a plan's success lay in garnering the support of Great Britain. Were that forthcoming, the Germans might come on side, along with France's friends in eastern Europe. Then, if Russia could be enlisted in the same pact, Hitler would see the implications at once. He could make the plan work by accepting the territorial status quo in the east – thus furthering Germany's own security – or he could withdraw from something which had the potential to become a device for encircling Germany.[41] A day or so later, Barthou told Léger that he was now resolved on this initiative. Having in any case to send a formal reply to a recent British communication on disarmament, he would use the opportunity to indicate French acceptance of German rearmament. But only within the framework of a new arms convention. The same day, 16 April, the minister conveyed his decision to Henri Béranger, chairman of the Senate's Foreign Affairs committee, and to Jean Fabry, chairman of the Chamber's Army committee. Both seemed to like the initiative.[42]

Premier Doumergue did not. Supported, if not incited, by Tardieu and Herriot, the two politically most powerful members of his cabinet, Doumergue decided otherwise. What was needed, he concluded, was for France to take the tough line, option four. The forthcoming reply to the British note should not renounce the idea of further disarmament negotiations, but it should again condemn Germany's repeated arms violations and make it clear that such conduct simply made it impossible for France to pin all hopes for her security on some elusive and distant disarmament convention.[43] Implicitly, this was to mean reaffirming the more traditional emphasis on alliance diplomacy and, more implicitly still, on the need to revitalize France's military capacity.

Convinced as he had been by contrary arguments, Barthou did not like what he was being told, and in front of the entire cabinet. It was a mistake, he believed – and as he had maintained earlier at Genoa – for France to run the risk of being held responsible for the collapse of the disarmament conference. Not only was this likely to play into Hitler's hands, but it was ill calculated to impress the British government. His views, however, persuaded few, one measure of which was the cabinet vote, which went strongly against him. Angered and mortified by the lack of support, he later confided that this had been one of the most unpleasant experiences of his entire political life. He contemplated resignation, but feared that such an act would precipitate yet another governmental and parliamentary crisis. Instead, he decided to stay on, doubtless with a view to containing the damage that might come from the note demanded by Doumergue – that which was despatched from the Quai d'Orsay on 17 April 1934.[44]

Having resolved to swallow his pride, the minister had no choice but to back the cabinet's collective decision and, accordingly, to deny his personal misgivings. Having told Fabry a day before that France had to say "yes" to German demands for further concessions on armaments, he now found it expedient to pose a rhetorical question to the Chamber's Foreign Affairs committee. "When one is inclined to say no, is it not better to say so outright?"[45] In short, he refused to admit to any divergence between his own views and the policy he had agreed to pursue. Before the committee, and the Chamber itself, he stressed the unanimity with which the contents of the April note had been agreed upon by the cabinet, and categorically denied suggestions that he had relented only as a gesture of cabinet solidarity. The most he was ever to concede publicly, and that only once, came in the form of an oblique reference to the world of political necessity. Had there been divisions in the cabinet, he said, it certainly would serve no purpose to admit them.[46]

That, at least, was true – unlike the rest. Nevertheless, this much can be said in mitigation of his lack of candour. Having previously signalled his views to at least three ministerial officials, as well as to the chairmen of two parliamentary committees, and sometimes in the presence of the journalist Geneviève Tabouis, his subsequent denials had very little to do with deception. Why he did not resign may be interpreted in ways for or against him, but his own predilections seem to have been an open secret. Certainly it seemed clear to the members of the Chamber's Foreign Affairs committee that the note of 17 April was not of Barthou's doing.

The committee was uncertain about what that note actually meant in any event, and rightly so. Prompted in part by the observation that the April note would neither stop German rearmament nor facilitate multilateral disarmament, the committee declined to endorse that note. It was prepared to go so far as to call it "a starting point," although it could not detect anything really new in substance. But it feared that what might have been gained by the appearance of some new vigour might also have been lost by the resentments kindled in Berlin and in London. This, of course, was precisely what Barthou himself feared, and why he would have opted for another kind of response. Given that perception, which grew in part from his scorn of bravado and empty gestures, it was not surprising that the minister would try to remove some of the sting from the note which carried his own signature. In his remarks to parliament, for example, what he stressed was not the novelty of the April note, but rather its continuity. By his telling, the note was entirely consistent with the policies of his precedessors, including their commitment to a disarmament convention, and was indeed a conciliatory document that left the doors wide open to any kind of peace initiatives.[47]

That all of this should have led to some confusion is not in the least surprising. For one thing, while privately Barthou said the note was an ill-advised departure from past policy, publicly he maintained there had been no departure at all. More perplexing still, this public claim brought no audible rebuke from a cabinet which, to the minister's chagrin, had earlier backed the note as a bold new beginning.

Furthermore, while that cabinet undertook little in the way of new defence initiatives in 1934 – action which might have lent substance to the rhetoric of 17 April – the principal opponent of the note, Barthou, was soon made out to be a diplomat of the old, confrontational school. The more he talked of Russia and an eastern pact, the more he was rebuked by some and applauded by others for reviving the old pre-war diplomacy. No doubt mindful of Barthou's role in 1913, when the Russian alliance had been reinforced and three-year service introduced, one deputy warned that this was the government's game – a return to the old patterns of alliances and military conventions, with all the hazards therein contained.[48] While this was certainly overstated, it does put one thing aright. It was not the April note that was especially significant, except in its suggestion of a new psychology. Rather it was the subsequent diplomatic initiatives undertaken by an ebullient and tenacious foreign minister nearly seventy-two years of age.

Even these, it should be said, were not entirely of his own doing, the groundwork for his late April visit to Warsaw and Prague having been laid by his predecessor, Paul-Boncour. What he had not begun himself, he nonetheless executed with some aplomb. In Poland this was no small achievement, for relations were sufficiently troubled that Joseph Beck, the foreign minister, made a point of missing Barthou's arrival at the Warsaw station. But by the time of his departure a few days later, Barthou had convinced himself that his visit had been a tonic for Franco-Polish relations. He had not secured Polish support for the eastern pact, or resolved an especially sensitive commercial dispute between the two countries, or even raised the delicate issue of Polish support for Soviet membership in the League; however, he had been assured that the recent Polish-German non-aggression pact had done nothing to undercut Poland's alliance with France and, in his turn, had offered assurances to an openly sceptical Marshal Pilsudki that the Doumergue government was determined to take a firmer line with Nazi Germany. Exchanges of this sort, facilitated by his vocal appreciation of Polish women and Polish vodka, had helped the minister restore an atmosphere of renewed conviviality. Moreover, his public and private acknowledgments of Poland's status as great power, and of her importance to the security of eastern Europe, were well calculated to appeal to Beck's personal as well as his national pride. All told, therefore, the visit convinced Barthou that the Polish alliance was still intact and fundamentally reliable.[49]

So too was that with Czechoslovakia, a country whose premier, Edouard Benes, was already a close personal friend. In Prague there was little to cloud Franco-Czech relations, although Barthou did try to prod the government to improve its relations with Poland, to reaffirm its commitment to an independent Austria, and to take the lead in defending the regional independence of the Balkan zone against Italian designs. Here, too, he made full use of his range of personal charm – from that of wit, raconteur, and ladies' man to savant and bibliophile – in order to reinforce the ties between nations with friendship of a more personal character.[50]

Barthou related his impressions of these visits to the Chamber's Foreign Affairs committee in early May 1934. Two months later, he reappeared before the same committee in order to bring its members abreast of still more recent travels, this time to Geneva, Bucharest, and Belgrade. In a careful *tour d'horizon*, he outlined the essential features of current French foreign policy. Significantly, he said nothing of Poland, with whom relations were once again badly inflamed, and next to nothing of Great Britain, dependence on whom might profitably be lessened by means of some productive French initiatives on the continent. What he stressed, however, was that his objective was not to create a system of blocs and counter-blocs. Rather, he pledged himself to a policy of "collaboration européenne" within the framework of the League of Nations.[51] In the interests of such a policy, the government had already made it clear that it would co-operate fully with Germany in preparing for the Versailles-envisaged plebiscite to determine whether or not the inhabitants of the Saar valley wished to be fully reunited with Germany. After the French had signalled this conciliatory intent, there were signs that some delegations at Geneva were a little more inclined to accept the French position on disarmament – namely that enhanced security arrangements across the entire continent were an essential prelude to any serious convention for multilateral disarmament.

For good reason, the minister felt no need to remind the committee of his own insistence on the word "serious," no need to say again in July what had been broadcast in June. For the fact is that he had created a small storm by the candour he had unleashed in Geneva. He had said then, categorically, that he wanted to see Germany return to the Disarmament Conference, entirely on her own volition. Thereafter, what should take place was serious and completely frank negotiations, not all of the smarmy public statements about goodwill and unanimity. Part of the problem in the past was this myth of accord when there was none, of unity despite its absence. In fact, he judged that all of the wonderful unanimity of the past had been thoroughly grounded in "misunderstandings and internal contradictions." Therefore, he concluded, "too bad, if I am not among the unanimous. ... In my own way, which may not be better but which at least is candid, I have spoken my mind."[52]

So his candour continued before the Foreign Affairs committee, as he moved on to the subject of the eastern regional security pact. Everything now rested with the Poles, Germans, and Russians. He had met Litvinov, the Soviet foreign minister, several times in Geneva during the months of May and June, and had duly informed Berlin of these contacts so as to scotch any rumour of some desire to encircle Germany. What was now envisaged was that Russia would join the League, and then inscribe herself in the eastern pact as a fully fledged League member. When asked what would happen if the Poles, Germans, or both rejected the idea of the eastern pact, Barthou replied that no firm contingency plan had yet been worked out. However, he did add that when discussing just such an eventuality in Belgrade, with King Alexander, he had reminded the monarch of the pre-war Franco-Russian alliance – suggesting thereby that it might be as possible for republican France to ally with Soviet Russia as it had done with Russia of the czars.[53]

Yugoslavia, he observed, was likely to be a key player in his efforts to preserve the peace, partly because he had a high regard for the leadership abilities of the young monarch, mainly because he saw that kingdom as central to any French attempt to enlist the support of Mussolini. Given the diplomatic accord between France and Yugoslavia, and the protracted discord between Yugoslavia and Italy, French hopes for Italian cooperation rested in turn on some kind of Italo-Yugoslav accommodation. If Russia was one ace the minister hoped to play in Geneva, Italy was a second.

His frequent talks in Geneva with Aloisi, the Italian delegate, had progressed satisfactorily in May and June, and it was already being projected that he would pay a visit to Mussolini's capital as soon as the international climate seemed right and certain issues had been resolved. All the signs were that the Duce remained opposed to any German move against Austria, and that he regarded Hitler as living in a dream world constructed by his own propaganda.[54] It was time, therefore, to iron out the differences between France and Italy, whether they touched upon Libya, Tunisia, or relative naval strengths, and it was time to push with renewed vigour for an Italo-Yugoslav settlement. As for a French accommodation with fascism, the minister said that the peace of Europe was worth the price. He had no illusions about the dictatorial nature of Italian fascism, and had commented on it publicly; however, he would gladly enlist one dictator to restrain another if he thought that such a strategy was in the interest of European peace.[55]

Clear as these remarks to the committee were, a low cloud of uncertainty still hung over the minister's intentions. It may have descended from deceit, but it was just as likely the result of his inability to foresee every curve that lay between him and his destination. More precisely, perhaps, it remained unclear which of two potential policies would ultimately be called upon. There was, on the one hand, the Barthou who remembered Briand, and the last war, and his son, and who as an aggrieved parent found the prospect of more military carnage too terrible to contemplate. It was he who spoke of European reconciliation, who decried useless and provocative posturing, and who insisted on the continuity of his policy back through Paul-Boncour to Briand. It was he who told a German diplomat in late May 1934:

I and my people do not desire war, but peace. I lost my son in the war. During the war I stated publicly: "Never shall this hand of mine touch the hand of a German." But after Versailles I changed my views and was the first French political leader to negotiate in Berlin with German political leaders. I desire an understanding with Germany, this I tell you eye to eye, as a man of honor.[56]

In keeping with this sentiment, and yet in the face of a Nazi regime already rearming, what made sense was to postpone disarmament discussions until collective security pacts obviated the need for large standing armies. That had been France's position all along, and Barthou never departed from it. So "security first," not constructed around potentially destructive alliance systems but rather, ideally, around collective security through the League. Indeed, Edouard Herriot took particular note of how strongly his colleague had associated French policy with the League and how vigorously he had resisted those in the Chamber who dismissed Geneva as being of no account.[57]

However, and as Barthou knew perfectly well, an eastern Locarno might lead to as many disappointments as those which had plagued the accord reached by Briand and Stresemann in the 1920s. In short, without a genuine regional pact, there would be no security for anyone, and no disarmament; and that failure in turn was likely to underscore the importance of traditional alliances – along the lines of those concluded after the war with Belgium, Poland, and Czechoslovakia – and in all probability to signal the beginning of a new arms race. Indeed, some were already persuaded that it was this second scenario that the government either wanted or at least expected to take shape. That is why, in May, one deputy had foreseen a return to 1913, and in July another had scolded Barthou for making a truculent speech in Bucharest which had sounded more like "bloc against bloc" than anything reminiscent of European collaboration.[58] Thus the distinction between what was desirable and what merely likely was too fine for some to appreciate, though not too fine for the minister to express with clarity. His personal view was that if the eastern pact fell through and Russia could not be enlisted in that way, some were certain to demand a straightforward Franco-Russian alliance in its place. Although he did not say quite as much on the subject of Italy, it is clear that the same logic held here as well, perhaps the more so given his express reference to a future visit to Rome.[59]

There was no mistaking the fact that events in the summer of 1934 were rapidly undermining hopes in League-sponsored security pacts. A man who had spent the last war castigating the Prussian-infected German character, Barthou had reason to think that the political descendants of the Kaiser were returning with a vengeance. In mid-July he and Léger listened to a radio broadcast in the library on the avenue Marceau, a broadcast in which Hitler sought to justify the massacre of potential rivals during the night of 30 June. Having listened while the appalling was brushed aside by the cynical, Barthou remarked on the renewed urgency with which Russia had to be brought into the League and enlisted for the security pact.[60] One week later, grief tinged by indignation prevented him from reading aloud a press statement to journalists assembled at the Quai d'Orsay. Chancellor Dollfuss of Austria had just been murdered by Austrian Nazis intent on delivering their country to Hitler. The minister's statement ended very simply: "Yes, it is true, so intense is my grief that I know I have lost a friend."[61] Later in the day he still could only manage to say that civilized society would not tolerate the use of assassination as a tool of international policy – a clear enough reflection of his view that Hitler had been behind the murder. More promising, however, was Mussolini's decision to mobilize troops on the Brenner frontier with Austria, as a clear warning that Italy would not tolerate a German attempt at an *Anschluss*.

In September Barthou made several trips to the League of Nations in Geneva. By then he had two principal objectives. First, he had to make a case strong enough to ensure Soviet admission to the League, a hurdle finally negotiated in mid-September. Although he was still pitching his arguments in terms of Russia's potential contribution to the eastern security pact, Polish and German animosity had already made such a pact even more problematical than it had been at the outset. Instead, and if necessary, League membership would lend

Russia the aura of respectability which might be required if talk turned to a straight bilateral accord. At the same time, Barthou plied • the Italian delegate with compliments and expressions of camaraderie, while nursing negotiations toward a new Anglo-French-Italian statement on the independence of Austria and promoting better relations between Italy and Yugoslavia.[62] Indeed, to Aloisi's annoyance, Barthou tried to present his projected visit to Rome not only as a step toward improved Franco-Italian relations but also as one that might initiate new accord between Italy and all of the Little Entente countries.

Less than two weeks after his final meeting with Aloisi on 26 September, Barthou made a point of reaffirming the context in which he had been working. In a public address of 3 October, pronounced in tribute to Théophile Delcassé, the minister praised his former cabinet colleague for his pre-war contribution to Franco-Italian and Franco-British relations. But this, he said, had not been designed as any preposition to war. On the contrary, despite what was sometimes said about one country's desire to encircle another, such had never been Delcassé's intention. His efforts had been aimed at no one.[63] Three days later, he went for a walk with the journalist Wladimir d'Ormesson, and delivered the same message, if less obliquely expressed. He had no wish to encircle Germany, and for the moment at least had very firm limits on how far he would go with the Soviet Union. He would welcome an era of reasonable negotiations with Germany, but the trick was always to find the mean between a dangerous optimism and a debilitating pessimism. That line, he believed, would be called a policy which combined prudence, confidence, and realism. "That's what I'm trying to accomplish."[64] It was with this in mind that he was going to be in Marseille on 9 October, to greet King Alexander at the start of his state visit to France. From that encounter might come new momentum for an Italo-Yugoslav understanding, and new possibilities for some Franco-Italian accord.

That such momentum had been built up by a septuagenarian was only remarkable to those unfamiliar with Barthou's energy. He was in splendid form thoughout the spring and summer of 1934, a condition which he attributed to his strict regimen of early nights, five o'clock risings, cold baths, morning calisthenics, and frequent walks. Nothing deterred him from his schedule, whether it meant saying good night at nine in the evening to the journalists accompanying him on the train to Warsaw or, once arrived, alerting Polish security men to be ready for a morning walk at five. Even on holiday, effort was his relaxation. That summer at Bürgenstock he had been hiking and swimming every day, working on Foreign ministry documents, and spending hours with so many of his favourite books that he had required assistance to get them back to Paris.[65]

It was a combination of physical and nervous energy, as evident in the elder man as it had been in the boy nicknamed "vif argent." He still had difficulty remaining immobile for long, as advertised by the constant fidgeting with his glasses, always resetting them with an index finger on the bridge of his nose. Indeed, so pronounced and familiar was the mannerism, this nervous "tic," that some joked about how he was forever imitating himself. Just as amusing, some found, was his continuing attachment to the enthusiastic but old-fashioned exclamation, "En toute bonne foi!"[66] Commonly, however, he provoked mirth by intent, for his wit, and his tongue, were as keen as ever. In the summer of 1934 he recalled for an appreciative audience of deputies how he had handled one British diplomat's misgivings about ministerial instability in France. I replied, he said, by suggesting that governments like ours seemed to be able to change ministers while retaining their policy. Others, like His Majesty's Government, often changed their minds without changing ministers. That kind of humour a French audience could find amusing, but reactions varied when he turned on occasion to ribald anecdotes at a dinner table or engaged in good-humoured but crude flirtations with the wives of diplomatic personnel. Some for example, were affronted when he, though a champion of the League, stooped in jest to likening that body to a "tired old virgin."[67]

What lay behind this recent predilection for the salacious remains a mystery, our previous speculation notwithstanding.[68] For the fact is that this was a man who was more than ever attached to a life of bourgeois domesticity. He had made a point of installing his mother-in-law in his residence after Alice's death, and whenever possible he declined invitations and evening engagements in favour of staying home.[69] There was, therefore, behind this sparkling bonhomie, behind the expansive raconteur and jester, a lonely man who was no stranger to melancholy. It was this Barthou whom close collaborators like Pierre Benoit and Louis Vitalis saw when doors closed on the library or on the office at the Quai d'Orsay. Georges Suarez saw it as well, laughter used as a disguise. Lonely as he was, Barthou never complained, but in depressed moments he could say, matter-of-factly, that he no longer had any personal reasons for living.[70]

That was only at low moments, and in October 1934 he had little time for depression. The demands of the Foreign ministry were only a part of it. For one thing, he was engaged in the preparation of a reception speech for the Duc de Broglie at the Académie Française.

He was also supervising the publication of a special edition of Hugo's *Fin de Satan* for *Le Livre contemporain*, working on a radio broadcast about Wagner and Baudelaire, and preparing a short piece on Juliette Drouet.[71] It did not help that he was suffering from a head cold and feeling miserable enough to contemplate backing out of the trip to Marseille. With that in mind, he phoned François Piétri, the naval minister, and asked if the latter might go alone to greet King Alexander. Piétri, correctly enough, suggested that this would be too much of a breach of protocol, to which Barthou replied with a quip. He would take his cough drops, but if he were to die of a cold on board the king's vessel he would count on the French navy to see that he was buried on land.[72] Having then arranged to take the night train to Marseille on the evening of 8 October, Barthou carried on with his final appointments of the day.

The last was with Gustave Samazeuil, the Béarnais musical composer upon whom Barthou relied for advance notice of foreign artists scheduled to perform in Paris. Their conversation concluded, the two men shook hands, Barthou closed the large double doors of his ministerial office, and the two men descended to the street. There the minister climbed into his chauffeured automobile and, with a wave and a smile, was off. Later that evening, at the Gare de Lyon, the Béarnais journalist Georges Coustel witnessed the minister's departure for the south. Barthou was dressed in his favourite grey tweed suit, in the lapel of which he was wearing the *grand cordon* of Yugoslavia. It was to be his burial suit.[73]

For some months prior to the royal visit the French security services had been aware of a possible threat to the king's life. By 5 October they had assembled a dossier which singled out as the most likely assassin a Yugoslav whom they knew under the name of Nalis Tikomir, and had forwarded the information to the authorities in Marseille. On the morning of 9 October, hours before the king's scheduled landing on the quayside, the commandant of the Marseille gendarmerie had circulated this information to all officers assigned to the security detail.[74] As one might have expected, the police had not kept the threat to themselves. Charles Rochat, Barthou's current *chef de cabinet*, had certainly received word of a possible attack on the king; and the king himself, long accustomed to death threats from exiled Croatian separatists, had even taken the precaution of having a bullet-proof vest especially made for his journey in France.[75]

But so much foresight was met by a series of cruel rebuffs. The vest would not fit under the admiral's uniform which the king had selected for wear on his arrival in the port of Marseille. The vehicles chosen for the motorcade from the quay were open-air limousines rather than hard-top sedans. And the police security screen along the motorcade route proved stunningly inadequate. Hardly had the king and Barthou installed themselves in the first vehicle than a man broke from the crowd lining the roadway, rushed to the slowly moving target car, and opened fire on the king. Within a matter of minutes the sovereign was dying, the assassin had been sabred to the ground by a mounted officer, and pandemonium had erupted amid a hail of police bullets. Some spectators were killed, others wounded. Barthou, who appears not to have been a target, staggered out of the vehicle and was seen groping on the pavement for his glasses, shaken but apparently unscathed. In fact, he had been hit in the arm, probably by a stray police bullet, and was starting to hemorrhage.[76]

Unknown to him, a humeral artery had been severed, a grave enough wound but one which a tourniquet could have contained until he had received hospital attention. Instead, the tragedy only quickened. Unable to gauge the gravity of his condition, partly from physiological shock and partly from a visual capacity that was acutely impaired without his spectacles, the minister was left in the chaos to make his own way to the nearest hospital. He arrived there by taxi, after a trip delayed by crowd-filled streets. There, he got out of the car, asked about the king, and just before fainting, said that he did not think his own wound was serious. Indeed, the earliest telephone messages received by Rochat in Paris said the same. The king, he knew, was already dead, but le patron seemed out of danger, a broken arm and substantial blood loss.[77]

The prognosis was good, and incorrect. Precisely what happened late that afternoon in the Saint-Charles hospital will never be known. Nor would knowing make a difference. There were reports that someone had applied a tourniquet while the minister was en route to the hospital, but below rather than above the wound. Another report suggested that treatment of any kind, including a transfusion, had been delayed until the arrival of a surgeon eminent enough to treat a statesman of such rank. It was then decided to repair the artery surgically, prior to which he was given the first transfusion. Piétri, having made his way to the hospital, was told the transfusion was being administered at that moment and that he would be able to see his colleague in less than an hour. But in the operating room Louis Barthou was dying. Semi-conscious, he mumbled a question about the king's condition and about his missing glasses. Vision misted over, he tried again to reach the bridge of his nose in that familiar, now unfinished gesture, as his hand fell back motionless.[78]

For a day and a half his body lay in state at the Marseille prefecture, beside that of the murdered king, while cabinet colleagues in Paris made preparations for the state funeral they thought he deserved. On 11 October, Herriot watched as Barthou's formaldahyde-injected body was collected from the funeral bier, arms pathetically limp, and moved to a special train bound for Paris. Later that day he and Tardieu returned to the capital with the coffin, descending at the Gare de Lyon to be met by Doumergue, other members of the cabinet, and a visibly shaken Léon Barthou. From there a procession accompanied the body back to the Quai d'Orsay, where it lay in the Salon de l'Horloge, surrounded by an honour guard.

Two days later, when the queues of citizens wishing to pay their respects had diminished, a funeral procession set out from the Foreign ministry to the esplanade of the Invalides, the very location where but three years before Barthou had delivered the funeral oration for Marshal Joffre. There, to the strains of Chopin's funeral march, they took him; and there it fell to Doumergue to remind the nation of the minister's long and dedicated service to his country, a service now twice exceptional. He had given his only son to France, the premier recalled, a loss from which he had never fully recovered; and now he had fallen himself in the service of his country. He had been a patriot of the first order, one who had only agreed to return to government in order to help restore the sense of national unity. It was up to those who survived him to see that this unity was made the more secure through the sacrifice of his death.

From there they took him to the adjacent church of Saint-Louis-des-Invalides. The frail Mme Mayeur was there, supported by Léon and Joseph Barthou, their widowed sister Clémence, the Gilbert cousins, the faithful valet Gustave. Still in a state of shock they sat in the front rows of the crowded church, steeling themselves against the emotions about to be released by wave upon wave of Barthou's favourite music. It began with the psalm *De Profundis*, sung by a soloist from the church of Saint-Clothilde; and then Fauré's *Libera Me, Domine*, performed by a singer from the Opera and accompanied by an orchestra assembled from the Conservatoire. Absolution was granted by the adjutant of the Archbishop of Paris, and then still more music, this time the *allegretto* movement from Beethoven's Seventh Symphony. Finally, the procession began its departure to the bars of Saint-Saëns's *Marche héroïque* – out through the Place Vauban and along the boulevards, the Invalides, Montparnasse, Port Royal, Saint Marcel, l'Hôpital, Henry IV, to the Bastille, and then the rue de la Roquette, the boulevard Ménilmontant, and the awaiting tomb at Père Lachaise.[79] There, on 13 October, all that remained of Louis Barthou returned to his wife and his son. Just before dusk, on the high ground, not far from where Balzac had buried Père Goriot.

Conclusion

> I'd give a handsome twenty-franc piece ... to be
> Barthou's confessor, to hear what he would say in the
> stillness of a church, behind the small wooden grill,
> just to know what he really thinks about himself, and
> others, and the events of our times.[1]

So Léon Daudet wrote in 1925. Within a year, however, his curiosity
had been slaked. Louis Barthou was the son on whom all the sins
of the Republic had been visited – debauched, dishonest, discredited.
For those who have followed the life of this, Daudet's nemesis, his
appraisal may well seem as foolish as it was malicious. This is not to
say that Barthou had no need of a confessor or, more important,
that this biography has made some priest redundant. Indeed, Barthou was personally convinced that every individual stands guard
over some inner, distant recess into which no one else can ever
penetrate.[2] At the same time, as a biographer himself, he also appreciated the challenge inherent in this genre of history and was
repeatedly drawn back to the study of those he considered men and
women of genius. Who knows what he would have thought about
having the tables turned, about becoming subject instead of student?
My guess is that he would have enjoyed the attention, but been
perplexed by the choice, for never would he have put himself on a
par with any of his own subjects. For good reason. But these are
three short words which invite two lengthier explanations, both of
which touch upon the biographer.

The first is the most personal. The introductory remarks to this
volume alerted the reader to an interpreter's presence and advised
that what followed was a sympathetic portrait. Some might judge
the warning extraneous, even ill advised, but few are now likely to
quarrel with the forecast. The fact is that for the better part of a
decade I have lived with Barthou, studied his published and unpublished writing, read some of his favourite authors, listened to
some of his preferred music. I have walked the streets of his youth

in Oloron, Pau, and Bordeaux, and the estate of his cherished Bürgenstock in Switzerland. I have listened to his tremulous tenor voice,
recorded in 1932 when he delivered a public eulogy for Anna de
Noailles; between my hands have passed books from his library,
the sword he designed for the Académie, the gun which killed
King Alexander, and the sabre which struck down the assassin. The
Madeleine where he was married, the Invalides chapel where musicians last played in his memory, the Académie Française where his
bust of Lamartine will be safe for ever, the granite tomb at Père
Lachaise, in each of these we have shared something. And within
me too there is an indebtedness to one whose knowledge and interests have helped instruct a foreigner in the richness of another culture. Of all this the reader has a right to be aware.

Second, the concept of "greatness" has played little part in the
selection of Louis Barthou as biographical subject. Although presented as a republican notable, a man closely associated with some
of the more significant "events" of the regime's history, no case is
made, no vocabulary employed, for making him larger than life or
greater than the events through which he lived. He was chosen in
the first instance because, like many apparently lesser peaks, he was
there, and not overrun by other sightseers. There was as well some
sense of a need for restitution, for flowers no longer appear on his
tomb on 9 October, the cairn in his memory at Bürgenstock has
been removed, and it is said that even the school children of Béarn
barely recognize his name. Perhaps too the choice had something
to do with a perceived irony. For all the suspicion in which historians
now hold "great man" explanations of history, too few of them can
resist the spell cast by figures already demonstrably famous. Finally,
and most likely of all, in Barthou there seemed to be the possibility
of a full-life construction, non-political as well as political, private as
well as public. It was this that became the generating force, not the
methodology which is traditional, but the concept of a "social" biography. Even this, I concede, is of limited novelty, reminiscent of
Bacon's remark about the essay: "the word is new, the thing is ancient." Nevertheless, as an expression of intent and objective, the
adjective may prove to be as useful to the reader as it has been to
the author.

If the biographer eschews great-man history, and any notion that
his or her subject is always in charge of events, what is left? Something both less and more grand. The subject, in this case Barthou,
reacquires a quality long apparent to him and to all of his contemporaries – that of an ordinary being, exceptional by moment or place,
but with feet unmistakably of clay. Yet it is that in which the humanist

finds greatness of another sort, the awesome complexities and contradictions of the human species. It is in that, too, that one may perceive the connection between a biographer's artistic goal of portraying a single human being, and the goal identified by novelists like de Maupassant.

At the same time, however, by respecting that quality of ordinariness, the biographer, as social scientist, is also well placed to observe the impact of social conditioning on the emergence of a subject's personality. Seldom, if ever, the sole master of his fate, that person absorbs much of the fibre of the society into which he has been thrust from the womb. If the evidence is up to it, there seems every reason to examine that process of absorption, for few would deny some kind of interrelationship between individuals and their times. Demonstrating it, to be sure, is much more taxing. To this task in turn must be added an equally arduous assignment, that of discerning whatever is unique within this socialized individual. Acculturated organisms though we may be, to borrow a phrase from Thomas Dewey, there are few who would wish to surrender all claims to individuality. And certainly neither Barthou nor his biographer is among them. In this, therefore, in all of this, lie the appeal and the challenge of biography. The object is to reconstruct one life by exploring the myriad intersections where the formative influences of society interact with that unique composition of personal characteristics which collectively is called personality.

"They raised me above their own station in life," wrote a seventy-year-old Barthou when recalling his parents.[3] It was as a child in Oloron-Sainte-Marie that he first discovered the thrill which accompanied personal achievement and advancement, and in the cause of which his father's industry and ambition served as inspiration. Indeed, to the end of his days Barthou continued to speak "with a good-natured pride of his father the cask-maker."[4] Expected to achieve as a student, first in Béarn and later in Bordeaux and Paris, this son and first-born did so in full measure. It was more than filial obedience, or simply a lack of imagination, for Barthou's interests carried well beyond the classroom, to politics, sport, music, autograph collecting, journalism, and young women. Education, his father had emphasized, was the portal to success, and hard work the key. But recreation, too, was essential, as a tonic for work and an antidote to tedium. And in the pastoral setting of Béarn, in resort centres like Pau and Eaux-Bonnes, it was not difficult to acquire an interest in the lifestyles of leisured visitors whose enjoyments ranged from those afforded by the casino and racetrack, to the bookshops and historical sites like the Château de Pau, to the lush foothill

country of the Pyrenees. It was to the latter kinds of attraction that
Barthou gravitated, to the book stalls of the city, to the rivers which
he thought had taught him an affinity for music, to the very mountains where he knew de Vigny and Hugo had wandered.

Even in the early days, however, there had been more to his work
and his pleasures than pure egocentrism. If he wished to get ahead,
to achieve social prominence and material success, it was not strictly
self that concerned him. To be sure, he showed no sign of ever
becoming a social crusader, one bent on eradicating economic in-
equalities among Frenchmen. But he did acquire from an early age
a passionate conviction that out of the humiliation of military defeat
in 1870 had emerged a progressive, fair-minded Republic. Whether
this had come from the lips of his father, from Georges Edet's furtive
reading of Hugo in the classroom, or from the newspaper accounts
of Gambetta's speeches in Paris, Barthou soon understood that the
Republic was good, that parliamentary democracy was France's hope,
that clericalism and royalism were to be resisted with the same determination as socialism. Then had come Emile Garet, the publisher
of *L'Indépendant*, a man who soon became one of Barthou's living
heroes, a republican to the core, but a man of inherent moderation
and acquired erudition in history and literature. It was he who had
taken "quicksilver" in hand, trained him in journalism, whetted his
interest in politics, and encouraged his candidacy for the municipal
council. Together they had fought against the demagoguery of Boulangism, the victory over which had sent Barthou to parliament in
1889.

There, brimming with a confidence furnished by distinguished
academic achievement and the electoral upset of Jacques LaCaze,
the young deputy encountered any number of comparable success
stories. Unique in parental influence and personal experience in
Béarn, he nonetheless found himself among so many others of similar age and bourgeois provenance, of comparable education and
historical appreciation. Royalists and Imperialists excepted, here was
a congregation of deputies who were intent on reasserting France's
position in the world under the auspices of a liberal-democratic
Republic. Some, certainly, were more intent than others on redis-
tributing the nation's wealth on a more equitable basis, but the majority were slowly turning their attention to the maintenance of social
order by means of gradual reform. Clericalism, for many, still remained the enemy and was the issue upon which they secured their
claim to being on the "left"; but this political defence of the Republic
against the right increasingly became associated with the need to
combat clerical- and socialist-inspired dissidence with labour and

educational reform, and sometimes with restrictive, punitive legislation.

It was in this current that Barthou found himself in the decades before World War One, one which used the law to repress anarchism, constrain the Church, and coerce striking public employees, one which used other law to promote better pension plans, safer and shorter working hours, improved health care and more developed social assistance programs. Belated, modest, and piecemeal though these reforms may now be judged, and derived as much from a concern for social order as from social conscience, they were the work of a generation of middle class deputies who had begun their careers with a conditioned animus against state intervention in the economy. In his initial reluctance to encourage such state intrusions, and in his gradual acceptance of the state's responsibility, Louis Barthou was very much a politician of his time.

That is to say that his personal political maturation was tied up with a broader, developing sense of *bourgeois oblige*, which in turn was linked to his personal good fortune. For in the 1890s marriage had vaulted him into the affluent middle class, at an age and in a manner that was entirely typical of the cadre of cabinet ministers. Now, class-secure, with a wealthy wife, an expensive apartment off the Champs-Elysée, and a country residence in the fashionable western suburbs, his confidence in the Republic seemed fully vindicated. Here was proof of a personal order that a regime, animated by the ideals of political democracy and governed by educated commoners of demonstrated competence, was receptive to newcomers who were themselves industrious and professionally trained. From that there followed a renewed conviction that this was a regime worth saving and serving, to ensure that extremists of whatever hue did not destroy something precious.

There is, therefore, a dual association at work. In the first instance, there is the ongoing, variegated transaction between Barthou and his times: whether it be in his attention to the current divorce, alcohol, and birth-rate issues, or in his acquired taste for Wagner, Hugo, bibliophilia, exercise, and mountain vacations. In the second, there is the link between the lifestyle of a lawyer-deputy who could now indulge himself as tourist, collector, concert-goer, and aviator, and his efforts as a legislator to maintain stability through the calculated use of the law, sometimes to curtail and sometimes to enlarge the freedoms of his fellow citizens. Republican democracy had a responsibility to effect progress under law, and a right to defend itself while doing so. When challenged years later to define what he meant by democracy, he said at seventy-two what he would have said

at thirty-two: "Monsieur, to be a workingman's son ... to have strug-
gled toward ... and to have reached, the position which I have occupied for many years in the counsels of the Republic, that is what
democracy is all about."[5]

Bourgeois democracy, some have called it, but it was the only kind
he knew or would countenance, for the adjective to him was no
pejorative. Bourgeois meant effort and application, a commitment
to family, traditional moral values, and social order, and an attendant
notion of personal honour and respectability. It also meant to those
like him, those of rich and elevated education, a commitment to the
humanist ideals of Western civilization. These included not only the
goal of social justice and human betterment, but a reverence for the
work of civilization's artists, those who over centuries had expressed
the dignity of the human condition and the belief in humanity's
unlimited potential.

Louis Barthou was not merely entertained by these, and emotionally consoled; he actually drew upon their counsels. In 1902, for
example, when making a case for reform of the divorce laws, he
drew upon the observations of writers like Voltaire and Courteline.
The following year, addressing the need for educational reform, it
was to de Tocqueville and Taine that he turned. For Barthou, Diderot had long since made the basic case for improved labour legislation, just as Lamartine had sage advice to offer on the importance
of sound Anglo-French relations, or Victor Hugo on the potential
of air technology. And if he believed that his understanding of human nature owed much to insights long since provided by Corneille,
Racine, and La Bruyère, he also found persuasive Renan's dictum
against trying to contain legitimate social grievance with repression.
Just as persuasive, and as hopeful, was Anatole France's confidence
in the halting but inexorable progress of humankind. Finally, while
not himself a religious man in any conventional sense, Barthou detected in music, Fauré's *Pénélope* in particular, proof positive of the
link between mortality and immortality.[6]

Inevitably, too, he saw in these his compatriots further evidence
of France's special genius. For if Barthou was a product of his family's
foyer, his region, his class, and his political generation, so was he also
the product of an idea: that of an eternal France, made great by
kings and revolutionaries, warriors and orators, administrators and
scientists, but left immortal by her poets, writers, artists, and musicians. So central were these to his concept of patriotism, of being
French, that any attempt to portray him in political terms alone
would collapse and fall away into a void. It was no accident that his
sole attempt at writing memoirs, following a forty-year career in

politics, should have been distinguished by the near absence of political personalities. Conversely, his *Promenades* are with Baudelaire and Bourget, Corneille and Coppée, Diderot and Donnay, de Maistre and de Musset, Racine, Richepin, and Rousseau, Sévigné, Stendhal, and Saint-Simon. This was not a France of his making. It was rather a patrimony, the first instalment of which he had received from the hands of his teachers and mentors in Oloron and Pau, received like all the boys of his class and many of his generation whether in Béarn, Lorraine, Normandy, or Auvergne. Again, something typical. But if custom explains the first sip, only personal taste would make it a habit. It is here that one crosses the frontier between society in the individual and the individual in society.

There are some who believe that character may be deduced by physiognomy, by body and facial contours. Psychologists may have their doubts, but not so caricaturists, and certainly not those who revelled in exaggerating the features of leading politicians of the Third Republic. In the case of Barthou, no caricaturist was more trenchant than Sennep, he who illustrated so many of the works written by Maurras and Daudet. Indeed, Daudet's "Médor" ("Fido") Barthou is remembered as much for the accompanying drawings by Sennep as for the acid engravings of the writer. For the "chien" Barthou was invariably presented as a little figure, small mouth smiling between full moustache, beard, and goatee, sometimes positioned on all fours, and always sporting a bedraggled tail.

Malicious as it was, there was something about the image that was compelling, and not only to members of the Action Française. Maurice Barrès had been one of the first to use the canine metaphor when treating Barthou, Briand, and Caillaux. But even friends liked the imagery, including Paul Flat, with his sense of the pointer ready to leap into action, and Alice, with her own image of the fox terrier. The portrait artist Cornélius van Dongen also captured on canvas something of the canine spirit – the alert, mischief-suggesting face, set behind a tightly trimmed grey beard and moustache, and above a wing collar and black bow-tie. The back is straight and the head erect, as if to ensure maximum height, while the suggestion of a slightly rounded belly and the hands in trouser pockets imply something casual, genial, and informal. The terrier at momentary ease.

What the body promised, character seemed to deliver. There was something playful, mischievous, about Louis Barthou. Contemporaries commonly remarked on the twinkle in the eyes, the ready smile, the talent for disarming quips, all of which suggested a man of abundant good nature. Some, of course, did not care for him at all, thought him superficial, *un homme léger*. His humour, too, they found tiresome, sometimes coarse, sometimes malicious. But others saw him as a refreshing free spirit, enjoying his wit, his light-hearted informality, and the ways he employed both to defray suspicions and defuse antagonisms. They appreciated the often self-deprecatory element in his humour, the jokes about his exercise ritual, his professed terror of ignorant visitors to his library, his Jacqueline on the rue Furstemberg, even the poor eyesight which, he confided, helped him avoid people he had no desire to recognize. There was something amusing too, as well as down-to-earth, in his futile efforts to imitate the sound of a camel, to gatecrash a formal reception for Victor Hugo, or to publicly humiliate whispering concert-goers.

The latter suggested, rightly enough, that there was another, less convivial side to this natural conciliator. When provoked, he could snap at the inattentive, call Jaurès a liar, threaten striking postal workers with jail, and write war propaganda calculated to excite hatred. He was not always mellow, as Anthony Eden discovered in February 1934. Barthou "makes long speeches at one," Eden complained, and generally was "bristly ... a nasty old man at heart."[7] Neither was he always modest and unassuming, a shortcoming typified by his too familiar boast about having been the youngest cabinet minister in the Republic's history, or his characterization of an electoral rival in 1904 as a nobody compared to himself. And certainly there were times when the pride became petulance, when little things did not go his way, when Combes had not acted on his prefectoral recommendations or when Louis Ducla had not given him advance notice of a de Vigny celebration in Béarn.[8] There were times, in short, when his sense of self-importance translated itself in ways that were not very becoming.

Those times, however, were doubly revealing. Undeniably, they betrayed flashes of intolerance, insensitivity, and immodesty. But they betrayed, too, a man bent on self-defence. Everyone who followed politics in France knew that Barthou's tongue could lash as well as charm. This was very much a part of his public persona, someone not always genial. But very few ever saw the private man in whose defence humour and anger both were often enlisted, or saw the cynicism which his aides knew was a third device for protecting what was a highly sensitive spirit. Wherever it had begun, with the bully in Oloron, the school chaplain in Pau, the circumstances surrounding his ministerial resignation in 1895, the Caillaux-Calmette affair, wherever and whenever, Louis Barthou used cynicism to deflect criticism and ward off disappointment. Not surprisingly, given the record. For in all the talk of his betrayal of others, there was something ironic. Having abandoned Dupuy and Méline on grounds of principle, at least as judged by his lights and our telling, he was made out to be inconstant and unprincipled. Accordingly, even friends like Waldeck-Rousseau, Caillaux, and Poincaré found it expedient to exclude him from their cabinets. Following these rejections came his persistent exclusion from a succession of wartime cabinets, partly because of unsubstantiated rumours of his role in the Caillaux affair of 1914 and partly because of demonstrably spurious doubts about his commitment to pursuing the war to the very end. Little wonder, therefore, that his closest collaborators were privy to a cynicism which pride usually denied public expression.

Only they witnessed the sensitive individual whom personal ambition and an array of social determinants had thrust into the turbulence of politics. Of course one did not have to be an insider to see him as a very emotional man, to see in his writings glimpses of a full-blown romanticist, to see in his eyes the tears called forth by Beethoven or Fauré. Strangers had seen him break down at a restaurant table, when talk had turned to Max, or when, at the tomb of the Unknown Soldier, it had fallen to him to speak of France's war dead. But it did take an inner circle of advisers – Olivier Sainsère, Pierre Roland-Marcel, Georges Lamirault, Louis Vitalis, Pierre Benoit, Maurice Reclus – to leave in written record or at least in the memories of their survivors the sense of Louis Barthou as *le patron*. These, and some journalist friends, particularly those of Béarnais origin, have left behind fragments of a man who commanded an affection and a loyalty which have endured for over fifty years.

What they remembered, remember still, is a man who was as constant as his critics made him fickle, sensitive to their needs, supportive of their careers, as generous with his time as with selected gifts from his library. Their stories are of the personal sort which never made the papers: a formally dressed Barthou laughing off the results of a serving accident, when an inexperienced waiter had managed to spill soup in his lap; Barthou laughing too as he provided a formal *laissez-passer* so that one of the young, and desperate, Lamirault daughters could use the ministerial staircase as the fastest route to a washroom. And if they remember as well how he liked to dominate table talk, or show off his exercise prowess at some dinner party, or tell risqué jokes, or firmly hasten the departure of guests inclined to stay too late, so they still recall his loyalty as a friend, his devotion to Alice, his pride in Max, the grief he expressed on losing one, and then the other, a grief from which they knew he never fully recovered.[9]

Constant to friends and family, Louis Barthou evinced one other iron loyalty, one which is at the core of what he represented and who he was. If he had been taught a love of France, and instructed in the need to defend the Republic, he brought to that task a temperament unique in its blend of qualities. If he found an early hero in Emile Garet, he did so because his own native centrism took him there; and in that moderation, that commitment to a gradual betterment of the human condition he heard the footsteps of earlier heroes: Mirabeau, Danton, Lamartine, moderates who had worked on the ground between those who wanted no change at all and those who wanted little to remain. It is here that one detects the governing principle of Barthou as historian and politician. Although he certainly found it flattering to be in the councils of the powerful, and at times manoeuvred to ensure that he was, it was not power he coveted.

Or if it was, it will take a Freudian to explain how. For this was one who began a ministerial career by declining the first invitation to join a cabinet, who nearly recanted on his first acceptance, and who resigned from that same cabinet rather than implement a policy with which he disagreed. In 1895 he turned down another ministerial invitation, and three years later watched impassively as his portfolio disappeared with the collapse of the Méline government. In 1910 he brought on his own fall from the Briand cabinet, this time by arguing against the severe measures which the premier proposed taking against striking rail workers; and in 1913 he precipitated the demise of his own government by refusing to compromise with the parliamentary opposition. Poincaré called it a suicide, and was perplexed by Barthou's apparent indifference to the loss of power. At Genoa in 1922 he finally conformed to his premier's instructions, but not before running the risk of being sacked; and if he satisfied the same Poincaré in 1923, in the buildup to the Ruhr occupation, by the spring of 1924 he was again courting the possibility of further reprimands. It was then, that summer, that he turned down Herriot's offer of the Finance portfolio, an action repeated once more in 1929 when Tardieu asked him to stay at Justice. Five years later, following a long cabinet meeting over the disarmament note of April 1934, he was again poised to resign from the cabinet, and relented only for fear that such an action would revive the ministerial instability of which he long had been such a vocal critic.

Doubtless there are less positive constructions which might be imposed on this précis of events, constructions which are abundant enough in many of his contemporaries' memoir accounts. Nevertheless, there is no danger of unanimity. But to marshal some against the others, the critics versus the defenders, would now serve little purpose. The fact remains that not even the latter made much of an effort to illuminate the principles according to which Barthou tried to lead his life. Until that is done, and as would be the case for most, there appears to be little beyond personal ambition and perhaps some opaque sense of service.

While eschewing the label of "great" man for Barthou, this study suggests that he was greater than that, and not merely in the sense of his role in important events – the legislation for miners' pensions, the state takeover of the western railway, the passage of the Moroccan protectorate, the three-year service law, the international role in the 1920s, the reinvigoration of French foreign policy in 1934. Underlying each of these was a commitment to defend a moderate, liberal, and democratic Republic, to combat extremism in any form, and slowly to nudge a unified, ordered society toward greater material prosperity, social justice, and national security. And to do so not only because this was the Republic, but because the nobility of the cause was worthy of France. It was for this that he lived, and in whose name he bled to death. Writing of another patriot who had just died from loss of blood, André Malraux recalled the old saying: "It takes at least an hour before the soul starts to come out."[10] Many hours later, I hope that of Barthou has begun to show.

Abbreviations

AF	Académie Française
Annales	*Journal de l'Université des Annales*
ARD	*Alliance Républicaine Démocratique*
AN	Archives Nationales
Ass. Nat.	Assemblée Nationale
BHVP	Bibliothèque Historique de la Ville de Paris
BN	Bibliothèque Nationale
Bull. du bib.	*Bulletin du bibliophile*
Cahiers	*Cahiers de Radio Paris*
DBFP	*Documents on British Foreign Policy*
DDB	*Documents Diplomatiques Belges*
DDF	*Documents Diplomatiques Français*
DGFP	*Documents on German Foreign Policy*
FHS	*French Historical Studies*
FNSP	Fondation Nationale des Sciences Politiques
FO	Foreign Office (Great Britain)
FRUS	*Foreign Relations of the United States*
JO	*Journal officiel*
MAE	Ministère des Affaires Étrangères
NR	*Nouvelle Revue*
Pau Catalogue	(See chapter 1, note 8.)
PRO	Public Record Office
RB	*Revue bleue*
RDDM	*Revue des deux mondes*
RF	*Revue de France*
RH	*Revue hebdomadaire*
RP	*Revue de Paris*
RRP	*Revue régionaliste des Pyrénées*

Notes

INTRODUCTION

1 Preface by Louis Barthou to Charles Mathiot, *Pour vaincre: vie, opinions et pensées de Lazare Carnot* (Paris: Flammarion 1917), x. All translations are by the author.
2 Barthou, *Sur les routes du droit* (Paris: Bloud et Gay 1918), 173.
3 "Quand un peuple conserve le culte du Beau, on peut être sûr qu'il est l'ami du Bien." See his preface in *Le musée du Louvre depuis 1914* (Paris: Demotte 1919), tome 1. He called Beethoven not a German soul, but "une âme humaine." See his "Autour de *William Shakespeare* de Victor Hugo," RP (1 Aug. 1920): 458.
4 Discours Claude Farrère, 23 April 1936, AF, 5.
5 Barthou preface for his own *Amours d'un poète* (Paris: Fayard 1929), 12.
6 Maupassant, "The Novel," used as a preface to his *Pierre and Jean* (Penguin 1979), 27.
7 Barthou preface, *Lettres de Robert Dubarle* (Paris: Perrin 1918), i.
8 Barthou preface for Jean-Serge Debus, *Métier d'Islande, Les trimardeurs de la mer* (Lille: *Mercure de Flandre* 1929), 11.
9 Barthou, *Promenades autour de ma vie: Lettres de la montagne.* (Paris: Les Laboratoires Martinet 1933), 216.
10 "Il n'y a pas de grand homme dont le véritable caractère ne se révèle ou ne se confirme par le choix qu'il a fait de ses amis." Barthou, "Leconte de Lisle et Jean Marras. Documents inédits," RDDM (15 November 1933): 306.
11 Nigel Nicolson, "Personal View," *Sunday Times*, 10 April 1988.
12 Nathan Leites's chapter on "Honesty and Lies" notwithstanding. Though it seems a little overdrawn to suggest that the French élite all

agree with Gide that "lying is something absolutely sacred," I have tried to stay on guard. See Leites, *The Rules of the Game in Paris* (Chicago: University of Chicago Press 1969), 304–11.

13 Quoted by Barthou in "Victor Hugo à douze ans", RH no. 2 (1914): 162.

14 Barthou, "Anatole France, commis-bibliothécaire au Sénat," RP 6 (1 December 1924): 490.

CHAPTER ONE

1 Barthou speech, "Discours ... pour les fêtes du centenaire d'Ernest Renan," AF, 2 September 1923, 22.

2 Barthou, *Notes de voyage: En Belgique et en Hollande, Trois jours en Allemagne* (Pau: Imprimerie Garet 1888), 5.

3 Octave Aubert, *Louis Barthou* (Paris: A. Quillet 1935), 22–3.

4 Barthou, *Notes de voyage*, 20. For further information on the conservative reaction to "modern" trends, see Charles Rearick, *Pleasures of the Belle Époque: Entertainment and Festivity in Turn-of-the-Century France* (New Haven: Yale University Press 1985), 32.

5 Isidore Barthou (1832–1915); Marie Octavie Barthou (1842–1919); Marie *Clémence* Barthou (1864–1948), who married Eugène Barès in 1886; Jean Victor *Joseph* Barthou (1886–1938); Grégoire *Léon* Antoine Barthou (1868–1943).

6 Barthou, *Promenades autour de ma vie: Lettres de la montagne* (Paris: Les Laboratoires Martinet 1933), 190.

7 Extrait des registres des actes de l'état civil de la ville d'Oloron Sainte Marie. This extract is dated 29 October 1913 and was included in Barthou's application for membership in the Société des Gens de Lettres. See their dossier "Louis Barthou." See also Maurice Donnay's reply to Barthou's reception speech at the Académie Française, 6 February 1919, and the two-page, handwritten biographical text supplied by Barthou to Donnay, and communicated to me by M. Castaing of the Maison Charavay.

8 Félix Barthe, "La vie Paloise de Louis Barthou," *L'Indépendant*, 17 October 1934; Jean-Jacques Cazaurang, "Louis Barthou," an introductory essay for the exhibition catalogue entitled *Louis Barthou, 1862–1934* (Pau: Conseil Général des Pyrénées Atlantiques 1984), 5–11. Subsequently referred to as *Pau Catalogue*.

9 Barthou, "Pour ceux qui avaient huit ans en 1870," in his *Lettres à un jeune français* (Paris: Éditions Pierre Lafitte 1916), 135–40; "Souvenirs de la Rue Sablière" in *Plaisir du Béarn* (Paris: Nouvelle Société d'Édition 1931), 25–37.

10 Barthou, "Pour ceux qui avaient huit ans," *Lettres*, 139. In 1891, re-calling his own school days in the same lycée, Barthou carried on the tradition of his boyhood by promising the assembled youths that they would be part of the revival of France and instruments of retribution. "Vous serez des soldats." His address was reported in *L'Indépendant* of 1 August 1891.

11 His remarks on physics come from his posthumous speech to the Academy of 31 January 1935, those on physical education from "Les sports bienfaisants," *Annales* (1 May 1917): 514; those on poetry and the celebrated Jean Moréas from "Discours au banquet Armand Godoy," *Le Manuscrit autographe* (October 1932): 87–8 and Barthou's funeral speech for Moréas, *Le Temps*, 3 April 1910. For information on Barthou's prize-winning academic performances, see *Pau Catalogue*, item 19:22, and Aubert, *Louis Barthou*, 19–20.

12 Regarding Spanish, see Jean-Marc De Launay, "Louis Barthou et l'Es-pagne," in *Barthou, un homme, une époque*, ed Michel Papy (Pau: J. et D. Editions 1986), 86. As for German, Aubert says that students in the lycée – where he was two years behind Barthou – considered those who had to take German to be "martyrisés." See Aubert, *Louis Barthou*, 22–3. Marcel Gilbert confirms Aubert's claim that Barthou spoke fluent Béarnais, and that he later made a point of conversing in German with his son, Max, whose own capacity in the language owed much to the presence of a German nanny. Interview, 4 May 1982.

13 Barthou, *Promenades*, 216.

14 For Barthou on Edet, "éducateur d'âmes," see *L'Indépendant*, 8 April 1904. On the influence of Hugo see Aubert, *Louis Barthou*, 9; Jules Bertaut, *Louis Barthou* (Paris: Sansot 1919), 4–6; Barthou, *Émile Garet, 1829–1912* (Pau: Imprimerie Garet 1912); Barthou, "Souvenirs de la Rue Sablière," *Plaisir du Béarn*, 35.

15 Barthou, *Promenades*, 220–1; Aubert, *Louis Barthou*, 12–13. Aubert later recalled that for Barthou "Gambetta était son dieu." See his *De l'histoire et des histoires: Souvenirs d'un journaliste* (Bordeaux: Éditions Delmas 1943), 26.

16 Barthou, *Notes de voyage*, 22, 24.

17 Aubert, *Louis Barthou*, 30. Aubert also reports that Barthou played the violin during his Pau and Bordeaux days. But this is a solitary claim, never mentioned by Barthou himself and unknown to Marcel Gilbert. Regarding Barthou's early Hugo collection, see "Souvenirs de la Rue Sablière," 36–7.

18 For his remarks on women, see Barthou's letter to his friend, Robert Lacoste, 24 May 1881, Fonds Lacoste, Departmental Archives, Pau. On pelote, see Cazaurang, "Louis Barthou," *Pau Catalogue*, 6. On stu-

dent politics, see Gilles Le Béguec, "Louis Barthou, patron et modèle politique," in *Barthou, un homme, une époque,* ed. Papy, 130–1.

19 Barthou to Lacoste, 24 May and 5 September 1881, Fonds Lacoste, Departmental Archives, Pau. See also Bertaut, *Louis Barthou,* 6–7; Aubert, *Louis Barthou,* 30–1.

20 *Pau Catalogue,* item 26:22.

21 Cazaurang, "Louis Barthou," *Pau Catalogue,* 6; Bertaut, *Louis Barthou,* 27; Aubert, *Louis Barthou,* 34–7.

22 Aubert, *De l'histoire,* 27.

23 Barthou, *Droit romain de la distinction des biens en meubles et immeubles: Droit français de l'origine de l'adage "vilis mobilium possessio" et de son influence sur le code civil* (Paris: Arthur Rousseau 1886), 223.

24 Barthou, "Les sports bienfaisants," *Annales* (1 May 1917): 516–17. In all probability this medical student was the friend Bouvie with whom Barthou exchanged letters during the First World War, letters published as "Paroles d'Union" in his *Lettres à un jeune français,* 129–46.

25 Maurice Martin Du Gard, *Les Mémorables,* 3 vols. (Paris: Flammarion 1957–78), 1:226. For assessments of Hugo's exceptional popularity among the young – unrivalled since that of Voltaire – see Priscilla Parkhurst Clark, *Literary France: The Making of a Culture* (Berkeley: University of California Press 1987), 140; also Albert Guérard, *France: A Modern History* (Ann Arbor: University of Michigan Press 1959), 335.

26 Aubert, *De l'histoire,* 29–30. See also Aubert's press account of this incident in *L'Indépendant,* 7–8 April 1895. For further information on the *Union de la Jeunesse Républicaine,* see the introductory remarks preceding Barthou's speech on Hugo at the Sorbonne in December 1891, in Barthou, *Victor Hugo, homme politique* (Paris: Union de la Jeunesse Républicaine 1892).

27 Barthou, *Notes de voyage,* 29, 33, 40.

28 Ibid., 42–3.

29 Pierre Miquel, *Poincaré* (Paris: Fayard 1961), 77.

30 Barthou, *Émile Garet,* 23–6, 24, 28.

31 Barthou, *Notes de voyage,* 52–77, 96.

32 Barthou preface for Charles de Bordeu, *La Terre de Béarn* (Paris: Éditions de l'Estampe 1927), vii.

33 Barthou, "Lettres d'Alfred de Vigny à Victor Hugo," RDDM (1 February 1925): 525; *En Marge des "Confidences." Lettres inédites de Lamartine* (Abbeville: F. Paillart 1913), 38–9.

34 Speech of Maurice Donnay, based on Barthou's notes, AF, 6 February 1919, 45.

35 Alice Barthou to Pierre Loti, undated letter, Collection Loti-Viaud.

36 See *Pau Catalogue,* item 25:22.

37 Jean Bousquet-Mélou, *Louis Barthou et la circonscription d'Oloron, 1889–1914* (Paris: Pedone 1972), 34, 36.

38 See in particular his front-page editorials in *L'Indépendant* of 15 October 1887, 7 March, 1–2 April, 25 May, 16–17 July 1888. For the latest scholarly work on Boulangism see William D. Irvine, *The Boulanger Affair Reconsidered: Royalism, Boulangism, and the Origins of the Radical Right in France* (New York: Oxford University Press 1989).

39 "Délibérations du Conseil Municipal," Archives municipales, Pau, 1888–89, D10/34. *Pau Catalogue*, item 96:34; Félix Barthe, "La Vie Paloise de Louis Barthou," *L'Indépendant*, 17 October 1934.

40 Barthou, *Le Politique* (Paris: Hachette 1923), 14, 16.

41 Ibid., 17.

42 In mid-July a report in *L'Indépendant*, which described Barthou's selection as candidate, informed readers that he had agreed to run only in the face of the "refus irréductible" of senior republican leaders.

43 Bousquet-Mélou, *Louis Barthou*, 50–61. For a brief description of the courts of first instance, usually located in the principal market town of the *arrondissement*, see Raymond Poincaré, *How France Is Governed*, translated by Bernard Miall (1913; Port Washington: Kennikat Press 1970), 248.

44 Michel Papy, "Les provinciaux et l'image du pouvoir: comment Louis Barthou fut perçu par les béarnais," in *Barthou, un homme, une époque*, ed. Papy, 214–15, 238.

45 Bousquet-Mélou, "Louis Barthou et ses électeurs de l'arrondissement d'Oloron, 1889–1922," in *Barthou, un homme, une époque*, ed. Papy, 49.

46 Bousquet-Mélou, *Louis Barthou*, 69–70.

47 Ibid., 34–5, 39, 67; Bousquet-Mélou, "Louis Barthou et ses électeurs," 47–54.

48 Bousquet-Mélou, *Louis Barthou*, 67–8; John Merle Rife, Jr, "The Political Career of Louis Barthou, 1889–1913" (Unpublished Ph.D. dissertation, Ohio State University 1964), 8–12.

49 Bousquet-Mélou, *Louis Barthou*, 66–7.

50 Barthou, *Promenades*, 181.

51 Aubert, *De l'histoire*, 62.

52 Barthou, *Promenades*, 183–4.

53 Of 13,730 unspoiled ballots, 7,033 had gone to Barthou and 6,697 to LaCaze. See *Pau Catalogue*, item 101:34. However, since his share of the vote was just a fraction above the mandatory, 51 per cent, Barthou did not have to submit to a second *scrutin*.

54 Barthou, *Promenades*, 187.

55 Barthou, *Le Politique*, 35.

56 See Garet's optimistic, touching editorial in *L'Indépendant*, 27 September 1889.

CHAPTER TWO

1 Barthou, "Discours ... à la Cité Universitaire," *Annales* 3 (1928): 400.

2 R.D. Anderson, *France, 1870–1914: Politics and Society* (London: Routledge and Kegan Paul 1977), 30–2.

3 Ibid., 31: Pierre Sorlin, *La Société française*, vol. 1 (1840–1914) (Paris: Arthaud 1969), 116.

4 Sorlin, *Société française*, 140: Hubert Bonin, *Histoire économique de la France depuis 1880* (Paris: Masson 1988), 24–40.

5 Sorlin, *Société française*, 124; Roger Price, *A Social History of Nineteenth-Century France* (New York: Holmes and Meier 1987), 56–7.

6 Sorlin, *Société française*, 123.

7 Roger Magraw, *France, 1815–1914: The Bourgeois Century* (Oxford: Oxford University Press 1986), 229–32; Sorlin, *Société française*, 150; Bonin, *Histoire économique*, 28–9.

8 Barthou's reception speech, 6 February 1919, AF, 29.

9 He was so convinced of this that in August 1890, speaking to a school assembly in Pau, the deputy assured the young men that France no longer suffered from inequality and privilege. "Il n'est pas d'ambition qui ne soit permise au plus humble." See *L'Indépendant*, 14 August 1890.

10 Sorlin, *Société française*, 123; Jules Bertaut, *Les Dessous de la "Troisième"* (Paris: Tallandier 1959), 191.

11 Ernest A. Vizetelly, *Paris and Her People under the Third Republic* (New York: Frederick Stokes 1918), 157, 161; Roger Price, *A Social History*, 66; Sorlin, *Société française*, 237; Brenda F. Nelms, "The Third Republic and the Centennial of 1789" (Unpublished Ph.D. dissertation, University of Virginia 1976).

12 Bertaut, *Les Dessous*, 97, 101–2.

13 Richard D. Mandell, *Paris 1900: The Great World's Fair* (Toronto: University of Toronto Press 1967), 21.

14 Eugen Weber, *France: Fin de Siècle* (Cambridge, Mass.: Harvard University Press 1986), 27–39; Bertaut, *Les Dessous*, 72–3.

15 Barthou, "Les Sports bienfaisants," *Annales* (1 May 1917): 516–17. See also "La Petite Reine" in Weber's *Fin de Siècle*, 197–205.

16 Bertaut, *Les Dessous*, 99.

17 Paul Flat speaks of two generations of Wagner devotees, the first of the mid-1870s, the second between 1885 and 1890. See *Souvenirs d'avant guerre pour servir après* (Paris: Plon 1916), 79–81. See also Weber, *Fin de Siècle*, 144–5.

18 Bertaut, *Les Dessous*, 198–9; Vizetelly, *Paris and Her People*, 183–4.

19 Barthou, *Le Politique* (Paris: Hachette 1923), 37.

20 Ibid., 36.

21 Ibid.; André Guérin, *La Vie quotidienne au Palais-Bourbon à la fin de la IIIe République* (Paris: Hachette 1978), 18–21; Georges Buisson, *La Chambre des députés* (Paris: Hachette 1924).

22 André Guérin, *La Vie quotidienne*, 22–3.

23 Barthou, *Le Politique*, 48.

24 Octave Aubert, *Barthou* (Paris: A. Quillet 1935), 71. For discussions of the bureaus, committees, and parliamentary groups, see Aubert's *Le Moulin parlementaire* (Paris: A. Quillet 1933), 168–75. See also Barthou's "Le Coeur de Jules Ferry," *Conférencia* (15 November 1934): 554–6.

25 Barthou, *Le Politique*, 46. See also Mattei Dogan, "Filières pour devenir ministre de Thiers à Mitterand," *Pouvoirs* 36 (1986): 52. For Barthou's involvement in the *commission du budget*, see *Le Temps*, 16 May 1891, 4; 19 November 1891, 4.

26 Mattei Dogan, "Political Ascent in a Class Society: French Deputies, 1870–1958," in *Political Decision-Makers*, ed. Dwaine Marvick (Chicago: Free Press of Glencoe 1961), 77.

27 Barthou, *Le Politique*, 18–19; Dogan, "Political Ascent," 67–70.

28 Dogan, "Political Ascent," 79.

29 Ibid., 73, 80–1.

30 Pierre Guiral and Guy Thuillier, *La Vie quotidienne des députés en France de 1871 à 1914* (Paris: Hachette 1980), 106.

31 Ibid., 108–9, 113.

32 Jean Bousquet-Mélou, *Louis Barthou et la circonscription d'Oloron, 1889–1914* (Paris: Pedone 1972), 85–8; Guiral and Thuillier, *La Vie quotidienne des députés*, 115–45.

33 Barthou, *Le Politique*, 5–7.

34 Guiral and Thuillier, *La Vie quotidienne des députés*, 207–9; Maurice Reclus, *La Troisième République, 1870–1918* (Paris: Fayard 1945), 251.

35 Guiral and Thuillier, *La Vie quotidienne des députés*, 219.

36 Barthou was not a Mason, and his attachment to the Catholic church appears to have been highly tenuous.

37 Guiral and Thuillier, *La Vie quotidienne des députés*, 137–8.

38 Barthou, *Le Politique*, 62.

39 Ibid., 125.

40 Ibid., 89.

41 Barthou, "Comment assurer à nos ministres la liberté d'action," RB (10 June 1911): 707–9; Guiral and Thuillier, *La Vie quotidienne des députés*, 265–70.

42 Jean Estèbe, *Les Ministres de la République, 1871–1914* (Paris: Presses de la Fondation Nationale des Sciences Politiques [FNSP] 1982).

43 Estèbe, *Les Ministres*, 99–101; Paul Gerbod, "The Baccalauréate and Its Roles in the Recruitment and Formation of French Elites in the Nineteenth Century," in *Elites in France*, ed Jolyon Howorth and Philip Cerny (New York: St Martin's Press 1981), 49; René Rémond, Aline Coutrot, Isabel Boussard, *Quarante ans de cabinets ministériels* (Paris: FNSP 1982), 70–1; Yves-Henri Gaudemet, *Les Juristes et la vie politique de la IIIe République* (Paris: PUF 1970).

44 Estèbe, *Les Ministres*, 104–9.

45 Ibid., 20–41.

46 Ibid., 24.

47 Ibid., 53–8.

48 Maurice Reclus, for instance, wrote of Barthou: "Il avait comme beaucoup de compatriotes d'Henry IV, la réputation (bien gratuite) d'être changeant et peu sûr." *La Troisième République*, 270.

49 Estèbe, *Les Ministres*, 87.

50 Ibid., 185.

CHAPTER THREE

1 Barthou, "Sur Anatole France," RF 3 (May-June 1926): 623.

2 See in particular the concluding chapter of Sanford Elwitt, *The Third Republic Defended: Bourgeois Reform in France, 1880–1914* (Baton Rouge: Louisiana State University Press 1986), 289–98; and Judith F. Stone, *The Search for Social Peace: Reform Legislation in France, 1890–1914* (New York: SUNY Press 1985), especially the introductory and concluding chapters, ix–xvii, 161–82.

3 Robert Elegant, *A Kind of Treason* (Penguin 1982), 244.

4 Barthou, "L'Esprit de la politique," *Conférencia* (1 March 1933): 279; *Lettres à un jeune français* (Paris: Éditions Pierre Lafitte 1916), 149.

5 Barthou, "Sur Anatole France," 602; "Discours sur Montaigne," *Annales* (1933), 473; preface for Robert Dubarle, *Lettres de guerre de Robert Dubarle* (Paris: Perrin 1918), i–ii; *Danton* (Paris: Albin Michel 1932), 162, 361; *Lamartine orateur* (Paris: Hachette 1916), 52. For the tensions inherent in modern liberalism, see Roger H. Soltau, *French Political Thought in the Nineteenth Century* (New York: Russell and Russell 1959), and the opening chapter of William Logue, *From Philosophy to Sociology: The Evolution of French Liberalism, 1870–1914* (De Kalb: Northern Illinois University Press 1983).

6 Jean Bousquet-Mélou, *Louis Barthou et la circonscription d'Oloron, 1889–1914* (Paris: Pedone 1972), 77. On 10 February 1890 Barthou voted with the majority to reaffirm a law from 1886 prohibiting members of former ruling families from returning to France. See John Merle Rife, Jr, "The Political Career of Louis Barthou, 1889–1913" (unpublished Ph.D. dissertation, Ohio State University 1964), 13–14.

7 Bousquet-Mélou, *Barthou*, 78.

8 Ibid., 78–80.

9 *JO*, Chamber Debates, 3 March 1890, 422–3.

10 Rife, "The Political Career," 35.

11 See Barthou's speech in the Vendée, *Le Temps*, 4 September 1894, 3.

12 Bousquet-Mélou, *Barthou*, 86–7; Rife, "The Political Career," 27–31. For suggestions that the Méline tariff of 1892 was itself equivocal, a compromise between free traders and protectionists, see Michael S. Smith, "Free Trade Versus Protection in the Early Third Republic," *FHS* 10, no. 2 (Fall 1977): 313; and Roger Magraw, *France, 1815–1914. The Bourgeois Century* (Oxford: Oxford University press 1986), 229.

13 Rife, "The Political Career," 33–5; Bousquet-Mélou, *Barthou*, 88–90.

14 Rife, "The Political Career," 23–5; Bousquet-Mélou, *Barthou*, 87.

15 Rife, "The Political Career," 13–17.

16 *JO*, Chamber Debates, 19 March 1892, 311–15.

17 Rife, "The Political Career," 18–19.

18 *JO*, Chamber Debates, 19 November 1892, 1640; Maurice Barrès, *Leurs figures* (Paris: Émile-Paul Frères 1917), 89.

19 Commission d'enquête (Panama), 25 November 1892–4 July 1893, cahiers 1–5, AN, series C, 5474. For press reports of his role on the commission, see *Le Temps*, 15, 18, 19 December 1892, 22, 29 January, 1 February, 22 March 1893; and *L'Indépendant*, 2 February 1893. See also Barrès, *Leurs figures*, 329.

20 Barthou, "Sous les griffes du Tigre," *Annales* (15 December 1929): 544. See also Adrien Dansette, *Les Affaires de Panama* (Paris: Perrin 1934), 177–8; Gaston Monnerville, *Clemenceau* (Paris: Fayard 1968), 186.

21 He received three thousand votes more than in 1889. *Pau Catalogue*, 36.

22 Barrès, *Leurs figures*, 89; Dansette, *Les Affaires de Panama*, ix–x; Charles Benoist, *Souvenirs de Charles Benoist*, 3 vols. (Paris: Plon 1933–34), 1:357.

23 Bousquet-Mélou, *Barthou*, 95; Rife, "The Political Career," 53.

24 *JO*, Chamber Debates, 23 November 1893, 99–104. See also his article entitled "Socialisme," in *L'Indépendant*, 9 December 1893.

25 Dansette, *Les Affaires de Panama*, 247.

26 Benoist, *Souvenirs*, 3:190.

27 *Le Temps*, 3 December 1893, 4; 1 November 1895, 4; Bousquet-Mélou, *Barthou*, 99; Rife, "The Political Career," 36, 64.

28 Recalling Dupuy's offer, Barthou later wrote: "À peine avais-je accepté que mon incompétence et les difficultés de ma fonction me remplirent d'effroi. Je songeais même à reprendre ma liberté." *Promenades autour de ma vie: Lettres de la montagne* (Paris: Les Laboratoires

Martinet 1933), 197. His letter of resignation was reproduced in
Le Temps, 15 January 1895, 1.

29 *JO*, Chamber Debates, 949–50; Rife, "The Political Career," 57.

30 On Barthou's trip to England, see the interview with him published
by *Le Temps*, 29 August 1894, 4; the report in *L'Indépendant*, 30 August 1894; and the report in *The Times*, 21 August 1894, 3.

31 *JO*, Chamber Debates, 17 November 1894, 1893–7.

32 *JO*, Chamber Debates, 22 December 1894, 2292–2301.

33 *JO*, Chamber Debates, 24 December 1894, 2320. See also Harvey
Goldberg, *The Life of Jean Jaurès* (Madison: University of Wisconsin
Press 1962), 130–2; Marcel Auclair, *Jean Jaurès* (Paris: Éditions du
Centenaire 1959), 147; Jean Rabaut, *Jaurès* (Paris: Perrin 1971), 101.

34 See *L'Indépendant*, 27 December 1894; also *Le Temps*, 24, 26 December
1894.

35 Rife, "The Political Career," 60–2.

36 *JO*, Chamber Debates, 14 January 1895, 51–60.

37 In October 1896 an article by a M. Cornudet in *La Lanterne* smeared
Barthou with indirect suggestions that he had engaged in insider
trading, made a personal profit on the shares of the Orléans and Midi
railways, and then resigned. A formal *jury d'honneur*, convened on
Barthou's request, found him to have been entirely beyond reproach.
The clearest report on this affair is in *L'Indépendant*, 21 October 1896,
13–19. More details can be found in a press dossier addressed to the
affair, in the Barthou press file (currently in five dossiers) at the
BHVP.

38 Rife, "The Political Career," 61–2.

39 For Barthou's own reference to his turning down of Bourgeois in November 1895, see *JO*, Chamber Debates, 16 December 1898, 2565. See
also *Le Temps*, 25 April 1898.

40 *JO*, Chamber Debates, 21 November 1895, 2439–41.

41 Pierre Miquel, *Poincaré* (Paris: Fayard 1961), 160.

42 Barthou was accompanied by Olivier Sainsère as *directeur du cabinet*,
and Georges Lamirault as *chef du secrétariat particulier*.

43 Georges Lachapelle, *Le Ministère Méline* (Paris: J.L. D'Artrey 1918),
20–1; *Le Temps*, 25 May 1896, 1.

44 Bousquet-Mélou, *Barthou*, 102.

45 *JO*, Chamber Debates, 21 and 28 March 1898, 1300–3, 1432–4.

46 Rife, "The Political Career," 64.

47 Ibid., 74.

48 Audition du ministre, Commission des finances, 21 Juin 1897, Sénat,
9–14; Bousquet-Mélou, *Barthou*, 102; Rife, "The Political Career," 80.

49 Barthou speech to the Ligue nationale de la prévoyance et de la mu-
talité, 29 May 1897, *JO*, *Lois et Décrets*, 3057–8. See also *Le Temps*,

15 June 1897, 4 April 1898, and a piece called "La Mutualité" in
Le Temps, 6 January 1910.

50 *JO*, Chamber Debates, 8 June 1896, 887.

51 Lachapelle, *Le Ministère Méline*, 116.

52 Ibid., 136.

53 See Rife, "The Political Career," 89, for Méline's remark. For that of
Anatole France, see *Penguin Island* (New York: Modern Library 1933),
178.

54 Lachapelle, *Le Ministère Méline*, 166–8.

55 See Herman Lebovics, *The Alliance of Iron and Wheat in the Third French
Republic, 1860–1914* (Baton Rouge: Louisiana State University Press
1988), 190–1. For a brief sketch of the "Progressistes," see Giselle and
Serge Berstein, *La Troisième République* (Paris: MA Éditions 1987), 250.

56 Guy Chapman, for instance, says that Barthou had resisted Méline's
pressure to use various government resources against the Radicals,
and Alexander Sedwick refers to appreciations that Barthou was
"soft" on the Radicals. See, respectively, Chapman's *The Dreyfus Case*
(London: Rupert Hard-Davis 1955), 208, and Sedwick's *The Ralliement
in French Politics, 1890–1898* (Cambridge, Mass.: Harvard University
Press 1965), 144–7.

57 Lachapelle, *Le Ministère Méline*, 169–70.

58 *JO*, Chamber Debates, 16 December 1898, 2465–9.

59 Lachapelle, *Le Ministère Méline*, 169–70. For a discussion of some of
the prefectoral casualties inflicted once Barthou had gone and the
Radicals returned to power, see Christophe Charle, *Les Élites de la République, 1880–1900* (Paris: Fayard 1987), 206.

60 See under "Le Projet Barthou," *Le Temps*, 1 June 1898, 4.

61 Lachapelle, *Le Ministère Méline*, 187. Years later, in an apparently
veiled reference to this experience, Barthou said that Méline was one
who understood "quand la collaboration ressemble à une servitude."
See his address on Méline, *JO, Lois et Décrets*, August 1918, 9787.

62 Lachapelle, *Le Ministère Méline*, 195; also the remarks of Jean-Marie
Mayeur in "Barthou et la 'question religieuse'" in *Barthou, un homme,
une époque*, ed. Michel Papy (Pau: J. et D. Éditions 1986), 142.

63 Bousquet-Mélou, *Barthou*, 112–14. For his remarks on this subject to
the *groupe des républicains progressistes*, see *Le Temps*, 26 October 1898,
4.

64 *JO*, Chamber Debates, 20 January 1899, 94; Bousquet-Mélou, *Barthou*,
114. For his formal deposition of 26 April 1899 on the Dreyfus affair,
see *L'Indépendant*, 28 April 1899.

65 In his formal resignation as leader of the Progressistes, Barthou also
stressed his concern with the fact that too many within their ranks
had backed Méline, rather than Émile Loubet, in his unsuccessful bid

for presidency of the Republic. See *Le Temps*, 19, 20 February 1899, and *l'Indépendant*, 20 February 1899.

66 R.D. Anderson, *France, 1870–1914: Politics and Society* (London: Routledge and Kegan Paul 1977), 19–20.

67 Barthou once described the ARD as having "aucune nuance exclusive" and as being less a party than "une sorte d'institution d'arbitrage." *Le Temps*, 15 December 1905, 1. See, as well, Rosemonde Sanson, "Louis Barthou, leader de l'Alliance Républicaine Démocratique, 1902–1914," in *Barthou, un homme, une époque*, ed. Papy, 104–7; Georges Lachapelle, *L'Alliance Démocratique: Ses origines, ses hommes, son rôle* (Paris: Grasset 1935), 7–20; Jean-Denis Bredin, *Joseph Caillaix* (Paris: Hachette 1980), 34.

68 Pierre Benoit, AF 23 April 1936, 41. Claude Farrère, Barthou's successor at the Académie Française, described this quality as "ce scepticism souriant." Ibid., 9.

69 Given the stringent Radical critique of Barthou's role in the 1898 elections, there were reports that they would withhold their support from any cabinet in which Barthou figured. See the report in *Le Temps*, 18 June 1899, 1.

70 Barthou, "Lettre politique," NR 8 (1901): 227–8; Bousquet-Mélou, *Barthou*, 118.

71 Barthou argued that neither the Falloux Law of 1850 nor subsequent legislation had ever given unauthorized congregations the right to teach. And now, that "right," simply acquired through neglect on the part of the state, had led to the current competition between Church-run lycées and those that were state-run. See his "Autour de la Loi Falloux," ARD, 22 May 1903, 16.

72 Ibid., 4.

73 *Pau Catalogue*, 37.

74 Rife, "The Political Career," 121–2.

75 Jean-Marie Mayeur, "Louis Barthou et la 'question religieuse,'" in *Barthou, un homme, une époque*, ed. Papy, 143. See also *Le Temps*, 14, 15 March 1903, 1.

76 Rife, "The Political Career," 124.

77 His reasons and justifications for so voting are developed at length in his speech to the Chamber of 12 March 1903, JO, Chamber Debates, 1129–35, and at greater length in his article, "La Révolution et la liberté d'enseignement," RP (1 February 1903): 493–507.

78 Mayeur, "Barthou et la 'question religieuse,'" in *Barthou, un homme, une époque*, ed. Papy, 146–8.

79 Bousquet-Mélou, *Barthou*, 130. For Barthou's own explanation of why he had chosen to run at the departmental level, see "Impression du candidat," *L'Indépendant*, 16 July 1904.

80 *JO*, Chamber Debates, 28 March 1905, 1117–24; Rife, "The Political Career," 123–37; *Le Temps*, 30 March 1905.

81 Poincaré, too, was also convinced about "le caractère doctrinal et systématiquement antilibéral du nouveau mouvement ouvrier." See Miquel, *Poincaré*, 213.

82 Rife, "The Political Career," 143–7, 160; Barthou, "Les Syndicats d'Instituteurs," *RP* (1 March 1906): 1–30; also his speech to the ARD, in *Le Temps*, 11 December 1907, 2.

83 For the *affaire des fiches* and General André, see Rife, "The Political Career," 133–5; and for Barthou on Émile Combes, see his speech "La Séparation," of 19 March 1905, to the Alliance Républicaine Démocratique. By late 1904 Barthou was displeased with Combes for personal reasons, principally because the latter had not been quick to act on Barthou's advice about certain promotion matters within the prefectoral administration. Barthou to Combes, 9 October 1904, 31, Fonds Émiles Combes, Archives Départementales, Charentes-Maritimes.

84 For his distinction, see his speech of 17 September 1905 to the ARD entitled "Patriotisme et Nationalisme." Some might call Barthou's patriotism the "new nationalism." See Eugen Weber, *The Nationalist Revival in France, 1905–1914* (Berkeley: University of California Press 1968), 2–3.

85 See *Le Temps*, 15 March 1906, 1. Barthou took with him to Public Works his brother Léon as *directeur de cabinet*, Georges Lamirault as *chef de cabinet*, and Maurice Reclus as the minister's *secrétaire particulier*.

86 Sanson, "Louis Barthou, leader de l'Alliance Républicaine ...," in *Barthou, un homme, une époque*, ed. Papy, 109–11; and the interview with Barthou on the subject of antimilitarism, *Le Temps*, 15 March 1906, 3.

87 *Pau Catalogue*, 38; Bousquet-Mélou, *Barthou*, 127–34.

88 Rife, "The Political Career," 162–3, 188.

89 Lachapelle, *L'Alliance Démocratique*, 24; Rife, "The Political Career," 167.

90 *JO*, Chamber Debates, 14 June 1909, 1446–7; 13 July 1909, 2058–67; *Le Temps*, 4 February 1907, 3; 25 February 1909, 1; 26 February, 4; 24 May, 1, 3; 7 June, 1; 21 June, 1; 10 July 1909.

91 *JO*, Chamber Debates, 19 March 1906, 772–6; see in particular for "la grèves des facteurs," *Le Temps*, 14, 15, 19, 20 April, 1 May, 6 June 1906.

92 *JO*, Chamber Debates, 28 March 1909, 1259; see also March–July, *Le Temps*.

93 Commission des chemins de fer, 18 January 1906–26 February 1907, and sous-commission des finances (Rachat de l'Ouest), 22 October 1907–25 February 1908, Sénat. See also Georges Bonnefous, *Histoire*

politique de la Troisième République 1 (Paris: PUF 1965), 44, 102–4, 156.

94 *JO*, Chamber Debates, 4, 5, 7 December 1906, 2891, 2917–31, 2994–3001; 9 July 1907, 1791; 11 July 1908, 1701–2; 10 December 1909, 3338–41.

95 *JO*, Chamber Debates, 10 December 1909, 3338–44; Commission des Travaux Publics, AN, series C7353, dossier "Chemins de fer," 16–76. See also Barthou's remarks on the *Rachat* in "La Situation," *Annales* (19 December 1920): 517.

96 Defined, of course, as he preferred: "un homme d'ordre qui accepte sans arrière pensée les institutions de son pays, et veut la paix sociale dans la liberté et dans l'union." Speech on the election of Henri-Robert, AF, 12 June 1924, 52.

97 "Tu ne songes qu'à satisfaire l'opinion du moment." Joseph Caillaux, *Mes Mémoires* (Paris: Plon 1947), 3:56.

98 AF, 12 June 1924, 44.

99 Sanson, "Louis Barthou leader de l'Alliance Républicaine ...," in *Barthou, un homme, une époque*, ed. Papy, 108.

CHAPTER FOUR

1 Quoted by Louis Latzarus in "Barthou," *Le Figaro*, 7 May 1914.

2 Barthou, *Le Politique* (Paris: Hachette 1923), 125.

3 Barthou, "Lettre politique," *NR* (1901): 23–9.

4 Reception speech by Farrère, AF, 23 April 1936, 5.

5 Barthou, "Patriotisme et Nationalisme," *ARD*, 17 September 1905, 1.

6 Gordon Wright, *France in Modern Times* (Chicago: Rand McNally 1974), 281.

7 Barthou, *L'Action syndicale (Loi du 21 mars 1884 – résultats et réformes)* (Paris: Arthur Rousseau 1904), 26–35, 303. In November 1905 he supported the postal agents' and sub-agents' right to unionize, but only after having secured their renunciation of the general strike as a political weapon. See Commission du Travail, 15 and 22 November 1905, AN, series C, 7338, dossiers 2934–5.

8 Barthou, *L'Action syndicale*, 47–100. See also his "Le syndicat obligatoire," *NR* (1901): 321–47.

9 Barthou, "Les Syndicats d'instituteurs," *RP* (March 1906): 22; and his remarks in parliament, *JO*, Chamber Debates, 7 May 1907, 915–16.

10 Barthou, "Les Syndicats d'instituteurs," 29. See also his "La Révolution et la liberté d'enseignement," *RP* (1 February 1903): 493–507.

11 Barthou, *L'Action syndicale*, 20–5, 194.

12 Barthou, "Le Syndicat obligatoire," 334.

13 Barthou, *L'Action syndicale*, 158–64, 226–7.

14 Barthou, "La Mère et l'enfant," 25 March 1911, Institut de Puéricul-
ture, 5, 12–13. For a broader treatment of male, republican attitudes,
see Marilyn Boxer, "Protective Legislation and Home Industry: The
Marginalization of Women Workers in Late Nineteenth-Early Twentieth Century France," *Journal of Social History* 20, no. 1 (Fall 1986):
45–66; Mary Lynn McDougall, "Protecting Infants: The French Campaign for Maternity Leaves, 1890s–1913," *FHS* 13, no. 1 (Spring
1988): 79–105.

15 Alain Becchia, "Les Milieux parlementaires et la dépopulation de
1900 à 1914," *Communications* 44 (October 1986): 203, 218–30. For
laws designed to assist large families and passed by the Barthou government in July 1913, see Richard Tomlinson, "The 'Disappearance'
of France, 1896–1940: French Politics and the Birth Rate," *Historical
Journal* 28, no. 2 (1985): 405–15. See as well Colin Dyer, *Population
and Society in Twentieth-Century France* (London: Hodder and Stoughton 1978); and John C. Hunter, "The Problem of the French Birth
Rate on the Eve of World War I," *FHS* 2, no. 4 (Fall 1962): 490–503.

16 *Le Temps*, 17 July 1906, 2. In August 1907 he was made the guest of
honour at the annual congress of the stenographers' union, expressly
as a measure of thanks for his initiative in hiring women. *L'Indépendant*, 20 August 1907.

17 Barthou, "La Mère et l'enfant," 6.

18 Barthou, "Autour du divorce," *NR* (15 December 1902): 436. For the
broader social context of the divorce issue, see Edward Berenson,
"The Politics of Divorce in France of the Belle Époque: The Case of
Joseph and Henriette Caillaux," *American Historical Review* no. 1 (February 1988): 31–55.

19 Barthou, "Autour du divorce," 444. See also his preface for Doctor B.
Roussy, *Éducation domestique de la femme et la rénovation sociale* (Paris:
Delagrave 1914).

20 Barthou, "Diderot et son oeuvre," *Revue pédagogique* (1913): 504–5.

21 Jean Bousquet-Mélou, *Louis Barthou et la circonscription d'Oloron, 1889–
1914* (Paris: Pedone 1972), 107. Once again, for a broader treatment
of marriage customs and conditions, see the chapter "Marriage and
Morals" in Theodore Zeldin, *France, 1848–1945*: vol. 1, *Ambition, Love
and Politics* (Oxford: Clarendon Press 1973), 287–90.

22 See the "Déclaration de Mutation par Décès," for Mme Louis Barthou
(15 January 1930), Monsieur Louis Barthou (9 October 1934),
Mme Mayeur (19 May 1940). Archives Départementales de la Seine,
Section des Impôts (Place Saint-Sulpice).

23 "Registre des mariages," 26 January 1895, Mairie du 5e arrondissement de Paris, *Pau Catalogue*, 23, and notes made at the time of the
Exposition in Pau in 1984.

24 Description of Mme Barthou's headdress comes from an interview with the late Mme Souchère, 30 October 1981.

25 "Registres des mariages," Paroisse de la Madeleine à Paris, 8e arrondissement, 29 January 1895, Archives de l'Archeveché de Paris. See also Robert J. Young, "Louis Barthou, portrait intime," in *Barthou, un homme, une époque*, ed. Michel Papy (Pau: J. et D. Éditions 1986), 258–9.

26 Jules Bertaut, *Les Dessous de la "Troisième"* (Paris: Tallandier 1959), 145–51.

27 Ibid., 181–90; Charles Rearick, *Pleasures of the Belle Époque: Entertainment and Festivity in Turn-of-the-Century France* (New Haven: Yale University Press 1985), 127–59.

28 Including the Barthou family, who had to be evacuated to the Justice ministry, some by boat, others "on men's backs." *The Times*, 29 January 1910.

29 See again Bertaut, *Les Dessous*, as well as Richard D. Mandell, *Paris 1900. The Great World's Fair* (Toronto: University of Toronto Press 1967) and Ernest A. Vizetelly, *Paris and Her People under the Third Republic* (New York: Frederic Stokes 1918).

30 *Le Temps*, 3 July 1907, 4.

31 For his efforts to control traffic, see *Le Temps*, 13 October 1909, 4, and 16 October 1909, 1. For the accident, see *Le Temps*, 8 March 1908, 3, and *The Times*, 7 March 1908.

32 Barthou, "Les Héros de l'air," *RB* (November-December 1915): 578.

33 « Un Ministre en ballon," *L'Illustration* (1 June 1907): 364. See also J.J. Cazaurang, "Deux pionniers de la locomotion aérienne: Les Frères Barthou," *Pyrénées* no. 3 (1984): 249–58.

34 Reception speech by Farrère, *AF*, 23 April 1936, 5.

35 *L'Indépendant*, 10 September 1908; *The Times*, 9 September 1908.

36 *Le Temps*, 2–3 January 1909, 2; *L'Indépendant*, 7 November 1908; *Pau Catalogue*, 29–30. Barthou's *double entendre* is found in a two-page biography, written in his own hand, though undated. I was able to consult this document thanks to the kindness of M. Castaing of the Maison Charavay.

37 *L'Indépendant*, 27 and 30 July 1909.

38 Barthou, "Les Sports bienfaisants," *Annales* (1 May 1917): 513–27. As Marcel Spivak has written more recently, from 1872 onward the idea grew: "il faut à la France une jeunesse forte, dressée au maniement des armes." See his "Le développement de l'éducation physique et du sport français de 1852 à 1914," *Revue d'histoire moderne et contemporaine* 24 (1977): 35.

39 Barthou, "Les Sports bienfaisants," 525. One might speculate that Barthou knew that his friend Poincaré was committed to physical fitness. See Pierre Miquel, *Poincaré* (Paris: Fayard 1961), 339.

40 Barthou, *Promenades autour de ma vie: Lettres de la montagne* (Paris: Les Laboratoires Martinet 1933), 133. For further information on the perceived connection between patriotism and physical conditioning, see Robert A. Nye, *Madness and Politics in Modern France: The Medical Concept of National Decline* (Princeton: Princeton University Press 1984), 310–29.

41 Latzarus, "M. Barthou," *Le Figaro*, 7 May 1914; Léon Daudet, *L'Agonie du régime* (Paris: Nouvelle Librairie Nationale 1925), 43–4.

42 Benoist, *Souvenirs de Charles Benoist*, 3 vols. (Paris: Plon 1933–34), 3:191–3.

43 See chapter 3, pages 61, 63, notes 79 and 83.

44 Response by Pierre Benoit, AF, 23 April 1936, 41; Louis Vitalis, "L'Ami," *In Memoriam du Livre Contemporain* (Paris 1935), 7.

45 Barthou, "Beethoven," *Impressions et essais* (Paris: Bibliothèque Charpentier 1914), 113.

46 Barthou, "Pour qu'on écoute: À Madame X," *Impressions*, 105–10.

47 Interview with Mme Souchère, 30 April 1982. Response of Godoy to Barthou's speech at a banquet honouring the poet. See *Le Manuscrit autographe* (October 1932): 92–3.

48 Barthou, "Pour qu'on écoute," 107.

49 Barthou, "Richard Wagner cinquante ans après sa mort," *Les Annales politiques et littéraires* (10 February 1933): 155.

50 See for example Eugen Weber, *France: Fin de siècle* (Cambridge, Mass.: Harvard University Press 1986), 192.

51 See Barthou's seventh letter, from Dresden, 7 September 1902, and his sixth letter, from Vienna, 31 August 1902, in *Impressions*, 38–40, 45.

52 *L'Illustration*, 4, 11, 18 March 1911, and reprinted as "Au Soudan Égyptien" in *Impressions*, 56–95.

53 Barthou, "Au Soudan Égyptien," *Impressions*, 56–7, 62–3.

54 See, for instance, his remarks to the departmental council in Pau, when he spoke of their great inheritance from statesmen like Gambetta, writers like Hugo, philosophers like Renan, and scientists like Berthelot and Pasteur. *Le Temps*, 28 September 1909, 4.

55 Barthou, second letter, Berlin, 9 May 1901, *Impressions*, 10–11.

56 Barthou, sixth letter, Vienna, 31 August 1902, *Impressions*, 10–11.

57 Barthou, "Corneille," *Impressions*, 156; "Après avoir lu La Bruyère," *Lettres à un jeune français* (Paris: Éditions Pierre Lafitte 1916), 210, and for Pascal, ibid., 62–3; "Diderot et son oeuvre" (1913), 502.

58 Barthou, "Discours sur Napoléon," *La Vie des peuples* 4 (1921): 7; remarks on Sainte-Beuve in Barthou's *Rachel* (Paris: Librairie Alcan 1926), 34–5; and on Chateaubriand in "Ce que Napoléon aurait fait sur la Marne," *Conférencia* (5 September 1931): 261.

59 Barthou's response to the reception speech of Joseph Bédier, AF,

3 November 1921; also his "Des Musardises à Chantecler," *Cahiers* (June 1932): 535–57.

60 François Marin, "Louis Barthou et Anatole France," *RRP* 241–2 (January-June 1984): 33.

61 Barthou, "Anatole France sans la politique," *Conférencia* (1 May 1925): 453.

62 Barthou, "Sur Anatole France," *Revue de France* no. 3 (May-June 1926): 607.

63 Barthou, "Anatole France sans la politique," 454–5.

64 Barthou preface for N. Serban, *Pierre Loti, sa vie et son oeuvre* (Paris: Les Presses Françaises 1924), x.

65 Barthou's memorial speech on Loti at Hendaye, AF, 7 September 1930, 7.

66 André Gaudelette de la Morlière, "Présence de Louis Barthou," *Journal de Vichy*, 27 June 1952.

67 Coppée to Barthou, 11 May 1896, 28 November 1898; Erlanger to Barthou, 27 September 1906, Collection Roland-Marcel.

68 Barthou to Porte-Riche, 25 February 1906, n.a.f. (Porto-Riche), f. 348, BN; Barthou to Victor du Bled, 6 July 1907, n.a.f. 24412 (du Bled), f. 36, BN.

69 Barthou to Loti, 11 July 1908, Collection Loti-Viaud; Debussy to Barthou, 28 December 1908, Collection Roland-Marcel.

70 Jean Toulet, "Louis Barthou, une époque de la bibliophilie" in *Barthou, un homme, une époque*, ed. Papy, 187–96; and Robert J. Young, "La Cité des livres: Louis Barthou (1862–1934)," *Bull. du bib.* no. 4 (1983): 448–59. See also Barthou's contribution to *Les Obsèques d'Édouard Pelletier* (Paris: Imprimerie Nationale 1914), 29–34; and "Sur Marius Michel" in *Plaisir du bibliophile* (Spring 1927): 67–73.

71 This, the best known, was designed for Barthou by Jean-Louis Forain, and executed by the engraver Pierre Bouchet. The interpretation offered here is a derivative of a number of conversations with Parisian bibliophiles and booksellers. A second *ex libris*, rarely seen, was designed by Bouchet. It features another nude female, this time perched on the well's edge, deeply engaged in a book which she has chosen at the expense of the vanity-associated mirror discarded at her feet. I owe a very special debt of thanks to Mme Pierre Bouchet for having presented me with her husband's original sketch.

72 Barthou, *Mirabeau* (Paris: Hachette 1913). Barthou was an active member of the Société de l'histoire de la Révolution, through which he was in frequent contact with professional historians like Alphonse Aulard and Camille Bloch. See *Le Temps*, 26 March 1912, 3.

73 Barthou, *Mirabeau*, 169, 216–17.

74 Ibid., 79, 273, 290. The friendly journalist P.B. Gheusi drew public attention to a number of these similarities, in a manner possibly calcu-

lated to assist Barthou's contemplated candidacy for the Académie Française. See his "Mirabeau et M. Barthou," *NR* no. 8 (July-August 1913): 19–34.

75 Barthou, *Mirabeau*, 258.

76 Of de Mun he wrote, "Le terrible problème de la responsabilité des classes dirigeantes ou possédantes s'imposa à Albert de Mun." See "Albert de Mun," *RDDM* (15 March 1923): 278.

CHAPTER FIVE

1 Barthou, "Quand Lyautey Parle," *RDDM* (15 May 1927): 259.

2 Jean Bousquet-Mélou, *Louis Barthou et la circonscription d'Oloron, 1889–1914* (Paris: Pedone 1972), 151–3.

3 Ibid., 174–5. Barthou's electoral *profession du foi* is reproduced in *L'Indépendant*, 16 April 1910.

4 For information on these parliamentary groups, see Alain Bomier-Landowski, "Les Groupes parlementaires de l'Assemblée Nationale et de la Chambre des Députés de 1871 à 1940," in *Sociologie électorale*, ed. F. Goguel and G. Dupeux (Paris: Colin 1951), 75–89. On the 1910 election results, see Georges Bonnefous, *Histoire politique de la Troisième République*, vol. 1, *L'Avant-guerre, 1906–1914* (Paris: PUF 1965), 184–5.

5 Bernard Oudin, *Aristide Briand* (Paris: Laffont 1987), 188; John Merle Rife, Jr, "The Political Career of Louis Barthou, 1889–1913" (unpublished Ph.D. dissertation, Ohio State University 1964), 191–5.

6 *The Times*, 21 October 1910. In March 1913, Premier Barthou urged the railway companies to rehire those strikers who had not been reinstated following the strike of 1910. See *JO*, Chamber Debates, 29 March 1913, 1307.

7 This came up during Barthou's testimony before the parliamentary Rochette commission. See *Le Temps*, 25 March 1914, 2.

8 Joseph Caillaux, *Mes Mémoires* (Paris: Plon 1947), 3:56.

9 Barthou, "Ministère de l'intérieure," *RH* no. 4 (1911): 608–37.

10 Barthou, "Comment assurer à nos ministres la liberté d'action," *RB* (10 June 1911): 707–9.

11 Ibid., 707.

12 Caillaux, *Mes Mémoires*, 3:54.

13 Caillaux to Barthou, 24 October 1911, Collection Roland-Marcel. See also Jean-Claude Allain, *Joseph Caillaux*, 2 vols. (Paris: Imprimerie Nationale 1978), 1: 96–8.

14 Barthou, "Discours," *ARD*, 17 November 1911, 4–5.

15 For this emphasis on domestic politics, see David E. Sumler, "Domestic Influences on the Nationalist Revival in France, 1909–1914," *FHS* 6, no. 4 (Fall 1970): 517–37; Frederic Seager, "Joseph Caillaux as Pre-

mier, 1911–1912: The Dilemma of a Liberal Reformer," *FHS* 11, no. 2 (Fall 1979): 239–57; Donald G. Wileman, "Caillaux and the Alliance, 1901–1912: The Evolution of a Disillusioned Conservative," *Canadian Journal of History* 23, no. 3 (December 1988): 355–73.

16 Rosemonde Sanson, "Louis Barthou, leader de l'Alliance Républicain ...," in *Barthou, un homme, une époque*, ed. Michel Papy (Pau: J. et D. Éditions 1986), 109–10.

17 Barthou, "Discours," *ARD*, 17 November 1911.

18 *Le Temps*, 9 December 1911, 3.

19 See Rudolf Binion, *Defeated Leaders: The Political Fate of Caillaux, Jouvenel and Tardieu* (New York: Columbia University Press 1960), 48–9; Jean-Denis Bredin, *Joseph Caillaux* (Paris: Hachette 1980), 141; Keith A. Hamilton, "The 'Wild Talk' of Joseph Caillaux: A Sequel to the Agadir Crisis," *International History Review* 9, no. 2 (May 1987): 195–226.

20 See, for example, his praise of the government in a speech delivered at Anjou. *Le Temps*, 16 April 1912, 1.

21 Poincaré does not comment on the exclusion of Barthou in 1912, but he does discuss his friend's political liabilities in connection with the circumstances of March 1913. See his *Au service de la France*, 10 vols. (Paris: Plon 1926–33), 3: 158. On the range of factors which may explain cabinet inclusion or exclusion, see Serge Berstein, "Le Ministre ...," *Pouvoirs* (1986): 23.

22 Rife, "The Political Career," 206; *Le Temps*, 18 April 1912, 3.

23 *JO*, Chamber Debates, 1 July 1912, 1849–54, 1874; also *Le Temps*, 3 July 1912, 6; and *The Times*, 2 July 1912, 5.

24 "Louis Barthou au-dessus des nuages," *Le Temps*, 18 August 1913, 3.

25 *Impressions et essais* was actually published in 1913, but Barthou admitted that he had delayed the distribution so as not to distract attention from his *Mirabeau*. See *Le Temps*, interview of 18 August 1913. Also "L'Avocat et le juge dans le répertoire classique," *Annales* (1 March 1912): 303–16; *En Marge des "Confidences", Lettres inédites de Lamartine*, Les Amis d'Édouard, no. 18 (Abbeville: F. Paillart 1913), 1–43; "Victor Hugo, correcteur d'épreuves," *RH* (August 1912) and reprinted in *Impressions et essais*, 239–71; "Dédicaces, lettres et autographes," *RH* (March 1912), and reprinted in *Impressions*, 272–99.

26 Pierre Benoit, *AF*, 23 April 1936, 43.

27 Jules Bertaut, *Louis Barthou* (Paris: Sansot 1919), 36–7; Latzarus, "M. Barthou," *Le Figaro*, 7 May 1914; P.B. Gheusi, *Les Chefs: Études politiques et de théâtre* (Paris: Flammarion n.d. but circa 1913–14), 8.

28 *Annuaire du Cinquantenaire, 1951–1953: Le Livre Contemporain* (Paris: Siège Social 1953), 13–35.

29 Alfred-Jousselin, "La Mission Champlain," *Le Monde illustré* no. 2878

(25 May 1912): 340–1; Gabriel Hanotaux, *Carnets, 1907–1925* (Paris: Pedone 1982), 82.

30 See articles by Gaston Deschamps, *Le Temps*, 10 May 1912, 2; 18 May, 1; 19 May, 1; 21 May, 2; 4 June, 3. See also the Toronto *Globe*, 6 May, the Montreal *Devoir*, 29 April, 2, 3, 4, 6, 7, 11 May; *New York Times*, 29 April, 1, 2, 3, 5, 9 May.

31 See Deschamps's "Pélcrinages français," *Le Temps*, 4 June 1912, 3; and Barthou, "Les Quarantes sont quarante," *Cahiers* (August 1930): 698.

32 Poincaré, *Au service*, 3:157–8.

33 "La Crise ministérielle," *Le Temps*, 22 March 1913, 3.

34 *Le Temps*, 22 March 1913, 1, 3; 26 March, 6. See also Georges Michon, *La Préparation à la guerre: La loi de trois ans, 1910–1914* (Paris: Marcel Rivière 1935), 150; and Jean-Jacques Becker, "Les 'Trois Ans' et les débuts de la première guerre mondiale," *Guerres mondiales et conflits contemporains* no. 145 (1987): 7–26.

35 Michon, *La Préparation*, 143–5; General Adolphe Messimy, *Mes Souvenirs* (Paris: Plon 1937), 116. See also Jean Doise and Maurice Vaïsse, *Diplomatie et outil militaire, 1871–1969* (Paris: Imprimerie Nationale 1987), 173–5.

36 Barthou, *Promenades autour de ma vie: Lettres de la montagne* (Paris: Les Laboratoires Martinet 1933), 49–51. See also his interview with *Le Figaro*, 26 January 1916.

37 *JO*, Chamber Debates, 25 March 1913, 1194.

38 See Barthou's deposition of 23 December 1919, submitted in connection with the treason trial of Caillaux. Deposition 29, Fonds Roche-Caillaux, dossier 6, FNSP.

39 Poincaré, *Au service*, 3:189–91, 194–7; Maurice Paléologue, *Journal, 1913–1914* (Paris: Plon 1947), 102–6. For more assurances of the government's peaceful intentions, see Barthou's interview with an Italian journalist as reported in *L'Indépendant*, 3 September 1913.

40 At the end of March, Barthou had been careful to warn parliament that such a measure might prove necessary. Instead of tempering resistance, however, his forewarning seemed only to stiffen opposition in the Army commission. See the minutes of the committee meeting for 27 March 1913, Commission de l'Armée, AN, series C, 7421, dossier 365, no. 1.

41 See *The Times*, 5 May, 7; 16 May, 5; 30 May, 7; *Le Temps*, 25 May, 1; 31 May, 6.

42 See again the Army commission meeting of 27 March 1913, for his rationale on article 33. AN, series C, 7421, dossier 365, no. 1; and *Le Temps*, 19 March, 2; 17 May, 3; 30 May, 1.

43 *JO*, Chamber Debates, 27 May 1913, 1565–6 (Dumont), 1567, 1580–2 (Barthou); *Le Temps*, 28 May 1913.

44 *Le Temps*, 19, 20 May, 1; Caillaux, *Mes Mémoires*, 3:58.

45 "M. Barthou's Financial Policy," *The Times*, 30 May 1913, 7.

46 See chapter 2, page 30 note 27.

47 Caillaux, *Mes Mémoires*, 3:59, 70.

48 Barthou to Loti, 12 June 1913, Collection Loti-Viaud; Alice Barthou to [unidentified], 14 August 1913. This letter, now part of a private collection, was shown to me prior to sale by M. Castaing of the Maison Charavay, to whom I express thanks.

49 *The Times*, 28 May 1913.

50 *JO*, Chamber Debates, 2 June 1913, 1666; *The Times*, 3 June 1913, 7.

51 Barthou, *Promenades*, 59; *JO*, Chamber Debates, 2 June 1913, 1667.

52 See his speech to the *Conférence corporative des voyageurs*, in *Le Temps*, 16 June 1913, 3.

53 Barthou, *Le Politique* (Paris: Hachette 1923), 56; preface to Henri Robert, *Les Grands Procès de l'histoire* (Paris: Payot 1931), xii.

54 Barthou, *Mirabeau* (Paris: Hachette 1913), 304.

55 Bertaut, *Barthou*, 26; Ignotus, "Louis Barthou," *RP* (1922): 79.

56 Jean Vignaud, "Les Nouveaux Immortels: Louis Barthou," (1918): 346.

57 Barthou, *Le Politique*, 49. For his sympathetic portrait of Charles Floquet, see his speech at Saint-Jean-Pied-de-Port, *JO*, *Lois et Décrets*, 12 July 1912, 6070–1.

58 Vignaud, "Les Nouveaux Immortels," 346.

59 Paul Flat, "Un Orateur jugé par un homme d'état," *RB* no. 17 (2–9 September 1916): 513–14.

60 See his two key interventions in *JO*, Chamber Debates, 26 June 1913, 2231, 2233–4, 2238–9; 4 July 1913, 2459.

61 Interview with M. André Schuck, 24 March 1982. This was a story told to Schuck by Vitalis himself in the 1950s.

62 The original, hand-corrected address is in the archives of the Société des Gens de Lettres. Part of this speech was reproduced in *Le Temps*, 7 July 1913, 3.

63 Jean Lefranc, "Louis Barthou ...," *Le Temps*, 18 August 1913, 3.

64 Ibid.

65 Ignotus, "Louis Barthou," 80.

66 "Paroles nécessaires," *Le Temps*, 11 November 1913, 1.

67 *Le Temps*, 30 November 1913, 3.

68 For Barthou's qualified support for the return of *scrutin de liste*, see *JO*, Chamber Debates, 25 March 1913, 1195. See also *Le Temps*, 6 November 1913, 1.

69 See the premier's speech at Saint Germain-en-Laye, *Le Temps*, 11 November 1913, 3.

70 *JO*, Chamber Debates, 27–8 November 1913, 3613–14, 3647–63; and the article "L'Emprunt" in *Le Temps*, 30 November 1913, 1.

71 See the editorial "Contradiction," *Le Temps*, 27 December 1913, 1; and the text of Barthou's speech to the *Comité*, in *Le Temps*, 21 November 1913, 3.

72 See minutes of Commission du Budget (1910–14), sessions of 14, 17, 19, 20, 21, 24, 28 November 1913, AN, series C, 7427; and *Le Temps*, 21 November 1913, 1; *The Times*, 21 November, 7 and 28 November, 7.

73 *The Times*, 21 November 1913, 7.

74 Ibid., 2 December 1913, 8. His decision to allow the government to stand or fall on the tax exemption was announced to the local republican committee in Pau, the Comité Mascuraud, and reported in *Le Temps*, 21 November 1913, 3.

75 Poincaré, *Au service*, 3:313, 337.

76 Ibid., 313.

77 Barthou's speech to the Comité Mascuraud, *Le Temps*, 21 November 1913, 3. Even in May 1913 Barthou seems to have been preparing himself philosophically for defeat, judging by remarks made to his Béarnais friends of "La Garbure." See Aubert's account of this social gathering, *L'Indépendant*, 17 May 1913.

78 Ibid., also *The Times*, 2 December 1913, 8.

79 Speech to the Ligue de l'Enseignement, *Le Temps*, 30 November 1913, 3.

80 "Journée parlementaire," *Le Temps*, 4 December 1913, 3; Allain, *Caillaux*, 1:260–2.

81 *JO*, Chamber Debates, 2 December 1913, 3731; *Le Temps*, 4 December 1913, 3.

82 Poincaré, *Au service*, 3:339. Georges Louis later reported Poincaré's frustration, attributing to the president the view that Barthou and Dumont had made many mistakes on financial issues, "malgré mes incessantes recommandations." See *Carnets de Georges Louis*, 2 vols. (Paris: Rieder 1926), 2:94–5.

83 "Rapport sur la candidature ... de M. Louis Barthou," December 1913, Archives de la Société des Gens de Lettres. The letters of Rostand and Hervieu were published in *L'Indépendant*, 23–4 November 1913.

CHAPTER SIX

1 Barthou quoting Danton, in his *Danton* (Paris: Albin Michel 1932), 308.

2 The appellation is attributed to Charles Benoist, in Aubert's *De l'histoire et des histoires: Souvenirs d'un journaliste* (Bordeaux: Éditions Delmas 1943), 106.

3 See "Constitution de la fédération des gauches," *Le Temps*, 15 January 1914, 3.

4 G. Bonnefous's account in *Histoire politique de la Troisième République*: vol. 1, *L'avant-guerre, 1906–1914* (Paris: PUF 1965), 369–88, is consistent with the interpretation advanced by Barthou in speeches of 26 January and 6 February 1914, *Le Temps*, and with that paper's editorial entitled "Les Audacieux" of 27 January. For an account much more sympathetic to Caillaux, see Gerd Krumeich, *Armaments and Politics in France on the Eve of the First World War* (Leamington Spa: Berg Publishers 1984), 157–9.

5 *Le Temps*, 16 February 1914, 2. See also his attacks in the Chamber, *JO*, Chamber Debates, 5 March 1914, 1333–4; and for signs of Jaurès's discomfort with Caillaux's apparent compromises, see G. Bonnefous, *Histoire politique (1906–1914)*, 387.

6 The phrase was that of Barthou. See *Le Temps*, 6 February 1914, 6.

7 Even Léon Daudet, a man of acid tongue, described Calmette as one who "excellait à dissiper les malentendus, à réconcilier, à amadouer." See his *L'Entre-Deux-Guerres* (Paris: Nouvelle Librairie Nationale 1915), 164.

8 *Le Temps*, 13 February 1914, 3.

9 To this point, there seems to be agreement among Poincaré, Caillaux, and Barthou. See Poincaré, *Au service de la France* (Paris: Plon 1926–33), 4: 34–5; Caillaux, *Mes Mémoires* (Paris: Plon 1947), 3: 108–10; Barthou's testimony of 24 March 1914, before the Rochette commission. See Commission d'enquête (Rochette) (1914), AN, series C, 7454, dossier 1690 bis, no. 10.

10 Caillaux, *Mes Mémoires*, 3:118–19; this charge was made by Henriette Caillaux in the course of the trial proceedings. Barthou acknowledged a chance encounter with Mme Gueydan, since they lived on the same street, but denied having been shown any letters. See an excerpt of his court deposition, *Le Temps*, 2 April 1914, 6.

11 Poincaré, *Au service*, 4:79–80. The Fabre note, it should be recorded, though dated March 1911, was only submitted in 1912, to Briand, as justice minister in the Poincaré cabinet, and reportedly as a person-to-person initiative rather than a formal, registered complaint.

12 See Poincaré, *Au service*, 4:83–4; Caillaux, *Mes Mémoires*, 3:121. For the latter's absence of reference to any meeting with Poincaré on Saturday, 14 March, see ibid., 119.

13 Barthou's deposition to the Rochette commission does not mention his having seen Calmette on Monday, 16 March, an encounter which – given the tragic circumstances – it seems likely he would have recalled for the commission.

14 *JO*, Chamber Debates, 17 March 1914, 1693–5.

15 See Benjamin F. Martin, *The Hypocrisy of Justice in the Belle Époque* (Baton Rouge: Louisana State University Press 1984), 169–206; Jean-

Claude Allain, *Joseph Caillaux* (Paris: Imprimerie Nationale 1978), 1:391–436.

16 Caillaux, *Mes Mémoires*, 3:121, 131–8, 174. The motives attributed to Poincaré, according to this version, are retribution for Caillaux's resistance to the three-year law and, perhaps more important, apprehension about the minister's projects for a progressive income tax and a sharp new tax on capital.

17 Caillaux, *Mes Mémoires*, 3:54–7, 109–10, 131–2, 136. Undeniably, these memoirs are ambiguous on the subject of Barthou. Sometimes he is seen as vulgar, mean-spirited, and small-minded; sometimes he is a man of very great talent and considerable finesse. See as well Allain, *Caillaux*, 2:394.

18 In May 1914 he told Ribot about Barthou's alleged role. See *Journal d'Alexandre Ribot et correspondances inédites, 1914–1922* (Paris: Plon 1936), 7. The "confession" leak came in 1926 when a journalist, clearly acting on Poincaré's behalf, told Caillaux the story of Barthou's admission to the president on 17 March 1914. See Caillaux, *Mes Mémoires*, 3:131.

19 Poincaré, *Au service*, 4:32, 50, 58, 63, 88; viii, 61. He strengthens the impression further by injecting here a note of disgust at Barthou's alleged manoeuvrings to secure a chair in the Académie Française.

20 Notes journalières (Mars-Août 1914), BN, Papiers Poincaré, n.a.f. 16027, 17 March, 20–2.

21 Firmly, but not uncritically, on Poincaré's side are Gordon Wright, *Raymond Poincaré and the French Presidency* (New York: Octagon Books 1967 reprint), 107–8; Gerd Krumeich, "Raymond Poincaré et l'affaire du 'Figaro,'" *Revue historique* 264 (October-December 1980): 361–73; Becker, "Les 'Trois Ans'" et les débuts de la première guerre mondiale," *Guerres mondiales* (1987): 18.

22 For a direct attribution of the Calmette campaign to the "Élysée" see Victor Margueritte, *Aristide Briand* (Paris: Flammarion 1932), 148.

23 See Bernard Oudin, *Aristide Briand, biographie* (Paris: Laffont 1987), 250–1; also Vercors, *Moi Aristide Briand* (Paris: Plon 1981), 138.

24 Barthou testimony, Rochette commission, 24 March 1914, AN, C7454, dossier 1690 bis, no. 10, 1826.

25 Ibid., 1827–8.

26 Ibid., 1881. The deposition can also be found in *Le Temps*, 25 March 1914, 1.

27 Ibid., 1885. This confirmation allowed Calmette to make frequent allusions to this document in his article of 10 March. See Krumeich, *Armaments and Politics*, 175.

28 Barthou deposition, Rochette commission, AN, C7454, dossier 1690 bis, no. 10, 1931–2.

29 Ibid., 1881.

30 Caillaux confirms both of these conversations. The only difference is that he claims Barthou mentioned Gueydan's arsenal of letters, whereas Barthou always denied any knowledge of such a collection. See Caillaux, *Mes Mémoires*, 3:109–10, 118–19. Barthou's clearest statement on a personal warning to Calmette comes in the excerpt from his deposition which was published in *Le Temps*, 9 April 1914, 6.

31 Barthou testimony, Rochette commission, AN, C7454, dossier 1690 bis, no. 10, 1883–7. Presumably this is why on 14 March Poincaré recorded Barthou's conviction that Calmette would not publish the Fabre note. See Poincaré, *Au service*, 4:80.

32 Poincaré, *Au service*, 4:90.

33 Barthou testimony, Rochette commission, AN, C7454, dossier 1690 bis, no. 10, 1892–5, 2025–6.

34 Maurice Barrès, *Dans le cloaque. Notes d'un membre de la commission d'enquête sur l'affaire Rochette* (Paris: Éditions de l'*Écho de Paris* 1914), 24–5.

35 There was an incident in 1916 when Poincaré heard rumours that Barthou was blaming him for Calmette's campaign, a rumour that the president neither verified nor mentioned again. See *Au service*, 8:61.

36 See "Nouvelle déposition de M. Barthou," *Le Temps*, 25 July 1914, 2, 6.

37 See his speech to the Parti Républicain Démocratique, the text of which is reproduced in *Le Temps*, 4 April 1914, 3.

38 Jean Bousquet-Mélou, *Louis Barthou et la circonscription d'Oloron, 1889–1914* (Paris: Pedone 1972), 176–7. His electoral *profession de foi* is reproduced in *Le Temps*, 18 April 1914, 3.

39 Eugen Weber, *The Nationalist Revival in France, 1905–1914* (Berkeley: University of California Press 1968), 137; R.D. Anderson, *France, 1870–1914: Politics and Society* (London: Routledge and Kegan Paul 1977), 28.

40 Letter of 20 July 1914, AF Archives, dossier 2GB2.

41 Poincaré, *Au service*, 5:477–8.

42 Barthou recalled this conversation in a public lecture of 6 May 1915. See dossier "pièces diverses" in the Barthou files, BA 257 (Provisoire), Archives de la Préfecture de Police.

43 Pierre Loti, "Un Petit Hussard," *Illustration* (26 December 1914): 495; Yvonne Sarcey, "La Mort d'un Enfant: À Mme Louis Barthou," *Annales* (27 December 1914): n.p.

44 Pierre Espil, "Une Amitié complexe: Louis Barthou-Pierre Loti," RRP (January-June 1984): 27.

45 L.L. Klotz, *De la guerre à la paix* (Paris: Payot 1924), 14–15; Charles Benoist, *Souvenirs de Charles Benoist* (Paris: Plon 1933–34), 3:211.

46 Loti, "Un Petit Hussard," 495.

47 Barthou to Georges Cain, 5 December 1914, Dossier Charavay (1981).

48 See Poincaré, *Au service*, 5:509; press coverage in *Le Temps* of 17 December, 3, and 18 December, 5, and *Le Figaro*, 17 December, 3, and Rostand's tribute to Max, also in *Figaro*, 15 January 1915; and *L'Indépendant*, 19 December.

49 Her detachment and accelerating religiosity are both remarked on by Marcel Gilbert and Mme Roland-Marcel, during interviews with the author of 4 May and 27 April 1982 respectively. See also Becker,   .
    "Louis Barthou devant la guerre," in *Barthou un homme, une époque,* ed. Michel Papy (Pau: J. et D. Éditions 1986), 164, note 12; Espil, "Une Amitié complexe," 27.

50 Alice to Loti, 9 February 1909, and two wartime, but undated, letters, one written from Eaux-Bonnes. Collection Loti-Viaud.

51 Barthou to Loti, 15 May 1918, Collection Loti-Viaud.

52 Alice Barthou, "La Maison enchantée," *RH* (October 1918): 444.

53 Lesley Blanch, *Pierre Loti: The Legendary Romantic* (New York: Harcourt, Brace, Jovanovich 1983), 310.

54 Loti to Alice, undated, Collection Roland-Marcel.

55 Alice-Louis Barthou, *Au Moghreb parmi les fleurs* (Paris: Grasset 1925), 9; and her "La Maison enchantée," 450–6.

56 Opening a gift copy of Loti's "Petit Hussard" article, "J'ai pleuré, je pleure, et je vous embrasse avec tout mon pauvre coeur meurtri ..." Barthou to Loti, 5 July 1916, Collection Loti-Viaud.

57 "Allocution funèbre," AF Archives, dossier 1G7 (Barthou); also Farrère's reception speech, AF, 23 April 1936.

58 Ugo Ojetti, "Le souvenir de Louis Barthou," October 1934, press clipping of undetermined origin, dossier Barthou, Bibliothèque Historique de la Ville de Paris.

59 Barthou, "Avant-propos d'après guerre," in his *Lettres à un jeune français* (Paris: Éditions Pierre Lafitte 1916), 235.

60 Barthou to Lyautey, 13 March 1919, AN, Papiers Lyautey, carton 717.

61 Barthou to Loti, 2 October 1916, 18 September 1919, Collection Loti-Viaud.

62 Poincaré, *Au service*, 6:230, 316, 327; vii, 186; Barthou to Loti, 3 November 1915, Collection Loti-Viaud, in which he sees the Socialists as punishing him for the three-year law, and Caillaux as exacting his revenge.

63 In late October he wrote bitterly to Briand: "Tu m'a lâché, toi, Briand, et à cause de la loi de trois ans!" see Oudin, *Briand*, 279. See also Poincaré, *Au service*, 6:222–3, 267, 276.

64 See Dossier "Commission supérieure consultative ..." carton 32, AN, Papiers Millerand; *Le Figaro*, 9, 23 August 1914; Barthou, "En souvenir du Capitaine ... de Chinchilla," *Lettres à un jeune français*, 229.

65 Gabriel Hanotaux, *Carnets, 1907–1925* (Paris: Plon 1925), 162. See also "Le congrès franco-italien de Cernobblo," *Le Temps*, 18 September 1915, 2.

66 Poincaré, *Au service*, 8:236, 241, 244, 257.

67 Ibid., 9:32–3.

68 Barthou, "Pour la santé de nos soldats," *Le Monde illustré* (4 November 1916): 263–4.

69 Barthou, "Sur le front italien," in his *Lettres à un jeune Français* 114–15; and "Autour de la Suisse Hospitalière," in ibid., 176. See also *Le Temps*, 29, 30 July 1916.

70 Poincaré, *Au service*, 7:318. See also the report on the Comité de l'effort de la France et de ses alliés in *The Times*, 16 August 1916, 5.

71 See his *Lettres* (1916); his *L'Heure du droit: France, Belgique, Serbie* (Paris: Georges Crès 1916); and his *Sur les routes du droit* (Paris: Bloud et Gay 1917).

72 Barthou, "La Victoire française," "Pour la Belgique," in *L'Heure du droit*, 5, 81–2.

73 See his "Sur le front anglais de la Somme," and "L'Épreuve alsacienne," in *Lettres à un jeune Français*, 205, 92; "La Victoire française" and "Paroles pour la France," *L'Heure du droit*, 15, 37; "L'Effort italien," in *Sur les routes du droit*, 248.

74 Barthou, "Toute la France pour toute la guerre," "Le Soldat français," in *Sur les routes du droit*, 38–132; *Le Temps*, 28 October 1916, 3; "L'Emprunt de la victoire," *L'Heure du droit*, 52–4; "Souscrire, c'est combattre," *Annales* (11 November 1917): 414.

75 Barthou, "Aux vaillantes," *NR* 29 (1917): 15–17; "L'Effort de la femme française," in *Sur les routes du droit*, 133–71; and *Le Temps*, 20 April 1917, 4.

76 Barthou, "Les Sports bienfaisants," *Annales* (1 May 1917): 513.

77 Barthou to Loti, 6, 13, 17 June 1917, Collection Loti-Viaud.

78 Poincaré, *Au service*, 9:276; Ribot, *Journal*, 197.

79 Poincaré, *Au service*, 9:283.

80 Ibid., 9:371.

81 David Watson, *Georges Clemenceau: A Political Biography* (London: Eyre Methuen 1974), 265.

82 Becker, "Louis Barthou devant la guerre," in *Barthou, un homme, une époque*, ed. Papy, 162. The irony is that Painlevé, much influenced by advisers sympathetic to a negotiated peace, had felt politically compelled to take Barthou as foreign minister – a man whom he knew to be against "a compromise peace." See D. Stephenson, *French War Aims against Germany, 1914–1919* (Oxford: Clarendon Press 1982), 91–2.

83 J.-B. Duroselle, in his new biography, *Clemenceau* (Paris: Fayard 1988), says nothing about this alleged misgiving. By inference, it seems only

that Clemenceau wanted Pichon at the Foreign ministry, a post Barthou apparently wanted to retain. See page 633.

84 Barthou to Anatole France, 26 September 1917, BN, Papiers Anatole France, n.a.f. vol. 15430, f. 188; and France to Barthou, 11 October 1917, Collection Lamirault.

85 Poincaré, *Au service*, 9:288–9, 338; Ribot, *Journal*, 205, 230–1.

86 Barthou, "L'Amérique Latine," in *Sur les routes du droit*, 254; "Le dernier quart d'heure," *Lectures pour tous* (1 October 1917): 5; JO, Chamber Debates, 25 October 1917, 2779; and *Le Figaro*, 26 October 1917.

87 Barthou, "Aux morts pour la patrie," *Le Temps*, 3 November 1917, 4. For the origins and employment of the term *jusqu'auboutiste*, see Catherine Slater, *Defeatists and Their Enemies: Political Invective in France, 1914–1918* (Oxford: Oxford University Press 1981), 139–54.

88 Audition of foreign minister Barthou, 12 November 1917, Commission des Affaires Étrangères, Archives du Sénat.

89 Barthou speech on Ribot, 12 June 1924, AF, 47; Ribot, *Journal*, 236–7, 239, 242; Poincaré, *Au service*, 9:321.

90 Poincaré, *Au service*, 9:321.

91 Ibid., 9:332; "French War Aims," *The Times*, 17 October 1917, 7.

92 Poincaré, *Au service*, 9:357–8.

93 Duroselle, *Clemenceau*, 633.

94 Poincaré, *Au service*, 9:366–71.

95 The italics are those of Barthou in *Le Politique*, 101. Note: Jean-Jacques Cazaurang says categorically that Léronensius is indeed Barthou himself. See his "Louis Barthou," *Pau Catalogue*, 9.

96 Barthou to France, 21 February 1918, BN, Papiers Anatole France, n.a.f. vol. 15430, f. 194.

97 Barthou to France, 6 April 1918, ibid., f. 197.

98 Barthou to France, 26 April 1918, ibid., f. 200. Barthou to Loti, telegrams of 18 March, 23 April, 12 May. A letter of 21 April reports that the operation on Alice was performed in her mother's apartment; another letter, of 24 May, reports the maid's operation. Collection Loti-Viaud.

99 Barthou, "Une Lettre d'Amérique," *Annales* (26 May 1918): 432; "L'Erreur de nos ennemis," *Lectures pour tous* (1 June 1918): 1162–4.

100 Barthou to Loti, 6 June 1918, Collection Loti-Viaud.

101 Poincaré, *Au service*, 10:155, 198.

102 Ibid., 10:163–4, 360–1.

103 Barthou, "Sous les griffes du Tigre," *Annales* (15 December 1929): 543; "De la guerre à la paix," ibid. (2 December 1932): 471.

104 Barthou preface for his *Sur les routes du droit*, 5.

105 From Lamartine's poem "L'Isolement." See Barthou, "À l'ombre du clocher de Milly: Lamartine intime," *Conférencia* (1 March 1917):

258; "L'Élection de Lamartine à l'Académie Française," *RP* (15 September 1916): 303–23; "Victor Hugo à douze ans," *RH* no. 2 (1914): 161–90; "La Jeunesse de Victor Hugo," *Lectures pour tous* (15 July 1914): 1690–7; *Les Obsèques d'Édouard Pelletan* (Paris: Imprimerie nationale 1914); "Lamartine et la *politique rationale*," in *A. Lamartine, 1833–1913* (Paris: Plon 1914), 9–32; "Un Discours inédit de Lamartine," *Annales de l'Académie de Mâcon* (1914–15), 64–84; *Autour de Baudelaire* (Paris: Maison du Livre 1917).

106 Barthou, *Lamartine orateur* (Paris: Hachette 1916), 32–3.

107 Ibid., 163.

108 He was elected by twenty of the twenty-seven votes cast. See "Minutes des procès-verbaux. Correspondance 1918," AF Archives, Carton 5B41; Poincaré, *Au service*, 10:156; *Le Temps*, 3 May 1918.

109 Barthou reception speech, AF, 6 February 1919, 5.

110 Donnay response, ibid., 60.

CHAPTER SEVEN

1 Barthou, *À la mémoire de Delcassé: Discours ... le 3 Octobre 1934* (Paris: Société d'Éditions Géographiques, Maritimes et Coloniales 1935), 19–20.

2 See chapter 5, page 100.

3 Maurice Paléologue, *Journal, 1913–1914* (Paris: Plon 1947), 163, 205–6. Barthou's marginal involvement in the diplomacy of 1913 is even more evident in Paléologue's "Comment le service de trois ans fut rétabli en 1913," *RDDM* (1, 15 May 1935): 67–94, 307–44.

4 Gerd Krumeich, *Armaments and Politics in France on the Eve of the First World War* (Leamington Spa: Berg Publishers 1984), 17–18, 232–3.

5 See his deposition of 23 December 1919, in connection with the Caillaux treason trial. Fonds Roche-Caillaux, dossier 6, FNSP. Also Paléologue, *Journal*, 211; and chapter 5, pages 105–6.

6 Barthou, "Une Lettre d'Amérique," *Annales* (May 1918); preface for Paul Gauthier, *Leçons morales de la guerre* (Paris: Flammarion 1919), iii; Chamber Foreign Affairs Committee, 2 November 1918, AN, C7491, 35–6.

7 Poincaré, *Au service de la France* (Paris: Plon 1926–33), 10:163–4.

8 See meetings of 3, 7, 8 May 1918, Chamber Foreign Affairs committee, AN C7491.

9 Ibid., 2 August 1918, 61.

10 Ibid., 31 October and 2 November.

11 Ibid., 24 January 1919.

12 Ibid., 5 February 1919.

13 For his impressions of Doumer, see "Au seuil du nouveau septennat," *Annales* (1 June 1931): 509–10.
14 Barthou, "Crimes et châtiments. Notre victoire," *RH* no. 5 (1919), 141–59.
15 See meetings of 27 November 1918 and 20 January 1919, Foreign Affairs Committee, AN, C7491.
16 Chamber Peace Treaties committee, 8–9 July 1919, AN, C7773. See also Pierre Miquel, *La Paix de Versailles et l'opinion publique française* (Paris: Flammarion 1972), 549.
17 Peace Treaties committee, 8–9 July 1919, AN, C7773. Marshal Ferdinand Foch had served as commander-in-chief of the allied armies during the last year of the war.
18 Ibid., 16 July 1919.
19 Ibid., 17 July 1919.
20 See ibid., meetings of 25, 28 July and 1 August.
21 Barthou, *Le Traité de paix* (Paris: Bibliothèque Charpentier 1919), 4, 174. See also *JO*, Chamber Debates, 2–3 September 1919, 4099–4114, 4124–9; and 18 September, 4422–3.
22 Ibid., 10, 49, 65, 155–6.
23 Barthou to Loti, 2 September 1919, Collection Loti-Viaud; *JO*, Chamber Debates, 24 September 1919, 4543–52.
24 Georges Lecomte described Barthou's hearing as exceptional. He heard everything around him, Lecomte said, even whispers, and what he did not hear, he seemed to deduce. See his "Louis Barthou à l'Académie," *Illustration* (hors-série, October 1934); n.p.
25 See *JO*, Chamber Debates, 24 September 1919, 4553; Barthou, *Le Politique* (Paris: Hachette, 1923), 68; and Graham to Curzon, 25 September 1919, *Documents on British Foreign Policy*, 1st series, vol. 5, no. 146, 574–7.
26 See Barthou's "Sous les griffes du Tigre," *Annales* (15 December 1929): 543–5; "L'Esprit de la politique," *Conférencia* (1 March 1933): 267–82; "De la guerre à la paix," *Annales* (2 December 1932): 471–2.
27 *JO*, Chamber Debates, 25 March 1920, 711–18.
28 Ibid., 717–18.
29 Chamber Foreign Affairs committee, 14, 30 April and 17, 27 May 1920, Ass. Nat.
30 Barthou, "La Situation," *Annales* (20 June, 24 October 1920): 324–5.
31 Ibid.
32 Barthou, "La Situation," *Annales* (8 August 1920): 104–5; (19 September 1920): 224–5.
33 Ibid. (18 July 1920): 44–5; (9 January 1921).
34 Ibid. (1 August 1920): 84–5; (14 November): 386–7; (21 November): 406–7.

35 Ibid. (11 July 1920): 23–3; (1 August): 84–5; (22 August): 144–5; (5 September): 184–5.

36 J.J. Cazaurang, "Un Ouvrage peu connu de Louis Barthou," RRP (July-December 1977): 176–7.

37 Barthou, "Les Raisons de la France," Annales (14 April 1933): 413–14.

38 Barthou to Lyautey, 9 November 1920, Papiers Lyautey, AN; Barthou to Loti, 21 April 1921, Collection Loti-Viaud. See also Barthou, "La Situation," in Annales of 28 November, 12 December 1920, and 16 January 1921. Barthou had served during the war, and in the immediate post-war period, as president of the Comité de l'Orient, an organization which represented French business interests in the Turkish empire. See Christopher M. Andrew and A.S. Kanya-Forstner, France Overseas: The Great War and the Climax of French Imperial Expansion (London: Thames and Hudson 1981), 125, 199.

39 JO, Chamber Debates, 22 April 1921, 1883.

40 Barthou, "La Situation," Annales (January 1921); also JO, Chamber Debates, 17 December 1920, 3731–2.

41 Barthou to Loti, 23 January 1921, Collection Loti-Viaud. On the constitution of this cabinet, and British appraisals of Barthou, see Hardinge to Curzon, 17, 18 January 1921, PRO, FO 371, 6981, W650/247/17, W715/247/17.

42 Barthou to Lyautey, 26 May 1921, AN, Fonds Lyautey.

43 Chamber Army committee, 21 February 1921, Ass. Nat. and 23 February 1921, Senate Army committee, Sénat.

44 Army Committee, 23 February 1921, Sénat.

45 Barthou to Loti, 13 May 1921, Collection Loti-Viaud. See also Judith M. Hughes, To the Maginot Line (Cambridge, Mass.: Harvard University Press 1971), 119–20.

46 Serge Berstein, "Le Rôle politique national de Louis Barthou de 1919 à 1934," in Barthou un homme, une époque, ed. Michel Papy (Pau: J. et D. Éditions 1986), 119.

47 See Army committee, 21 February 1921, Ass. Nat.; Army committee, 23 February, Sénat.

48 Army committee, 8 June 1921, Sénat.

49 JO, Chamber Debates, 4 March 1921, 1109–12; Army committee, 21 February 1921, and 23 November, Ass. Nat., Finance committee, 17 October 1921, Ass. Nat.

50 Army committee, 6 July 1921, Ass. Nat.

51 JO, Lois et Décrets, 28 August 1921, 10020. His position, though appropriately not his language, has been adopted by Dan P. Silverman, Reconstructing Europe after the Great War (Cambridge, Mass.: Harvard University Press 1982), v–vi.

52 JO, Lois et Décrets, 12 September 1921, 10479.

53 Barthou, "Discours sur Napoléon," *La Vie des peuples* no. 4 (1921): 11.

54 Barthou, "La Situation," *Annales* (18 July 1920), 44–5; (8 August 1920), 104–5.

55 Louise Weiss, *Mémoires d'une européenne*, 3 vols. (Paris: Payot 1968–70), 2:159; Sir John Wheeler-Bennett, *Knaves, Fools and Heroes in Europe between the Wars* (London: St Martin's Press 1974), 161. Georges Bonnet also refers to Barthou's rumoured role, in *Quai d'Orsay* (Isle of Man: Times Press 1965), 50; as does Édouard Bonnefous, *Histoire politique de la Troisième République*: vol. 3, *L'Après guerre, 1919–1924* (Paris: PUF 1959), 299.

56 See Vercors, *Moi Aristide Briand* (Paris: Plon 1981), 224–30; Pierre Miquel, *Poincaré* (Paris: Fayard 1961), 440; Jacques Chabannes, *Aristide Briand, Le Père de l'Europe* (Paris: Perrin 1973), 213–30.

57 Carole Fink, *The Genoa Conference: European Diplomacy, 1921–1922* (Chapel Hill: University of North Carolina Press 1984), 85, 139.

58 For instance when, on 11 April, he agreed to a delay in the conference proceedings on the request of the Russian Chicherin. See Barthou to Poincaré, 6 May 1922, MAE série Y, Conférence de Gênes, vol. 29: 34. For his complaints about the quality of the instructions, see telegram of 11 April and note of 13 April, ibid., 32:82.

59 Barthou to Poincaré, 16 April, and Poincaré to Barthou, 17 April, MAE, Y, vol. 29: 191, 222.

60 See communications of 19, 20, 21 April, between Poincaré and Barthou, MAE, Y, vol. 30: 57, 112–16, 200.

61 Once again, see the exchanges of 22–3 April 1922, MAE, Y, vol. 31: 8–11, 33–4.

62 Barthou to Poincaré, 25, 29 April, MAE, Y, vol. 31: 79, 99–100.

63 Poincaré to Barthou, 30 April, MAE, Y, vol. 31: 141–4; Barthou to Poincaré, ibid., 151.

64 Weiss, *Mémoires*, 2:160–1, 169. Less acerbic in tone, sixty years later, Mme Weiss displayed no sign of any second thoughts on Barthou. Interview of 3 May 1982.

65 Jean de Pierrefeu, *La Saison diplomatique. Gênes (Avril-Mai 1922)* (Paris: Éditions Montaigne 1928), 148–52; also his "Un Touriste à Gênes," *Illustration* (29 April 1922), 377–8. For similarly sympathetic reports of Barthou's role at Genoa, see *L'Indépendant*, 15, 25 April 1922.

66 Weiss, *Mémoires*, 2:169–72. See also Paul Cambon, *Correspondance, 1870–1924*, 3 vols. (Paris: Grasset 1940), 3:408. Charles Benoist was another who thought Barthou exaggerated and exploited his role as middleman between Lloyd George and Poincaré. See *Souvenirs de Charles Benoist* (Paris: Plon 1933–34), 3:195.

67 Pierrefeu, *La Saison diplomatique*, 166–7.

68 Poincaré to Barthou, 5 May 1922, MAE, Y, vol. 32: 174–8.

69 Barthou to Poincaré, 6 May 1922, MAE, Relations Commerciales, Conférence de Gênes, vol. 97: 67. See also Barthou, "De Bossuet à Briand en passant par Moscou," *Annales* (15 January 1930).

70 The two best accounts of Barthou's role at Genoa, and the dilemmas he faced thanks to "l'incompréhension totale de Paris," are Renata Bournazel, *Rapallo: Naissance d'un mythe* (Paris: FNSP and Colin 1974), 151–74; and Stephen A. Schuker, *The End of French Predominance in Europe: The Financial Crisis of 1924 and the Adoption of the Dawes Plan* (Chapel Hill: University of North Carolina Press 1976), 205–7.

71 Pierrefeu claims that the British account derived from the senior French journalist André Géraud (Pertinax). He suspects that Barthou had primed Géraud so as to ensure that Lloyd George was hauled up abruptly. Such, at least, is the implication in *La Saison diplomatique*, 183–204.

72 Weiss, *Mémoires*, 2:171. Barthou first informed Poincaré of his issued denial, and then two days later sent the minutes of the meeting to Paris – minutes which do have Lloyd George saying: "Peut-être eut-on à un tournant dans l'histoire des relations franco-britanniques" and Barthou protesting that he "n'aurait pas voulu entendre de telles paroles!" See Barthou to Poincaré, 9, 11 May 1922, MAE, Relations Commerciales, Conférence de Gênes, vol. 97: 149–50, 207–22.

73 Poincaré had hoped Viviani would take the Reparations Commission, and that Barthou would go to Berlin as ambassador. However, Viviani declined the offer because of commitments in Geneva, and Barthou refused the embassy posting because Alice could not bear being among Germans. See Bernard Auffray, *Pierre de Margerie et la vie diplomatique de son temps* (Paris: Librairie Klincksieck 1976), 399.

74 *The Times*, 6 October 1922, 9.

75 Délégation française à la commission des réparations, 17 October 1922, AN, AJ5 535.

76 In fact, Bradbury predicted they were heading for a "breaking point," despite conciliatory behaviour from Barthou. Treasury to FO, 23 October 1922, PRO, FO 371, 7486, C 14509/99/18. For reports on Barthou's performance in Berlin during the Commission's visit there, see Saint-Quentin to Poincaré, 1 November 1922, MAE, Z (Réparations), vol. 476: 93–5.

77 René Girault, Robert Frank, *Turbulente Europe et nouveaux mondes, 1914–1941* (Paris: Masson 1988), 133. Such an operation was first discussed in detail during a joint session of the Chamber's Finance and Foreign Affairs committees on 7 June 1922. See Denise Artaud, "À propos de l'occupation de la Ruhr," *Revue d'histoire moderne et contemporaine* 17 (January-March 1970): 3; and Georges Soutu, "Le coke dans les relations internationales en Europe de 1914 au plan Dawes," *Rela-*

tions internationales no. 43 (Autumn 1985): 249–67. By 23 November everything was in place, as Poincaré made clear to a special Franco-Belgian meeting in Paris, a meeting attended by Louis Barthou. MAE, Z (Réparations), vol. 476: 212.

78 Poincaré to the London embassy, 29 November 1922, MAE, Z, vol. 476: 241. Barthou's perspective is best developed in his very lengthy history/report of 15 June 1924, MAE, Z, vol. 488: 22–3.

79 Délégation française, Commission des Réparations, 26 December 1922, AN, AJ5 535.

80 Barthou to Lyautey, 2 January 1923, AN, Fonds Lyautey.

81 Commission des Réparations, 8–9 January 1923, AN, AJ5 535.

82 *Le Temps*, 25 April 1923, 2. In March he had published a front-page article defending the occupation. See *L'Indépendant*, 7 March 1924. For Poincaré's own reluctance to resort to the occupation, see Sally Marks, "The Misery of Victory: France's Struggle for the Versailles Treaty," *Historical Papers*, Canadian Historical Association (1986): 117–33.

83 Barthou, "Les Espérances Françaises," RH (1924): 131–58; also a long report on his speech of 25 January 1924, Crewe to FO, PRO, FO 371, 9730, C2540/32/18.

84 Délégation française, Commission des Réparations, 9 April 1924, AN, AJ5 536. For the suggestion that Barthou was a moderating influence on Poincaré – in connection with the Committee of Experts – see Paul Reynaud, *Mémoires*: vol. 1, *Venu de ma montagne* (Paris: Flammarion 1960), 174.

85 Jacques Bariéty has argued, without any reference to Barthou, that Poincaré was coming round to a more flexible stance on his own initiative. See *Les Relations franco-allemandes après la première guerre mondiale, 10 novembre 1918–10 janvier 1925* (Paris: Pedone 1977), 265, 274.

86 Impressions of this exchange derive once again from Barthou's comprehensive report of 15 June 1924, MAE, Z (Réparations), vol. 488: 13–49. Stéphane Lauzanne later told readers of *Le Matin*: "C'est à M. Barthou que nous devons le plan Dawes." Reprinted in *L'Indépendant*, 22 April 1925.

87 For Poincaré's apprehensions (and implicit complaints), see his note to Barthou, 12 April 1924, MAE, Z, vol. 488: 38–41. See also Édouard Herriot, *Jadis*, 2 vols. (Paris: Flammarion 1948–52), vol. 2, *D'une guerre à l'autre*, 133. One might also note that *Le Temps*, 20 July 1926, carried a report that Herriot had offered Barthou the Finance portfolio in 1924, but that the latter had declined on the grounds of insufficient experience for such a ministry.

88 Délégation française, Commission des Réparations, 9 August; 8, 11 September 1924, AN, AJ5 536.

89 Ibid., 9 December 1924.

90 Ibid., 24 August 1926. These judgments were echoed by Marshal Pétain, who said of him: "Nul mieux que lui ne savait entretenir la conversation, élever le débat, empêcher les apartés, provoquer la gaieté." See General Laure, *Pétain* (Paris: Berger-Levrault 1941), 410.

91 See the first note for this chapter.

CHAPTER EIGHT

1 As quoted by Georges Coustel, "Sur Louis Barthou. Anecdotes et souvenirs," *La République des Pyrénées*, undated press clipping, in "Dossier de presse: Tome B," Bibliothèque municipale de Pau.

2 Commission des Réparations, 24 August 1926, AN, AJ5 536.

3 Serge Berstein, "Le Rôle politique," in *Barthou, un homme, une époque*, ed. Michel Papy (Pau: J. et D. Éditions 1986), 124.

4 Barthou, "La Situation," *Annales* (19 December 1920): 517.

5 Paul Reynaud, *Mémoires*, 2 vols. (Paris: Flammarion 1960–63), 1: 137–8.

6 Barthou, *Le Politique* (Paris: Hachette 1923), 32. A typical generational perspective consistent with Ortega y Gasset's generational theory. See Julian Marias, *Generations: A Historical Method*, trans. Harold Raley (University, Alabama: University of Alabama Press 1967), 69–106.

7 Barthou, *Le Politique*, 86–9; "La Situation," *Annales* (4 July 1920): 2–3; "Propos Libres," *Annales* (15 October 1930): n.p.

8 *Pau Catalogue*, 40; *Le Temps*, 17 July 1922; *l'Indépendant*, 18 July 1922.

9 Barthou reception speech, 6 February 1919, AF, 17.

10 Barthou, "La Politique reprend ses droits," *RP* (15 February 1919): 677.

11 Ibid., 678–9; "La Situation," *Annales* (26 September 1920): 244–5.

12 Barthou, "La Situation," *Annales* (26 September 1920): 244. See also the same column of 27 June, 3, 24, 31 October 1920.

13 Barthou to Lyautey, 9 December 1919, AN, Fonds Lyautey.

14 Barthou, "La Situation," *Annales* (5 September 1920): 184; "Crimes et châtiments," *RH* (1919): 157.

15 Barthou, "Pierre Loti – *Mon Frère Yves*," *Conférencia* (1 September 1933): 269–82; "Pierre Loti," *RDDM* (15 February 1930): 952–72; "Pierre Loti," in *Le Livre du centenaire: Cents ans de vie à la Revue des deux mondes* (Paris: Hachette 1929), 479–88; "Discours ... réception de M. Albert Besnard," 10 June 1926, AF, 29–63; "Discours ... à Hendaye," 7 September 1930, AF; preface for N. Serban, *Pierre Loti. Sa Vie et son oeuvre* (Paris: Les presses françaises 1924), i–xiii; *Pêcheur d'Islande de Pierre Loti: Étude et analyse* (Paris: Librairie Mellottée 1929).

16 François Marin, "Louis Barthou et Anatole France," *RRP* January-June 1984): 34–5.
17 Barthou, "Anatole France sans la politique," *Conférencia* (1 May 1925): 472; "Anatole France, commis-bibliothécaire au Sénat," *RP* 6 (1 December 1924): 481–90; *Bibliothèque de M. Louis Barthou*, 4 vols. (Paris: Auguste Blaizot 1935), 2, no. 946, France to Barthou, 1 January 1915, 230.
18 Barthou, "Anatole France sans la politique," 460; "Sur Anatole France," *RF* 3 (May-June 1926): 601–30; "Anatole France – *Les Dieux ont soif*," *Conférencia* (1 May 1933): 477–91.
19 Barthou to Lyautey, 31 August 1922 and 27 August 1924, AN, Fonds Lyautey.
20 In particular, see Valéry's inscription for his *Odes, Aurore, La Pythie, Palme* in vol. 1, no. 373, of *Bibliothèque Barthou*. Though undated, the inscription seems to have been done between 1922, when Barthou was at Justice, and 1925, when Valéry entered the Académie. Note also the entry of March 1922 where Valéry is identified as Barthou's most recent literary passion, in Maurice Martin du Gard, *Les Mémorables*, 3 vols. (Paris: Flammarion 1957–78), 2:221–2.
21 See chapter 6, pages 128–9, note 33. Also Aubert, *De l'histoire et des histoires: Souvenirs d'un journaliste* (Bordeaux: Éditions Delmas 1943), 97.
22 Jourdan, "Louis Barthou et le département des Basses-Pyrénées, 1919–1934," in *Barthou, un homme, une époque*, ed. Papy, 68 and his endnote 97. Note the absence of a single reference to Barthou in Marguerite Léon-Bérard's "Souvenir de mon père," *RDDM* (1 July 1968): 43–56. See also *L'Indépendant*, 23 December 1926, for open reference to this continuing tension. For more recent treatment of the "rupture," see Pierre Arette Lendresse, *Léon Bérard, 1876–1960* (Pau: J. et D. Éditions 1988), 48–50.
23 Aubert, *De l'histoire*, 143; Lendresse, *Léon Bérard*, 34. Madame Roland-Marcel, while confirming the war issue, gives more emphasis to the basic incompatibility of their personalities. "Il y avait une antinomie entre eux complète." Interview, 27 April 1982.
24 Aubert, *De l'histoire*, 196.
25 Barthou, *Le Politique*, 94.
26 *JO*, Chamber Debates, 21 June 1927, 2002. For further information on the Philippe Daudet affair and ensuing events, see Éric Vatré, *Léon Daudet ou le libre réactionnaire* (Paris: Éditions France-Empire 1987), 160–82; also the background report prepared by the British embassy in Paris. Phipps to Austen Chamberlain, 15 June 1927, PRO, FO 371, 12637, W5495/5495/17.
27 *JO*, Chamber Debates, 21 June 1927, 2002.

28 Reynaud, *Mémoires*, 1:143. Dossier "Philippe Daudet," and report of July 1929 on Léon Daudet, Archives de la Préfecture de Police, BA1 (1583). For other academicians attacked by Daudet, see his *Verts de l'Académie et vers de presse* (Paris: Éditions du Capitole 1930); for other politicians, see his *Député de Paris* (Paris: Grasset 1933).

29 Daudet, *L'Agonie du régime: Panorama des hommes, des clans et des crimes, 1919–1925* (Paris: Nouvelle Librairie Nationale 1925), 43–4. Émile Henriot described Daudet as an excellent portrait painter of those he liked, but a devastating caricaturist of his opponents – one with a talent for the "trait excessif ... déformant." See Henriot, *Maîtres d'hier et contemporain* (Paris: Albin Michel 1956), 292–3.

30 See unsigned press clipping from *Action française*, 19 July 1927, in "Dossier Barthou," Préfecture, BA257; also Charles Maurras, *Le Bibliophile Barthou* (Paris: Éditions du Capitole 1929), 177.

31 Daudet, "Barthou et les papiers secrets de Hugo," *Action française*, 7 July 1927.

32 Daudet, *Le Garde des seaux: Louis Barthou* (Paris: Éditions du Capitole 1930), 118–24; *Souvenirs politiques* (Paris: Éditions Albatros 1974), 197, 206.

33 Daudet, *Garde des seaux*, 120, 123, 173. See also his *La Police politique* (Paris: Denoël et Steele 1934).

34 Zeldin identifies three large loopholes in French libel laws in this period – the infrequency of conviction by juries, the opportunity for right of reply (which allowed for the original accusations to be repeated), and the sense that alleged defamation against public office holders was usually only an expression of freedom of information for voters. See Theodore Zeldin, *France, 1848–1945*: vol. 2, *Intellect, Taste and Anxiety* (Oxford: Clarendon Press 1973), 548–9. This is a judgment confirmed by the distinguished historian of the French press M. Pierre Albert, in an interview of 25 February 1982.

35 Martin du Gard, *Les Mémorables*, 2:307.

36 Barthou, *Émile Garet* (Pau: Imprimerie Garet 1912), 24; *Autour de Baudelaire* (Paris: Maison du Livre 1917), 28; "Fêtes du centenaire d'Ernest Renan," 2 September 1923, AF, 35; "Inauguration ... Méline," 28 August 1928, JO, *Lois et Décrets*, 9787; *Le Maréchal Joffre* (Paris: Plon 1931), 26.

37 René Rémond, "Louis Barthou historien," and Jean Estèbe, "Louis Barthou écrivain," in *Barthou, un homme, une époque*, ed. Papy, 206, 202.

38 Barthou, "Impressions brèves d'un vieux bibliophile," *Illustration*, Noël 1928, n.p.

39 I am indebted to a number of people in Paris who, in the course of casual conversation, spoke with good-natured candour of fellow bib-

liophiles. My thanks to Mme Pierre Bouchet, Messieurs Benoit-Cattin, Schuck, and Droin of *Le Livre contemporain*, M. Castaing of Charavay, M. Kieffer of the Librairie Kieffer.

40 Zeldin says that "wives were so keen to transform themselves from brides into matriarchs that adultery and prostitution were essential to the working of the system." See *Ambition, Love and Politics*, 303–5; also Paul Allard, *Les Favorites de la Troisième République* (Paris: Éditions de la France 1942).

41 Anonymous, "Louis Barthou," in *Ceux qui nous mènent* (Paris: Plon 1922), 4–5. The sole exception is the refuted allegation which emerged in the Cornudet affair. See chapter 3, page 49, note 37.

42 Daudet, *Garde des seaux*, 100–1; Octave Homberg, *Les Coulisses de l'histoire* (Paris: Fayard 1938), 42; Léon Noel, *La Tchécoslovaquie devant Munich* (Paris: Plon 1982), 167; Geneviève Tabouis, *Vingt ans de "suspense" diplomatique* (Paris: Albin Michel 1958), 200. See also Hervé Lucbéreilh, "Louis Barthou, orateur et bibliophile," RRP (January-June 1984): 63.

43 Though this evidence is similarly impressionistic, it is worth recording that Maître Marcel Gilbert believes Barthou enjoyed "beaucoup de succès féminins." Mme Lamarque recalls that in Pau Barthou had the reputation of being a bit of a woman-chaser; Mme Roland-Marcel also thinks it quite probable that Barthou was no stranger to sexual affairs outside his marriage. Interviews, respectively, of 4 May 1982, 7 April 1982, 27 April 1982. It should be noted that the man each remembers was the Barthou of the post-1914 period.

44 Army committee, 6 July 1921, Ass. Nat. For a series of press reports on his attacks on the communists in 1926, see *L'Indépendant*, 14 June 1926.

45 *JO*, Chamber Debates, 10 May 1927, 1359; and 10 June, 1831–2.

46 *JO*, Chamber Debates, 10 June 1927, 1832. For the legal action undertaken by the Justice ministry against Doriot, see *Le Temps*, 21–2, 26 May; 8, 9, 12, 14 June 1927.

47 *L'Humanité*, 11 June 1927.

48 *JO*, Chamber Debates, 14 June 1918, 1938.

49 Legislation committee, 17 July 1929, Ass. Nat.

50 Though this is not to be taken at face value, Barthou once laughingly dismissed the impact of the hostile press by describing an old "dodge" learned from Clemenceau: "do not read the papers, particularly do not read those that attack you. The most important thing for a political leader is to have a reliable friend who can be trusted to sift the papers." D'Abernon to FO, 9 November 1922, PRO, FO 371, C15606/99/18.

51 Jean Toulet, "Louis Barthou, une époque de la bibliophilie," in

Barthou, un homme, une époque, ed. Papy, 187–96; Robert J. Young, "La Cité des Livres," *Bull. du bib.* no. 4, (1983): 448–59; *Bibliothèque de M. Barthou,* 4 vols; Seymour de Ricci, *Quelques Bibliophiles:* vol. 3, *Louis Barthou* (Paris: Plaisir du Bibliophile 1927).

52 Seymour de Ricci, "Louis Barthou, bibliophile," *Nouvelles littéraires* (13 October 1934): n.p.

53 Jean Toulet, "Louis Barthou ... bibliophile," in *Barthou, un homme, une époque,* ed. Papy, 195.

54 Interview with Madame Pierre Bouchet, 8 June 1982.

55 Barthou, "De Villon à Montaigne," *Conférencia* (15 May 1920): 522.

56 Expressly on this theme, see his "La Séparation," *ARD* (19 March 1905): 1; "Quand Lyautey Parle," *RDDM* (15 May 1927): 256.

57 Barthou, *Rachel* (Paris: Librairie Alcan 1926).

58 Barthou, *La Vie amoureuse de Richard Wagner* (Paris: Flammarion 1925), 106.

59 Barthou's response to Alfred Besnard, 10 June 1926, AF, 61.

60 Barthou, *La Vie amoureuse,* 113–14.

61 Barthou, *Le Neuf Thermidor* (Paris: Hachette 1926), 16. Barthou remained active in the Société de l'histoire de la Révolution Française, as is evidenced by reports in *Le Temps,* 23, 30 April 1929. See also chapter 4, pages 89–90, note 72.

62 "Gardez-nous vos jeudis, Monsieur," he told Henri Robert when the latter entered the Academy, 12 June 1924, AF, 72. See also his "Les Quarantes sont quarante," *Cahiers* (August 1930): 695–703. On Barthou as grammatical stickler, see *Le Temps,* 13 April 1921, and Maxime Weygand, *Mémoires,* vol. 2 (Paris: Flammarion 1957), 362–3.

63 These included Maurice Donnay, Alfred Capus, Robert de Flers, Henri Régnier, Jean Richepin, Jules Cambon, and Gabriel Hanotaux. See Horace de Carbuccia, *Le Massacre de la victoire, 1919–1934* (Paris: Plon 1973), 33.

64 George Lecomte, "Louis Barthou à l'Académie," *L'Illustration* (October 1934): n.p.; Abel Hermant, "Louis Barthou," unidentified press clipping from "Dossier Barthou" in BHVP.

65 Carbuccia, *Le Massacre,* 43–4; Martin du Gard, *Les Mémorables,* 2:304; Maurice Donnay, "Louis Barthou," unidentified press clipping from "Dossier Barthou" in BHVP.

66 Marc Martin, "'La grande famille': L'Association des journalistes parisiens, 1885–1939," *Revue historique* (January-March 1986): 149, *Le Temps,* 22 January 1925, 3.

67 Barthou preface for Stéphane Lauzanne, *Sa Majesté la presse* (Paris: Fayard 1925), 15; "L'Esprit de la politique," *Conférencia* (1 March 1933): 274.

68 Barthou preface for Henri Robert, *Les Grands Procès de l'histoire* (Paris: Payot 1931), xiv.

69 Maurice Donnay to Barthou, 23 April 1927; Jules Cambon to Barthou, 13 September 1921; Caillaux to Barthou, 19 August, 17 September, 15 November 1927; 20, 23 January and 4 September 1928. Collection Roland-Marcel; Barthou to Lyautey, 7 August 1926, AN, Fonds Lyautey.

70 Derème to Barthou, 19 June 1927, Collection Roland-Marcel; Barthou to Derème, 8 June, 4 July 1927, in J.A. Catala, *Le Bibliophile et le poète: Trente cinq lettres de Louis Barthou à Tristan Derème (1919–1934)* (Bordeaux: Imprimerie Taffard 1966), 7–12; Barthou to Lucien Pallez, 19 April 1927, "Dossier Louis Barthou," Fonds Ritter, Archives départementales des Pyrénées Atlantiques; Barthou to M. Léautaud, June-July 1928, "Louis Barthou. Correspondance," Série Léautaud, Bibliothèque Jacques Doucet.

71 *Le Livre contemporain* (Annuaire 1953), 20–1; Raymond Hesse, *Histoire des sociétés de bibliophiles en France de 1820 à 1930*, 2 vols. (Paris: Giraud Badin, 1929–31), which shows Barthou as being a member as well of "Hippocrate et ses amis," and "Société de Saint-Éloy." Seymour de Ricci says Barthou first joined, in 1889, the oldest of the French bibliophilic societies, "Les Amis des Livres." See *Quelques Bibliophiles*, 4.

72 Derème to Barthou, 20 October 1927, Collection Roland-Marcel; André Gaudelette de la Morlière, "Présence de Louis Barthou," *Journal de Vichy*, 27 June 1952; Émile Henriot, "Les Amis des livres," *Le Figaro littéraire*, 13 October 1934. See Barthou's presentation volume to Finaly of *Le Traité de paix*, bound by Marius Michel and containing the original manuscript of his report on Versailles, Bib. Ass. Nat. For his gift to the Academy of two volumes of letters written by Sully-Prudhomme to Alice's grandmother, Mme Alice Amile Amiel, see "Dossier Louis Barthou," BHVP.

73 Gustave Samazeuil, "Le Mélomane," *Le Figaro littéraire* (13 October 1934).

74 See police report of 5–15 January 1929, "Barthou," Préfecture, BA257; Charles Maurras, "Pujo reste avec les Apaches," *L'Action française*, 1 July 1927. For Tardieu's offer of a post, communicated by Étienne Clémentel, see *Le Temps*, 2–3 November 1929, 2, 1.

75 "Une Française au grand coeur," *L'Illustration* (25 January 1930): 135; *Le Temps*, 18 January 1930, 8. *L'Indépendant*, 16, 17 January 1930.

76 Ugo Ojetti, "Le Souvenir de Louis Barthou," unidentified press clipping, "Dossier Barthou," BHVP.

77 Barthou, *Le Politique*, 11–14. Here I infer from his positive appraisal of such women that Alice was among them.

78 Interview with Madame Souchère, 30 April 1982.
79 Pierre Benoit, "Souvenirs," *Le Figaro littéraire* (13 October 1934).
80 Barthou to Suzanne Cappiello, 28 January 1930, Collection Cappiello. See also a letter of 21 September 1929, in which he refers to his wife's suffering.
81 See untitled, unidentified press clipping of a piece by A. Chesnier du Chesne, in "Dossier Barthou," BHVP.

CHAPTER NINE

1 Barthou, "1934. La Paix ou la guerre," *Annales* (29 December 1933): n.p.
2 Barthou, "Propos Libres: La Paix légale et morale des consciences," *Annales* (1 February 1930): n.p.
3 Barthou, "Propos Libres ...," *Annales* (1 March 1930): 208. See also the same column for 15 March and 1 April; and also Monique Claque, "Vision and Myopia in the New Politics of André Tardieu," *FHS* 8, no. 1 (Spring 1973): 105–29.
4 Barthou, "Propos Libres ...," *Annales* (1 December 1930): n.p.
5 See the explanatory note accompanying his "La Vertu à l'Académie," *Annales* (15 December 1930); and "French Cabinet Crisis," in *The Times*, 8 December 1930, 12. The principal source of cabinet instability between 1928 and 1932, we are told, was the unwillingness of republican moderates like Barthou, Poincaré, and Leygues to envisage a coalition without the Radicals, with whom they felt a greater ideological affinity than they did with Tardieu's forces on the right. See Jean-Marie Mayeur, *La Vie politique sous la troisième république* (Paris: Éditions du Seuil 1984), 302.
6 In fact, Barthou intervened rarely in Senate debates during the 1930s.
7 Barthou, *Le Maréchal Joffre* (Paris: Plon 1931); also "Ce que Napoléon aurait fait sur la Marne," *Conférencia* (5 September 1931): 259–74; *Lyautey et le Maroc* (Paris: Éditions du *Petit Parisien* 1931); "Le 'Sourire' de Lyautey au Maroc," *RDDM* (1 December 1930): 580–90.
8 Barthou to Lyautey, 4 January 1932, AN, Fonds Lyautey. See also his "Sophie et Gabriel," *RP* (15 July 1931): 241–64.
9 See the report on his lecture to the Société de l'Histoire de la Révolution Française, at their accustomed venue of the Sorbonne, in *Le Temps*, 16 April 1932.
10 Barthou, *Danton* (Paris: Albin Michel 1932), 361.
11 Barthou, "Impressions de Bayreuth," *Annales* (1 September 1930): 193–5; "Richard Wagner cinquante ans après sa mort," *Annales*

(10 February 1933): 153–5; "Au retour de Bayreuth," *Cahiers* (1930): 577–83; "Richard Wagner et Judith Gauthier," *RP* (1, 15 August 1932): 481–98, 721–52.

12 Henry Malherbe, "Louis Barthou et la musique," *Feuilleton du Temps* (17 October 1934); Gustave Samazeuil, "Le Mélomane," *Le Figaro littéraire* (13 October 1934); Samazeuil, "Un Hommage à Louis Barthou," *La République des Pyrénées*, 26 November 1964; *Le Temps*, 29 October 1933, 3; Barthou preface for Léon Constantin, *Berlioz* (Paris: Éditions Émile-Paul Frères 1934), i–vii.

13 Barthou preface for Svend Dahl, *Histoire du livre de l'antiquité à nos jours* (Paris: Jules Lamarre 1933), v–vii; "L'Évolution artistique de la relieure," *Illustration* (Noël 1930); "Édouard Rahir," *Bull. du bib.* (1930): 101–12; "Un Décor de l''Odyssée' par F.L. Schmied," *Illustration* (September-December 1932).

14 Barthou, "Aristide Briand," *Annales* (15 March 1932): 231–2; "Discours au banquet Armand Godoy," *Le Manuscrit autographe* (October 1932): 89; "Anatole France – Les Dieux ont soif," *Conférencia* (1 May 1933): 477–91.

15 Barthou, "Souvenirs de la Rue Sablière," in *Plaisir du Béarn*, 25–37; préface for Pierre Daguerre, *Béarn et Béarnais* (Pau: Éditions de L'Indépendant 1933), i–vi, *Promenades autour de ma vie: Lettres de la montagne* (Paris: Les Laboratoires Martinet 1933), 14.

16 Barthou, "Le Général Lyautey jugé par ses lettres," *RH* 9 no. 3 (1920): 268; Pierre Tranchesse, "Promenade autour d'un livre," *RRP* (January-June 1984): 5–21.

17 Barthou, *Promenades*, 80–1, 112–13, 150.

18 Ibid., 81, 106, 193, 198.

19 Ibid., 118, 193.

20 Compte d'exécution testamentaire de la succession de Monsieur Barthou, 10 May 1937. This document includes the *testament mystique* of 5 March 1930, two codicils of August 1932, both prepared at the Hotel Bürgenstock; and a third codicil, dated 13 October 1933, which added the name of Louis Loriot to the three originally designated executors: Louis Vitalis, Georges Lamirault, and Pierre Roland Marcel.

21 Formule de Déclaration de mutation par Décès de Louis Barthou, décédé, 9 octobre 1934, Archives des direction de l'Enregistrement. See also Barthou's summary verdict in *Promenades*, "Les bibliothèques d'État ressemblent trop à des cimetières ...," 157.

22 Barthou to Mme Mayeur, 9 August 1932, Collection Marcel Gilbert.

23 Barthou, *Promenades*, 27–8.

24 Barthou, "Propos Libres ...," *Annales* (1 October 1930): 288; "Au seuil du nouveau septennat," *Annales* (1 June 1931): 509.

25 Barthou, "Aristide Briand," *Annales* (15 March 1932): 231–2.

26 Barthou, "Propos Libres ...," *Annales* (15 April 1932): 358; (15 July 1930): n.p.

27 Barthou, "Propos Libres ...," *Annales* (1 October 1930): 288: (1 November 1930): n.p.

28 Interview with Maître Marcel Gilbert, 20 November 1981. For further evidence that Barthou was sure in late 1933 that he would never be called back to power – and with no trace of regret – see Marcel Prévost, "Portrait de Louis Barthou," *L'Indépendant*, 4–5 March 1934.

29 Barthou, "1934. La Paix ou la guerre," *Annales* (29 December 1933): n.p.

30 Foreign Affairs committee, 2 February 1934, Communiqués (1934–39), Sénat.

31 Foreign Affairs committee, 2 March 1934, Ass. Nat., 24.

32 André François-Poncet, *Souvenirs d'une ambassade à Berlin* (Paris: Flammarion 1946), 173. Ambassador Phipps described the note as more "cassant" in tone than its predecessors, but acknowledged that it might be useful, "since this government was suggesting that it was strong enough to reach an agreement with Germany over disarmament." Phipps (Berlin) to Simon, 14 February 1934, PRO, FO 800 (Simon Papers), 289.

33 Foreign Affairs committee, 2 March 1934, Ass. Nat. 16; *Le Temps*, 7 March 1934, 3; Fernand de Brinon, "Après les voyages de M. Barthou," *RP* (1934): 526. For Eden's account of Barthou's withering candour, see the report on the Anglo-French meetings in Paris in February 1934. Tyrell to Simon, 18 February 1934, *DBFP* 2nd series, vol. 6, no. 297, 435–42, and 1 March, no. 324, 493–501.

34 Foreign Affairs committee, 2 March 1934, Ass. Nat., 2–28.

35 Ibid., 24.

36 Ibid., 9 May 1934, 33–5.

37 François-Poncet, *Souvenirs*, 175–6; Jules Laroche, *La Pologne de Pilsudski: Souvenirs d'une ambassade, 1926–1935* (Paris: Flammarion 1953), 154. Geneviève Tabouis, *Vingt ans de "suspense" diplomatique* (Paris: Albin Michel 1958), 167. On the generally conciliatory inclinations of Quai officials, see the Belgian appraisal in "Exposé," 24 April 1934, *DDB*, vol. 3, no. 127, 357.

38 Barthou to Lyautey, 15 April 1934, AN, Fonds Lyautey.

39 François-Poncet, *Souvenirs*, 176; Laroche, *La Pologne*, 154; Jacques Fischer, *Doumergue et les politiciens* (Paris: Éditions Le Jour 1935), 57–8, 150, 152.

40 Several years earlier a British report had discussed Léger's influence on Briand, and vice versa, and characterized Léger as a "most helpful

and greatly valued friend to His Majesty's Embassy." See Tyrrell
(Paris) to Henderson, 15 December 1930, PRO, FO 371, 14905,
w13446/198/17. For a German view on Léger's thinking see Köster to
Berlin, DGFP, series C, vol. 3, 123–6.

41 Tabouis, *Vingt ans*, 171. For more on Briand's perceived impact on
Barthou's foreign policy, see Vercors, *L'après Briand* (Paris: Plon
1982), 68–70. Henri Marchat, one of Briand's *chefs de cabinet*, also believed that Barthou's policy was in the tradition of Briand. Interview
of 12 February 1982, Saint Jean d'Angély.

42 Tabouis, *Vingt ans*, 171; Jean Fabry, *De la Place de la Concorde au Cours
de l'Intendance* (Paris: Éditions de France 1942), 55. A month later,
René Massigli acknowledged that Barthou had resisted the note of
17 April, and had it "clearly in mind not to close the door against any
possible future negotiations." Consul (Geneva) to London, 15 May
1934, PRO, FO 371, 18525, w4714/1/98. The Americans were similarly
convinced of Barthou's opposition to the note, as were the Belgians.
See, respectively, Straus to Washington, 20 April 1934, *Foreign Relations of the United States*, vol. 1 (1934), 52–3; and "Exposé," DDB, vol. 3:
358.

43 See Doumergue's note to Barthou, 16 April 1934, DDF, 1ᵉ, vol. 6,
no. 97, 246–7, as well as the preceding "compte rendu" of the ad hoc
national defence study committee, convened on Barthou's request,
14 April, DDF, no. 93, 220–37.

44 "Communication," 17 April 1934, DDF, vol. 6, no. 104, 270–2. See also
Tabouis, *Vingt ans*, 170; Maurice Vaïsse, "Louis Barthou et la note du
17 avril 1934," in *Barthou, un homme, une époque*, ed. Papy, 167–72;
and Robert J. Young, *In Command of France. French Foreign Policy and
Military Planning, 1933–1940* (Cambridge, Mass.: Harvard University
Press 1978), 52–75.

45 Foreign Affairs committee, 9 May 1934, Ass. Nat., 40; also Jean Fabry, *J'ai connu ... 1934–1945* (Paris: Descamps 1960), 44, as well as his
De la Place de la Concorde, 55.

46 *JO*, Chamber Debates, 25 May 1934, 1261.

47 Ibid., 9 May 1934, 33–49; Foreign Affairs committee, 6 July 1934,
Ass. Nat., 65–71; Maurice Vaïsse, *Sécurité d'abord: La politique française
en matière de désarmement, 9 décembre 1930–17 avril 1934* (Paris: Pedone
1981), 511. For a Belgian appraisal of Barthou's efforts to recoup any
losses incurred by the note, see Note of 3 May 1934, DDB, vol. 3,
no. 128, 363–5.

48 Foreign Affairs committee, 16 May 1934, Ass. Nat., 1–2.

49 Foreign Affairs committee, 9 May 1934, Ass. Nat., 5–23, 56–7, 65–6;
Laroche to Quai, 24 April, DDF, vol. 6, no. 133, 333–6; Barthou to

Corbin, ibid., no. 299, 637–40; Laroche, *La Pologne*, 155–70. In fact, Franco-Polish relations quickly soured; see Barthou to Laroche, 22 June, DDF, vol. 6, no. 373, 704–5.

50 Tabouis, *Vingt ans*, 174–8; Léon Noel, *La Tchécoslovaquie d'avant Munich* (Paris: Publications de la Sorbonne 1982), 61–2, 165–7. For Léger's appraisal of the eastern tour, see Clerk to Simon, 5 May, *DBFP*, vol. 6, no. 418, 688–9. The most authoritative secondary account of the tour is now Piotr S. Wandycz, *The Twilight of French Eastern Alliances 1926–1936. French-Czechoslovak-Polish Relations from Locarno to the Remilitarization of the Rhineland* (Princeton: Princeton University Press 1988), 335–56.

51 Foreign Affairs committee, 6 July 1934, Ass. Nat., 32. For confirmation of this commitment, see Ambassador Köster's report on a conversation with Barthou in mid-June. Köster to Berlin, 15 June 1934, *DGFP*, C, vol. 3, 7–10; and also Ribbentrop's report on his talk with Barthou on 18 June, ibid., 75–82.

52 Massigli to Quai, 5 June 1934, MAE, série SDN, sous-série II (Désarmement), vol. 891: 49.

53 Foreign Affairs committee, 6 July 1934, Ass. Nat., 99. See also the account of Barthou's talk with Litvinov in Geneva, prepared by Bargeton, 18 May 1934, *DDF*, vol. 6, no. 221, 496–502.

54 Foreign Affairs committee, 6 July 1934, Ass. nat., 41–2. For Barthou's view on Franco-Italian relations, see his note to Chambrun (Rome), 15 June 1934, *DDF*, vol. 6, no. 340, 710–11.

55 Foreign Affairs committee, 6 July 1934, Ass. Nat., 41–2; Barthou, "La Crise d'autorité," *Annales* (13 January 1933): 31–2; Baron Aloisi, *Journal (1932–1936)* (Paris: Plon 1957), 189–200. For Barthou's perception of Italo-Yugoslav relations, see Patteson (Geneva) to Simon, 18 September 1934, *DBFP*, 2nd series, vol. 12, no. 97, 99–100.

56 Von Lersner (Geneva) to Berlin, 31 May 1934, *DGFP* C, vol. 2, no. 475, 859.

57 Édouard Herriot, *Jadis*, 2 vols. (Paris: Flammarion 1948–52), 2:433.

58 Foreign Affairs committee, 6 July 1934, Ass. Nat., 58. For the clearest exposition of Barthou's association of Eastern Locarno and disarmament, see the minute by Bülow, appended to his circular of 7 June 1934, *DGFP*, C, vol. 2, no. 486, 881.

59 Ibid., 105. The belief that Barthou was indeed thinking more along the lines of traditional diplomacy is given some support by J.B. Duroselle, *La Décadence, 1932–1939* (Paris: Imprimerie nationale 1979), 121.

60 Tabouis, *Vingt ans*, 194. For the disgust expressed by Barthou toward this recent Nazi violence, see Straus to Washington, 4 September 1934, *FRUS* 1934, vol. 1, no. 1183, 573.

61 Barthou dossier, 25 July 1934, MAE, Papiers 1940 (Rochat), vol. 3 (1933–34); Tabouis, *Vingt ans*, 196.

62 Aloisi, *Journal*, 215–16, 221–3.

63 Barthou, *À la mémoire de Delcassé* (Paris: Société d'éditions géographiques, maritimes et coloniales 1935), 21.

64 Wladimir d'Ormesson, "L'Intérêt général," unidentified press clipping in "Dossier Barthou," BHVP. Ribbentrop was satisfied that Barthou was genuinely interested in détente and not confrontation. See Klaus Hildebrand, "La Politique française de Hitler jusqu'en 1936," in *La France et l'Allemagne, 1932–1936* (Paris: Éditions du CNRS 1980), 364.

65 Tabouis, *Vingt ans*, 176, 178. See also Barthou dossier, 20, 24 August 1934, MAE, Papiers 1940 (Rochat), vol. 3 (1933–34), dossiers 95–6.

66 Maurice Martin du Gard, *Les Mémorables*, 3 vols. (Paris: Flammarion 1957–78), 1:222.

67 Foreign Affairs committee, 6 July 1934, Ass. Nat., 22; Tabouis, *Vingt ans*, 200; Tabouis, *Ils l'ont appelée Cassandre* (New York: Éditions de la Maison Française 1942), 188–9.

68 See chapter 8, pages 190–1. Some presumably younger writer for *Spectator* went so far as to suggest that Barthou's entire generation was inclined to see everything "sub specie fornicationis." See John Rison Jr, "The Foreign Policy of Louis Barthou, 1933–1934," (Unpublished doctoral dissertation, University of North Carolina 1958), 227–8, note 8.

69 "Je ne dine plus dehors," he wrote to Lyautey on 16 January 1934. See AN, Fonds Lyautey. See also his letters of 19 November 1933 and 19 January 1934 to Mme Bour, BN, n.a.f. ffs 30–41.

70 Georges Suarez, "Louis Barthou chez lui," *Annales* (18 May 1934): 533–4.

71 See the reception speech, delivered by Paléologue, 31 January 1935, AF, 3–27; *Annuaire ... Livre contemporain*, 29; "Wagner et Baudelaire, *Cahiers* (November 1934): 1059–66; "Le Dévouement de Juliette," *Lisez-moi historique* (20 May 1935): 758–62.

72 François Piétri, "Souvenir de Barthou," RDDM 5 (1961): 69.

73 Gustave Samazeuil, "Un hommage à Louis Barthou," *La République des Pyrénées*, 26 November 1964; Georges Coustel, "Le Buste de Louis Barthou," from *La République des Pyrénées*, October 1957, in "Dossier de Presse/tome B, Bibliothèque municipale de Pau.

74 "Louis Barthou," E A/104 12, Préfecture de Police; "Rapports des préfets et des commissaires spéciaux," Sûreté Générale, Ministère de l'Intérieur, AN, F7, carton 14754; "Assassinat du Roi Alexandre," Service Historique de l'Armée de Terre, 7N 2520.

75 Sir John Wheeler-Bennett, *Knaves, Fools and Heroes in Europe between the Wars* (London: St Martin's Press 1974), 171–2. See also the com-

munication from the Interior ministry to the Prefecture of police, 20 August 1934, in the Barthou dossier, Préfecture de Police, BA 257. Charles Rochat spoke to the Gilbert family about the risks attendant on the Marseille trip. Interview with Marcel Gilbert, 20 November 1981.

76 "L'Attentat de Marseille d'Octobre 1934," *L'Aurore* (21 October 1977); Alain Decaux, *Les Assassins* (Paris: Perrin 1986), 85–129; Jacques de Launay, *Les Grandes Controverses de l'histoire contemporaine* (Paris: Albin Michel 1971), 244–9; Édouard Calic, *Heydrich, l'homme clef du IIIe Reich* (Paris: Laffont 1985), 149–66; Stephen Graham, *Alexander of Yugoslavia* (New Haven: Yale University Press 1939), 239–51.

77 Barthou dossier, 9 October 1934, MAE, Papiers 1940 (Rochat), vol. 3 (1933–34), dossiers 97–101.

78 See Tabouis, *Vingt ans*, 210–11; Piétri, "Souvenir de Barthou," 70–3; Jones, "The Foreign Policy of Louis Barthou," 522–5; François Broche, *Assassinat de Alexandre 1er et Louis Barthou* (Paris: Balland 1977), 105; Louis Proust, "Les grands parlementaires de la IIIe République que j'ai connu: Louis Barthou," *Journal de Vichy* 23 July 1952; interview with Mme Suzanne Taillefer (née Lamirault), 5 May 1982.

79 See Barthou dossiers, at Préfecture de Police, E A/104 12 and BHVP.

CONCLUSION

1 Léon Daudet, *L'Agonie du régime: Panorama des hommes, des clans, et des crimes, 1919–1925* (Paris: Nouvelle Librairie Nationale 1925), 43–4.

2 Barthou, *Promenades autour de ma Vie: Lettres de la montagne* (Paris: Les Laboratoires Martinet 1933), 216.

3 Ibid., 190.

4 Henry Bidou, "Louis Barthou," *Vu* (12 October 1934): n.p. It appears that Isidore Barthou made his own casks for the hardware store.

5 Geneviève Tabouis, *Vingt ans de "suspense" diplomatique* (Paris: Albin Michel 1958), 174.

6 Barthou, *Promenades*, 150.

7 Eden to Simon, 18 February 1934, PRO, FO 800 (Simon), 289. Eden experienced, however, a marked change of heart, describing Anglo-French relations as "better, essentially franker, than I had ever known them." He makes a point of saying that Barthou's death moved him "personally as well as politically ... I bitterly regretted a man who had, I thought, become a friend." See Earl of Avon, *The Eden Memoirs: Facing the Dictators* (London: Cassell 1962), 108–9.

8 The incident with Ducla occurred in March 1925. See Michel Fabre, "Un politique et un poète," RRP (January-June 1984): 51–2.

9 I shall take this final opportunity to express my thanks once again for the exceptionally gracious assistance of Mme Pierre Roland-Marcel, Mme Suzanne Taillefer (née Lamirault), the late Mme Jacqueline Souchère (granddaughter of Olivier Sainsère), and Maître Marcel Gilbert.

10 André Malraux, *L'Espoir* (Paris: Éditions Gallimard 1937), 162.

Source Materials

1 PRIMARY SOURCES

Unpublished Primary

As indicated in the final chapter, the Barthou estate was not placed in the hands of his surviving brothers or sister – each of whom was without issue – but rather in those of four executors: Georges Lamirault, Louis Loriot, Pierre Roland-Marcel, and Louis Vitalis. The latter, evidently, became the principal figure, and it was he who took charge of the *patron*'s private papers.

Precisely what was kept from 1934 remains a mystery; however, even in the years immediately preceding his death in 1973, M. Vitalis acknowledged to Jean Bousquet-Mélou that some kind of collection still existed, at least for the period of the inter-war years. Regrettably, sometime between the reported exchange and 1973, M. Vitalis seems to have destroyed whatever collection then remained. Accordingly, it is all but certain that a Barthou *fonds*, properly called, does not now and will never more exist. It is this archival consideration which made imperative the casting of a wide net, one capable of drawing in information on Barthou's multifaceted public and private life.

One of the earliest, and certainly one of the most pleasant, assignments was to locate individuals who had been associated with Barthou in one way or another. In the form of interviews, sometimes supplemented by correspondence and sometimes by access to their private collections, the following individuals provided invaluable assistance. To each I express my profound thanks for their gracious hospitality: Maître Marcel Gilbert of Paris, and Mesdames Lamarque and Pourtalet of Pau, all being cousins of Louis Barthou; Mme Roland-Marcel and Mme Vitalis, the widows of two of the aforementioned executors; Mme Suzanne Taillefer and Marc Lamirault, daughter and grandson respectively of Georges Lamirault; the late Mme Jacqueline Souchère, granddaughter of Barthou's pre-1914 collaborator and close personal friend, Olivier Sainsère; M. and Mme Pierre Loti-Viaud, he being the grandson of Pierre Loti; M. Marcel Ribière, one of Poincaré's *chefs de cabinet*, and M. Henry Marchat, whose father was a longtime friend of Barthou and who was himself one of Briand's cabinet directors; the distinguished journalist, the late Mme Louise Weiss; M. Robert Dauchez, the notary responsible for processing the Barthou estate; Mme Monique Cappiello, daughter-in-law of the artist Leonetto, with whom Alice and Louis Barthou were on very friendly terms; Mme Pierre Bouchet, widow of the printer-engraver Pierre Bouchet, to whom Barthou gave much custom in the last two decades of his life; the bibliophiles Messieurs Benoit-Cattin, Schuck, and Droin, all of whom have been officers of Le Livre Contemporain; M. Castaing of the manuscript house of Charavay, and M. René Kieffer, the Paris book-dealer; Mme Geneviève Agnel, cousin of the writer Hughes Le Roux, with whom the Barthou family were particularly close; and Mrs Marielle Griffiths (née Bonnemaison), goddaughter of Alice Barthou.

Supplementing the information provided by the foregoing is that contained in various "Dossiers Barthou" from the following archives and libraries: Préfecture de Police, Société des Gens de Lettres, Bibliothèque Historique de la Ville de Paris, Archives départementales des Pyrénées Atlantiques, Bibliothèque municipale de Lucerne, Bibliothèque municipale d'Oloron-Sainte-Marie, Bibliothèque municipale de Pau, and the Archives de l'Académie Française. While I am grateful for the services provided by each of these institutions, I owe a particular debt of thanks to M. François Marin, director of the Pau municipal library, and to Mme Lafitte-Larnaudie, director of the archives at the Académie Française. In addition, I express thanks to the secrétariat administratif de l'Archevêché de Paris for supplying a copy of the Barthou marriage certificate from the Madeleine, and to the retired archivist, M. Pierre Froger (Direction de l'Enregistrement) for copies of the Déclarations de Succession for Alice, Louis, and Léon Barthou as well as that for Mme Mayeur.

Fortunately, many Barthou letters have survived, however dispersed they may be through the following, publicly held private collections. At the Archives Nationales, in the private paper series AP, I have canvassed the following holdings: Marshal Lyautey, Alexandre Millerand, Louis Marin, André Tardieu, Albert Thomas, Paul Painlevé, Paul Deschanel, and Louis Madelin. I take this opportunity to thank Mme Tourtier-Bonazzi for her generous and informed assistance.

At the Bibliothèque Nationale, apart from the Poincaré papers, in which there is no Barthou correspondence, there are letters scattered through the following collections: Frédéric-Auguste Casals, Joseph Reinach, Victor du Bled, Gaston Paris, Jehan Rictus, famille Porto-Riche, Eugène Carré, Anatole France (fonds Jacques Lion, Seymour de Ricci), Louis Bour, Jacques Rouché, Charles Pomaret, Yvette Guilbert, Scheurer-Kestner, Mme Bulteau, Paul Boyer.

At the Académie Française I examined the fonds Lavedan, Goyau, Regnier, and Reclus; and at the Assemblée Nationale, that of Jean Locquin; at the Fondation Nationale des Sciences Politiques, that of Émile Pillias and Roche-Caillaux; and at the Bibliothèque Jacques Doucet, that of Victor Giraud, Paul Valéry, and Natalie Clifford Barney, as well as the collections bearing the name of Mataresse and Léautaud. For access to the Doucet materials, and for his additional council, I thank its director, M. François Chapon.

Barthou letters are also to be found in the collection Émile Combes, in the Archives départementales de la Charente-Maritime; in the Fonds Paul Lacoste and Ritter in the Archives départementales des Pyrénées Atlantiques. In connection with the latter, I wish to acknowledge the exceptionally kind and efficient assistance of Mme Anne-Catherine Marin.

Finally, some Barthou letters are located in various private fonds within the series Papiers d'Agents at the archives of the French foreign ministry. Of particular note are the papers of Camille Barrère, Gabriel Hanotaux, and Édouard Herriot. There are also two letters and some assorted notes in the papers of Charles Rochat, themselves located in the series called Papiers 1940.

In addition to the foregoing materials, there is a substantial amount of archival documentation relevant to Barthou in various official series. At the Archives Nationales, the following have proven useful:

SERIES C (Commissions parlementaires, 1889–1919)
5474 Commission d'enquête (Panama)
7454 Commission d'enquête (Rochette)
5613(2), 5673, 7338 Commission du Travail (1894–1905)
7353 Commission des Travaux Publics (1906–10)
6410 Commission des élections législatives. Basses Pyrénées (1906)
7427 Commission du Budget (1910–14)
7421 Commission de l'Armée (1913)
7477 Déclarations ministérielles (1913)
7472 Commission de l'Enseignement Public et Beaux Arts (1913)
7475 Légion d'Honneur (1913)
7488, 7490 Commission des affaires extérieures (1918–19)
7773 Commission des Traités de Paix (1919)

SERIES AJ5 (Délégation Française à la Commission des Réparations)
535–6 Procès-verbaux (1920–26)
317 Conférences de Gênes, des Ambassadeurs

SERIES F7 (Ministère de l'Intérieur. Sûrêté Générale)
14683 Lettres et menaces
14754 Événements de Marseille. Attentat, Rapports (1934)
14755 Projets d'attentats contres les personnalités françaises (1931–36)

The documentation for series C at the Archives Nationales is continued for the post-1920 period in the form of parliamentary committee materials retained in the archives of the Assemblée Nationale. It was there that the following were consulted:

Commission des affaires étrangères (1920–24, 1934)
Commission de la Législation civile et criminelle (1920–22, 1926–29)
Commission des Finances (1921–24)
Commission d'Alsace et Lorraine (1922–24)
Commission de l'Armée (1921)
Bulletin des Commissions (1926–34)

The Senate also retains its own archives, depositing very little at the Archives Nationales. Records for the pre-1914 parliamentary commissions are spotty, in part a reflection of the ad hoc character of the committees themselves in that period; and the inter-war collection suffers from some major gaps as well. The following, however, were of some value, most of which involve auditions of Barthou as cabinet minister.

Commission ... des chemins de fer (1894–95)
Commission ... des chemins de fer (1906–7, 2 vols.)
Sous-Commission des finances (Rachat de l'Ouest, 1907–8)
Commission des Finances (1896–99)
Commission des affaires étrangères (1934). Communiqués.
Commission des affaires étrangères (1917)
Commission de l'Armée (1921)
Commission de législation civile et criminelle (1922)
Commission de la Marine (1934)

In the archives of the French foreign ministry there are a number of series which contribute to an understanding of Barthou's political and diplomatic career. Chief among them are: series Y (International, 1918–40) and series Relations Commerciales (1918–40), both of which are rich in materials for the Genoa conference; series z (Reparations), in particular carton 504, which derives from the Reparations Commission, 1921–28; series Société des Nations (SDN), sous-série II (Désarmement); and the two series, Papiers d'Agents and Papiers 1940, previously mentioned.

Apart from work undertaken in Paris archives, I have also drawn selectively from official series in other repositories, including: the "Délibérations du Conseil municipal de Pau (1888–89)," a municipal archive housed in the Pau municipal library; the two-volume photographic album registered as "Élection et personnel ... Louis Barthou, 1913–1921" in the municipal archive of Oloron-Sainte-Marie; "Délibérations du Conseil Général des Basses Pyrénées" (1913–1934) and series J (Dons et Acquisitions), both of which are found in the Archives des Pyrénées Atlantiques; the dossier "Assassinat du Roi ... 1934" in series 7N 2520, Service Historique de l'Armée de Terre; the General Correspondence Series, Foreign Office 371, at the Public Record Office, London, England.

Published Primary

Next in importance is the published parliamentary material and the newspaper press. As for the former, I have worked through the Chamber debates from 1889 to 1934 and the Senate debates from 1930 to 1934, both as recorded in the *Journal officiel*, and through the companion series, *Lois et Décrets*, for the texts of his extraparliamentary speeches as minister.

As for the press materials, I have conducted a careful survey of the centrist paper *Le Temps*, from 1889 to 1934, and a comparable survey of the local

L'Indépendant des Basses Pyrénées. Together, these two have provided an excellent coverage of virtually every aspect of Barthou's public life, political and non-political. In addition, more selective use has been made of *Le Figaro*, *L'Illustration*, *L'Alliance Républicaine Démocratique*, *L'Action française*, and *L'Humanité*, the latter two especially for the period of the mid-1920s to the early 1930s when Barthou had become a principal target of their criticism. Even more selective use has been made of several North American newspapers for their coverage of Barthou's visit to the United States and Canada in 1912: the *New York Times*, *Le Devoir* (Montréal), and the *Globe* (Toronto). Finally, use has been made of diverse press clippings which are to be found in various Barthou dossiers previously mentioned.

Of a very different order, I have canvassed the familiar pre- and post-1914 collections of diplomatic documents: *Documents diplomatiques français*, *Documents on British Foreign Policy*, *Documents on German Foreign Policy*, *Documents diplomatiques belges*, *Foreign Relations of the United States*.

2   BARTHOU BIBLIOGRAPHY

The most important source of published material for Barthou is the huge corpus of work written by him in the form of books, articles, and published speeches. Despite the extensive references which follow, I make no claim to their being exhaustive. What is here, I have read. However, there were a few items which simply proved too elusive to locate. Should there ever be a reader interested in compiling a still more complete list, he or she would be advised to integrate the following references with those of Bernard Del Socorro and Jean-François Saget in the bibliography which figures in *Barthou, une époque, un homme*, ed. Michel Papy (1986), 307–39. Between us, I believe we have reconstituted most of Barthou's publications, although nothing would now induce me to believe in the possibility of a truly definitive record of his work.

Attention is also drawn to the series of articles which Barthou contributed to *Les Annales*, principally in 1920–21 and 1929–30. I do so for two reasons. The first is simply to observe that the provision or non-provision of page references is explained by the inconstant publishing policy of that periodical rather than eccentricity on my part. Second, unlike the chapter notes where, for reasons of brevity, I have often cited only the column titles – either "La Situation" or "Propos-Libres" – here I have deleted those titles in favour of providing the more helpful titles of the articles themselves. The dates of publication provide a point of reference between these two systems.

Finally, since all of the following publications are those of Louis Barthou, I will mention here the two works published by Madame Alice-Louis Barthou: "La Maison enchantée," RH (October 1918): 443–52, and *Au Moghreb parmi les fleurs* (Paris: Grasset 1925).

Books and Brochures

Droit romain: De la distinction des biens en meubles et immeubles. Droit français: De l'origine de l'adage "Vilis mobilium possessio" et de son influence sur le code civil. Thèse de doctorat. Paris: A. Rousseau 1886.

Notes de voyages: En Belgique et en Hollande, trois jours en Allemagne. Pau: Imprimerie Garet 1888.

Victor Hugo, homme politique. Paris: L'Union de la Jeunesse Républicaine 1892.

L'Action syndicale (Loi du 21 mars 1884. Résultats et réformes. Paris: A. Rousseau 1904.

Émile Garet, 1829–1912. Pau: Imprimerie Garet 1912.

En marge des "Confidences": Lettres inédites de Lamartine. Abbeville: F. Paillart [Les Amis d'Édouard no. 18] 1913.

Mirabeau. Paris: Hachette 1913.

Impressions et essais. Paris: Bibliothèque Charpentier 1914. Includes: "En Allemagne et en Autriche"; "Au Soudan Égyptien"; "Pour qu'on écoute: À Madame X."

L'Heure du droit: France. Belgique. Serbie. Paris: George Crès 1916. Includes: "La Victoire française"; "Paroles pour la France"; "L'Emprunt de la victoire"; "L'Année décisive"; "Ceux de l'Argonne et ceux de Verdun"; "Pour la Belgique"; "Pour la Serbie."

L'Effort Italien. Paris: Bloud et Gay 1916.

Lamartine orateur. Paris: Hachette 1916.

Lettres à un jeune français. Paris: Éditions Pierre Lafitte 1916. Includes: "Le Flambeau sacré"; "De Philippe à Guillaume"; "Sur les neutres"; "Officiers et soldats"; "Les Bienfaits de la tolérance"; "Il y a du devoir partout"; "De Marceau à nos jours"; "La leçon des morts"; "Les Mauvaises Rumeurs"; "L'Union sociale"; "Des Pâques sanglantes aux pâques fleuries"; "L'École du front"; "Quelques prédictions de Lamartine"; "En Belgique: Socialistes et évêques"; "Autour de la frontière d'Espagne"; "L'Épreuve alsacienne"; "Sur le front Italien; "Chez d'Annunzio"; "À propos de Lord Kitchener"; "Paroles d'union"; "L'Esprit de parti et l'esprit national"; "Pour ceux qui avaient huit ans en 1870"; "De Mirabeau à nos jours"; "La Contagion sublime"; "Le Deuxième Anniversaire"; "Autour de la Suisse neutre"; "Autour de la Suisse hospitalière"; "L'Élite qui meurt"; "Dans un hôpital"; "Cheminots et postiers"; "Les Faussaires allemands d'Ems à Nuremberg"; "Après avoir lu La Bruyère"; "Comme nos instituteurs se battent"; "La Marseillaise de la paix"; "En souvenir du Capitaine Don Annibal de Chinchilla"; "Avant-propos d'après-guerre"; "La Femme française"; "Conseils à un jeune engagé volontaire."

Autour de Baudelaire: "Le Procès des Fleurs du Mal". Victor Hugo et Baudelaire. Paris: Maison du Livre 1917.

Sur les routes du droit. Paris: Bloud et Gay 1917. Includes: "Qui est responsable de la guerre?"; "Toute la France pour toute la guerre"; "Le Soldat français"; "L'Effort de la femme française"; "Déclaration des pères et mères de famille dont les fils sont morts pour la patrie"; "La Belgique héroïque"; "L'Effort italien"; "L'Amérique latine"; "La Guerre actuelle et les prédictions de Lamartine"; "Le Patriotisme au théâtre."

Les Dons américains. Paris: Imprimerie nationale 1918.

La Bataille de Maroc. Paris: Édouard Champion 1919.

Le Traité de paix. Paris: Bibliothèque Charpentier 1919.

Le Politique. Paris: Hachette 1923.

Autour de Lamartine. Paris: Payot 1925.

Lettres inédites d'Alfred de Vigny à Victor Hugo (1820–1831). Paris: Émile-Paul Frères 1925.

Pierre Loti (Juin 1923). Paris: Les Presses françaises 1925.

Victor Hugo élève de Biscarrat. Paris: Champion [Les Amis d'Édouard, no. 80] 1925.

La Vie amoureuse de Richard Wagner. Paris: Flammarion 1925.

Rachel. Paris: Félix Alcan 1926.

Le Général Hugo (1773–1828): Lettres et documents inédits. Paris: Hachette 1926.

Le Neuf Thermidor. Paris: Hachette 1926.

Paroles vécues. Paris: Figuière 1928.

Pêcheur d'Islande de Pierre Loti: Étude et analyse. Paris: Librairie Mellottée 1929.

Les Amours d'un poète. Paris: Fayard 1929.

Lyautey et le Maroc. Paris: Éditions du *Petit Parisien* 1931.

Le Maréchal Joffre. Paris: Plon 1931.

Danton. Paris: Albin Michel 1932.

La Vie ardente de Wagner. Paris: Flammarion 1932.

Promenades autour de ma vie: Lettres de la Montagne. Paris: Les Laboratoires Martinet 1933.

À la mémoire de Delcassé. Paris: Société d'éditions géographiques, maritimes et coloniales 1935.

Articles and Speeches

"L'Évolution des idées politiques de Victor Hugo." RB 23 (1892): 75–81.

"Discours ... lors de l'installation de la commission sur les caisses de secours." JO, *Lois et Décrets* (19 August 1894): 4132–3.

"Discours ... à l'inauguration du monument du président Sadi Carnot." JO, *Lois et Décrets* (30 June 1896): 3576–7.

"Discours ... prononcé à Oloron." JO, *Lois et Décrets* (18 October 1896): 5755–8.

"Discours prononcé ... à la cérémonie funèbre ... Bazar de la Charité." *JO*, *Lois et Décrets* (May 1897): 2662–3.

"Discours prononcé ... au banquet de la Ligue nationale de la Prévoyance et de la Mutualité." *JO, Lois et Décrets* (29 May 1897): 3057–8.

"Le Syndicat obligatoire." *NR* 8 (1901): 321–47.

"Lettre politique." *NR* 8 (January 1901): 23–9.

"Des atteintes à la liberté du travail." *NR* 8 (February 1901): 321–35.

"Discours." *ARD* (6 June 1902): 3–4.

"Autour du divorce." *NR* (15 December 1902): 433–45.

"La Révolution et la liberté d'enseignement." *RP* (1 February 1903): 493–507.

"Thiers et le loi Falloux." *NR* 23 (March-April 1903): 1–22.

"Autour de la loi Falloux." *ARD* (22 May 1903): 1–18.

"La Séparation." *ARD* (19 March 1905): 1.

"Patriotisme et nationalisme." *ARD* (17 September 1905): 1.

"Les Syndicats d'instituteurs." *RP* (1 March 1906): 1–30.

"Benjamin Franklin." *Le Temps* (28 April 1906).

"Corneille." *Le Temps* (7 June 1906).

"Discours ... prononcé à l'Institut de droit international." *JO, Lois et Décrets* (30 March 1910): 2663.

"Jean Moréas." *Le Temps* (3 April 1910).

"Ministère de l'intérieur." *RH* (April 1911): 608–37.

"Comment assurer à nos ministres la liberté d'action." *RB* (10 June 1911): 707–9.

"Sur un manuscrit de Lamartine: 'Milly ou la Terre natale.'" *RB* (1 July 1911); reprint *Impressions et essais*, 167–80.

"Beethoven." *Annales* (15 August 1911): 208–19.

"Discours." *ARD* (17 November 1911): 4–5.

"Chateaubriand et Victor Hugo." *RB* (9 December 1911); reprint *Impressions*, 204–38.

"Dédicaces, lettres et autographes." *RH* (March 1912); reprint *Impressions et essais*, 272–300.

"L'Avocat et le juge dans le répertoire classique." *Annales* (1 March 1912): 303–16.

"Jules Favre." *Le Temps* (28 June 1912).

"Discours prononcé à l'inauguration du monument Floquet." *JO, Lois et Décrets* (12 July 1912): 6070–1.

"Victor Hugo, correcteur d'épreuves." *RH* (August 1912); reprint *Impressions et essais*, 239–71.

"Diderot et son oeuvre." *Revue pédagogique* (1913): 501–9.

"Discours prononcé aux obsèques de M. Alfred Picard." *JO, Lois et Décrets* (16 March 1913): 2383.

"Discours." *ARD* (1 March 1914): 6–9.

"Vers la Russie nouvelle." *Le Monde illustré* (18 April 1914): 256.

"La Jeunesse de Victor Hugo." *Lectures pour tous* (15 July 1914): 1690–7.

"Victor Hugo à douze ans." *RH* no. 2 (1914): 161–90.

"Discours." In *Les Obsèques d'Édouard Pelletan*, 29–34. Paris: Imprimerie nationale 1914).

"Lamartine et la *politique rationnelle*." In A. *Lamartine, 1833–1913*, 9–32. Paris: Plon, 1914.

"Un Discours inédit de Lamartine." *Annales de l'Académie de Mâcon* (1914–15). 64–84.

"Vers la victoire." *RB* (May-June 1915): 193–7.

"Paroles pour la France." *Le Monde illustré* (6 November 1915): 41–2.

"Les Héros de l'air." *RB* (November-December 1915): 577–81.

"Ce que nous donnera la victoire: La paix française." *Lectures pour tous* (1 February 1916): 646–51.

"La Belgique héroïque." *Conférencia* (July-December 1916): 385–402.

"L'Élection de Lamartine à l'Académie française." *RP* (15 September 1916): 303–23.

"Pour la santé de nos soldats." *Le Monde illustré* (4 November 1916): 263–4.

"Le Suffrage des morts: Lettre ouverte à Maurice Barrès." *Annales* (26 November 1916): n.p.

"Comment les civils peuvent-ils le mieux servir le pays?" *RH* (December 1916): 5–22.

"À l'ombre du clocher de Milly: Lamartine intime." *Conférencia* (1 March 1917): 257–74.

"Les Sports bienfaisants." *Conférencia* (1 May 1917): 513–27.

"Le Dernier Quart-d'heure." *Lectures pour tous* (1 October 1917): 3–5.

"Souscrire, c'est combattre." *Annales* (11 November 1917): 414.

"Aux vaillantes." *NR* (1917): 15–17.

"Une Lettre d'Amérique." *Annales* (26 May 1918). 432.

"L'Erreur de nos ennemis." *Lectures pour tous* (1 June 1918): 1162–4.

"Les Amours d'un poète." *RP* (15 July 1918): 225–52.

"L'Alsace-Lorraine rédimé et rédemptrice." *Le Monde illustré* (14 September 1918): 2.

"*In corporo sano*." *Annales* (20 October 1918).

"Victor Hugo: Carnets et dessins inédits." *RDDM* (15 December 1918), 721–62.

"Crimes et châtiments: Notre victoire." *RH* (1919): 141–59.

"Discours ... pour la réception de M. Louis Barthou, 6 février 1919." AF. Paris: Firmin-Didot 1919.

"La Politique reprend ses droits." *RP* (15 February 1919): 673–86.

"Discours en honneur des écrivains français tombés pour la patrie, 9 avril 1919." AF. Paris: Firmin-Didot 1919.

"Un Voyage romantique en 1836." *RH* (1920): 405–19.

"Rabelais." *Conférencia* (15 February 1920): 237–54.

"Opinion sur Jean Moréas." *Revue critique des idées et des livres* (10 March 1920): 657–8.

"De Villon à Montaigne." *Conférencia* (15 May 1920): 522–34.

"Comment voyageait Jean de La Fontaine." *Le Monde illustré* (15 May 1920): 261–4.

"Si l'Amérique découvrait la France." *Lectures pour tous* (June 1920): 1162–7.

"Lamartine et Victor Hugo." *Annales* (13 June 1920): n.p.

"Paix du dehors et paix du dedans." *Annales* (20 June 1920): n.p.

"La Question des fonctionnaires." *Annales* (27 June 1920): n.p.

"Essai impartial de psychologie parlementaire." *Annales* (4 July 1920): 2–3.

"La Résurrection du peuple tchèque." *Annales* (11 July 1920): 22–3.

"Des vainqueurs au vaincu." *Annales* (18 July 1920): 44–5.

"Y-a-t-il encore un traité de Versailles?" *Annales* (25 July 1920): 64–5.

"Autour de *William Shakespeare* de Victor Hugo: Documents inédits." *RP* (1 August 1920): 449–86.

"Le Tournant russe." *Annales* (1 August 1920): 84–5.

"La Dernière Concession." *Annales* (8 August 1920): 104–5.

"Si chacun, à sa place, faisait son métier." *Annales* (15 August 1920): 124–5.

"Autour des divisions de l'Entente." *Annales* (22 August 1920): 144–5.

"Les Vraies Bases de l'Entente Cordiale." *Annales* (29 August 1920): 164–5.

"Le Général Lyautey jugé par ses lettres." *RH* (September 1920): 249–69.

"L'Heureuse Ténacité de M. Millerand." *Annales* (5 September 1920): 184–5.

"Quelques regards sur le dedans et sur le dehors." *Annales* (12 September 1920): 204–5.

"De Spa à Aix-les-Bains par Lucerne." *Annales* (19 September 1920): 224–5.

"À Monsieur le Président de la République." *Annales* (26 September 1920): 244–5.

"La Première Semaine d'un septennat." *Annales* (3 October 1920): 264–5.

"De Paris à Orléans par Berlin, Oppeln et Bruxelles." *Annales* (10 October 1920): 284–5.

"Maupassant inédit: Autour d'"Une Vie."" *RDDM* (15 October 1920): 746–7.

"De la nécessité et des conditions d'une politique continue." *Annales* (17 October 1920): 304–5.

"Quelques raisons internationales de la nécessité de l'union nationale." *Annales* (24 October 1920): 324–5.

"Autour d'un album romantique, 25 Octobre 1920." AF. Paris: Firmin-Didot 1920.

"Politique radicale et politique nationale." *Annales* (31 October 1920): 345.

"Gambetta." *Le Monde illustré* (6 November 1920): 295.

"Quelques réflexions sur quelques alliés." *Annales* (7 November 1920): 366.

"Du Général Wrangel au Président Harding." *Annales* (14 November 1920): 386–7.

"De l'apothéose aux difficultés." *Annales* (21 November 1920): 406–7.

"Il n'y a que l'imprévu qui arrive." *Annales* (28 November 1920): 406–7.

"De Rome à Athènes." *Annales* (5 December 1920): 446–7.

"Paris-Londres aller et retour." *Annales* (12 December 1920): 466–7.

"Coups d'oeil sur l'intérieur." *Annales* (19 December 1920): 517–18.

"À la recherche d'une majorité qui se cherche." *Annales* (2 January 1921).

"L'Année décisive de la paix." *Annales* (9 January 1921).

"Victor Hugo: Les batailles littéraires." *Conférencia* (15 January 1921): 89–99.

"Le Chemin est long des paroles aux actes." *Annales* (16 January 1921).

"Les Raisons et les leçons d'une crise." *Annales* (23 January 1921).

"Victor Hugo: L'Académie et l'exil." *Conférencia* (1 February 1921): 133–44.

"Victor Hugo: Pendant et après l'exil." *Conférencia* (15 February 1921).

"Discours sur Napoléon." *La Vie des peuples* no. 4 (1921): 7–11.

"Le Génie latin." *Annales* (24 July 1921).

"Discours ... à l'occasion de l'inauguration du monument érigé à Flirey à la mémoire des morts des dix-sept divisions américaines." JO, *Lois et Décrets* (28 August 1921): 1019–20.

"Discours ... à Meaux à la cérémonie anniversaire de la bataille de la Marne." JO, *Lois et Décrets* (12 September 1921): 10478–9.

"Discours ... à l'occasion de l'inauguration du monument de Paul Déroulède à Metz." JO, *Lois et Décrets* (20 October 1921): 11927–9.

"Discours ... réponse à M. Joseph Bédier, 3 Novembre 1921." AF. Paris: Firmin-Didot 1921.

"Mésaventures d'un chef d'oeuvre." RF (May-June 1922): 54–64.

"L'Homme politique." RH (1923): 387–92.

"Albert de Mun." RDDM (15 March 1923): 273–300.

"Solemnité organisée par l'Union Latine en l'honneur de Virgile, 20 Mars 1923." AF Paris: Firmin-Didot 1923.

"La Présidente Brisson." RF (May-June 1923): 180–8.

"Quelques souvenirs: Gabriel d'Annunzio." *Annales* (10 June 1923).

"Discours ... pour les fêtes du centenaire d'Ernest Renan, 2 Septembre 1923." AF. Paris: Firmin-Didot 1923.

"Lettre à Adolphe Brisson." *Annales* (23 September 1923): 324.

"À propos d'un mot de Roty." *RF* (September-October 1923): 412–18.

"Lettres inédites de Lamennais à Saint-Victor." *RDDM* (1 November 1923): 162–200.

"Autour de dix vers d'André Chénier ... qui sont d'Anatole France." *RP* (15 December 1923): 721–7.

"Les Espérances françaises." *RH* (1924): 131–58.

"Discours ... pour la réception de M. Henri-Robert, 12 June 1924." *AF*. Paris: Firmin-Didot 1924.

"Quelques réflexions sur le *Neveu de Rameau*." *RF* (November-December 1924): 544–52.

"Anatole France, commis bibliothécaire au Sénat." *RP* (1 December 1924): 481–90.

"Une Plaquette unique de Victor Hugo." *Bull. du bib.* (1 January 1925): 5–9.

"Le Général Hugo, 1773–1828. *Demain* (January 1925): 5–63.

"Lettres inédites d'Alfred de Vigny à Victor Hugo." *RDDM* (1 February 1925): 513–38.

"Le Général Hugo et ses fils." *Demain* (March 1925): 5–75.

"Anatole France sans la politique." *Conférencia* (1 May 1925): 453–72.

"Hommage à Albert Samain." *Mercure de Flandre* (August 1925): 13.

"Lamartine et Aimé Martin." *RP* (1 October 1925): 481–9.

"Les 'Cartellistes' de Clermont-Ferrand au lendemain du 30 Prairial an VII." *RF* (September-October 1925): 365–80.

"Réponse à 'Aimez-vous notre époque?'" *Annales* (6 December 1925).

"Les Anglais chez eux: Victor Hugo et l'Angleterre." *Conférencia* (1 January 1926): 61–74.

"La Vie artistique de Rachel." *RDDM* (1 January 1926): 93–113; (15 January 1926): 371–91.

"Sur Anatole France." *RF* (May-June 1926): 601–30.

"Discours ... pour la réception de M. Albert Besnard, 10 Juin 1926." *AF*. Paris: Firmin-Didot 1926.

"Discours ... l'inauguration du monument élevé à la mémoire d'Alfred Mézières, 10 Octobre 1926." *AF*. Paris: Firmin-Didot 1926.

"Au lendemain du neuf Thermidor." *RP* (12 October 1926): 721–35.

"Discours ... l'inauguration du monument élevé à la mémoire de Paul Deschanel, 24 Octobre 1926." *AF*. Paris: Firmin-Didot 1926.

"Discours ... à l'occasion de l'anniversaire de Washington." *JO, Lois et Décrets* (26 February 1927): 2440.

"Sur Marius Michel." *Plaisir du bibliophile* (Spring 1927): 67–73.

"Lamartine au pilori du travail forcé." *RH* (1927): 5–18.

"Quand Lyautey parle." *RDDM* (15 May 1927): 241–64.

"Discours ... funérailles de M. Le Marquis Robert De Flers, 4 Août 1927." *AF*. Paris: Firmin-Didot 1927.

"Discours ... à l'occasion de l'inauguration du monument du sergent Bernès-Cambot." *JO, Lois et Décrets* (28 September 1927). 10134–5.

"Discours ... à l'inauguration du monument aux morts de la ville de Pau." *JO, Lois et Décrets* (16 November 1927): 11749–50.

"Discours ... l'inauguration de la statue élevée à la mémoire de Paul Déroulède, 20 November 1927." AF. Paris: Firmin-Didot 1927.

"Réponse à l'exposé d'Alfredo Rocco." *Revue politique et parlementaire* no. 136 (1928): 184–7.

"Discours ... à la Cité Universitaire." *Annales de l'Université de Paris* 3, no. 4 (1928): 397–400.

"Méditation pascale sur l'autorité des préfets." RF (May-June 1928): 158–66.

"Discours à l'inauguration de la statue de Jules Méline." *JO, Lois et Décrets* (August 1928): 9787.

"Discours ... réception de M. Maurice Paléologue, 29 Novembre 1928." AF. Paris: Firmin-Didot 1928.

"Impressions brèves d'un vieux bibliophile." *L'Illustration* (Noël 1928).

"En marge des *Nuits*." *Le Manuscrit autographe* (March 1929): 1–12.

"Autour d'un exemplaire des 'Essais' de Montaigne de 1580." *Bull. du bib.* (1 December 1919): 534–41.

"La Transmission du pouvoir." *Annales* (1 December 1929): 405–6.

"Sous les griffes du Tigre." *Annales* (15 December 1929): 543–5.

"Thiers, Historien de la Révolution et de l'Empire." *La Révolution française: Revue d'histoire contemporaine* (1929): 360–61.

"Pierre Loti." In *Le Livre du centenaire: Cent ans de vie française à la Revue des Deux Mondes*, 479–88. Paris: Hachette 1929.

"Les Torts ne sont pas réciproques." *Annales* (1 January 1930).

"De Bossuet à Briand en passant par Moscou." *Annales* (15 January 1930).

"Au retour de Bayreuth." *Cahiers* (1930): 577–83.

"La Paix légale et morale des consciences." *Annales* (1 February 1930).

"M. André Tardieu se porte bien." *Annales* (15 February 1930).

"Pierre Loti." RDDM (15 February 1930): 952–72.

"Réflexions prudentes sur l'imprudence d'une crise." *Annales* (1 March 1930): 207–8.

"Quelques citations d'actualité." *Annales* (15 March 1930): 257–8.

"Vers la concentration républicaine." *Annales* (1 April 1930): 307–8.

"Le Risque qu'il faut courir." *Annales* (15 April 1930): 357–8.

"Équipe double et bouchées triples." *Annales* (1 May 1930): 417–18.

"Discours ... l'inauguration d'une statue élevée en l'honneur du Maréchal Joffre, 21 Juin 1930." AF. Paris: Firmin-Didot 1930.

"Du Cap Nord au Palais Bourbon." *Annales* (15 July 1930).

"Les Quarantes sont quarante." *Cahiers* (August 1930): 695–703.

"Une Clôture qui ne clôt rien." *Annales* (1 August 1930).

"Affaires de femmes." *Annales* (15 August 1930).

"Impressions de Bayreuth." *Annales* (1 September 1930): 193–5.

"Discours ... l'inauguration d'une plaque commémorative apposée sur la maison de Pierre Loti, Hendaye, 7 Septembre 1930." AF. Paris: Firmin-Didot 1930.

"Impressions béarnaises sur la situation européenne." *Annales* (1 October 1930): 287–8.

"Lettre d'un sénateur de gauche à un député du centre." *Annales* (15 October 1930).

"Autour de *Mireille*." *Cahiers* (1930): 293–302.

"Préciser c'est presque prévoir." *Annales* (1 November 1930).

"Que voulez-vous que je vous dise?" *Annales* (15 November 1930).

"Quand l'artichaut perd une feuille." *Annales* (1 December 1930).

"Le 'Sourire' de Lyautey au Maroc, 1912–1918." RDDM (1 December 1930): 580–90.

"Rapport sur les prix de vertu, 4 Décembre 1930." AF. Paris: Firmin-Didot 1930.

"La Vertu à l'Académie." *Annales* (15 December 1930).

"L'Évolution artistique de la reliure." *L'Illustration* (Noël 1930).

"Édouard Rahir." *Bull. du bib.* (1930): 101–11.

"Souvenirs de la Rue Sablière." *Plaisir du Béarn* (Paris: Nouvelle Société d'Édition 1931): 25–37.

"La Vérité dans Ramuntcho." *Cahiers* (1931): 391–8.

"Pierre Loti et le pays basque." *Cahiers* (1931): 5–13.

"Au seuil du nouveau septennat." *Annales* (1 June 1931): 509–10.

"Sophie et Gabriel." RP (15 July 1931): 241–64.

"Grandeur et servitude coloniales." *Annales* (15 August 1931): 144–5.

"Ce que Napoléon aurait fait sur la Marne." *Conférencia* (5 September 1931): 259–74.

"Pierre Loti à bord du 'Redoutable': Notes inédites." RF (1 January 1932): 35–46.

"Les Forces spirituelles de la Belgique." *Conférencia* (20 January 1932): 109–25.

"Aristide Briand." *Annales* (15 March 1932): 231–2.

"Les Forces spirituelles de l'Italie." *Conférencia* (20 April 1932): 415–30.

"Des Musardises à Chantecler." *Cahiers* (June 1932): 535–57.

"Avez-vous lu *Hans d'Islande*?" RP (15 June 1932): 721–45.

"Richard Wagner et Judith Gauthier." RP (1 August, 15 August 1932): 481–98, 721–52.

"Un Décor de l'"Odyssé' par F.L. Schmied." *L'Illustration* (September-December 1932).

"Discours au banquet Armand Godoy." *Le Manuscrit autographe* (October 1932): 86–91.

"Devant la statue de Clemenceau." *Annales* (2 December 1932): 471–2.

"La Crise d'autorité." *Annales* (13 January 1933): 31–2.

"Benjamin Constant contre les discours écrits." *RF* (January-February 1933): 39–51.

"Richard Wagner cinquante ans après sa mort." *Annales* (10 February 1933): 153–5.

"L'Esprit de la politique." *Conférencia* (1 March 1933): 267–82.

"Pourquoi reculer pour mal sauter?" *Annales* (17 March 1933): 293–4.

"Les Raisons de la France." *Annales* (14 April 1933): 413–14.

"Hommage de la France à l'Amérique." *Le Manuscrit autographe* (April 1933): 55–6.

"Anatole France – *Les Dieux ont soif.*" *Conférencia* (1 May 1933): 477–91.

"Discours ... l'inauguration d'une plaque sur la maison ... de M. Anatole France, 20 Mai 1933." AF. Paris: Firmin-Didot 1933.

"Discours ... réapposition d'une plaque sur la maison de ... Sainte-Beuve, 11 Juin 1933." AF. Paris: Firmin-Didot 1933.

"Pierre Loti – *Mon Frère Yves.*" *Conférencia* (1 September 1933): 269–82.

"Leconte de Lisle et Jean Marras: Documents inédits." *RDDM* (15 November 1933): 306–26.

"Discours sur Montaigne." *Annales de l'Université de Paris* (1933): 466–74.

"Autour de Victor Hugo, raconté par un témoin de sa vie." *Bull. du bib.* (20 November 1933): 489–92.

"1934: La Paix ou la guerre." *Annales* (29 December 1933).

"À propos d'un inédit de Victor Hugo." *Bull. du bib.* (20 January 1934).

"Marchand à Fachoda." *RF* (January-February 1934): 749–59.

"Cosima Wagner." *Conférencia* (1934): 296–322.

"Wagner et Baudelaire." *Cahiers* (November 1934): 1059–66.

"Le Coeur de Jules Ferry." *Conférencia* (15 November 1934): 551–65.

"Discours ... réception du Duc de Broglie, 31 Janvier 1935." AF. Paris: Firmin-Didot 1935.

"Le Dévouement de Juliette." *Lisez-moi historique* (20 May 1935): 758–62.

Prefaces

André, Louis. *La Récidive: Théorie ... des lois préventives ou répressive de la récidive.* Paris: Chavalier-Marescq 1892.

Aubert, Octave. *La Sentinelle.* Paris: Librairie Juven 1899.

Roussy, B. *Éducation domestique de la femme et rénovation sociale.* Paris: Librairie Delagrave 1914.

Flat, Paul. *Vers la victoire.* Paris: F. Alcan 1915.

Lacour-Gayet, M.G. *Les Roumains de Transylvanie sous le joug Magyar.* Paris: Plon-Nourrit 1915.

Maurevert, Georges. *L'Alcool contre la France*. Paris: Société Générale d'Éditions Illustrées 1915.

Abensour, Léon. *Les Vaillantes: Héroïnes, martyres et remplaçantes*. Paris: Librairie Chapelot 1917.

Mathiot, Charles. *Pour vaincre: Vie, opinions et pensées de Lazare Carnot*. Paris: Flammarion 1917.

Dubarle, Robert. *Lettres de guerre de Robert Dubarle*. Paris: Perrin 1918.

Demotte, M. *Le Musée du Louvre depuis 1914*. Paris: Demotte 1919.

Gaultier, Paul. *Leçons morales de la guerre*. Paris: Flammarion 1919.

Jonnesco, Thomas. *La Question roumaine*. Paris: Payot 1919.

Bienfait, Valmyre. *Comme ceux de quatre-vingt-douze*. Mulhouse: Ernest Maininger 1920.

Castell, Alexandre. *La Suisse et les Français*. Paris: G. Crès 1920.

Martchenko, M. *La Catastrophe austro-hongroise*. Paris: Berger-Levrault 1920.

Henri-Robert. *Les Grands Procès de l'histoire*. Paris: Payot 1921.

Anonymous. *Les Basses Pyrénées*. Paris: *L'Illustration*, October 1922.

Diderot, D. *Le Neveu de Rameau*. Paris: Pelletan 1922.

Chénier, André. *Oeuvres poétiques*. Paris: Société des Amis des Livres 1923.

Bertholini, Jean. *Wagner et le recul du temps*. Paris: Albin-Michel 1924.

Serban, N. *Pierre Loti: Sa Vie et son oeuvre*. Paris: Les presses françaises 1924.

Lauzanne, Stéphane. *Sa Majesté la presse*. Paris: Fayard 1925.

Meunier, Dauphin. *Autour de Mirabeau*. Paris: Payot 1926.

Bordeu, Charles. *Le Terre de Béarn*. Paris: Éditions de l'Estampe 1927.

Lyautey, Hubert. *Paroles d'action: Madagascar, Sud-Oranais, Oran, Maroc, 1900–1926*. Paris: Colin 1927.

Anonymous. *Catalogue des livres de F.L. Schmied*. Paris: Presses de F.L. Schmied 1927.

–*Exposition rétrospective: Marius Michel, Mai-Juin 1927*. Paris: Palais des Beaux Arts 1927.

Laronze, Georges. *Histoire de la Commune de 1871*. Paris: Payot 1928.

Ricolfi, Humbert. *Le Code de justice militaire du 9 mars 1928*. Paris: Charles-Lavauzelle 1928.

Debus, Jean-Serge. *Métier d'Islande: Les Trimardeurs de la mer*. Lille: Mercure de Flandre 1929.

Jaulme, André. *Les Beaux Livres d'autrefois: Le XVe Siècle*. Paris: Henry Babou 1929.

Guérin, Maurice. *Le Centaure et la bacchante*. Paris: Le Livre Contemporain 1931.

Mauclair, Camille. *Louis Legrand*. Paris: H. Babou 1931.

Cleray, Edmond. *L'Affaire Favras, 1789–1790*. Paris: Éditions des Portiques 1932.

Walter, Gérard. *Les Massacres de septembre*. Paris: Payot 1932.

Daguerre, Pierre. *Béarn et Béarnais*. Pau: Éditions de L'Indépendant 1933.

Dahl, Svend. *Histoire du livre de l'antiquité à nos jours*. Paris: Jules Lamarre 1933.

Junca, F., and G. Parrel. *L'Éducation vocale: Manuel à l'usage des membres de l'enseignement*. Paris: Fernand Nathan 1933.

Libron, F., and H. Clouzot. *Le Corset dans l'art et les moeurs du XIIIe au XVe siècle*. Paris: F. Libron 1933.

Rossel, Virgile. *Le Peuple roi, ou grandeur et misères de la démocratie*. Paris: Marcel Rivière 1933.

Constantin, Léon. *Berlioz*. Paris: Éditions Émile-Paul Frères 1934.

Mickiewicz, Adam. *Pan Tadeusz*. Paris: Félix Alcan 1934.

Anonymous. *Catalogue de la bibliothèque du feu Édouard Rahir*. Paris: F. Lefrançois 1935.   •

Prod'homme, J.G. *Les Sonates pour piano de Beethoven*. Paris: Delagrave 1937.

3   WORKS ON BARTHOU

Anonymous. "Jean-Louis Barthou." *Les Hommes du jour* (10 April 1909).

– "Monsieur Louis Barthou et la guerre." *Les Hommes du jour* (3 June 1916).

– "Louis Barthou." *Ceux qui nous mènent* (Paris: Plon 1922), 3–14.

– "M. Louis Barthou, Sénateur." *L'Ame gauloise* (January 1930).

– "La Tragédie du 9 octobre." Paris: *L'Illustration*, Octobre 1934.

– *Le Président Louis Barthou à l'Institut Français de Hautes Études en Roumanie*. Bucharest: Typographies Roumaines S.A. Rahouei 1934.

– *In Memoriam Louis Barthou, 1862–1934*. Paris: Le Livre Contemporain 1935.

– *Bibliothèque de M. Louis Barthou*. 4 vols. Paris: A. Blaizot 1935–37.

– *Inauguration du monument Louis Barthou*. Pau: Marrimpouey 1971.

– *Louis Barthou*. Pau: Association régionaliste du Béarn, du Pays basque et des contrées de l'Adour. Numéro spéciale de la *Revue régionaliste des Pyrénées* (January-June 1984).

– *Louis Barthou, 1862–1934*. Pau: Conseil Général des Pyrénées Atlantiques 1984.

Aubert, Octave. *Louis Barthou*. Paris: A. Quillet 1935.

Bastid, Paul. "La Paix est blessé." *Vu* (12 October 1934): n.p.

Becker, Jean-Jacques. "Louis Barthou devant la guerre de 1914–1918." In *Barthou, un homme*, ed. Michel Papy, 153–66.

Bérard, Léon. *Hommage au Président Louis Barthou de l'Académie Française*. Pau: G. Lescher-Moutaoué 1934.

Berstein, Serge. "Le Rôle politique national de Louis Barthou de 1919 à 1934. "In *Barthou, un homme*, ed. Michel Papy, 115–28.

Bertaut, Jules. *Louis Barthou*. Paris: Sansot 1919.

Bidou, Henry. "Réception de M. Barthou à l'Académie." *RDDM* (15 February 1919): 945–9.

– "Louis Barthou." *Vu* (12 October 1934): n.p.

Blaizot, Georges. "Louis Barthou bibliophile." *Bulletin de la librairie ancienne et moderne* (October 1963): 205–8.

Bousquet-Mélou, Jean. *Louis Barthou et la circonscription d'Oloron, 1889–1914.* Paris: Pedone 1972.

– *Louis Barthou et la naissance du syndicalisme à Oloron.* Pau: Imprimerie commerciale des Pyrénées 1972.

– "Louis Barthou et ses électeurs de l'arrondissement d'Oloron (1889–1922)." In *Barthou, un homme,* ed. Michel Papy, 47–54.

Brinon, Fernand de. "Après les voyages de M. Barthou." *RP* (1 August 1934): 526–42.

Brisson, Adolphe. "Souhaits de bienvenue." *Annales* (13 February 1916): 177.

Broche, François. *Assassinat de Alexandre 1er et Louis Barthou: Marseille, le 9 octobre 1934.* Paris: Balland 1977.

Cahuet, Albéric. "M. Louis Barthou à l'Académie." *Le Monde illustré* (18 February 1919).

– "Un Trésor du bibliophilie et d'histoire littéraire." *L'Illustration* (23 March 1935): 351–3.

Catala, Jules-André. *Le Bibliophile et le poète: trente cinq lettres de Louis Barthou à Tristan Derème, 1926–1934.* Bordeaux: Imprimerie Taffard 1966.

Cazaurang, Jean-Jacques. "Un Ouvrage peu connu de Louis Barthou: *L'Action syndicale.*" *RRP* (July-December 1977): 169–77.

– *Le Béarnais Louis Barthou vu par le Lorrain Raymond Poincaré.* Pau: L'Auteur 1982.

– "Deux pionniers de la locomotion aérienne: Les frères Barthou." *Pyrénées* (September 1984): 249–58.

Chastenet, Jacques. *Discours (lors de l') inauguration du monument de Louis Barthou.* Paris: Firmin-Didot 1963.

– *Discours (lors de l') inauguration d'une effigie de Louis Barthou.* Paris: L'Institut 1971.

Chaumeix, André. "Barthou." *Larousse mensuel illustré* (May 1935): 97–98.

Colombani, Roger, and Jean-René Laplayne. *La Mort d'un Roi: La vérité sur l'assassinat d'Alexandre de Yougoslavie.* Paris: Albin Michel 1971.

Coustel, Georges. "Léon Barthou." *La République des Pyrénées* (9 January 1954).

– "Louis Barthou. Ce que fut l'ami." *La République des Pyrénées* (10 May 1963).

Daudet, Léon. *Le Garde des seaux Louis Barthou.* Paris: Éditions du Capitole 1930.

Decaux, Alain. "Alexandre 1er meurt à Marseille." In his *Les Assassins,* 85–129. Paris: Plon 1986.

Delaunay, Jean-Marc. "Louis Barthou et l'Espagne." In *Barthou, un homme*, ed. Michel Papy, 85–100.

Donnay, Maurice. *Réponse ... au discours de M. Louis Barthou*. Paris: Firmin-Didot 1919.

Doumic, René. "Raymond Poincaré et Louis Barthou." *RDDM* (1 November 1934): 238.

Ducla, Louis. "Causerie. Autour de l'actualité." *RRP* (February-April 1934): 345–54.

– "Louis Barthou." *RRP* (August-October 1934): 437–43.

– "Le Centenaire de Louis Barthou." *RRP* (January-June 1962): 1–8.

– "Le Centenaire de Louis Barthou au Musée béarnais." *RRP* (January-June 1963): 17–22.

– "Hommage à Louis Barthou." *RRP* (January-June 1968): 1–5.

Duroselle, Jean-Baptiste. "Louis Barthou et le rapprochement franco-soviétique en 1934." *Cahiers du monde russe et soviétique* (October-December 1962): 525–45.

– "Barthou et les alliances contre Hitler." In *Barthou, un homme*, ed. Michel Papy, 173–84.

Espil, Pierre. "Une Amitié complexe: Louis Barthou – Pierre Loti." *RRP* (January-June 1984): 23–30.

Estèbe, Jean. "Louis Barthou écrivain." In *Barthou, un homme*, ed. Michel Papy, 197–204.

Exbrayat, Jules. *Louis Barthou de l'Académie Française, 1862–1934*. Paris: Fequet et Baudier, [Bibliophiles Franco-Suisses] 1934.

Fabre, Michel. "Un Politique et un poète (Louis Ducla)." *RRP* (January-June 1984): 49–59.

Farrère, Claude. *Discours prononcé dans la séance publique tenue par l'Académie française le 23 avril 1936*. Paris: Firmin Didot 1936.

Flat, Paul. "Un Orateur jugé par un homme d'état." *RB* (2–9 September 1916): 513–17.

French, G.S. "Louis Barthou and the German Question of 1934." *Canadian Historical Association Report* (1964): 120–35.

Gaudelette de La Morlière, André. "Présence de Louis Barthou." *Journal de Vichy* (27 June 1952).

Gheusi, P.B. "Mirabeau et M. Barthou." *NR* (July-August 1913): 19–34.

Henriot, Émile. "Au milieu de ses livres." In *In Memoriam*, 25–32.

Hérault, Marc. *La Mort tragique du roi Alexandre 1er de Yougoslavie et de M. Louis Barthou*. Paris: Les Amitiés franco-yougoslaves 1935.

Herriot, Édouard. "Louis Barthou." *Le Journal* (13 October 1934).

Herzog, Wilhelm. *Barthou*. Zurich: Die Liga 1938.

Ignotus. "M. Louis Barthou." *RP* (1 November 1922): 77–81.

– "Louis Barthou, Raymond Poincaré." *RP* (November-December 1934): 5–20.

Jones, John Rison, Jr. "The Foreign Policy of Louis Barthou, 1933–1934." University of North Carolina: Unpublished Ph.D dissertation 1958.

Jourdan, Jean-Paul. "Louis Barthou et le département des Basses-Pyrénées, 1919–1934." In *Barthou, un homme*, ed. Michel Papy, 55–82.

La Mazière, Pierre. "Réception de M. Barthou à l'Académie." *Le Monde illustré* (8 February 1919).

Latzarus, Louis. "Louis Barthou." *Le Figaro* (7 May 1914).

Launay, Jacques de. "L'Attentat de Marseille (9 octobre 1934)." In *Les Grandes Controverses de l'histoire contemporaines, 1914–1945*, 244–9 Lausanne: Éditions Rencontre, 1964.

Le Béguec, Gilles. "Louis Barthou, Patron et modèle politique." In *Barthou, un homme*, ed. Michel Papy, 129–36.

Lecomte, Georges. "Hommage du Livre Contemporain." In *In Memoriam*, iii–viii.

– "Louis Barthou à l'Académie." *L'Illustration* (October 1934).

Lefranc, Jean. "M. Louis Barthou au-dessus des nuages (Burgenstock)." *Le Temps* (18 August 1913): 3–4.

Loti, Pierre. "Un Petit Hussard (Max Barthou)." *L'Illustration* (26 December 1914): 495.

Lucbereilh, Hervé. "Louis Barthou, orateur et bibliophile." *RRP* (January-June 1984): 61–6.

Malherbe, Henri. "Louis Barthou et la musique." *Le Temps* (17 October 1934).

Marin, François. "Louis Barthou et Anatole France." *RRP* (January-June 1984): 31–42.

Martin Du Gard, Maurice. "Louis Barthou." *RRP* (February-April 1928): 589–94.

– "Louis Barthou." *Les Nouvelles littéraires* (14 April 1934).

Maurras, Charles. *Le Bibliophile Barthou*. Paris: Éditions du Capitole 1929.

Mayeur, Jean-Marie. "Louis Barthou et la 'question religieuse.'" In *Barthou, un homme*, ed. Michel Papy, 139–52.

Monzie, Anatole de. "L'Orateur." In *In Memoriam*, 9–16.

Papy, Michel, ed. *Barthou, un homme, une époque*. Pau: J. et D. Éditions 1986.

– "Les Provinciaux et l'image du pouvoir: Comment Louis Barthou fut perçu par les béarnais." In *Barthou, un homme*, 213–48.

Piétri, François. "Souvenir de Barthou." *RDDM* (May 1961): 65–75.

Pinon, René. "Chronique de la quinzaine: Louis Barthou et Raymond Poincaré." *RDDM* (1 November 1934): 237–40.

Proust, Louis. "Les Grands Parlementaires de la IIIe République que j'ai connu: Louis Barthou." *Journal de Vichy* (12, 17, 23 July 1952).

Prévost, Marcel. "Les Lettres." In *In Memoriam*, 17–24.

Rémond, René. "Louis Barthou historien." In *Barthou, un homme*, ed. Michel Papy. 205–10.

Ricci, Seymour de. *Quelques bibliophiles*: vol. 3, *M. Louis Barthou*. Paris: *Plaisir de bibliophile* 1927.

– "Louis Barthou, bibliophile." *Les Nouvelles littéraires* (18 October 1981)

Rife, John Merle, Jr. "The Political Career of Louis Barthou, 1889– 1913." Unpublished Ph.D dissertation, Ohio State University 1964.

Ritter, Raymond. "Louis Barthou et le Béarn." *Pyrénées* (April-June 1963): 73–81.

Roche, Émile. "Caillaux et Louis Barthou." *RDDM* (August 1977): 330–2.

Saget, Jean-François. "Louis Barthou et l'Indépendant des Basses-Pyrénées." In *Barthou, un homme*, ed. Michel Papy, 355–400.

Samazeuilh, Gustave. "Ses prédilections dans la musique." In *In Memoriam*, 45–52.

– "Le Mélomane." *Le Figaro littéraire* (13 October 1934).

– "Un hommage à Louis Barthou." *La République des Pyrénées* (26 November 1964).

Sanson, Rosemonde. "Louis Barthou, leader de l'Alliance républicaine démocratique." In *Barthou, un homme*, ed. Michel Papy, 103–14.

Sarcey, Yvonne. "La Mort d'un enfant: A Mme Louis Barthou." *Annales* (27 December 1914).

Suarez, Georges. "M. Louis Barthou chez lui." *Annales* (18 May 1934): 533–4.

Tabouis, Geneviève. "Louis Barthou au fauteuil de Vergennes." *Aux carrefours de l'histoire* no. 69 (1963): 37–47.

Thibaudet, Albert. "Réflexions." *Nouvelle Revue française* (1 January 1935): 124–30.

Toulet, Jean. "Louis Barthou, une époque de la bibliophilie." In *Barthou, un homme*, ed. Michel Papy, 187–96.

Tranchesse, Pierre. "Promenade autour d'un livre." *RRP* (January-June 1984): 5–21.

Tudesq, André-Jean. "La Presse et la mort de Louis Barthou." In *Barthou, un homme*, ed. Michel Papy, 249–54.

Vaïsse, Maurice. "Louis Barthou et la note du 17 avril 1934." In *Barthou, un homme*, ed. Michel Papy, 167–72.

Valriant, Jane. "Louis Barthou." *RRP* (July-December 1956): 150–4.

Vanderem, Fernand. "Les Ventes de la bibliothèque Barthou," *Bull. du bib.* (1935–36).

Verne, Henri. "Le Protecteur des arts." In *In Memoriam*, 33–41.

Vignaud, Jean. "Louis Barthou." *RB* (1–8 June 1918), 345–7.

Vitalis, Louis. "L'Ami." In *In Memoriam*, 3–8.

Vogel, Lucien. "Dernier entretien" *Vu* (12 October 1934).

Young, Robert J. "La Cité des livres": Louis Barthou (1862–1934)." *Bull. de bib.* no. 4 (1983): 448–59.

– "Louis Barthou, portrait intime." In *Barthou, un homme*, ed. Michel Papy, 255–74.

4   OTHER WORKS

Memoirs, Diaries, Speeches, Recollections

Aloisi, Baron. *Journal (25 juillet 1932–14 juin 1936)*. Paris: Plon 1957.

Aubert, Octave. *De l'histoire et des histoires. Souvenirs d'un journaliste*. Bordeaux: Éditions Delmas 1943.

Auriol, Vincent. *Hier ... demain*. 2 vols. Paris: Charlot 1945.

Avon, Earl of. *The Eden Memoirs: Facing the Dictators*. London: Cassel 1962.

Barrès, Maurice. *Mes cahiers*. Paris: Plon 1963.

Benoist, Charles. *Souvenirs de Charles Benoist*. 3 vols. Paris: Plon 1933–34.

Bérard, Armand. *Un Ambassadeur se souvient:* vol. 1, *Au Temps du danger allemand*. Paris: Plon 1976.

Béraud, Henri. *Les Derniers Beaux Jours*. Paris: Plon 1953.

Beuve-Méry, Hubert. *Réflexions politiques, 1932–1952*. Paris: Seuil 1951.

Bonnet, Georges. *Vingt ans de vie politique, 1918–1938*. Paris: Fayard 1969.

– *Quai d'Orsay: Forty-Five Years of French Foreign Policy*. Isle of Man: Times Press 1965.

Brinon, Fernand de. *Mémoires*. Paris: LLC 1949.

Caillaux, Joseph. *Mes Mémoires*. 3 vols. Paris: Plon 1942–47.

Cambon, Paul *Correspondance, 1870–1924*. Paris: Grasset 1940–46.

Carbuccia, Horace de. *Le Massacre de la victoire, 1919–1934*. Paris: Plon 1973.

Chastenet, Jacques. *Quatre fois vingt ans, 1893–1973*. Paris: Plon 1974.

Child, Richard W. *A Diplomat Looks at Europe*. New York: Duffield and Co. 1925.

Combes, Émile. *Mon Ministère, 1902–1905*. Paris: Plon 1956.

Daudet, Léon. *Souvenirs politiques*. Paris: Éditions Albatros 1974.

Donnay, Maurice. *Mon Journal, 1919–1939*. Paris: Fayard 1953.

Escholier, Raymond. *Souvenirs parlés de Briand*. Paris: Hachette 1932.

Fabre-Luce, Alfred. *Vingt-cinq années de liberté*. 3 vols. Paris: Juillard 1962–64.

Fabry, Jean. *De la Place de la Concorde au cours de l'Intendance*. Paris: Éditions de France 1942.

– *J'ai connu ... 1934–1945*. Paris: Éditions Descamps 1960.

Flandin, Pierre-Étienne. *Politique française, 1919–1940*. Paris: Éditions Nouvelles 1947.

Flat, Paul. *Souvenir d'avant-guerre pour servir après*. Paris: Plon 1916.

François-Poncet, André. *Souvenirs d'une ambassade à Berlin*. Paris: Flammarion 1946.

Gamelin, General Maurice. *Servir*. 3 vols. Paris: Plon 1946.

Gheusi, P.-B. *Cinquante ans de Paris: Mémoires d'un témoin, 1889–1939:* vol. 2, *Leurs femmes*. Paris: Plon 1940.

Guyot, Yves. *Trois ans au ministère des travaux publics*. Paris: Léon Chailley 1896.

Hanotaux, Gabriel. "Les carnets de Gabriel Hanotaux." *Revue d'histoire diplomatique* (1977): 5–141: (1979): 47–181.

– *Carnets, 1907–1925*. Paris: Plon 1925.

Herriot, Édouard. *Jadis*. 2 vols. Paris: Flammarion 1948–52.

Homberg, Octave. *Les Coulisses de l'histoire*. Paris: Fayard 1938.

Jouvenel, Bertrand de. *D'une guerre à l'autre*. 2 vols. Paris: Plon 1941.

Judet, Ernest. *Ma politique, 1905–1917*. Paris: Société mutuelle d'édition 1923.

Kayser, Jacques. *Ruhr ou Plan Dawes? Histoire des Réparations*. Paris: Delpeuch 1925.

Klotz, L.L. *De la guerre à la paix*. Paris: Payot 1924.

Laroche, Jules. *Quinze ans à Rome avec Camille Barrère, 1898–1913*. Paris: Plon 1948.

– *Au Quai d'Orsay avec Briand et Poincaré, 1913–1926*. Paris: Hachette 1957.

– *La Pologne de Pilsudski: Souvenirs d'une ambassade, 1926–1935*. Paris: Flammarion 1953.

Lazareff, Pierre. *Dernière Édition*. Montréal: Valiquette n.d.

Lebrun, Albert. *Témoignage*. Paris: Plon 1945.

Lémery, Henry. *D'une république à l'autre: Souvenirs de la mêlée politique, 1894–1944*. Paris: La Table Ronde 1964.

Léon, Paul. *Du Palais Royal au Palais Bourbon*. Paris: Albin Michel 1947.

Léon-Bérard, Marguerite. "Souvenir de mon père." RDDM (1 July 1968): 43–56.

Loucheur, Louis. *Carnets secrets, 1908–1932*. Paris: Brepols 1962.

Louis, Georges. *Les Carnets de Georges Louis*. 2 vols. Paris: F. Rieder 1926.

Loustaunau-Lacau, Georges. *Mémoires d'un français rebelle, 1914–1948*. Paris: Laffont 1958.

Martin Du Gard, Maurice. *Les Mémorables*. 3 vols. Paris: Flammarion 1957–78.

Messimy, General Adolphe. *Mes souvenirs*. Paris: Plon 1937.

Meyer, Arthur. *Ce que je peux dire*. Paris: Plon 1912.

Millerand, Alexandre. *Pour la défense nationale: Une année au ministère de la guerre*. Paris: Fasquelle 1913.

Monzie, Anatole de. *L'Entrée au forum*. Paris: Albin Michel n.d.

Morand, Paul. *Journal d'un attaché d'ambassade*. Paris: Gallimard 1963.

Mordacq, General. *Le Ministère Clemenceau: Journal d'un témoin*. 4 vols. Paris: Plon 1930–31.

Noel, Léon. *La Tchécoslovaquie d'avant Munich*. Paris: Publications de la Sorbonne 1982.

Paléologue, Maurice. "Comment le service de trois ans fut rétabli en 1913." RDDM (1, 15 May 1935): 67–94, 307–44.

– *An Intimate Journal of the Dreyfus Case*. New York: Criterion Books 1957.

– *Journal, 1913–1914*. Paris: Plon 1947.

Pange, Jean de. *Journal, 1927–1936*. 3 vols. Paris: Grasset 1964–70.

Paul-Boncour, Joseph. *Entre deux guerres.* 3 vols. Paris: Plon 1946.

Pierrefeu, Jean de. *La Saison diplomatique: Gênes, avril-mai 1922.* Paris: Éditions Montaigne 1928.

– "Un Touriste à Gênes." *L'Illustration* (29 April 1922): 377–8.

Poincaré, Raymond. *Au service de la France.* 10 vols. Paris: Plon 1926–33.

Raphael-Leygues, Jacques. *Chroniques des années incertaines, 1935–1945.* Paris: Éditions Franc-Empire 1977.

Reynaud, Paul. *Au coeur de la mêlée, 1930–1945.* Paris: Flammarion 1951.

– *Mémoires.* 2 vols. Paris: Flammarion 1960–63.

Ribot, Alexandre. *Lettres à un ami: Souvenirs de ma vie politique.* Paris: Éditions Bossard 1924.

– *Journal d'Alexandre Ribot et correspondance inédites, 1914–1922.* Paris: Plon 1936.

Roche, Émile. *Avec Joseph Caillaux: Mémoires, souvenirs et documents.* Paris: Publications de la Sorbonne 1980.

Seydoux, François. *Mémoires d'outre-Rhin.* Paris: Grasset 1975.

Seydoux, Jacques. *De Versailles au Plan Young.* Paris: Plon 1932.

Siegfried, André. *Mes souvenirs de la IIIe République: Mon père et son temps: Jules Siegfried, 1836–1922.* Paris: PUF 1952.

Tabouis, Geneviève. *Vingt ans de "suspense" diplomatique.* Paris: Albin Michel 1958.

– *Ils l'ont appelée Cassandre.* New York: Éditions de la Maison Française 1942.

Tirard, Paul. *La France sur le Rhin.* Paris: Plon 1930.

Vansittart, Robert *The Mist Procession.* London: Hutchinson 1958.

Weiss, Louise. *Mémoires d'une européenne.* 3 vols. Paris: Payot 1968–70.

Wheeler-Bennett, Sir John. *Knaves, Fools and Heroes in Europe Between the Wars.* London: St Martin's Press 1974.

Weygand, General Maxime. *Mémoires:* vol. 2, *Mirages et réalité.* Paris: Flammarion 1957.

Contemporary Studies (pre-1945)

Allard, Paul. *Les Favorites de la Troisième République.* Paris: Éditions de la France 1942.

Aubert, Octave. *Le Moulin parlementaire: Plus de son que de farine.* Paris: Librairie Quillet 1933.

Bainville, Jacques. *The French Republic, 1870–1935.* London: Jonathan Cape 1940.

Barrès, Maurice. *Dans le cloaque: Notes d'un membre de la commission d'enquête sur l'affaire Rochette.* Paris: Éditions de l'Écho de Paris 1914.

– *Leurs Figures.* Paris: Émile-Paul Frères 1917.

Barthélemy, Joseph. *Essai sur le travail parlementaire et le système des commissions.* Paris: Delagrave 1934.

Bertaut, Jules. *Le Paris d'avant-guerre.* Paris: La Renaissance du Livre 1919.

Buisson, Georges. *La Chambre et les députés*. Paris: Hachette 1924.

Dansette, Adrien. *Les Affaires de Panama*. Paris: Perrin 1934.

D'Ormesson, W. *France*. London: Longmans 1939.

Daudet, Léon. *L'Entre-Deux-Guerres: Souvenirs des milieux littéraires, politiques, artistiques et médicaux de 1880 à 1905*. Paris: Nouvelle Librairie Nationale 1915.

– *L'Agonie du régime: Panorama des hommes, des clans et des crimes, 1919–1925*. Paris: Nouvelle Librairie Nationale 1925.

– *Verts d'Académie et vers de presse*. Paris: Éditions du Capitole 1930.

– *Député de Paris, 1919–1924*. Paris: Grasset 1933.

– *La Police politique*. Paris: Denoël et Steele 1934.

Echeman, Jacques. *Les Ministères en France de 1914 à 1932*. Paris: Marcel Rivière 1932.

Fischer, Jacques. *Doumergue et les politiciens*. Paris: Éditions *Le Jour* 1935.

Golob, Eugene O. *The Méline Tariff: French Agriculture and Nationalist Economic Policy*. 1944; New York: AMS Press 1968.

Halévy, Daniel. *La République des comités: Essai d'histoire contemporaine de 1895 à 1934*. Paris: Grasset 1934.

Hanotaux, Gabriel. *Mon Temps*. 2 vols. Paris: Plon 1933–38.

Lachapelle, Georges. *Le Ministère Méline: Deux années de politique intérieure et extérieure*. Paris: J.L.L. D'Artrey 1928.

– *L'Alliance Démocratique: Ses origines, ses hommes, son rôle*. Paris: Grasset 1935.

Micaud, Charles A. *The French Right and Nazi Germany, 1933–1939*. Durham, NC: Duke University Press 1943.

Michon, Georges. *La Préparation à la guerre: La Loi de trois ans, 1910–1914*. Paris: Marcel Rivière 1935.

Pertinax. *The Gravediggers of France*. New York: Doubleday 1944.

Poincaré, Raymond. *How France Is Governed*. Port Washington, NY: Kennikat Press 1970. Translated and reprinted from 1913 original.

– *Histoire politique: Chroniques de quinzaine*. 3 vols. Paris: Plon 1920–21.

Tardieu, André. *L'Heure de la décision*. Paris: Flammarion 1934.

Vizetelly, Ernest A. *Paris and Her People under the Third Republic*. New York: Kraus reprint 1971.

Biographical Works

Allain, Jean-Claude. *Joseph Caillaux*. 2 vols. Paris: Imprimerie nationale 1978–81.

Auclair, Marcelle. *Jean Jaurès*. Paris: Éditions du Centenaire 1959.

Auffray, Bernard. *Pierre de Margerie (1861–1942) et la vie diplomatique de son temps*. Paris: Librairie Klincksieck 1976.

Belperron, Pierre. *André Maginot*. Paris: Plon 1940.

Binion, Rudolph. *Defeated Leaders: The Political Fate of Caillaux, Jouvenel, and Tardieu*. New York: Columbia University Press 1960.

Blanch, Lesley. *Pierre Loti: The Legendary Romantic*. New York: Harcourt, Brace, Jovanovich 1983.

Bredin, Jean-Denis. *Joseph Caillaux*. Paris: Hachette 1980.

Calic, Édouard. *Heydrich, l'homme clef du Reich*. Paris: Laffont 1985.

Chabannes, Jacques. *Aristide Briand: Le Père de l'Europe*. Paris: Perrin 1973.

Chirron, Yves. *Barrès: Le Prince de la jeunesse*. Paris: Perrin 1986.

Duroselle, J.-B. *Clemenceau*. Paris: Fayard 1988.

Ellis, Jack D. *The Early Life of Georges Clemenceau, 1841–1893*. Lawrence: Regents Press of Kansas 1980.

Eubank, Paul. *Paul Cambon, Master Diplomatist*. Norman: University of Oklahoma Press 1960.

Fraser, Geoffrey, and Thadée Natanson. *Léon Blum – Man and Statesman*. New York: Lippincott 1938.

Goldberg, Harvcy. *The Life of Jean Jaurès*. Madison: University of Wisconsin Press 1962.

Graham, Stephen. *Alexander of Yugoslavia: The Story of the King Who Was Murdered at Marseilles*. New Haven: Yale University Press 1939.

Griffiths, Richard. *Marshal Pétain*. London: Constable 1970.

Holt, Edgar. *The Tiger: The Life of Georges Clemenceau, 1841–1929*. London: Hamish Hamilton 1976.

Kupferman, F. *Pierre Laval*. Paris: Masson 1976.

Laure, General. *Pétain*. Paris: Berger-Levrault 1941.

Lendresse, Pierre Arette. *Léon Bérard, 1876–1960: Le Combat politique d'un avocat béarnais*. Pau: J. et D. Éditions 1988.

Le Révérend, André. *Un Lyautey inconnu: Correspondance et journal inédits, 1874–1934*. Paris: Perrin 1980.

Margueritte, Victor. *Aristide Briand*. Paris: Flammarion 1932.

Marquardt, Steve R. "Joseph Reinach (1856–1921): A Political Biography." Unpublished Ph.D. dissertation. University of Minnesota 1978.

Miquel, Pierre. *Poincaré*. Paris: Fayard 1961.

Noel, Léon. *Camille Barrière: Ambassadeur de France*. Paris: Tardy 1948.

Monnerville, Gaston. *Clemenceau*. Paris: Fayard 1968.

Oudin, Bernard. *Aristide Briand, biographie*. Paris: Laffont 1987.

Planté, Louis. *Un Grand Seigneur de la politique: Anatole de Monzie*. Paris: Clavreuil 1955.

Porter, Charles. *The Career of Théophile Delcassé*. Westport, Conn.: Greenwood Press 1975, from 1936 original.

Rabaut, Jean. *Jaurès*. Paris: Perrin 1971.

Schmidt, Martin E. *Alexandre Ribot: Odyssey of a Liberal in the Third Republic*. The Hague: Nijhoff 1974.

Sorlin, Pierre. *Waldeck-Rousseau*. Paris: Colin 1966.

Sternhell, Zeev. *Maurice Barrès et le nationalisme français*. Paris: Colin 1972.

Vercors. *Moi, Aristide Briand*. Paris: Plon 1981.

– *L'Après Briand, 1932–1942*. Paris: Plon 1982.

Watson, David. *Georges Clemenceau: A Political Biography.* London: Methuen 1974.

Historical Articles

Artaud, Denise. "À propos de l'occupation de la Ruhr." *Revue d'histoire moderne et contemporaine* 17 (January-March 1970): 1–21.

Bariéty, Jacques. "Les Partisans français de l'entente franco-allemand et la 'prise du pouvoir' par Hitler, avril 1932–avril 1934. In *La France et l'Allemagne entre les deux guerres mondiales,* ed. J. Bariéty, A. Guth, and J. M. Valentin, 21–30. Nancy: Presses universitaires de Nancy 1987.

Becchia, Alain. "Les Milieux parlementaires et la dépopulation de 1900 à 1914." *Communications* 44 (Octobre 1986): 201–46.

Becker, Jean-Jacques. "Les 'Trois ans' et les débuts de la première guerre mondiale." *Guerres mondiales et conflits contemporains* no. 145 (January 1987): 7–26.

Benoît-Lévy, Jean. "L'Oeuvre sociale de la troisième république." In *L'Oeuvre de la Troisième République* 161–87. Montreal: L'Arbre 1945.

Berenson, Edward. "The Politics of Divorce in France of the Belle Époque: The Case of Joseph and Henriette Caillaux." *American Historical Review* 93, no. 1 (February 1988): 31–55.

Berstein, Serge. "Le Ministre sous les IIIe et IVe Républiques." *Pouvoirs* 36 (1986): 15–27.

Bomier-Landowski, Alain. "Les Groupes parlementaires de l'Assemblée nationale et de la Chambre des Députés de 1871 à 1940." In *Sociologie électorale,* ed. François Goguel and Georges Dupeux, 75–89. Paris: Colin 1951.

Boxer, Marilyn. "Protective Legislation and Home Industry: The Marginalization of Women Workers in Late Nineteenth-Early Twentieth Century France." *Journal of Social History* 20, no. 1 (Fall 1986): 45–66.

Clague, Monique. "Vision and Myopia in the New Politics of André Tardieu." *FHS* 8, no. 1 (Spring 1973): 105–29.

Clissold, Stephen. "The Marseilles Murders, 1934." *History Today* 29 (October 1979): 631–8.

Cross, Gary. "Les Trois Huits: Labor Movements, International Reform, and the Origins of the Eight-Hour Day, 1919–1924." *FHS* (Fall 1985): 240–68.

Dogan, Mattei. "Filières pour devenir ministre de Thiers à Millerand." *Pouvoirs* 36 (1986): 43–60.

– "Political Ascent in a Class Society: French Deputies, 1870–1958." In *Political Decision-Makers,* ed. Dwaine Marvick, 57–90. Illinois: Free Press of Glencoe, 1961.

Duroselle, J.-B. "Les Milieux gouvernementaux français en face du problème allemand en 1936." In *La France et l'Allemagne, 1932–1936,* 373–96. Paris: Éditions du CNRS 1980.

Elwitt, Sanford. "Social Reform and Social Order in Late Nineteenth Century France: The Musée Social and Its Friends." *FHS* 11, no. 3 (Spring 1980): 431–51.

Heinberg, J. Gilbert. "The Personnel of French Cabinets, 1871–1930." *American Political Science Review* 25 (1931): 389–96.

Hildebrand, Klaus. "La Politique française de Hitler jusqu'en 1936." In *La France et l'Allemagne, 1932–1936,* 339–72. Paris: Éditions du CNRS 1980.

Hunter, John C. "The Problem of the French Birth Rate on the Eve of World War I." *FHS* 2, no. 4 (Fall 1962): 490–503.

Jacobson, Jon. "Strategies of French Foreign Policy after World War I." *Journal of Modern History* 55, no. 1 (March 1983): 78–95.

Krumeich, Gerd. "Raymond Poincaré et l'affaire du 'Figaro.'" *Revue historique* 264 (October–December 1980): 361–73.

Marks, Sally. "The Misery of Victory: France's Struggle for the Versailles Treaty." *Historical Papers,* Canadian Historical Association (1986): 117–33.

Martin, Marc. "'La Grande Famille': L'Association des journalistes parisiens, 1885–1939." *Revue historique* 557 (January–March 1986): 1929–57.

Mayran, Jacques. "Le Métro avant Zazie." *Historia* no. 176: 76–83.

McDougall, Mary Lynn. "Protecting Infants: The French Campaign for Maternity Leaves, 1890s–1913." *FHS* 13, no. 1 (Spring 1988): 79–105.

Michel, Henri. "Conclusion." In *La France et l'Allemagne, 1932–1936,* 397–403. Paris: Éditions du CNRS 1980.

Reid, Donald. "Putting Social Reform into Practice: Labor Inspectors in France, 1892–1914." *Journal of Social History* 20, no. 1 (Fall 1986): 67–88.

Seager, Frederic. "Joseph Caillaux as Premier, 1911–1912: The Dilemma of a Liberal Reformer." *FHS* 11, no. 2 (Fall 1979): 239–57.

Smith, Michael S. "Free Trade versus Protection in the Early Third Republic: Economic Interests, Tariff Policy, and the Making of the Republican Synthesis." *FHS* 10, no. 29 (Fall 1977): 293–314.

Soutou, Georges. "Le Coke dans les relations internationales en Europe de 1914 au plan Dawes (1924)." *Relations internationales* no. 143 (Autumn 1985): 249–67.

Spivak, Marcel. "Le Développement de l'éducation physique et du sport français de 1852 à 1914." *Revue d'histoire moderne et contemporaine* 24 (1977): 28–48.

Sumler, David E. "Domestic influences on the Nationalist Revival in France, 1909–1914." *FHS* 6, no. 4 (Fall 1970): 517–37.

Tomlinson, Robert. "The 'Disappearance' of France, 1896–1940: French Politics and the Birth Rate." *Historical Journal* 28, no. 1 (1985): 405–15.

Weiss, John H. "Origins of the French Welfare State: Poor Relief in the Third Republic, 1871–1914." *FHS* 13, no. 1 (Spring 1983): 47–78.

Wileman, Donald G. "Caillaux and the Alliance, 1901–1912: The Evolution of a Disillusioned Conservative." *Canadian Journal of History* 23, no. 3 (December 1988): 355–73.

Historical Studies

Anderson, R.D. *France, 1870–1914: Politics and Society.* London: Routledge and Kegan Paul 1977.

Andrew, Christopher. *Théophile Delcassé and the Making of the Entente Cordiale.* London: Macmillan 1968.

Andrew, Christopher, and A.S. Kanya-Forstner. *France Overseas: The Great War and the Climax of Imperial Expansion.* London: Thames and Hudson 1981.

Bariéty, Jacques. *Les Relations franco-allemandes après la première guerre mondiale, 10 novembre 1918–10 janvier 1925.* Paris: Pedone 1977.

Becker, Jean-Jacques. *1914. Comment les Français sont entrés dans la guerre.* Paris: FNSP 1977.

Bernard, Philippe. *Nouvelle histoire de la France contemporaine: La fin d'un monde, 1914–1929.* Paris: Seuil 1975.

Berstein, Serge. *Histoire du Parti Radical: La recherche de l'âge d'or.* Paris: FNSP 1980.

– *Édouard Herriot ou la République en personne.* Paris: FNSP 1985.

Berstein, Serge, et Giselle Berstein. *La Troisième République.* Paris: MA Éditions 1987.

Bertaut, Jules. *Les Dessous de la "Troisième."* Paris: Tallandier 1959.

Bonin, Hubert. *Histoire économique de la France depuis 1880.* Paris: Masson 1988.

Bonnefous, Édouard. *Histoire politique de la Troisième République*: vol. 3, *L'Après-Guerre, 1919–1924.* Paris: PUF 1959.

Bonnefous, Georges. *Histoire politique de la Troisième République*: vol. 1, *L'Avant-Guerre, 1906–1914.* Paris: PUF 1965.

Bournazel, Renata. *Rapallo: Naissance d'un mythe.* Paris: FNSP et Colin 1974.

Bredin, Jean-Denis. *The Affair: The Case of Alfred Dreyfus.* New York: Braziller 1986.

Broche, François. *Assassinat de Alexandre 1er et Louis Barthou.* Paris: Balland 1977.

Burns, Michael. *Rural Society and French Politics: Boulangism and the Dreyfus Affair.* Princeton, NJ: Princeton University Press 1984.

Chapman, Guy. *The Dreyfus Case: A Reassessment.* London: Hart-Davis 1955.

Charle, Christophe. *Les Élites de la République, 1880–1900.* Paris: Fayard 1987.

Chastenet, Jacques. *Histoire de la Troisième République*, 7 vols. Paris: Hachette 1952–63.

Clark, Priscilla Pankhurst. *Literary France: The Making of a Culture*. Berkeley: University of California Press 1987.

Colombani, Roger, and Jean-René Laplayne. *La Mort d'un roi: La Vérité sur l'assassinat d'Alexandre de Yugoslavie*. Paris: Albin Michel 1971.

Curtis, Michael. *Three against the Republic: Sorel, Barrès and Maurras*. Princeton: Princeton University Press 1959.

Debu-Bridel, Jacques. *L'Agonie de la Troisième République, 1929–1939*. Paris: Éditions du Bateau Ivre 1948.

Decaux, Alain. *Les Assassins*. Paris: Perrin 1986.

Derfler, Lesley. *President and Parliament: A Short History of the French Presidency*. Boca Raton: University Press of Florida 1983.

Doty, C. Stewart. *From Cultural Rebellion to Counterrevolution: The Politics of Maurice Barrès*. Athens: Ohio University Press 1976.

Doise, Jean, et Maurice Vaïsse. *Diplomatie et outil militaire, 1871–1969*. Paris: Imprimerie nationale 1987.

Dupeux, Georges. *French Society, 1789–1970*. London: Methuen nd.

Duroselle, J.-B. *La France et les Français, 1914–1920*. Paris: Éditions Richelieu 1972.

– *La Décadence, 1932–1939*. Paris: Imprimerie nationale 1979.

Dyer, Colin. *Population and Society in Twentieth-Century France*. London: Hodder and Stoughton 1978.

Elwitt, Sanford. *The Third Republic Defended: Bourgeois Reform in France, 1880–1914*. Baton Rouge: Louisiana State University Press 1986.

Estèbe, Jean. *Les Ministres de la République, 1871–1914*. Paris: FNSP 1982.

Fink, Carole. *The Genoa Conference: European Diplomacy, 1921–1922*. Chapel Hill: University of North Carolina Press 1984.

Gaudemet, Yves-Henri. *Les Juristes et la vie politique de la IIIe République*. Paris: PUF 1970.

Guérard, Albert. *France: A Modern History*. Ann Arbor: University of Michigan Press 1959.

Guérin, André. *La Vie quotidienne au Palais-Bourbon à la fin de la IIIe République*. Paris: Hachette 1978.

Guiral, Pierre, and Guy Thuillier. *La Vie quotidienne des députés en France de 1871 à 1914*. Paris: Hachette 1980.

Hatzfeld, Henri. *Du pauperisme à la sécurité sociale, 1850–1940*. Paris: Colin 1971.

Henriot, Émile. *Maîtres d'hier et contemporain*. Paris: Albin Michel 1956.

Howorth, Jolyon, and Philip Cerny, eds. *Elites in France: Origins, Reproduction and Power*. New York: St Martin's Press 1981.

Hughes, Judith M. *To the Maginot Line: The Politics of French Military Preparations in the 1920s*. Cambridge, Mass.: Harvard University Press 1971.

Irvine, William D. *The Boulanger Affair Reconsidered: Royalism, Boulangism, and the Origins of the Radical Right in France*. New York: Oxford University Press 1989.

Jacobson, Jon. *Locarno Diplomacy: Germany and the West, 1925–1929*. Princeton: Princeton University Press 1972.

Keeton, Edward David. *Briand's Locarno Policy: French Economics, Politics, and Diplomacy, 1925–1929*. New York: Garland 1987.

Kieger, John F.V. *France and the Origins of the First World War*. London: Macmillan 1983.

Krumeich, Gerd. *Armaments and Politics in France on the Eve of the First World War: The Introduction of Three-year Conscription, 1913–1914*. Leamington Spa: Berg Publishers 1984.

Larkin, Maurice. *Church and State after the Dreyfus Affair: The Separation Issue in France*. New York: Barnes and Noble 1974.

Launay, Jacques de. *Les Grandes Controverses de l'histoire contemporaine, 1914–1945*. Lausanne: Éditions Rencontre 1964.

Lebovics, Herman. *The Alliance of Iron and Wheat in the Third French Republic, 1860–1914*. Baton Rouge: Louisana State University Press 1988.

Leites, Nathan. *The Rules of the Game in Paris*. Chicago: University of Chicago Press 1969.

Logue, William. *From Philosophy to Sociology: The Evolution of French Liberalism, 1870–1914*. Dekalb: Northern Illinois University Press 1983.

Lottman, Herbert R. *The Left Bank: Writers, Artists, and Politics from the Popular Front to the Cold War*. London: Heinemann 1982.

Machin, Howard. *The Prefect in French Public Administration*. London: Croom Helm 1977.

Magraw, Roger. *France, 1815–1914: The Bourgeois Century*. Oxford: Oxford University Press 1986.

Mandell, Richard D. *Paris 1900: The Great World's Fair*. Toronto: University of Toronto Press 1967.

Manévy, Raymond. *La Presse de la IIIe République*. Paris: J. Foret 1955.

Marias, Julian. *Generations: A Historical Method*. University, Ala.: University of Alabama Press 1967.

Martin, Benjamin F. *The Hypocrisy of Justice in the Belle Époque*. Baton Rouge: Louisiana State University Press 1984.

Mayeur, Jean-Marie. *La Vie politique sous la troisième République*. Paris: Seuil 1984.

Mayeur, Jean-Marie, and Madeine Rebérioux. *The Third Republic from Its Origins to the Great War, 1871–1914*. Cambridge: Cambridge University Press 1984.

McDougal, Walter A. *France's Rhineland Diplomacy, 1919–1924*. Princeton: Princeton University Press 1978.

McManners, John. *Church and State in France, 1870–1914*. New York: Harper and Row 1972.

Miquel, Pierre. *La Paix de Versailles et l'opinion publique française*. Paris: Flammarion 1972.

Nelms, Brenda F. *The Third Republic and the Centennial of 1789*. New York: Garland 1987.

Nye, Robert A. *Crime, Madness and Politics in Modern France: The Medical Concept of National Decline*. Princeton: Princeton University Press 1984.

Osborne, Thomas R. *A Grande École for the Grands Corps: The Recruitment and Training of the French Administrative Elite in the Nineteenth Century*. Boulder, Col.: Social Science Monographs 1983.

Partin, Malcolm O. *Waldeck-Rousseau, Combes, and the Church: The Politics of Anti-Clericalism, 1899–1905*. Durham, NC: Duke University Press 1969.

Persell, Stuart M. *The French Colonial Lobby, 1889–1938*. Stanford: Hoover Institution Press 1983.

Pitts, Vincent J. *France and the German Problem: Politics and Economics in the Locarno Period, 1924–1929*. New York: Garland 1987.

Price, Roger. *A Social History of Nineteenth-Century France*. New York: Holmes and Meier 1987.

Rearick, Charles. *Pleasures of the Belle Époque: Entertainment and Festivity in Turn-of-the-Century France*. New Haven: Yale University Press 1985.

Reclus, Maurice. *La Troisième République de 1870 à 1918*. Paris: Fayard 1945.

Rémond, René, Aline Coutrot, and Isabel Boussard. *Quarante ans de cabinets ministériels*. Paris: FNSP 1982.

Rostow, Nicolas. *Anglo-French Relations, 1934–36*. London: Macmillan 1984.

Schuker, Stephen A. *The End of French Predominance in Europe: The Financial Crisis of 1924 and the Adoption of the Dawes Plan*. Chapel Hill: University of North Carolina Press 1976.

Scott, W.E. *Alliance against Hitler*. Durham, NC: Duke University Press 1962.

Sedgwick, Alexander. *The Ralliement in French Politics, 1890–1898*. Cambridge, Mass.: Harvard University Press 1965.

Shorrock, William I. *From Ally to Enemy: The Enigma of Fascist Italy in French Diplomacy 1920–1940*. Kent, Ohio: Kent State University Press 1988.

Silverman, Dan P. *Reconstructing Europe after the Great War*. Cambridge, Mass.: Harvard University Press 1982.

Slater, Catherine. *Defeatists and Their Enemies: Political Invective in France, 1914–1918*. Oxford: Oxford University Press 1981.

Soltau, Roger H. *French Political Thought in the Nineteenth Century*. New York: Russell and Russell 1959.

Sorlin, Pierre. *La Société française*. 2 vols. Paris: Arthaud 1969.

Sternhell, Zeev. *Maurice Barrès et le nationalisme français*. Paris: Colin 1972.

Stevenson, D. *French War Aims against Germany, 1914–1919*. Oxford: Clarendon Press 1982.

Stone, Judith F. *The Search for Social Peace: Reform Legislation in France, 1890–1914*. New York: SUNY Press 1985.

Sudik, Thomas J. "The French Administration of Fine Arts, 1875–1914." Unpublished Ph.D. dissertation, University of North Carolina 1979.

Suleiman, Ezra N. Elites in French Society: The Politics of Survival. Princeton: Princeton University Press 1978.

Soucy, Robert. Fascism in France: The Case of Maurice Barrès. Berkeley: University of California Press 1972.

Sutton, Michael. Nationalism, Positivism and Catholicism: The Politics of Charles Maurras and French Catholics, 1890–1914. Cambridge: Cambridge University Press 1982.

Trachtenberg, Marc. Reparations in World Politics: France and European Economic Diplomacy, 1916–1925. New York: Columbia University Press 1980.

Vaïsse, Maurice. Sécurité d'abord: La Politique française en matière de désarmement, 9 décembre 1930–17 avril 1934. Paris: Pedone 1981.

Vatré, Éric. Léon Daudet ou le libre réactionnaire. Paris: Éditions France-Empire 1987.

Wandycz, Piotr S. The Twilight of French Eastern Alliances, 1926–1936: French-Czechoslovak-Polish Relations from Locarno to the Remilitarization of the Rhineland. Princeton: Princeton University Press 1988.

Weber, Eugen. The Nationalist Revival in France, 1905–1914. Berkeley: University of California Press 1968.

– Peasants into Frenchmen: The Modernization of Rural France, 1870–1914. Stanford: Stanford University Press 1976.

– France: Fin de Siècle. Cambridge, Mass: Harvard University Press 1986.

Wishnia, Judith. "French Fonctionnaires: The Development of Class Consciousness and Unionization, 1884–1926." Unpublished Ph.D. dissertation, SUNY at Stony Brook 1978.

Wohl, Robert. The Generation of 1914. Cambridge, Mass.: Harvard University Press 1979.

Wormser, Georges. Le Septennat de Poincaré. Paris: Fayard 1977.

Wright, Gordon. Raymond Poincaré and the French Presidency. New York: Octagon Books 1967.

– France in Modern Times. Chicago: Rand McNally 1974.

Young, Robert J. In Command of France: French Foreign Policy and Military Planning, 1933–1940. Cambridge, Mass.: Harvard University Press 1978.

Zeldin, Theodore. France 1848–1945. 2 vols. Oxford: Clarendon Press 1973.

Index